OUR MAN DOWN IN HAVANA

OUR MAN

DOWN IN

HAVANA

The Story Behind Graham Greene's
Cold War Spy Novel

CHRISTOPHER HULL

PEGASUS BOOKS
NEW YORK LONDON

Our Man Down in Havana

Pegasus Books Ltd
148 West 37th Street, 13th Floor
New York, NY 10018

Copyright © 2019 by Christopher Hull

First Pegasus Books hardcover edition March 2019

Interior design by Sabrina Plomitallo-González, Pegasus Books

ISBN: 978-1-64313-018-7

10 9 8 7 6 5 4 3 2 1

Printed in the United States of America
Distributed by W. W. Norton & Company, Inc.

In remembrance of:

My father Oswald Hull (1919–2007): geographer, historian
My student Emma Galton (1994–2018): bright sunflower

CONTENTS

✳

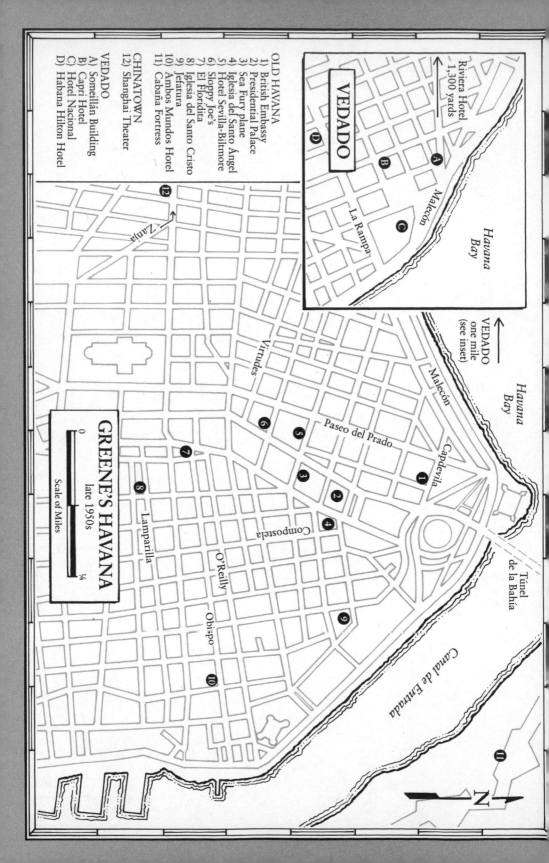

GREENE'S HAVANA
late 1950s

Scale of Miles
0   ¼

OLD HAVANA
1) British Embassy
2) Presidential Palace
3) Sea Fury plane
4) Iglesia del Santo Angel
5) Hotel Sevilla-Biltmore
6) Sloppy Joe's
7) El Floridita
8) Iglesia del Santo Cristo
9) Jefatura
10) Ambos Mundos Hotel
11) Cabaña Fortress

CHINATOWN
12) Shanghai Theater

VEDADO
A) Someillán Building
B) Capri Hotel
C) Hotel Nacional
D) Habana Hilton Hotel

VEDADO

Riviera Hotel
1,300 yards

Malecón

Havana
Bay

La Rampa

VEDADO
one mile
(see inset)

Havana
Bay

Malecón

Capdevila

Túnel
de la Bahía

Paseo del Prado

Virtudes

Compostela

Zanja

Lamparilla

O'Reilly

Obispo

Canal de Entrada

N

GULF
of
MEXICO

Straits of Florida

ATLANTIC
OCEAN

BAHAMAS

Havana

Sierra
Maestra

Santiago
de Cuba

HAITI

CARIBBEAN
SEA

JAMAICA

CUBA

0   100

Scale of Miles

SANTIAGO DE CUBA

0   ¼

Scale of Miles

San Francisco

Plaza
de
Marte

Enramadas

Heredia

Calvario

Pío Rosado

SANTIAGO DE CUBA
1) San Francisco Church
2) 26 de Julio safehouse
3) Parque Céspedes
4) Santiago Cathedral
5) Casa Granda Hotel
6) Moncada Barracks

INTRODUCTION

INTRODUCTION

Graham Greene later confessed that "a sense of mischief and irresponsibility" had stirred in him. Maybe a U.S. immigration official roused his renowned anti-Americanism with the question "Ever been a member of the Communist Party?"[1] While he could not have anticipated that a student prank at twenty years old would provoke immigration problems three decades later, the well-traveled British writer surely knew a candid answer would cause trouble. His four-week membership of the party at Oxford in 1925 had unintended consequences, as would this encounter with overzealous officialdom at San Juan Airport in 1954.

During the late 1940s and early 1950s, Joseph McCarthy's anticommunist paranoia stoked hot the temperature of the Cold War. The Republican senator was engaged in a high-profile witch hunt to drag out alleged reds from under many beds in the United States. For example, the House of Representatives' Un-American Activities Committee summoned scores of writers, film directors, and actors from the U.S. entertainment industry to appear and face an "Are you now or have you ever . . . ?" line of questioning.

Following Greene's affirmative reply to U.S. Immigration in Puerto Rico, they deported him to Haiti and onward to Cuba, an unplanned visit just ten days after an uneventful one-night stay. His eye-opening return to Havana inspired him to resurrect a decade-old outline for an espionage story, originally set in Estonia before the Second

World War. In fact, an unintended consequence of his 1954 deportation was one of his most iconic novels, set in the Caribbean fleshpot "where every vice was permissible and every trade possible."[2]

The spy fiction satire *Our Man in Havana* hit bookshops in early October 1958, just twelve weeks before Fidel Castro led his bearded rebels to victory in the Cuban Revolution on January 1, 1959. The "our man" of the novel is James Wormold, an expatriate vacuum cleaner salesman living in Havana, recruited by the British Secret Service for their Caribbean network. He invents subagents and intelligence in order to increase his remuneration and fund his spoiled daughter's extravagant tastes. One bogus subagent flies over the "snow-covered mountains of Cuba" in an attempt to obtain photographic evidence of strange constructions.[3] His Secret Service superiors in London swallow his phony reports of military installations, and the sense of farce increases.

Greene's fictional account of invented intelligence not only encapsulated the period's tension and East-West paranoia but also accomplished something far more fascinating. It managed to presage in an almost psychic manner the Cold War's most perilous event: the Cuban Missile Crisis.

Much like his writing contemporary Ian Fleming, Greene knew the political and espionage worlds he portrayed extremely well. Both Greene and Fleming had worked for British intelligence during the Second World War. In the 1950s, they both introduced MI6 (the Secret Intelligence Service, or SIS) agents as main protagonists in new novels at the height of the Cold War. The two authors both named their fictional spies James and gave each a Double 0 code name. Ian Fleming's agent was the suave James Bond, 007, who led a glamorous lifestyle and enjoyed multiple sexual liaisons with attractive women, many of them fellow spies. Beginning with his first appearance in 1953's *Casino Royale*, which kicked off a long series of novels, Bond drove a Bentley (among other classic British cars) and drank "shaken not stirred" martinis.

Graham Greene's fictional protagonist, on the other hand, is the austere James Wormold, agent 59200/5. British intelligence services employ him as their man in Havana, where he has lived alone with his teenage daughter, Milly, since his American wife abandoned them. He has a limp, drives an ancient Hillman, and his only extravagance is the frozen daiquiri he drinks at a street bar every morning with his German friend Dr. Hasselbacher. Meanwhile, the local police captain, a sadistic torturer on the payroll of the island's ruthless dictator, is trying to seduce Wormold's sixteen-year-old convent-school daughter. Plain James Wormold was the antithesis of debonair James Bond.

Wormold's spy persona owed something to Greene's own Second World War experience in the Secret Intelligence Service, first in the forlorn outpost of Freetown in Sierra Leone, and later at a Mayfair desk working under notorious Soviet mole Kim Philby. Greene later drew on episodes from his SIS work and the impending Cold War in his espionage fiction.

The odd-sounding name "Wormold" mimicked the name of one of his romantic rivals, Brian Wormald. The former Anglican priest competed with him for the attentions of Catherine Walston, Greene's American-born goddaughter and his mistress between 1946 and the late 1950s.[4] The name itself conveys the decay and disorientation of an old worm, a moldy worm, or the worm (aka spy) that turned. Although in the case of the Cambridge Spies—most notorious among them Kim Philby, Guy Burgess, and Donald Maclean—their turning by the NKVD (Soviet secret police agency, forerunner of the KGB) occurred before the British government recruited them to work at its heart: in the Foreign Office, the Security Service (MI5, responsible for intelligence within the UK), and the Secret Intelligence Service (SIS/MI6, responsible for intelligence outside the UK).

Ian Fleming's James Bond caught the attention of the mass reading public; his series of novels later turned into a successful and continuing film franchise. *Our Man in Havana* would find a film life as well. Just six months after publication, film director Carol Reed and screenwriter Graham Greene arrived in post-revolutionary Havana to shoot a black-and-white adaptation of the novel. This was the same directing/screenwriting partnership behind *The Third Man*, the critically acclaimed 1949 film set in postwar Vienna. Famed for its resonant zither music score and a memorable performance from Orson Welles, *The Third Man* was a classic of film noir. Despite the star billing of British actors Alec Guinness and Noël Coward, the Reed/Greene collaboration *Our Man in Havana* failed to command anything approaching the same critical reception or attention. Both works excel, however, in evoking the atmosphere of time and place: the postwar ruins of Vienna, and the pre-revolutionary decadence of Havana.

Compared to Ernest "Papa" Hemingway's lengthy presence in Havana, Greene's multiple visits there are largely overlooked and certainly less celebrated. Defying advice in Greene's novel that it was "a city to visit, not a city to live in," the giant of American literature lived in Havana from the late 1930s until 1960, following initial visits in 1928 and 1932. He resided at the Ambos Mundos hotel in Old Havana before acquiring a house on the city's outskirts. When he was not standing at his typewriter hammering out novels, the all-action author was hooking four-hundred-plus-pound blue marlin from his beloved boat *Pilar*, in a period when the Florida Straits were teeming with giant fish. Furthermore, as opposed to Greene's single spy fiction satire, Hemingway set several novels and short stories in and around the island. These included *To Have and Have Not* (1937), *The Old Man and the Sea* (1952), and the posthumous *Islands in the Stream* (1970).

Greene only visited Cuba, although nobody—until now—has fathomed how many times, least of all perhaps the author himself. When his diligent secretary Miss Josephine Reid examined the British author's files in 1972 to list his numerous journeys abroad, she arrived at the figure of six visits to the island between 1954 and 1966.[5] This ignored the fact that Greene made three separate visits to Cuba in 1954 alone. In fact, his first two very brief visits appear to have escaped both the author's own memory and the attention of his biographers, including his "official biographer," Norman Sherry. On these occasions, Havana was merely a stopping-off point en route to somewhere else.

In total, Greene visited the island twelve times, beginning with a very brief stop in 1938. The most significant of the three short stays in 1954 was his second, following his deportation from Puerto Rico, the unplanned visit that opened his eyes to Cuba's "vicious" nature. His investigative trip in 1957, when he definitively began to write *Our Man in Havana*, was also crucial, as were his tours of the island in 1963 and 1966, when a British newspaper commissioned him to report on Cuba under Fidel Castro's communist rule. The fact that Greene kept a diary during these four visits and wrote to confidants such as mistresses Catherine Walston and Yvonne Cloetta, aid our analysis of the trips. These invaluable sources add important information to a new introduction he wrote for his novel, first drafted in 1963 and later included in his second autobiography, *Ways of Escape*.

There is a Hemingway cult in Havana, with Hemingway tours, a marina carrying his name, and even a Papa Doble cocktail in his honor. A life-sized statue of El Floridita's most famous client props up one end of its mahogany bar, setting in bronze his larger-than-life presence in Havana. Unacknowledged, however, are Greene's many visits to his preferred watering and feeding hole. The two Anglo-Saxon drinkers did not clink glasses there, which is probably just as well. When a journalist introduced them to each other on the film set of *Our Man in Havana* at Sloppy Joe's bar in 1959, the encounter was as frosty as one of Hemingway's double-frozen daiquiris, his favorite cocktail at the Floridita just three and a half blocks away. Greene's lunchtime cocktail of choice was the dry martini. Unlike the intricate preference of Fleming's literary creation, he liked his martinis prepared with only gin and a smear of vermouth.[6] Greene's consumption of very dry martinis assuaged his depression and stirred his creative albeit hypercritical juices.

Thanks to this new study of Greene in Cuba, we can reimagine his tall shadow stalking the streets of Old Havana and Santiago de Cuba. Over lunch in a dark corner of the Floridita restaurant, for example, he leans into a very dry martini and eavesdrops, his piercing blue eyes observant, the mind racing. Pencil in hand, his silhouette scrawls the salient details of your conversation and physical appearance on the end flyleaf of a French treatise about love.

Greene's novel portrayed Havana before the collision between capitalism and communism in Cuba. As he wrote the first draft of *Our Man in Havana*, a trinity of swanky modernist hotels opened in the Vedado district of the city. Yet twelve weeks after the novel's publication, the Cuban Revolution interrupted the island at an advanced stage of capitalist development. Charismatic revolutionary Fidel Castro soon called an end to Cuba's six-decades-long political and economic accommodation with its traditional ally, the United States. Havana jumped out of bed with its close northern neighbor and embraced Cold War archenemy Moscow instead. In a futile and perhaps vindictive attempt to avenge the infidelity, Washington imposed a trade blockade against the island. This, along with local Soviet-style central planning and prioritization of the countryside over the city, hindered Havana's further economic development. Thus the pre-revolutionary backdrop of Carol Reed's black-and-white CinemaScope film endures decades later, albeit in less pristine form. Elements that did not survive include the nude revues and casinos of Greene's and Reed's pre-revolutionary Havana. They disappeared when Fidel Castro eliminated them and other vestiges of capitalist vice in the Revolution's early years.

Our Man in Havana also renders its Cold War context brilliantly. Many of the period's global events occurred during the gestation and writing of the spy fiction satire. For example, both superpowers, as well as Britain, carried out hydrogen bomb tests as the postwar arms race heated up in the 1950s. Of course, the technological race also extended into space. Just five weeks before Greene began writing *Our*

Man in Havana in Havana itself, the Soviet Union stunned the world—but particularly their U.S. geopolitical rivals—when they launched Sputnik into orbit on October 4, 1957. It was the first man-made object to leave Earth's atmosphere. Another USSR satellite entered the cosmos a month later, although Sputnik II was less successful for its sole passenger. Stray dog Laika perished during the mission.

Britain's postwar leaders, meanwhile, continued to believe their country could punch above its weight. Ian Fleming perpetuated this delusion in his escapist James Bond novels. While the country had emerged victorious from two world wars and held a permanent seat on the United Nations Security Council, its ability to project power globally had diminished considerably. This was plain for all to see when Prime Minister Anthony Eden deceived his own cabinet to order a British military invasion of Egypt after its government nationalized the partially British-owned Suez Canal in 1956. When Washington strongly opposed the action, Eden had little option but to order a humiliating withdrawal. The Suez Crisis laid bare the plain reduction in Britain's scope to take military action independent of U.S. support.

International political bungling matched that in the intelligence world. Two senior British diplomats defected to the Soviet Union in 1951 before they could be unmasked as KGB penetration agents working at the heart of the Foreign Office. Much like the country's self-assurance about its global power status, the affair underlined the delusion that the Secret Intelligence Service was more leak-proof than its allies' and enemies' intelligence services. Former intelligence officer Greene therefore used *Our Man in Havana* to satirize Britain's self-delusion about its standing in the world, the ineptness of government departments, and the cover-ups they concoct to distract from their cock-ups.

Our Man in Havana is also a novel with an afterlife, prescient about not only the most perilous episode of the Cold War but also other future failures of government and intelligence. Furthermore, the title continues to resonate with readers and nonreaders alike. In the worlds of media and diplomacy, for example, "our man/our woman" denotes ad infinitum a correspondent or a diplomat abroad, anywhere from Accra to Zagreb. Some might suffer from a drinking problem or existential despair, and a recall home or transfer to another foreign posting can occur at any time. However, what our men and women all have in common is an umbilical link with their head office, to which they regularly report on conditions abroad.

During a period of the Second World War, Greene was SIS's man in Freetown. Unfortunately, the mundane truth of the matter was that there was very little of substance to report to London from this inconsequential spot on the West African coast. When he tried to add excitement to his small corner of the intelligence world, his superiors vetoed his inspired idea to establish a brothel and hoover up loose pillow talk from foreign clientele. Nevertheless, he did later resurrect the fun and practicable idea in a little-known stage play, *A House of Reputation*. A more successful and hopefully now better-known legacy of his unglamorous experience in British intelligence is the 1958 novel under examination here.

In 1985, one devoted reader returned his dog-eared paperback copy of *Our Man in Havana* to its author with a glowing tribute. His inscription began:

> There are books which you forget as soon as you've read them, there are some which make you read them a second time and a third time. And as to this one—I've been rereading it all my life both on Earth and in space. I've learnt it by heart.

Georgy Grechko was no ordinary Graham Greene fan. As well as sharing the author's initials, he was a decorated hero of the Soviet space program. While orbiting Earth in Soyuz missions and the Salyut space station, the USSR cosmonaut was evidently engrossed in the novel. (He also enjoyed listening to big bands like the Glenn

Miller Orchestra. After all, is there any mood music more fitting in the cosmos than "Moonlight Serenade"?) Grechko confessed to visiting all the places in Havana described in the novel and returned his "most valuable thing" to Greene with gushing gratitude just six years before the end of the Cold War.[7] He was not alone in identifying multiple layers of meaning in a novel that bears repeated reading.

SYNOPSIS

Our Man in Havana's backdrop is 1950s Cuba, an exotic fleshpot and gambling spot in the Caribbean where civil disturbances are perturbing tourists. There are early hints of global power politics when Wormold's German drinking companion, Dr. Hasselbacher, tells him before ordering another Scotch, "We none of us have a great expectation of life nowadays" [. . .] "We live in an atomic age, Mr. Wormold. Push a button piff bang where are we?"[8] It is the height of the Cold War and even in remote outposts like tropical Cuba, people fear the H-bomb threat and nuclear war.

A spruce-looking Englishman "wearing an exclusive tie" disturbs Wormold's routine existence when he walks into his shop in downtown Havana.[9] He is no ordinary customer and asks Wormold a few too many questions about his personal circumstances and the workings of a new Atomic Pile vacuum cleaner. He then leaves the shop as briskly as he entered it. Wormold's straitened economic circumstances play on his mind. His daughter's seventeenth birthday approaches, and a bank clerk reminds him about an overdraft when he goes to deposit a small check.

Wormold soon bumps into the Englishman again at Sloppy Joe's. In the bar's toilets, the well-dressed man identifies himself as Hawthorne, head of the British Secret Service's Caribbean network. He wishes to recruit Wormold as "our man in Havana." They arrange to meet in his hotel, the Sevilla-Biltmore, in room 501. There he gives

Wormold his code number and explains his salary and expenses. He also outlines the tools of the trade, including secret ink and a book code using Lamb's *Tales from Shakespeare*,* both used to communicate secure messages to his intelligence handlers.

Wormold makes clumsy attempts to recruit subagents at the country club, where Milly wants to stable a horse with the help of her suitor, Captain Segura of Havana's police force. After receiving his first secret message from London—and having failed to recruit a single subagent—he explains his dilemma to Hasselbacher over a daiquiri at the Wonder Bar. The German doctor suggests Wormold take their money and use his imagination. After all, he says, the "[k]ingdoms, republics, powers" of the world that exploit ordinary men do not deserve the truth, and Wormold's lies will do no harm.[10]

Wormold follows Hasselbacher's advice and uses a list of country club members to invent subagents, including engineer Cifuentes and Professor Sanchez. Moreover, he later dreams up a dancer named Teresa from the Shanghai Theater, "mistress simultaneously of the Minister of Defense and the Director of Posts and Telegraphs." He then makes an annual visit to retailers outside Havana, and two police officers assault him in Santiago when they find him in the street late at night without papers. He returns to Havana and finds Hasselbacher distraught. Someone has ransacked his home. A perturbed Wormold now decides to embellish reports from his invented subagents. Using the Atomic Pile vacuum cleaner as a model, he sketches "big military installations under construction in mountains of Oriente Province," with scaled drawings of a "large concrete platform" and "strange machinery in transport." The SIS chief C in London is impressed by what he believes may be "something so big that the H-bomb will become a conventional weapon," and praises Hawthorne for recruiting a gifted agent.[11]

---

* Greene refers to the book as "Lamb's *Tales from Shakespeare*" throughout *Our Man in Havana*, crediting authorship only to Charles Lamb. This ignores the fact that Charles's sister Mary Lamb co-authored the book with him.

London wants photographic evidence and sends a secretary and a radio operator to assist their man in Havana with his burgeoning network of subagents. Wormold meets his new secretary during Milly's seventeenth birthday celebrations at the Tropicana nightclub. Beatrice Severn endears herself to them both when she intentionally sprays uninvited guest Captain Segura with a soda siphon. Under pressure from Beatrice and London for photographic evidence, Wormold pretends to organize an overflight of the installations in the mountains. He entrusts the mission to invented subagent Raul Dominguez of Cubana Airlines, a pilot fond of whisky. By now, Wormold and Beatrice are falling for each other, even as she realizes he has created a web of lies and fiction. However, fiction suddenly merges into reality when Hasselbacher invites Wormold and Beatrice to his apartment for drinks and he receives a phone call informing him that one of his patients has died in a car crash near the airport. His name happens to be Raul, the same as Wormold's fake pilot. Then another subagent, in a case of mistaken identity, is the victim of a failed assassination attempt.

Beatrice decides they must warn their other agents against the mysterious enemy that is targeting them. She and Wormold rush to the Shanghai Theater to find nude dancer Teresa. There is a girl there called Teresa and they smuggle her out. They next drive on to the address of Professor Sanchez, who happens to be entertaining a mistress. Reports of their movements reach Captain Segura, and he hauls in Wormold and Beatrice for questioning, playing them a telephone recording of a man with a stammer telling Hasselbacher of Raul's fatal car accident. When Segura releases them, Wormold goes to confront the German doctor at his home about the recording of Raul and a copy of Lamb's *Tales from Shakespeare* that Hasselbacher has in his possession.

Henry Hawthorne urgently summons Wormold to Jamaica and tells him that the enemy will try to poison him at a forthcoming traders' lunch. Wormold is naturally reluctant to attend the event, but Hawthorne insists. On the return plane journey, he meets a rival vacuum cleaner salesman, the pipe-smoking Carter, who will attend the same lunch. Wormold notices Carter's stammer at the event and accidentally knocks his whisky to the floor as he rises to give his lunch speech. A dachshund under the table laps up the poisoned spirit and promptly expires.

Segura visits Wormold to ask for his daughter's hand in marriage. He also requests that Wormold accompany him to the Wonder Bar to identify a dead body. It is Hasselbacher. This third successive death—Raul, the dog, and now Hasselbacher—means Greene's comic story has taken a further sinister twist. Wormold comes clean with Beatrice about his invented agents and tells Milly to invite Segura to their home. Wormold challenges him to a game of draughts with the checkers replaced by whisky miniatures he has collected over the years. Twelve bourbons confront twelve Scotch, and the players are to drink each lost piece. Segura's alcohol consumption renders him unconscious, and Wormold borrows the police captain's pistol. He telephones Carter and invites him out to go "round the spots" of Havana.[12] Carter reluctantly agrees and Wormold confronts him about Hasselbacher's killing. They exchange shots. Wormold fires the first and last bullets and kills Carter.

The game is now up for Wormold. The British ambassador calls him to the embassy after hearing concerning reports from Segura and the Foreign Office and suggests he return to London forthwith. Segura arrives to bid farewell to Wormold and Milly at the airport and hands him an empty bullet casing. In London, he has to face his intelligence masters, who know that all his reports were pure fiction. They place Wormold on their domestic training staff. In a final twist of black comedy, SIS recommends Wormold for an OBE to cover up the whole embarrassing affair.

FICTION VERSUS FACT

As one contemporary review noted, the novel is one of "unaccommo-dating realism."[13] The division between fiction and reality is blurred, and it is sometimes difficult to know where one ends and the other begins. Much of the novel came from reality. Greene drew from characters in his own life, as well as his travels, including several visits to Cuba before the 1959 Revolution. He journeyed to the island in November 1957 to begin researching and writing his novel in the midst of a civil insurrection that led to revolution. This included flying to the heart of conflict in the east of the island to make contact with Fidel Castro's rebel movement. Furthermore, he discreetly involved himself in both Cuban and British politics when he made an indirect intervention to halt British arms sales to the island's military dictatorship as it struggled to defeat Castro's bearded guerrillas in the hills.

Greene's interest in Cuba did not wane with the publication of his novel and the triumph of the Cuban Revolution—although its new rulers did eliminate some aspects of pre-revolutionary Cuba that Greene had enjoyed. Authoritarian rule also resumed, but in a different guise.

In April 1959, he spent several days on the film set of Carol Reed's production of *Our Man in Havana*. He returned for two weeks in 1963 and again in 1966, his longest trip of all, to report on the progress of the Cuban Revolution for a British newspaper. He traveled the length of the island in a chauffeured Packard with three Cubans: a writer/journalist, a poet, and a photographer. In addition, after several frustrated efforts, he eventually met and talked at length with revolutionary leader Fidel Castro on the last evening of his three-week stay.

On his final visit in 1983, he arrived as an unofficial emissary of the Central American peace process. He stayed just twenty-four hours, meeting Fidel Castro again, this time in the company of the Nobel Prize–winning Colombian author Gabriel García Márquez. Based on annotations in the diaries he kept, Greene revealed his attitude toward Castro's radical revolution. For example, while impressed by some social advances, he was disturbed to learn about coercive attempts to reeducate Cubans deemed outside the revolutionary process.

What follows then is the story behind a story, and the story that follows the story: about how Graham Greene arrived on holiday in Havana by mistake and stumbled upon the ideal background for a spy satire. The story within and beyond *Our Man in Havana* involves espionage, a love affair, travel, anticommunism, anti-Americanism, the Cold War, capitalism, gambling and prostitution, civil war, manic depression, drugs (prescription and non), dry martinis, torture, arms sales, revolution, puritanism, and communism, roughly in that order. It is the story of how Greene became politically involved in Cuba and how his fictional story mimicked his own intelligence work in Sierra Leone and London. Most of all, the story reveals how his iconic novel proved more prophetic than even its author could have imagined.

2

A WRITING LIFE

Born in Edwardian England in 1904 to an upper-middle-class family, Henry Graham Greene grew up in the Hertfordshire market town of Berkhamsted, twenty-six miles northwest of London. His parents were first cousins, both descended from a prosperous brewing family in Bury St. Edmunds, a business that later became Greene King IPA. Graham's mother was a first cousin of Robert Louis Stevenson, the Scottish author of *Treasure Island* (1883) and *Strange Case of Dr. Jekyll and Mr. Hyde* (1886). An uncle on his father's side had prospered in the Brazilian coffee business, and his branch of the family, the "Hall Greenes," lived in a large house on the edge of Berkhamsted. Graham was the fourth of six children belonging to the less wealthy but more intellectually gifted "School House Greenes." Nevertheless, a typical coterie of maids, nannies, and other servants assisted with domestic duties in the more modest of the town's two Greene households.

His childhood was at turns both happy and unhappy. He had many relations to play with in a large family, but he was a sensitive child who did not enjoy sports. Difficulties related to loyalty surfaced when, at thirteen, he became a boarder at the private, all-boys Berkhamsted School, where his father was headmaster. As well as the new torment he suffered in senior school due to a lack of privacy and his dormitory companions' scatological behavior, some classmates viewed young Greene as his strict father's spy. He developed "divided loyalties" due to the duality of not belonging fully to either side; he could not ally himself with other pupils without betraying either his father or his elder brother (who was head of house), while some classmates regarded him as "a collaborator in occupied territory." A green baize door that separated his family's living quarters from the institutionalized school came to symbolize a transitional frontier. In his adult life and in his books, the crossing of frontiers became a common theme, as did the role of a double agent.[1]

One classmate, Lionel Carter, identified and exploited this conflict of loyalties. Alongside another classmate, he inflicted psychological as opposed to physical bullying on Greene that caused him profound anguish. Even so, he admired Carter's ruthlessness and acknowledged the tacit understanding between "the torturer and the tortured."[2] He later employed this experience and the name Carter in *Our Man in Havana*. Disreputable character William Carter is an agent working for the other side, and toward the end of the novel, Wormold avenges Carter's killing of his friend Hasselbacher by shooting him dead. Captain Segura—based on real police torturer Esteban Ventura—also explains the "mutual agreement" in torture and the existence of a "torturable class" in society.[3]

Greene found escape from mental torment in books from the school's well-stocked library. Adventure melodramas by such authors as Stanley Weyman, John Buchan, and H. Rider Haggard engrossed him. He also marveled at the new century's inventions. Indeed his life from 1904 to 1991 spanned all decades of the twentieth century and paralleled technological developments such as airplane flight, motion pictures with sound, the jet engine, and the atom bomb. One of his most prized childhood books was *The Pirate Aeroplane* (1913) by Captain Charles Gilson. When asked by the *School House Gazette* about his greatest aim in life, young Greene replied, "To go up in an aeroplane."[4] He was able to fulfill this ambition on numerous occasions, even flying supersonic on the Concorde in his seventies. A fastidious traveler, he admired the plane's speed but detested its food and narrow seats.[5]

Nearby Berkhamsted Common provided an ideal hiding place for playing truant from school. Its First World War practice trenches represented both danger and escape. On the eve of a new term at the end of one summer holiday, Greene's mental anguish came to a head. He left a runaway note and escaped to the dense undergrowth of the Common, where his older sister found him gorged on blackberries two hours later.[6]

Concern for his sixteen-year-old son's troubled psychological state led his father to seek the advice of Greene's older brother Raymond, a trainee doctor. Following Raymond's advice, their father made the bold and progressive decision to send his son to London for psychoanalysis. There he spent some of the happiest months of his life, living in the Lancaster Gate home of psychoanalyst Kenneth Richmond. He enjoyed breakfast in bed, studying alone in Kensington Gardens rather than at school, and mingling with a different circle of adults. Among Richmond's acquaintances were the novelist J. D. Beresford and the poet Walter de la Mare.

During much of the six-month period, Greene also fantasized about the psychoanalyst's beautiful wife, Zoe. Influenced by Jungian and Freudian theories, Richmond asked his patients to recount their dreams and advised Greene to invent if he was unable to remember them. Taking the doctor at his word, the young patient took the plunge one morning and described the analyst's naked wife to him, her breast hovering over his face.[7] These experiences with psychoanalysis instilled in Greene a lifelong fascination with the subconscious and dreams. Moreover, the idea to invent when he lacked source material provided inspiration for his later spy novel set in Havana.

Greene's pretty half-German first cousin Ave also arrived to stay at Richmond's house during this time, and he turned his attentions to her. On free afternoons, they visited the Old Bailey to witness the country's leading murder trials from its public galleries.[8] He was already interested in the darker side of life.

He returned to Berkhamsted from London feeling more worldly and confident. While his parents allowed Greene to return to the family side of the school's green baize door, regular episodes of manic depression continued to haunt him. He described the acute adolescent boredom he suffered in physical terms, akin to a balloon swelling ever larger in his head until it felt ready to burst.[9]

Greene went up to Balliol College at Oxford University for the autumn term in 1922. Unlike his school days at Berkhamsted, his undergraduate studies afforded him freedom and privacy. With a generous spending allowance from his father to support him, he enjoyed long walks, made literary contacts, and became assistant editor on a new literary magazine. He was a contemporary but not a close acquaintance of Evelyn Waugh. They socialized in different circles: Waugh in a clique of homosexual aesthetes, and Greene in a smaller, "belligerently heterosexual" set.[10] Both groups drank regularly, at any time of the day, and often to excess. Demonstrating enterprise and keenness for others to finance his foreign travel, a published article in the *Weekly Westminster Gazette* funded a weeklong summer trip to Ireland at the end of his first year of studies in 1923.[11]

During a family holiday in Norfolk the following summer, he developed an all-consuming crush for his sister Elisabeth's governess, when he spotted her exposed thigh as she lay on a beach. Despite the fact she was engaged to be married and ten years older than him, Greene bombarded her with letters and verse.[12]

Frustration at unrequited love and a craving for excitement to assuage his manic depression led him to try to deflate the aforementioned swollen balloon in his head. He experimented with Russian roulette on Berkhamsted Common and at Headington in Oxford. His weapon was a .32-caliber Smith & Wesson revolver, a present from a cousin on leave from the First World War to his brother Raymond that he had discovered in a corner cupboard of their shared bedroom at Berkhamsted.[13] Some have questioned whether the revolver was authentic and if it fired anything more than blanks. Yet

Greene insisted into old age that he really did spin its six chambers behind his back, insert its muzzle into his right ear, and pull the trigger.[14] These were not attempts at suicide, but desperate injections of elation to provide distraction from what he described as boredom.

Pulling the trigger awoke manic jubilation, "as if carnival lights had been switched on in a drab street. [His] heart knocked in its cage, and life contained an infinite number of possibilities."[15] He estimated a total of six experiments with Russian roulette at long intervals of around a month, pulling the trigger a fifth and a final sixth time on Berkhamsted Common. Feeling no more excitement than taking an aspirin for a headache, he lay down the revolver forever.[16]

In his final year at university he joined the Oxford branch of the Communist Party as a prank in January 1925, with fellow Berkhamsted alumnus and university student Claud Cockburn. They hoped to gain a free trip to Moscow and Leningrad seven years and three months after the October Revolution. Denied that chance, Greene embarked on a ten-day visit to Paris and the city's Communist headquarters as a card-carrying member of the Communist Party. On his first full evening a workers' meeting bored him, so he sought distraction at a topless revue, noticed the maturity of street prostitutes, and witnessed a couple copulating from the window of his shabby hotel.[17] As opposed to Greene's short-term membership, Cockburn later became a committed party member, reporting from the Spanish Civil War for the British Communist Party newspaper *The Daily Worker*.

During his final months at Oxford, Greene received a private letter from a twenty-year-old secretary at Blackwell Publishers. Vivienne Dayrell-Browning was a recent convert to Catholicism and worked with children's books and poetry. She wished to chastise him for a film review he had written that linked sex and religion. Like Greene, she had a passion for verse. Blackwell had actually accepted a volume of his verse, *Babbling April*, the previous autumn. It was published in May 1925, two months after her letter. Following his initial invitation to Vivienne for tea, and as their courtship developed, Greene inundated her with letters, verse, and telegrams. Unlike the short-lived infatuation with his sister's governess, this developed into a reciprocal loving relationship.[18]

He graduated from Oxford with a second-class degree in modern history in 1925. After finding work as a trainee sub-editor on the *Nottingham Journal*, he received religious instruction from a Catholic priest in the East Midlands city. He converted to Catholicism in a simple baptism ceremony at Nottingham Cathedral in February 1926, hoping to understand his Catholic-convert girlfriend with gray-green eyes (and soon-to-be wife) Vivienne (later shortened to Vivien).

Later that year, Greene began work as a sub-editor for *The Times* in London, where he honed his economical writing style. In fact, his fictional prose would mimic that of his mother's cousin Robert Louis Stevenson, with passages of descriptive action notably light on adjectives and adverbs. Indeed, admirers lauded Greene for this, for his skill in narrative, and for telling realistic and believable stories with credible characters. Like the titles of his novels, many of his characters' names endure in Britain's national consciousness, like the scar-faced gangster Pinkie Brown in *Brighton Rock* and Vienna's returned-from-the-dead racketeer Harry Lime in *The Third Man*.

Although Greene's native England served as the backdrop for several of his novels, about a third have settings in Africa, Southeast Asia, and Latin America. An overarching theme in his books is the individual's consciousness, especially as affected by religious faith and doubt, a theme manifested through portrayals of good and evil, attitudes to politics, and common dilemmas such as loyalty and betrayal toward people, institutions, and country. His written work and persona popularized the adjective *seedy*. Indeed, seediness imbues many of his novels. A frequent personage in his stories is the hunted man, or a man posted abroad in a situation of existential despair—often with a drinking problem.

Greene would directly experience the Second World War, the Cold War, and other insurgencies through his work in British intelligence and as an investigative newspaper correspondent and novelist. His readership readily identified with his portrayal of generational angst in a century of social flux and devastating wars.

His first novel was the well-received thriller *The Man Within* (1929). Eager to forge a full-time writing career and encouraged by positive reviews, he resigned from *The Times* in 1929, against the advice of friends and colleagues. A publisher's advance allowed him to produce two further books, but neither was as accomplished as his first effort. He then wrote the more commercially appealing *Stamboul Train* (1932), titled *Orient Express* in the United States, a glamorous, cross-border train journey thriller set in politically turbulent Europe. Like many of his subsequent novels, a successful film adaptation followed, bringing extra income. He continued to establish himself as an author with the publication of *It's a Battlefield* (1934), *England Made Me* (1935), and *A Gun for Sale* (1936), but with a wife and now two small children to support, he struggled financially.

OUR MAN IN TALLINN

Another world war with Germany loomed during the mid-to-late 1930s, as Adolf Hitler rose to power and rearmed Nazi Germany, a period when Greene's younger brother Hugh was the *Daily Telegraph*'s first assistant correspondent in Berlin. Greene visited his brother en route to Estonia in 1934, traveling first by train to Riga and thence by plane to Tallinn. Greene was reading a Henry James novel to pass the time, and by chance, another passenger was also reading a James novel. The fellow James fan was absorbed in *The Ambassadors* (1903), and a conversation revealed that the man, Peter Leslie, was the British vice-consul in Estonia.

Greene was reading James's *The Portrait of a Lady* (1881), though he sought a particular type of lady in Tallinn, on the recommendation of another lady, the Baroness Budberg, a Russo-Baltic exile and mistress of novelist H. G. Wells, among other lovers. She later spied for both MI5 and Stalin's KGB. The baroness had told Greene about a brothel in the Estonian capital run by the same family for three hundred years.[19] Alas, Greene would not find the long-established outlet for the world's oldest profession, if it existed. A chemist shop stood at the corner address, owned by ten generations of the same Hungarian family since 1585.

Still, Greene's trip had led him to an interesting acquaintance. Though bachelor Peter Leslie had a solitary bearing, he had a colorful past. They shared a taxi from the aerodrome and enjoyed a vodka supper. Greene learned that following work as an Anglican clergyman, Leslie had converted to Catholicism during the First World War. He had lived in Tallinn for twelve years, had represented a munitions company as an armaments salesman, and owned shares in a South African mine. There is also ample evidence that Leslie worked for the British intelligence services while posted in Estonia.[20]

Given what Greene learned about him during a fortnight together in Tallinn and the fact that he later set a film outline, *Nobody to Blame*, in the city in the prewar period, it is a safe assumption that Leslie was an inspiration for that story. Although the character of Richard Tripp sold Singer sewing machines, his invented agents were involved in arms sales. Though Greene changed the background location of the story from Tallinn to Havana after his visits to Cuba in 1954, it is logical that Greene's stay in Tallinn and his chance encounter with Leslie contributed to his composition of James Wormold and his espionage satire *Our Man in Havana*.

In the 1920s and 1930s, many of Greene's contemporaries made hazardous trips to far-flung parts of the world to discover new lands, as well as themselves. In the winter of 1934–35—with H. Rider Haggard's *King Solomon's Mines* (1885) at the forefront of his mind—Greene made a risky journey by foot into West Africa alongside his cousin Barbara to gather material for a travelogue *Journey Without Maps* (1936). He obtained a commission from the Anti-Slavery

Society and a contract from Heinemann publishers. Only rudimentary maps of Liberia and Sierra Leone existed for this perilous enterprise. When Greene contracted tropical fever during the three-month trip, local bearers had to haul him through the jungle. He came close to death. It was his first journey outside Europe, but only one of the many in his life to poor and troubled parts of the world.

Greene began to work as a film critic for *The Spectator* and *Night and Day*, a *New Yorker*–style magazine, between 1935 and 1940, viewing and writing reviews for over four hundred films. It was in this period that his antagonism toward the United States first became apparent in print. His stance cost him dearly following a successful libel suit by Twentieth Century Fox, spurred on by Greene's review of *Wee Willie Winkie* (1937), in which he dared to suggest that the "dubious coquetry" and "well-shaped and desirable little body" of the film studio's curly-haired child star Shirley Temple appealed to "middle-aged men and clergymen." Earlier savage Greene reviews had annoyed Hollywood, but this time they sought revenge. As he wrote to his younger brother Hugh, "The little bitch is going to cost me about £250 if I'm lucky." He was, in fact, unlucky and only half right, because he subsequently had to contribute £500 (£32,000 today [prices in parentheses adjusted for inflation]) toward the £3,500 (£240,000) High Court ruling against *Night and Day*. The judgment accelerated the closure of the magazine only six months after its inception.[21]

His first Catholic novel, *Brighton Rock* (1938), brought Greene his first big success and fame. It exposed the violent underworld of the coastal East Sussex resort where Greene had spent periods of convalescence, first as a sickly child and then in adulthood following an appendix operation. Later, when he was an established author, he would escape his family and London to cure writer's block in the seaside town. *Brighton Rock*'s main character is the villainous Pinkie Brown, a scar-faced gang leader and doubting Catholic, who seduces Rose, an innocent waitress and fellow believer. After the Second

World War, the novel became a successful film, shot on location in Brighton and starring Richard Attenborough as Pinkie. It is a classic British film noir, but Greene blamed the period's strict censorship for watering down evil Pinkie's religious sensibility.

MEXICO'S LAWLESS ROADS

While writing *Brighton Rock*, publishers in Britain (Longman) and the United States (Viking) commissioned Greene to travel to Chiapas and Tabasco in southern Mexico and report on the socialist government's persecution of Catholics, nearly thirty years after the outbreak of the Mexican Revolution. His long-planned journey occurred in 1938, too late to witness the worst period of anticlerical violence, so he penetrated Mexico's interior to seek out remaining pockets of religious persecution. His first visit to Latin America was a purgatorial experience, and one he would recall two decades later in Cuba during its 1956–58 insurrection. The poverty he encountered as he traveled by mule and plane through remote Mexico was as extreme as anything he had witnessed in West Africa.[22]

His arduous five-week visit led to two books: his second travelogue, *The Lawless Roads* (1939), and *The Power and the Glory* (1940), one of his best-known novels. It describes a whisky priest who finds himself a lone representative of the Catholic Church in a Mexican state that refuses to recognize either the power or the glory of the church. *The Lawless Roads* relates his Mexican journey and the religious persecution carried out to varying degrees of harshness by local governors. Socialist-run states were particularly repressive and puritanical toward priests and locals. He described Villahermosa in Tabasco as "the puritan as well as the Godless state." To escape the prevailing atmosphere of hate, he read Trollope, while to find relief from extreme tropical heat and ravenous mosquitoes he mimicked locals and swayed in a rocking chair. Vultures on rooftops were another foreboding presence.[23] He made a modest attempt to learn Spanish in Mexico through twenty Berlitz lessons, but during this and future visits to Latin America he never progressed beyond the present tense.[24]

The specter of the Spanish Civil War hovered over his return sea voyage from the port of Veracruz on the Gulf of Mexico in April/May 1938. Russian revolutionary leader Leon Trotsky had journeyed in the opposite direction the year before. In 1940, one of Joseph Stalin's agents would dispatch Lenin's former associate and ex-commander of the Red Army in Mexico City, planting an ice pick in the back of Trotsky's skull.

On the Hamburg-bound German liner *Orinoco*, Greene heard a BBC radio broadcast from London in Spanish about Franco's advancing forces. Some fellow passengers in his six-berth cabin were volunteers in berets headed for the war in Spain, suspicious of their English traveling companion. Only after their final port of call before crossing the Atlantic did they reveal themselves as Falangists, off to fight for the Fascist cause with cries of "*Arriba España, Viva Franco.*" According to *The Lawless Roads*, they barricaded the cabin door while in port to prevent anyone leaving. After departing port, one of the ship's cooks jumped overboard rather than face returning home. Despite circling for five hours, the crew failed to locate him.[25]

The port of call was Havana, a destination described several times in *The Lawless Roads*. In Veracruz, a Pennsylvanian with "insomniac eyes" had warned Greene about the "awful" Cuban capital, worse even than Paris because of "the things they show you." A bishop described a colleague's experiences in Havana, apparently the worst place in the Catholic world for missions, "where hardened racketeers of the brothel and dance-hall and cocktail lounge wept."[26] Greene can only have gained a very wicked impression of Havana from such reports. In fact, its vicious reputation was a legacy of centuries past. From the 1560s until the 1780s, the Spanish grand fleet anchored in Havana's port every year to await treasure ships from mainland Spanish America and escort their riches eastward across the Atlantic to Seville or Cadiz. The old walled city's character transformed during the transient annual residence of five to six thousand sailors when gambling, prostitution, and criminality escalated, despite the presence of a permanent Spanish garrison.[27]

As opposed to his published travelogue, Greene's handwritten "Mexican Diary" gives us a different, if very brief, account of the *Orinoco*'s scheduled stop at the port of Havana. It demonstrates that nobody prevented him leaving the third-class cabin. Instead, a short annotation on May 3, 1938, reports: "Havana. Had to go with the 2 women. A lousy town of touts."[28] His first-ever visit thus merited no more than a negative five-word description. The impression is of a brief disembarkation in female company, where he was unable to stray from Old Havana's port area and only encountered locals making a living on the street. This is all we know about his all-too-brief first taste of Cuba. Subsequent visits in the mid-1950s made a far more positive impression and induced him to return time after time.

In his diary, much like his published travelogue, Greene's obsession is with one particular fellow passenger rather than Havana. He is a big, pale German in loose-fitting clothes named Kruger, a man detectives had accompanied aboard days earlier. During the two-week transatlantic voyage, Kruger recounted to Greene in disjointed Conradian fashion his travels of the previous twenty-five years. It was such an incredible story that Greene believed every word of it, piecing it together in the epilogue of *The Lawless Roads*. Kruger's global odyssey had taken the adventurer from merchant seamanship to circus work to service in the Foreign Legion, from Germany to New York, to Liverpool, the East, to Alexandria, and back to Germany again.[29] Most recent was Kruger's release from a five-month prison stretch, after plainclothes police found him on Mexico's Pacific coast without papers. He was grateful to be alive and free, so when they passed the mist-shrouded Azores in the mid-Atlantic, Kruger advised Greene to suppress his worries and simply contemplate life.

When contemplating Havana from the balustrade of the Hamburg-bound liner, however, the German lamented the city's surfeit of "drink and women." His immediate plan was to jump ship at Lisbon in order to avoid imprisonment in Germany.[30]

While he hated Mexico, *The Lawless Roads* demonstrates that Greene loathed the United States even more. In fact, he had arrived in Mexico via the United States, traveling overland with Vivien from New York to New Orleans. From there, his wife returned home, while he headed south to cross the border at Laredo, Texas. In his travelogue, Greene describes the inertness of U.S. advertising for "the drugstore and the Coca-Cola, the hamburger, the sinless graceless chromium world." He also had the United States in mind because of the ongoing lawsuit over Shirley Temple.[31]

This first of many visits to Latin America was also Greene's first experience of the conflict between revolutionary communism and traditional Catholicism, contextualizing his views on the region for the rest of his life. His political thinking at the time was "neither subtle nor deep." In fact, he appeared to detest consumerism as much as authoritarian communism or fascism.[32] What impressed him most was the faith of Mexicans in the face of cruel persecution. Stuck in Mexico City twenty-five years later on the way to economically blockaded Cuba in 1963, he recalled how he had been young and poor when he first visited Mexico. He remembered "the swaggering pistoleros" in Chiapas, the "politicos" who had corrupted the country's revolution, but also the pious yet downtrodden ordinary Mexicans.[33]

He also evoked these experiences in Tabasco in 1938 during curfew hour in Santiago de Cuba in November 1957. In fact, the 1950s were for Greene a decade of obsessive travel to escape his troubled personal life, a trigger for his manic depression. He sought danger in order to experience risk and take him away from himself. It was for this reason that he flew to eastern Cuba in the midst of an armed insurrection. He planned to interview its leader, a lawyer-turned-rebel named Fidel Castro.

PART I

BEFORE THE CUBAN REVOLUTION

BROTHER, SISTER, BROTHER, SPY

Greene returned home to find London on a war footing. The Officers Emergency Reserve draft board summoned and interviewed the author about war service but granted him time to complete two unfinished novels. Despite owning a large family home in Clapham, he rented a studio in Bloomsbury. Fueled by Benzedrine, he toiled there on both *The Confidential Agent* (1939), a novel influenced by the Spanish Civil War, and *The Power and the Glory*. There was financial pressure to provide for his family, and the extra stimuli induced him over six weeks to write two thousand words each morning instead of his customary five hundred. He composed his Mexican novel at a less frantic pace in the afternoons. During this period, he became acquainted with his landlady's daughter, stage designer Dorothy Glover, and began an affair that outlasted the war. He dedicated the first, shorter title to her.

Like many other families, he evacuated his wife and children to the countryside after Germany's invasion of Poland and the declaration of war in September 1939. A yearlong hiatus known as the Phoney War commenced when Britons feared military invasion and aerial bombardment but neither ensued. Still, defense preparations radically altered London's cityscape. Stacks of sandbags stood outside public buildings and antiaircraft guns, tents, and trenches appeared on Clapham Common, an urban park opposite his Queen Anne house. Londoners carried gas masks, while barrage balloons floated over the city on long cables. Their deployment would provide limited protection against low-level and vertical bombing raids by Hitler's Luftwaffe.

With the country braced for war, Greene started work at the Ministry of Information. Based in Bloomsbury at Senate House, a towering neo-Georgian building requisitioned from the University of London, his job was to produce and commission wartime propaganda for home and abroad. Perversely, rather than fearing conflict and death, the unnerving danger of wartime London thrilled him. He experienced the early war through evening volunteer work as an air-raid warden during the Blitz from September 1940 to May 1941. He often performed these duties alongside Dorothy, by then a regular cohabitant. Their Post No. 1 lay under the School of Tropical Medicine on Gower Street, with three beats bordered by Torrington Place, New Oxford Street, Russell Square, and Tottenham Court Road. There he saw many of the horrors perpetrated by Nazi Germany's nightly bombing raids on the capital. His main duties as a warden were to enforce a blackout and assist citizens to shelters in their sector. Amid the chaos and minutiae of war, the keen-eyed writer noticed how prostitutes from a Tottenham Court Road milk bar used an air-raid shelter opposite for late-night work.[1]

On the other side of the city, his Clapham Common house suffered a direct hit at one thirty a.m. on October 18, 1940, with severe damage to its rear and interior. The bomb wrecked many of his home's contents, including valuable antiques and Vivienne's collection of Victorian dolls, but not his prized books. Scavengers pillaged much of what remained.[2]

The bomb also destroyed one of his most treasured possessions, a long, thin strip of paper that hung from his lavatory wall. It dangled there for a symbolic rather than a practical purpose. This was the writ served on Greene by Shirley Temple's legal representative after he accused Twentieth Century Fox of exploiting her "for immoral purposes."

Greene recognized some positive outcomes in the partial ruin of his Clapham family home. Rather than being a personal tragedy, it released him from the financial burden of a mortgage and precluded living with his wife and children. Journalist and writer Malcolm Muggeridge was a contemporary of Greene's, and their wartime careers progressed in tandem. They worked at the Ministry of Information by day and as fire wardens at night, sharing sausage suppers at Greene's mews flat near the ministry. Muggeridge later described the Blitz as "a kind of protracted debauch, with the shape of orderly living shattered, all restraints moved." He saw Greene soon after his home's partial destruction and reported him quite unperturbed by its demise. Later in their careers, after training, SIS would post Greene to Sierra Leone and Muggeridge to Mozambique. During the war, they would work as intelligence colleagues in St. Albans and London.[3]

Aesthetic aspects of the London Blitz enthralled both men. There were nightly blackouts to confound Luftwaffe navigators, while wailing sirens announced incoming raids. Defensive searchlights, falling incendiary devices, and buildings in flames lit up the night sky. The intermittent explosion of landing bombs alternated with the rattle of ground-based antiaircraft fire. This sensory overload brought a welcome distraction from boredom and stimulated the manic side of Greene's personality. Despite long and dull interludes, "moments of excitement [and] beauty" interrupted them. He described stargazing as he strolled down the middle of an empty Oxford Street, as incendiary devices floated down like "chandelier flares."[4] In fact, the random nature of bombing and death mimicked the Russian roulette he had played in his youth. Any one of Hitler's bombs could have ended his life in a flash.

Infidelity had already saved him once. When a bomb wrecked his Clapham home, he was in Dorothy Glover's company in Bloomsbury. Risk added frisson to their illicit relationship—and particularly their lovemaking. With his wife and children evacuated to the countryside, the couple enjoyed nights of the Blitz together, the earth literally moving beneath them. Greene would later recall how the dawn sound of brushes sweeping up broken glass provided the realization they had survived another night's bombing.[5]

It was in this period that SIS vetted Greene, although he was initially unaware of his induction into the world of secret intelligence. Spying, however, was not new to him or his family. At Oxford in 1924, he had initiated contact with the German embassy and proposed a fact-finding trip to explore conditions in the occupied Ruhr, where the French were attempting to set up a separatist "Revolver Republic" due to the nonpayment of World War I indemnities to France and Belgium. With the embassy's consent and funding, he traveled to the Rhine with two German-speaking companions, his cousin Tooter and Claud Cockburn. Their boyish escapade led to the publication of a pro-German propaganda piece in the *Oxford Chronicle* to gratify their financial sponsors.[6] The foreign jaunts to Germany and France (as a pseudo-communist) in his final two years at Oxford demonstrated a predilection for adventures abroad when paid for by somebody else. An uncle, also Graham Greene (1857–1950), had worked in the Foreign Intelligence Department from 1885, and later as a close adviser to First Lord of the Admiralty Winston Churchill during the First World War.[7] In the 1930s, his younger brother Hugh probably undertook intelligence work for the British government while Berlin correspondent for the *Daily Telegraph*.

HERBERT GREENE AND INTELLIGENCE

One older brother was definitely a spy for Japan in the mid-1930s. Herbert was the black sheep of the family and had been an embarrassment to them for years, traipsing around the world to fail in one fanciful scheme after another. Through family connections in the late 1920s, he worked in Brazil and Argentina in South America but proved generally irresponsible, especially with money. With his father's financial support, he moved onto Southern Rhodesia, where a tobacco farm collapsed and a chicken farm crashed when TB killed all the chickens.[8]

MI5 documents at the National Archives in Kew Gardens reveal how Herbert first approached the Japanese military attaché in London in January 1934 with an offer to spy for them. He told Captain Arata Oka about his family connections, including his uncle Sir Graham Greene, former permanent secretary at the Admiralty, and his five years' experience working for another uncle's coffee business in South America. The Japanese naval attaché saw an advantage in Herbert's suggestion of a posting to the "America of the almighty dollar." Once there, he could "mingle with big men in public life" and report back to Tokyo on the U.S. navy's strength. Furthermore, through his membership in the Queen's Club, a private sports club in West Kensington, he enjoyed "the entrée to any society." The Japanese codenamed their new man in London MIDORIKAWA, or "green river" in English.[9] They soon discovered he was a river that ran dry.

The British intelligence services soon became aware of Herbert Greene's activities, because he provided the information to MI5 himself. He offered to supply intelligence on the Japanese to the American naval attaché, and then pass everything to the British. His foolhardy triple-agent plan appalled MI5 and they implored him to abandon it, not least because he lacked the slightest ability to carry it out. He was unhappy about their rejection of his offer and their instruction to return the £150 (£10,000) in £5 notes already received from Captain Oka for services rendered.[10] Further MI5 research into his background in *Who's Who* discovered he was one of four sons of Berkhamsted School headmaster Charles Henry Greene. It also revealed that one of his brothers was Graham Greene, sub-editor of *The Times* from 1926 to 1930, and now an author. An official commented that the Greenes were "a gifted family."[11]

The least gifted among them was feckless Herbert, particularly in the intelligence world. When MI5 operatives tailed his movements around London, they found he was spending excessive amounts of time in public houses and with Japanese friends at the Queen's Club. The morning of August 15, 1934, started with a fifteen-minute walk with his dog at 8:25 a.m., a thirty-minute visit to the club with his dog at 10:40 a.m., and then a visit to the Bell and Anchor public house. Afterward, he took a bus to Piccadilly, where he loitered in the vicinity before entering the Sutherland public house. He then posted several letters in a pillar box, loitered again, and returned to the same pub. After a visit to the Dutch Club, he returned once more to the Sutherland. At midday, he "surreptitiously" handed a letter to a newspaper vendor, before calling in at five separate pubs: the Rayners, the Cock and Lion, the Pontefract Castle, the Bunch of Grapes, and the Three Compasses. After using a public telephone at Marble Arch Station, he returned to his Barons Court home, took his dog for two afternoon walks, and made a final evening visit to the Queen's Club.[12]

His meager intelligence yield led Captain Oka to inform his unproductive agent in December 1934 that he would be reducing his monthly pay to £30 (£2,000) because he was "rather disappointed with the results." Several of Oka's English friends had in fact supplied the naval attaché with better information, all of it free of charge, and leading to far superior pro-Japanese propaganda in British newspapers.[13]

A few years later, in 1937, Herbert lent his dubious espionage talents to the Republican side in the Spanish Civil War. He set out three times that year from the East Sussex port of Newhaven, driving down to Spain through France, the last time in his Morris 8.[14] These experiences led to his only published book, *Secret Agent in Spain*, reviewed rather negatively by Malcolm Muggeridge in the *Daily Telegraph* in 1938.[15] In order to publicize the book, the British Communist Party's newspaper had published a sensationalist report on its front page, headlined "'I was in the pay of Japan': A Secret Agent Tells His Story to

The Daily Worker." It reported how a high-ranking British Admiralty official's nephew had been receiving "expenses" to the tune of £800 (£52,000) per year for espionage work on Japan's behalf. The resulting pro-Japanese propaganda in the "incorruptible" British press principally targeted the United States.[16] According to a letter from Greene to younger brother Hugh, his Berkhamsted School and Oxford University contemporary Claud Cockburn had written the story. He was diplomatic correspondent for the *Daily Worker* and had spent time in Spain alongside Herbert, reporting on the country's civil war under the pseudonym Frank Pitcairn. Instead of paying Herbert for the story, he had added insult to injury by borrowing five shillings from him.[17]

In November 1937, the hapless Herbert Greene called at the Admiralty "in a state of considerable agitation and poured out an incoherent story." Creditors were chasing him and he was about to be declared bankrupt. After giving up "a good job with the Japanese Attaché at the express wishes of the Admiralty," he now wanted them to intercede with his creditors and find him employment. After all, he was "well qualified" for a job. During his three trips to Spain, he had made the acquaintance of several "Admiralty men" who were "fools." Could they help? They could not, and they warned him about making unsubstantiated public statements about the Admiralty.[18]

Herbert's personnel file at MI5 grew bulkier during the course of the Second World War. Early in the war he served in the Pioneer Corps, but "gave a great deal of trouble" and was "considered unreliable in every way." He was also suffering from a serious drinking problem. He wrote to army officials in July 1940 from Huyton Camp near Liverpool, begging for release from his posting at a "semi-penal battalion." In a fit of desperation, he listed for army authorities a series of misdemeanors he wished to bring to their attention:

* His commanding officer was forging mileage claims.
* Adjutant and warrant officers were drinking rum intended for dispatch riders.

* Officers were tampering with gasoline stocks and using them for
   private purposes.
* Officers were drawing both their own and the men's meat rations.

Suffice to say, with such a bounder in their midst, the army authorities discharged Private Herbert Greene on medical grounds in
October 1941 and declared him "permanently unfit for military
service."[19] That did not deter him from approaching MI5 again in
1942, when one official described him as "a general nuisance and,
judging from his past, a dangerous man." With considerable justification, they decided the service "should keep right out of any deal-
ings with him." However, they continued to trail Herbert Greene. By
September 1942, the East Sussex Constabulary was unable to detect
any suspicious activities. He appeared to be lying low, cycling the
county's country lanes to gather food for his burgeoning colony of
rabbits. Herbert was still frequenting public houses by day, but he
wasn't conversing with troops or discussing the war or politics with
fellow drinkers.[20]

When a member of MI5 spoke to Hugh Greene in 1943 about
sensational press reports concerning espionage for the Japanese by a
man with his surname, he admitted without hesitation that Herbert
was his brother. He advised the official to place "little reliance" on
the accuracy of his intelligence. Furthermore, while his brother "was
not a reliable or a pleasant character," neither was he a "danger to
security." Reports later in the year described Herbert working satisfactorily with his wife at a hostel for evacuee children at Reigate. At
that point, the intelligence reports in Herbert Greene's personal file
run dry.[21]

Graham himself must have learned about Herbert's degenerate
activities from the press, his brother Hugh, and Claud Cockburn.
Herbert inspired the character Anthony Farrant in his brother's 1935
novel *England Made Me*, about a scoundrel who involves himself in
one dodgy scheme after another as he chases an elusive fortune.[22] One

of Farrant's former occupations is that of vacuum cleaner salesman, sharing that profession of course with Greene's later Havana-based character James Wormold.

Three years after the publication of *England Made Me*, Greene received a visit at his Clapham home from bohemian hack and Fitzrovia barfly Julian Maclaren-Ross. He startled Greene when he told the author how he dabbled in door-to-door vacuum cleaner sales in Bognor Regis, carrying the unassembled parts of the appliance in a golf bag.[23] Maclaren-Ross's later novel *Of Love and Hunger* (1947) portrayed this world of domestic vacuum cleaner sales in coastal West Sussex towns, involving doorstep attempts to charm skeptical housewives and housekeepers into accepting a "dem"—a living room demonstration of a deftly assembled appliance. During one such dem in Maclaren-Ross's novel, one stubborn gatekeeper tells the principal salesman of the novel, Richard Fanshawe:

> "But I don't understand. I had the carpet cleaned. Two days ago. I had a woman in."

> "This dirt didn't accumulate in two days, Miss Tuke," I told her. "It's been in your carpet for years. The ordinary methods of cleaning won't remove it."

His sales pitch continues as he tries to persuade Miss Tuke, against her better judgment, to buy a vacuum cleaner through an installment plan.[24] In such a way, the worlds of his feckless brother Herbert and dubious salesmanship combined to implant themselves in Graham Greene's subconscious two decades before he penned *Our Man in Havana*.

Yet when he came to describe the gestation of his character James Wormold, an amateur spy with little inherent talent for the profession, Greene failed to mention his brother Herbert. Conspicuous by its absence is any reference to his brother's ineffectual intelligence efforts in anything the novelist wrote about the creation of *Our Man in*

Havana and the novel's deceitful agent Wormold. When inventing him, however, he must surely have had Herbert in mind. He evidently chose to remain resolutely loyal to his brother by never mentioning Herbert in the same breath as his fictional spy with inventive tendencies.

Greene did join forces with younger brother Hugh in 1957 to ridicule their older sibling in their tongue-in-cheek anthology of espionage writing, *The Spy's Bedside Book*. The collection contains all sorts of fanciful tales, most of them from well-known authors and adventurers such as Ian Fleming and his brother Peter, T. E. Lawrence, and W. Somerset Maugham, all of whom dabbled in and/or had written about the intelligence profession. *The Spy's Bedside Book* blurs the border between fiction and nonfiction in a comical yet troubling fashion. While many of its tales are on the face of it ludicrous, some possess a kernel of truth. Among its many bizarre tales about espionage through the ages is one contribution from Herbert Greene's *Secret Agent in Spain* under the subheading "A Spy Advertises." It reads:

> To anyone whom it may concern: I think it advisable to state that I have no documents of any importance in my own possession in connection with any other country of work I have undertaken. I am making this statement as, on January 4th, 1938, a friend and I left a certain Embassy in London. We were followed to Victoria Station, where I caught the 5.35 train. From then on, my memory is a blank until I found myself in hospital the following morning. Some papers of mine were missing. I will let the *Mid-Sussex Times* complete the story:

ACCIDENT IN MID-SUSSEX

> Mr W.H. Greene, of Oak Cottage, Plumpton, is in the Haywards Heath Hospital suffering from head injuries sustained in a motor

accident at Plumpton last week. He was found lying unconscious
near his damaged car.

—Herbert Greene[25]

Perhaps this was no accident, and British intelligence services targeted the treacherous Greene brother, inordinately keen to advertise
his role as a spy. On another occasion, according to *Secret Agent in
Spain*, "a very high official" had told Herbert at the Admiralty: "I
am warning you, Greene, that if you are not more careful you will
some day find yourself in the Thames."[26] While little that Herbert
ever said is credible, he was indeed involved in a motor accident that
left him feeling sorry for himself. He remained unapologetic about
his rogue spying activities.[27]

RECRUITMENT TO SIS

Younger Greene sibling Elisabeth was far more reliable than Herbert,
not to mention more intelligent. Despite Herbert's antics, SIS recruited
his sister in November 1938, providing Greene with an entrée into
British espionage. Elisabeth inducted her brother Graham and Malcolm Muggeridge into the Secret Intelligence Service through invitations to mysterious parties, and herself served in Cairo and Algiers
during the war. Greene described one Westminster gathering attended
by "members of some branch of intelligence" and a room full of
"sprawling grey-haired men speaking Russian." Despite the Blitz
and rationing, abundant quantities of liquor lent the party "an agreeable mist of drink." This washed down a rich spread of artichokes,
whitebait, and quail. A bald major with a hint of a foreign accent
approached the writer upstairs: "You're Greene, aren't you? You've
got your sister's eyes. But she . . . she prefers the Senior Service."[28]

Whatever the major meant, Graham joined Section V—the counterespionage section of SIS. Its primary function was "to obtain advance

information of espionage operations mounted against British territory from foreign soil."[29] Major Felix Cowgill headed Section V, the
leader described by Muggeridge as "a kindly, conscientious, nervous
man" with "the sallow face and withdrawn tired air that came of
long years of service in India."[30]

Greene first volunteered for service in Liberia. But due to his earlier travel book about the West African country, his posting changed
to Freetown in Sierra Leone.[31] SIS devised bespoke intelligence
training for the novelist, involving visits to Sections I–IV (Political,
Air, Naval, and Army, respectively), his own Section V (Counterespionage), and Section VI (Economic). Section V instructed him
in enemy methods, security, and the proper use of telephones. He
learned other tradecraft such as codes, wireless procedure, the use
of secret inks, and how to train agents, as well as the details of his
personal cover. Before departing for Africa, he underwent "the most
elementary instructions in soldiering" at Oxford's Oriel College so
that he could "wear battledress without embarrassment." This military training would enable him to be convincing while posing as
an army officer, his original cover plan.[32] Unfortunately, the impractical and physically weak Greene failed at motorcycle riding, and the
cold and squalid conditions laid him low with flu and bronchitis.[33]

Nevertheless, a few days after Japan's attack on Pearl Harbor in
December 1941, he again found himself departing Liverpool on a
cargo ship bound for tropical West Africa. This time his ship sailed
in convoy, as German submarine periscopes and torpedoes hunted
easy Allied prey in Atlantic waters. As a voracious reader and in
anticipation of both solitude and free time, Greene traveled with a
steel trunk crammed with books. Like his Mexican journey, he again
found escape and solace in Anthony Trollope, bringing seven of his
novels for the duration.

Upon arrival in Freetown, Greene received cover as a Department
of Overseas Trade (DoT) inspector and soon flew to Lagos in Nigeria
for a further three months of training. A world away from autumnal

Oxford, he spent his days coding and decoding and the evenings under a mosquito net. In addition to providing protection from malarial mosquitoes and sanctuary from a colonial lifestyle he detested, he liked to observe insects and reptiles as they devoured each other on the net. To counter tedium, he also hunted cockroaches by flashlight with a fellow trainee. He ate alongside somebody called Wormwold, who possibly inspired his naming of vacuum cleaner salesman as Wormold fifteen years later. Then, wandering home from a Ginger Rogers film one evening in the dark, he fell into a six-foot open drain filled with human excrement.[34] Suffice to say, his espionage reality was a world away from the fictional glamour of James Bond.

His subsequent existence at his appointed station in Freetown was also insalubrious. Objections from the DoT forced him to transfer his spurious attachment yet again, this time to the local CID Special Branch. In his "humid solitude," entertainment included the half-hour-long copulation of two flies on his bedroom staircase. However, there was less leisure time in Sierra Leone, and daily life in the West African colony was a struggle. Due to poor sanitation, all water required boiling. Locals used the area in front of Greene's home, a shack raised on stilts, as an open latrine. Heat and flies tormented him to the edge of folly. Rats swung on his bedroom curtains, while pi dogs howled at night in the lane behind his house. To complete the scene, three or four vultures habitually perched and squawked on his tin roof. Telephone calls at half-hour intervals interrupted him one day with an African voice proclaiming, "Heil Hitler." Meanwhile, basic items such as ink and condoms were scare commodities that arrived erratically by boat. Incoming and outgoing private letters—vital for his publications and sanity—took an age to arrive, while telegrams cost a small fortune to send. News of his father's death arrived by telegram an hour before a previously dispatched telegram to notify his son that he was ill.[35]

In one sense, Greene suffered the existential despair he apportioned to characters in his novels—foreigners, mostly men, surviving abroad in trying circumstances. To his older brother Raymond, a physician, he reported from "this colonial slum" that "you can't scratch yourself without going septic," while to Hugh, he complained about poor-quality export beer, the scarceness of whisky, "gin which is a depressant, and South African wines that make you feel like hell the next morning." He told his younger brother, "This place will be most amusing to look back on, I daresay, but it's extraordinary how dull and boring the bizarre can be at the time."[36] He was evidently able to extract both the fantastic and mundane aspects of his SIS work when he later set about re-creating some of them in *Our Man in Havana*.

Notwithstanding Greene's negative views about his contribution to British intelligence, he fell in love with Africa—its prevailing smell and murmur, its light and colors at dusk. But he rapidly tired of fellow English patriots in the British colony and neighboring territories, "of little plump men in shorts with hairless legs, and drab women." In a highly cynical mood, he poured scorn on Churchill's lauding of the West African war effort by boiling down the contribution of his fellow Europeans to "cowardice, complacency, inefficiency, illiteracy and thirst." At least the Africans, he wrote, "contribute grace." He considered his intelligence work futile and became nostalgic for the privations and perils of wartime London.[37]

Greene was 59200, the codename he later ascribed to Caribbean station chief Henry Hawthorne in *Our Man in Havana*. Like Hawthorne in the Caribbean, SIS officer Greene ran his station in Sierra Leone and recruited local agents (akin to Wormold) for his network and intelligence gathering. Therefore, they and not he ran the risks of an agent/spy working in the field. Before arrival of his codebooks by diplomatic bag, he employed a book code for communication, though not Charles Lamb's *Tales from Shakespeare*. He traveled with *Kindness in a Corner* (1930) by Dorset-based author T. F. Powys (1875–1953), after leaving a copy of the novel at London headquarters. Following the arrival of his codebooks, however, the impractical Greene misread technical instructions for his safe and locked the books inside. He would deploy the episode in *Our Man in Havana*, though Wormold forgets the safe's combination with his codebook inside. Greene had his safe carted up to Government House in Freetown and forced open with a blowtorch. Pretending it had suffered damage in transit, and while awaiting a replacement by convoy, he temporarily reverted to his laborious *Kindness in a Corner* book code.[38]

In this unglamorous corner of West Africa, the main function of Greene's intelligence work was to monitor the activities of the Abwehr (German military intelligence) and the Vichy French. He also reported and tried to prevent industrial diamond smuggling on Portuguese liners passing through Sierra Leone. By 1943, Germany possessed only eight months' remaining supply of this essential wartime commodity. Yet SIS's man in Freetown failed to discover a single diamond aboard a single vessel during his service there. His only real moment of excitement was ordering the navy to intercept a departing liner with a suspected spy on board. He questioned the Swiss businessman and borrowed his notebook for a few hours. Its only intriguing detail was the name and address of Greene's translator in France.[39]

One of his more outlandish plans was to establish a roving brothel in Portuguese Bissau, where prostitutes could pick up loose bar and pillow talk from clients, including holidaying Frenchmen and visitors from Senegal. The idea was a testament to Greene's vivid imagination and mischievous nature. He even found a patriotic French madam to run the brothel, but London vetoed his plan. It appeared that the French Deuxième Bureau had a monopoly on such intelligence-gathering establishments, and besides, according to Kim Philby, their bosses did not consider the plan "cost-effective."[40] One has to wonder whether such an ingenious scheme would not have paid for itself. Greene later wrote an unpublished play set in a brothel overseen by a madam, titled *A House of Reputation*.

Until his return to London, the name of his section head in SIS was unknown to him. Kim Philby later became notorious alongside Guy Burgess and Donald Maclean as one of the Cambridge Five. They had become committed communists at university in the early 1930s, only to be unmasked as Soviet moles at the heart of British intelligence decades later. Burgess and Maclean fled to the Soviet Union in 1951, and Philby escaped to Moscow in 1963 following years of newspaper speculation about the existence of a "third man." The headline term came from Greene's own 1949 film noir classic *The Third Man*, set in postwar Vienna.

Harold Adrian Russell (Kim) Philby (1912–88) was born in India, son of Harry St. John Bridger Philby (1885–1960), an Indian Civil Service officer and later a well-known Arabist. Kim attended Westminster School and in 1929 entered Trinity College, Cambridge, where he joined its Socialist Society. After Cambridge, he traveled to Vienna in 1933, where the NKVD talent spotted him. Philby aided Austrian socialists to escape persecution after the government crushed their uprising. Following the NKVD's definitive recruitment of Philby on a bench in London's Regents Park in June 1934, he severed his links with communism on their instruction. He then began to cultivate right-wing credentials in order to penetrate the British establishment. Philby feigned a pro-Franco stance as a journalist during the Spanish Civil War, first as a freelancer and then as foreign correspondent for *The Times*. SIS recruited him following further work in France as a correspondent at the start of the Second World War. They took the advice of Guy Burgess, his former student comrade and a fellow Soviet agent.[41]

In his autobiography *My Silent War*, Philby describes surprise at his ease of entry into the intelligence services. A cursory background check produced "the laconic statement: Nothing Recorded Against." During intelligence training, friend and MI5 officer Tomás "Tommy" Harris asked if Philby would like to employ his knowledge of Spain. Harris himself was half-Spanish and, like his father, a renowned art gallery owner and dealer in Spanish masters like El Greco. Nazi Germany was mounting various intelligence operations from Spain and Portugal, and Philby's recruitment to head the Iberian subsection was a sign of Section V's expanding work and importance.[42] Later, of course, SIS would uncover Philby as a Soviet mole and the organization's greatest traitor.

Greene, meanwhile, came to question the usefulness of his post in Sierra Leone and his contribution to the war effort. He ran agents near the border with Vichy-controlled French Guinea, but his immediate boss 1,200 miles away in Lagos refused him permission one day to travel for an important appointment. A row escalated that led to the interruption of Greene's and his subagents' pay. The novelist communicated his resignation to London, which HQ refused. Nevertheless, they now allowed him to deal directly with them and bypass Lagos.[43] The episode marked the beginning of the end for his intelligence service in the field. He soon returned home to work for Section V in England.

ROOM 51

Section V had already evacuated to St. Albans in London's commuter belt to avoid the Blitz and move closer to the all-important central registry. When he became head of the section in January 1941, Felix Cowgill prioritized strengthening British intelligence representation on the Iberian Peninsula in advance of Operation Torch, the Anglo-American landings in North Africa that eventually took place in November 1942. Good contacts already existed in the Western Mediterranean because of long-standing relationships with officers of the Deuxième Bureau. While working nominally for the new Vichy government, most were actually collaborating with "C," the head of SIS, Stewart Menzies. This practice of deception, or planting false intelligence with the enemy, became increasingly important as the war entered a more aggressive phase.[44]

Lisbon was a nest of spies in this period, with an atmosphere akin to that of the film *Casablanca* (1942). The titular city in Morocco is a staging post in the film for political refugees desperate for a visa that will first get them to Lisbon, and then to freedom beyond Europe's shores. During the Second World War, Allied and Axis officers and agents awkwardly cohabited the smoke-filled bars and cafeterias of the ostensibly neutral Portuguese capital, as well as the plush casinos of coastal resort Estoril. Locals, including officials in António de Oliveira Salazar's authoritarian government, could choose to ignore their foreign guests' intrigues, calculate with whom to fraternize, or hedge their bets on both sides. Many Abwehr agents faced similar dilemmas, especially as the war progressed and edged toward defeat for the Axis powers. A prime Section V objective was to convince some of them to turn against their Nazi handlers and work on Britain's side.

Greene's responsibility after he joined Section V in March 1943—under Kim Philby's supervision—was to monitor agent activity in Portugal and its possessions. Although access to SIS records is still closed, we are fortunate to have Philby's descriptions of Section V and its staff, gleaned from reports he sent to his Soviet handlers and accessed in Moscow. These reports highlight how Iberia was the stepping-stone for German agents departing the continent for the Americas and England, and a base for all German work against Britain. Furthermore, most neutral European-American shipping routes passed through the Iberian Peninsula, as well as most airlines and mail. Meanwhile, the Atlantic islands were important as a focus for German naval intelligence operations.[45]

Yet not one of Section V's six members was an experienced intelligence professional. They included Trevor Wilson, posted to Indochina after the war, where he hosted fellow Catholic Greene during several visits in the early 1950s. According to Philby, Wilson's "chief weakness" was women. Tim Milne, nephew of *Winnie the Pooh* author A. A. Milne, was a fellow alumnus of Westminster School and responsible for Enigma material. This consisted of German secret messages that British code breakers managed to decipher, unbeknownst to the enemy. Philby told his Soviet handlers his former school friend had a "very good brain" but was "inclined towards inertia." Unfortunately, there is no description of Greene as the report preceded him joining Section V. We do know, however, that the Soviets' codename for Greene was LORAN.[46]

When Nazi bombing raids reduced sharply, Section V returned to London in the summer of 1943. Greene and his colleagues worked in Room 51 of a large Edwardian house in Ryder Street, St. James's. He would adapt the room number for a scene in *Our Man in Havana*, when Hawthorne instructs Wormold how to use a book code and secret ink in room 501 of the Hotel Sevilla-Biltmore. Two collaborating organizations shared the Ryder Street house: the OSS (Office of Strategic Services, predecessors to the CIA) worked on the upper floor, headed by partly crippled Yale University professor of English and American studies Norman Pearson, and Section V, overseen by SIS chief Stewart Menzies, operated below them. C had an office on 54 Broadway's fourth floor, complete with a secret door to his residence. This obviated any need for him to leave the building. A red/green entrance light indicated permission to enter his main office, although not before visitors had run the gauntlet of formidable secretary and gatekeeper Miss Kathleen Pettigrew, the inspiration for Miss Moneypenny in Ian Fleming's Bond novels. To complete the picture, quilted leather padding insulated C's double-thickness door for sound.[47]

Greene had frequent interactions with Professor Pearson. They would often begin on the subject of literature and end with queries about some difficult-to-pronounce character in the backstreets of Lisbon. Greene was busy compiling a card index of suspected German agents in Portugal. This was a wider project of Cowgill's to reference all details about individual enemy intelligence officers, agents, and contacts, in so-called Purple Primers. Greene was careful to shield his Purple Primer on Portugal from Pearson's eyes. He was also compiling what he described as his "rarest first edition," a volume about the Azores that ran to only twelve copies. His contribution was introductory essays on land tenure and local government, while Philby wrote a section on radio communications.[48]

One name that surely figured within his card index was Paul Fidrmuc, agent OSTRO. Earlier in the war, another German agent in Lisbon was Juan Pujol García, the later decorated (by both sides) agent GARBO. In Greene's second autobiography, *Ways of Escape*, he described Abwehr agents involved in the "paying game" of "sending home completely erroneous reports based on imaginary agents." With Nazi fortunes in decline, he noted how "the conception of honour alters in the atmosphere of defeat."[49]

Fidrmuc was a Lisbon-based Czech businessman with a wide network of subagents, including five in Britain, and others in various parts of the empire, the Middle East, and the United States. He was parsimonious with information about these agents for a good reason: they were all figments of his imagination. His motivation was not to deceive the enemy and defeat the Nazi war machine but simply to make money. He was dangerous to SIS because his fabrications risked diluting the disinformation fed to the Germans by double agents under British control. His intelligence could turn out to be accurate and contradict what GARBO was telling his German handlers, discrediting the Catalan and even blowing his whole charade out of the water. Their dilemma was what to do with OSTRO. Should they bring him under the wing of SIS? Or bump him off? The British intelligence services chose neither option, though, like Wormold's falsehoods, they sometimes turned disconcertingly true. In early June 1944, Bletchley Park decrypted a message from OSTRO with information from an invented colonel on Montgomery's staff, identifying Normandy as the Allies' landing point. Alarmingly, the charlatan agent had unwittingly put the entire armed invasion of mainland Europe in jeopardy.[50]

Juan Pujol García was a much bigger fish whose inventions were more abundant and even more imaginative. His experiences in the Spanish Civil War led him to despise totalitarian regimes. Fortunately, he persisted when the British embassy in Madrid turned down his generous offer to spy for them against the Nazis. He instead pursued his ambition from a different angle, persuading a gullible German major working for the Abwehr in Madrid that he was about to investigate a currency racket in Britain for the Spanish security services. After promising to travel to Britain via Portugal, they hired him and equipped him with secret ink, one thousand pesetas, and a codename. He informed the major of his arrival in Britain, without leaving Lisbon. With considerable ingenuity, he started to fabricate intelligence about Britain for the Germans at a Lisbon public library, using secondhand books and newsreels. He gathered the names and addresses of British munitions companies and studied a German map of Great Britain. He also exploited two versions of the tourist book *Blue Guide to England* (in both English and French), a Portuguese study of the Frota Britânica (British fleet), and an Anglo-French vocabulary of military terms. He was hoodwinking the Germans without ever setting foot in Britain.[51]

In early 1942, decoders at Bletchley Park began to read Enigma traffic sent to Madrid from Lisbon about drunken orgies in Liverpool and major naval maneuvers on landlocked Lake Windermere. Copying the practice of the diplomatic corps in Madrid, who decamped to coastal San Sebastián during the stifling summer months, García reported in these communiques how London-based diplomats escaped to Brighton in the same fashion. Meanwhile, his expenses claims demonstrated a strange and erroneous conversion of British pence into shillings, and shillings into pounds. To the dismay of MI5 officials, SIS at first told them nothing about these reports. SIS wanted to keep the Catalan under their control in Lisbon, while MI5 sought to exploit him from Britain, from where his reports purported to originate. After lengthy discussions between the two rival intelligence services, MI5 smuggled García to Britain for two weeks of interrogation. Some officers were skeptical of his explanation and motivation, while one believed his "in some ways fantastic" account, since it was "very unlikely that anyone would invent a story so bizarre." MI5 installed their resourceful and soon-to-be prized agent in a safe house in the nondescript London suburb of Hendon.[52]

Once García was on British soil, MI5 changed his codename from BOVRIL to GARBO, in homage to screen actress Greta Garbo. They also appointed him a case officer, the Spanish-speaking Tomás Harris. GARBO and his Anglo-Spanish handler carefully set about expanding his ring of imaginary agents and subagents. He stayed clear of his own compatriots, claiming that "as a Catalan he distrusts all Spaniards." Multinational figments of his imagination would include a German-Swiss in Bootle who reported ship movements on the Mersey, an itinerant Gibraltarian waiter who spied on a subterranean munitions depot in the Chislehurst caves, and a Venezuelan in Glasgow who monitored airfields and Royal Navy sailings. He gilded the lily further by inventing "The Brothers in the Aryan World Order," a twelve-strong anti-Semitic group led by "Stanley" in Swansea. The illusory organization's mission was to topple Churchill's government and bring National Socialism to the Welsh valleys. By 1944, GARBO's fictional web of subterfuge boasted twenty-seven agents. He sent 315 invisible-ink messages from England overwritten by innocuous covering letters. Later, he communicated with Madrid predominantly through wireless messages. According to Tomás Harris, the enemy was unable to see through these colorful deceptions because his Nazi handler suffered a "characteristic German lack of sense of humour" that "blinded him to the absurdities."[53]

Worthless intelligence from GARBO's invented spy network reached German eyes and ears in a timely fashion, but anything important and correct would always arrive too late to be of any use. Too much false information would alert them to his subterfuge, so the British allowed a trickle of true but tardy truths to reach

Germany. GARBO's hoax reports bolstered Operation Fortitude, the biggest intelligence deception of the Second World War. It successfully convinced the Nazis that Allied forces were not amassing in the Southwest of England but in the North and the Southeast, in preparation for amphibious landings in Norway, Belgium, and Pas de Calais. This left Normandy's coastline weakly undermanned and exposed when the real invasion occurred there on D-Day, June 6, 1944. GARBO and his handlers transmitted truthful information about the Normandy landing point by wireless at three a.m. on the morning of the invasion, but there was no wireless operator there to receive it, and the message arrived far too late to be of use anyway. Thanks in great part to GARBO's credible deceptions, the Nazis remained convinced, even after D-Day, of an impending allied invasion near Calais and did not redeploy armed divisions from there to Normandy.[54]

Following their reverse on D-Day, the Nazis unleashed thousands of V-1 flying bombs and V-2 rockets against London, mostly from occupied northern France. Britons nicknamed the flying bombs "doodlebugs" on account of their distinctive buzzing, which cut out as they plunged to earth. Greene later wrote how he foresaw the terrifying new weapon: "I dreamed of a V.I missile some weeks before the first attack. It passed horizontally across the sky flaming at the tail in the very form it was to take."[55]

When the weapons actually materialized, renewed random destruction came as a shock. London's inhabitants, including Greene, had considered the Luftwaffe "defeated [and] unable to put on a show of this magnitude." The visual spectacle again bewitched him, this time the "curiously beautiful & fairy story effect" of "two tennis balls of red light" streaking across the London sky. On June 23, 1944, "a very near bomb" in adjacent Russell Square forced him and Dorothy into a cupboard beneath the stairs. Later that day, he inspected the "little pile of green metal" with German markings next to a destroyed garden shelter in the square. On Sunday, July 2, he counted twelve bombs between 1:45 and 1:55 a.m. The next day of torrential rain brought forty explosions. During brief intervals of sleep, Greene wrote in his diary, "one even dreamed one was in a raid—a worse raid." There was no respite, by day or by night.[56]

GARBO's foreign handlers asked him to reconnoiter and describe the location and extent of flying bomb damage in London. The Nazi desire to improve the aim and range of their bombs presented a large moral dilemma. To dissuade his enemy handlers, MI5 concocted a story that police had arrested and questioned GARBO while he investigated bomb damage in Bethnal Green. This alarmed the Germans, loath to lose an agent they considered a most valuable intelligence asset in Britain. They were relieved when they learned of his release and continuing service in the Nazi cause.[57]

The major deception of the war was complete. Yet two months after D-Day, the Führer and his subordinates still believed in GARBO and his subagents, a fictitious web that had extracted $350,000 ($5 million) from Nazi coffers. In continuing recognition of their collective war effort, Hitler bestowed on GARBO the highest Nazi military honor, the Iron Cross Class II. The British, meanwhile, awarded Juan Pujol García £15,000 (£600,000) and an MBE.[58] All in all, Nazi Germany would have been better advised never to attempt espionage against the British, given the counterproductive nature of the intelligence it reaped.[59]

British intelligence officers could pat themselves on the back. They had outwitted and conned their German enemies with aplomb. Their successful deciphering of Enigma coded messages had kept the British at least one step ahead of the Führer for most of the war. GARBO, in tandem with Tomás Harris, had proved a formidable double act, feeding the Nazis false intelligence and extracting large financial gain from them to boot. In truth, there was less reason to celebrate. Unbeknown to the British, Kim Philby was engineering an enormous coup at the heart of SIS under instructions from the KGB.

The world's widest and deadliest war ended in 1945, although a new global rivalry emerged in its wake. Joseph Stalin's Soviet Union came to lead a sphere of communist satellites in Eastern Europe, while the United States headed an alliance of capitalist countries in the West. The prevailing environment of mutual suspicion and paranoia would partly explain Greene's accidental visit to Cuba in 1954. In fact, his unplanned holiday in Havana would convince him to set an espionage satire in the "vicious" city.

4

COLD WAR SETTINGS

A few months after atomic bombs from an American B-29 devastated the Japanese cities of Hiroshima and Nagasaki in August 1945, George Orwell termed the new ideological confrontation between East and West a "cold war." He predicted how mutual possession of the atomic bomb and a monopoly over advanced technology would allow "monstrous super-states" to divide the world among themselves. Orwell claimed this would deprive exploited peoples of the means to revolt.[1] Forming the backdrop to his dystopian 1949 novel *Nineteen Eighty-Four*, a new, polarized world—based on technological prowess—threatened an oppressive and calamitous outcome. Early in *Our Man in Havana*, Hasselbacher reminds Wormold about the gloomy prospects for humanity when he asserts, "Reality in our century is not something to be faced."[2]

In his later autobiography *My Silent War*, Philby affirmed, "Long before the end of the war with Germany, senior officers in SIS began to turn their thoughts towards the next enemy."[3] Their Soviet counterparts were having just the same thoughts and wanted to exploit Philby's privileged position within SIS. In anticipation of the war's end, SIS reorganized and set up a new Section IX to deal with Soviet and communist activity. According to Philby, his Soviet handlers insisted he "must do everything, but *everything*" to become head of the new section. He therefore intrigued against Cowgill and convinced the service his boss was an impediment to smooth Anglo-American intelligence cooperation. Headed by Philby, Section IX later subsumed Section V, responsible "for the collection and interpretation of information concerning Soviet and Communist espionage and subversion in all parts of the world outside British territory."[4] It was a Soviet coup, at the heart of British intelligence.

Greene was implicated to the extent that he worked under Philby and might have suspected his treachery. Furthermore, he declined an offer of promotion to replace Philby as head of the Iberian subsection. He resigned from SIS altogether just weeks before the D-Day landings in 1944, raising suspicions about his motives. He later gave loyal support to Philby following his full exposure as a Soviet mole in 1963. In a controversial introduction to *My Silent War*, Greene wrote, "I saw the beginning of this affair—indeed I resigned rather than accept the promotion which was one tiny cog in the machinery of his intrigue. I attributed it then to a personal drive for power, the only characteristic in Philby which I thought disagreeable."[5] It was an odd time to resign, but it is perfectly plausible that Greene simply harbored no further service ambitions. He was ultimately dedicated to the profession of writing, not intelligence. He had only joined SIS because of the war, and Hitler's defeat was already in sight when he left.

Even so, Greene might well have suspected Philby's communist sympathies. Only seven years separated them. They both grew up during the period of the Bolshevik Revolution and its aftermath, and like many of their generation, they viewed communism as the only viable alternative to Western capitalism, a system discredited and thrown into turmoil by the Great War. Greene joined the Communist Party as "a joke" in January 1925, only a year after Lenin's death and a little over seven years after the October 1917 Revolution.[6] Philby later wrote how the rout of the Labour Party in 1931 convinced him that the British Left bore little resemblance to the movement elsewhere in the world.[7] Later in the 1930s, while Western European democracies acted weakly in the face of Hitler's aggression and Franco's advances in the Spanish Civil War, communism appeared the best bulwark against fascism. Furthermore, considering that every-body else in the intelligence services fell under the spell of Philby's innate charm, and nobody expressed any suspicion about his loyalty in 1944, should his seduction of Greene be any surprise?

Greene left SIS to return to the kind of work he had performed earlier in the war for the Ministry of Information. He now helped produce cultural propaganda in the Political Warfare Executive for distribution by plane over France. He also joined the board of Eyre & Spottiswoode publishers, making use of his wide knowledge of literature and the publishing business. During this period, he lived in Bloomsbury with Dorothy Glover, at a different address from earlier in the war, trusting to fate the random destruction of Hitler's V-1 bombs and V-2 rockets.

NOBODY TO BLAME

Greene was consistent in relating how the germ of the idea for his spy fiction satire *Our Man in Havana* first developed. In 1944, Bra-zilian director Alberto Cavalcanti asked him to write a film outline. Greene decided to write a Secret Service comedy and based the story on his wartime knowledge of duplicitous Lisbon-based agents who fed their German intelligence handlers with fictitious reports.[8]

The film treatment *Nobody to Blame* describes avid stamp col-lector and Singer sewing machines representative Richard Tripp "in some Baltic capital similar to Tallinn" in 1938–39. Agent B.720 wants to impress his much-younger wife due to fear of losing her. To augment his income and achieve this aim, he invents both subagents throughout Germany and a secret explosives factory near Leipzig, the latter a serious development due to the increasing threat of a Euro-pean war. Like in *Our Man in Havana*, Tripp's perturbed London bosses send their sewing machines rep agent Secret Service support under the guise of an office clerk and typist. The young clerk is in awe of the Tripps—Richard Tripp for his "experience and daring," his wife for her "legs and breasts." Another visitor from the service appears more interested in the local brothel life, and duly inspired, Tripp asks London to approve the recruitment of a "madame of a high class 'house.'"[9] In this way, the imaginative and dissembling agent mimicked Greene's own inspired but disregarded idea from his wartime service in West Africa.

Tripp informs London that both he and his wife are having affairs in order to extract important intelligence. His notional mistress is a cinema actress, while her imaginary lover works in the Foreign Ministry. This creates problems because his wife does not believe he is engaged in intelligence gathering during his nocturnal absences from home. Meanwhile, she begins a real relationship with somebody attached to the Ministry of Agriculture and Fisheries. Tripp's controllers in London get wind of his wife's affair and instruct him to fire her.[10]

The ending of the sketch is similar in some respects to its offspring *Our Man in Havana*. Comedy turns into melodrama when the Germans begin to take Tripp and his agents seriously and tail his movements. He wakes up at the German embassy after one of their thugs knocks him unconscious. They pressure him to betray his organization, but there is no organization to betray. So they give him an ultimatum: cooperate and go free, or suffer Gestapo interrogation as a spy when war breaks out. He chooses cooperation. They prepare a message for transmission with false information about a Nazi plan to invade Poland. Unfortunately, a gust of wind causes the real invasion plan to be confused with this false intelligence, which he redacts in secret ink and sends to London.[11]

Tripp's bosses recall him to London for a dressing-down over the hundreds of false reports received over the previous two years, including his final message. To mask their embarrassment, they decide to place him on their training staff and award him the OBE, the same punishment meted out to Wormold in *Our Man in Havana*.

Unlike Wormold's invented weapons site, however, Tripp might have performed a valuable service had it not been for "bungling in the British Embassy," where officials delayed communicating his final message with accurate information about the impending German invasion of Poland until after the event. Yet the Secret Service could at least claim it was informed.[12] On the face of it, the later Havana-based version of this espionage satire is far more entertaining, not to mention exotic.

THE THIRD MAN

Like Berlin in Germany, soldiers from victorious Britain, the United States, France, and the Soviet Union occupied Vienna after the war, the city divided into four separate zones with a jointly administered central district. The Austrian capital city was still very much in ruins when Greene visited in 1948, commissioned by Hungarian cinema mogul Alexander Korda to write a film for British director Carol Reed following their critical success with *The Fallen Idol* (1948). After Greene had written a film treatment, they traveled to Vienna to reconnoiter locations for *The Third Man* (1949), work on its screen-play, and act out scenes together. This was their customary method of collaboration. They frequented some of its more risqué venues, leading to the writer's dedication to Reed at the start of his pub-lished novella: "in memory of so many early morning Vienna hours at Maxim's, the Casanova, the Oriental."[13]

Greene met *Times* correspondent Peter Smolka, a friend of Phil-by's from his 1934 stay in the city. Smolka informed Greene about a police force that freely patrolled the sewers under the divided city and about a penicillin racket, both elements that he included in the film.[14] Reed then discovered zither player Anton Karas at a small beer and sausage restaurant in October 1948, and after experi-menting with a recording of his music during editing, decided that

Karas would provide the film's whole score. It was an inspired deci-sion—the music score for *The Third Man* is one of the most instantly recognizable of any film ever made.[15]

Greene had begun researching the story in Vienna itself in Feb-ruary 1948, and then started to write the treatment for the film in the company of his new mistress, Catherine Walston, in Italy, reading the finished story aloud to her in bed. But when he returned to Vienna a few months later with Reed and the film crew, they found the city described in his treatment much transformed. Ruins had disappeared, and former black market restaurants were now legal and serving pal-atable food. Greene found himself repeating to Reed over and again, "But I assure you Vienna was really like that—three months ago."[16]

The result of their efforts was a classic of twentieth-century film noir, and one of Greene's most enduring successes. According to him, the initial inspiration for the story came about after strolling down Piccadilly in Central London and entering a public lavatory. He noted down an idea on the flap of an envelope: "I had paid my last farewell to Harry a week ago, when his coffin was lowered into the frozen February ground, so that it was with incredulity that I saw him pass by, without a sign of recognition, among the host of strangers in the Strand."[17] This risen-from-the-dead character became Harry Lime, played superbly by Orson Welles. The friend who spots him is Amer-ican pulp fiction writer Holly Martins, played by Joseph Cotten.

Holly travels to Vienna to meet his old school friend Harry, only to hear about his death. He attends his funeral and learns about Harry's involvement in a racket to sell watered-down penicillin. Holly then spots Harry for a moment in a doorway, but Harry just as quickly melts into the night. Holly informs the British military policeman investigating Harry's case, but the policeman doesn't believe Holly until he spots a kiosk entrance to the city's sewers. He orders disin-terment of the body buried at the cemetery and discovers it is not Harry. Holly receives a message to meet Harry at the city's Ferris wheel, where, high above Vienna, his friend admits to the penicillin racket and offers to cut him in. His friend's ruthlessness disturbs Holly. The police await Harry at their next arranged meeting. He escapes through a street kiosk to the city's sewers, where the police chase and corner him. His friend Holly shoots him dead.

The Third Man is a rare case of a film that excels on virtually every level. Greene first turned a topical concept into a clever screenplay. Reed then elicited polished acting performances, married consummate direction with stunning photography, and accompanied it all with a memorable music score. Its portrayal of friendship, loyalty, morality, and power relations, set against the background of a bombed-out and divided city, resonated with audiences in early recovery from the traumas of a second deadly global conflict. Harry Lime's cynicism reflected that of many people toward governments that had marched them into the Second World War. Their contemporary world, just like Vienna, was turned upside down. It was no longer, as the opening voiceover narration informs us, an old city of "Strauss music" with "glamour and easy charm."[18] Instead it was a setting of ruins above ground, with rats (including Harry Lime) scurrying along pristine sewers below ground. While the city's shadowy streets were a living hell, life underground appeared almost celestial.

Many suspected that Harry Lime's name and character owed something to both Kim Philby and Graham Greene. It is true that the writer often created fictional amalgams of real people in his stories. Harry was Philby's real first name, and he had helped Austrian communists escape persecution through Vienna's sewers in 1934. Lime is also a shade of green, like the surname of his creator.

Greene was modest about *The Third Man*'s success, viewing it more as a "director's film" than a "writer's film." He actually appeared prouder of the previous year's *The Fallen Idol*, a more evenly matched writer/director collaboration with Carol Reed. It is possible that his modesty about the film noir classic sprung from the fact that he had purloined the essence of the story from somebody else. The story of an author who retraces a criminal's steps to enter his underworld closely resembled Eric Ambler's *The Mask of Dimitrios* (1939), a new realist approach to the spy thriller genre.[19] Greene had read the novel on convoy to West Africa in December 1941. Many consider Ambler's masterpiece, set in the Balkans, "the father of the modern spy novel." It certainly inspired many writers of the genre, including Greene and John le Carré.

REAL AFFAIRS

A pivotal moment in Greene's personal life occurred in 1946 when he met American-born Catherine Walston, his companion when writing *The Third Man*. She would have a massive emotional effect on him, their intense relationship lasting until the late 1950s. It was mainly a case of frustrated love, as Catherine was married to wealthy Labour politician Harry Walston, and she never came close to divorcing him and setting up home with Greene. Yet this was not for his lack of trying. The thousands of letters, telegrams, and postcards that he sent her during their lengthy love affair attest to his feelings for Catherine and their many liaisons, less frequent in later years.

Although a mutual friend had already introduced them, Catherine wrote to Greene's wife, Vivien, in 1946 to explain her conversion to Catholicism. She had read some of her husband's novels and wanted him to be her godfather. He agreed, and both Greene and Vivien visited Thriplow Farm, the Walstons' home near Cambridge. Catherine's effervescent behavior and good looks captivated Greene. When it was time for the couple to return home to Oxford, Catherine chartered a light aircraft from a nearby aerodrome and accompanied them on the flight. As they climbed into the single-engine Proctor V, a lock of Catherine's dark hair brushed Greene's face, as it did again during the short bumpy flight over snowy Cambridgeshire and Oxfordshire. After landing, Vivien walked ahead of them and Catherine kissed Greene on the mouth.[20] He was still married to

Vivien—and still in a relationship with Dorothy Glover—but a long and turbulent love affair had begun.

A first visit by Evelyn Waugh to the Walston home in 1948 opened his eyes to a slice of English society he had never experienced. The author of *Brideshead Revisited* (1945) described it as "very rich, Cambridge, Jewish, socialist, high brow, scientific, farming." In 1953, Catherine apparently viewed Greene as "very lonely and morose" and she attempted to "enliven him." Ian Fleming's wife, Ann, met Greene in Jamaica that year alongside Catherine and described him as "remote from all, totally polite and holding the cocktail shaker as a kind of defensive weapon." He also appeared "very over anxious" when mixing dry martinis.[21]

Like many depressives, Greene found solace in drink, but no cure. He was certainly fastidious about his favorite cocktail and liked his martinis so dry that mixing was not required. His daughter says his ideal dry martini in this period was a glass of gin with just "a drop" of vermouth "smeared around the rim of the glass."[22]

Catherine Walston provoked visceral reactions in Greene. Her personality and their relationship affected both his behavior and his writing. In many photographs of the couple together, he displays a carefree glee as opposed to his customary torment. A biographer of their long affair wrote, "Catherine was the dark river that runs through much of the most anguished, and joyful, vistas of Greene's finest work; a dark, twisting, dominating—occasionally sado-masochistic—sexual force."[23] Her rationing of their time spent together, often at her husband's behest, explains a lot of Greene's wanderlust in the 1950s. For example, he made several visits to Cuba in that decade, twice in her company. Conveniently, the Walstons owned an estate in St. Lucia in the Caribbean. While he often traveled abroad to meet her, he also sought to escape heartache—and England—when he could not be with her. When they were apart, he wrote to tell her how much he was missing her and to plead for further assignations. Yet he was not the only one to play away from home. While Catherine was having an affair with him, she was enjoying other extramarital relations. Intelligent and rich men fascinated her, both in and out of bed. She had a particular predilection for Catholic priests.

When Greene wrote *The End of the Affair* (1951) and dedicated it to "C" ("Catherine," in the U.S. edition), many assumed it was an autobiographical description of his affair with Catherine. After all, it was his first novel with a first-person narrative, written from the principal male character's point of view. Furthermore, it concerned a love triangle, in which writer Maurice Bendrix commences a love affair with the wife of an amiable but bland civil servant. Yet the assumption was a crass oversimplification. While Catherine may have influenced the main female character, the fact is she was just one of several women in Greene's unconventional private life who he amalgamated to form the fictional Sarah Miles. The novel is set in the Second World War and includes a scene where a bomb partially destroys Bendrix's home, replicating the fate of Greene's Clapham Common house. Of various female influences, he drew much from his lover Dorothy Glover as well as from Catherine Walston.[24]

Dorothy's doggedness and Greene's pity ensured their relationship ended slowly and painfully several years after the war. One day in 1947, for example, she suspected he was leaving the house for a tryst with her rival Catherine, and so hid his only pair of trousers to scupper the plan.[25]

In addition to his affair with Catherine, Greene's broader life also entwined with the Walston household. He became a frequent visitor to the Walston home in Cambridgeshire, enjoying regular sleepovers there. While Harry Walston at first came to terms with Greene and tolerated his presence, he later banned the writer from his house for periods of time. The Walstons also kept a small home above a hatters shop in St. James's Street, Mayfair. And Greene rented the flat next door. When they moved to an apartment at Albany nearby, he followed them there, too. For years, both men even shared the same secretary, Mrs. Young. Yet sometimes the movement was in the other direction.[26] Harry Walston did not just play the role of cuck-olded husband; he enjoyed a long affair with Greene's French literary agent, Marie Biche.

1950s WANDERLUST

Another aspect of Greene's manic depression and unstable private life was a propensity to long-haul travel. Greene later wrote in *Ways of Escape* that the 1950s were for him "a period of great unrest."[27] His manic depression and desire to be with his mistresses (or more generally pursue distractions from his tormented self) hardwired Greene as a long-haul air traveler. Risky, seedy, and distant trou-bled locations were a magnet to Greene throughout the decade and beyond.

A 1948 letter to his wife—to propose "an open separation"—spelled out his troubled self:

> [M]y restlessness, moods, melancholia, even my outside
> relationships, are symptoms of a disease & not the disease itself,
> & the disease, which has been going on ever since my childhood
> & was only temporarily alleviated by psycho-analysis, lies in
> a character profoundly antagonistic to ordinary domestic life.
> Unfortunately the disease is also one's material. Cure the disease
> & I doubt whether a writer would remain.[28]

He sought material and escape in a variety of distant locations. Even the flights themselves gratified him. Close friend Gillian Sutro, a fashion journalist and former actress, concluded that Greene relished air travel due to the inherent risk of an accident. For this maverick Catholic, each plane journey "carried hopes for him." As long as he had seen a priest beforehand and "cleansed the slate," it was "the

perfect way to die." Greene's Catholic faith precluded voluntary suicide.[29]

She also remarked that Greene set out on his journeys "with a
store/provision of French letters & ink refills for his fountain pen."[30]
Were it not for the weight of books he always carried, we might conclude he traveled lightly. When flying around the globe he liked to
collect complimentary miniature whisky bottles as mementoes, much
like the collection kept by Wormold. They served a fictional purpose in *Our Man in Havana*, replacing checker pieces in the drunken
draughts game between the protagonist and Captain Segura.

In this era, long-haul travel was prohibitively expensive.[31] Furthermore, Greene felt that circumstances beyond his control had delayed
and diminished his wealth. He had initially struggled to establish
himself as a writer in the 1930s, and when he finally achieved success with novels *Brighton Rock* and *The Power and the Glory*, the
Second World War interrupted his career. Always susceptible to the
temptations of money, he found offers of first-class, all-expenses
paid foreign trips irresistible.[32] In middle age, as in youth, he preferred others to finance his travel abroad.

Various newspapers, news magazines, and film companies commissioned many of Greene's expensive foreign trips. Far-flung destinations that decade included Malaya in 1950; Vietnam, where he spent
four winters between 1951 and 1955; and Kenya, where he reported
on its Mau Mau rebellion in 1953. Yet perhaps his most intriguing
commissions came from his former employer from the Second World
War, SIS. Greene's writing and journalism, and his fame, opened
doors for him abroad and gave him the perfect cover for informal
espionage. It was no coincidence that he often found himself in the
right place at the right time, visiting countries in the midst—or on the
cusp—of political unrest. In fact, he developed a habit and a reputation for it. One notable example was his arrival in Prague on the eve
of the communist-led Czech coup in February 1948.[33]

In the three categories of intelligence gathering, the writer was not in a position to provide electronic intelligence (ELINT), obtained from plane-, drone-, or satellite-mounted cameras. Also beyond his realm was signals intelligence (SIGINT), the interception of communications between people, often through surreptitious means (although he had performed this duty in his wartime SIS service in Sierra Leone). However, in the category of gathering human intelligence (HUMINT)—i.e., from human sources—the perceptive and well-connected Greene was a boon. SIS maintained a global network of informal intelligence gatherers. It commissioned them to perform specific duties or simply keep their eyes and ears open and undergo a friendly debriefing on their return home.[34]

If anyone queried why Greene was in a certain place or meeting a certain person, or generally asking too many questions, he could simply say he was researching an article or a novel. His human intelligence gathering was indeed an extension of his journalism or authorship. British author Frederick Forsyth, whose novels include *The Day of the Jackal* (1971) and *The Odessa File* (1972), himself carried out such work for SIS, first as a foreign correspondent in the 1960s, and later as an investigative novelist. He defined this type of espionage as "enhanced tourism."[35]

Small clues to Greene's enhanced tourism on Her Majesty's Secret Service appear in letters to Catherine. For example, in September 1957 he described "another drinking evening with F.O. [Foreign Office] man." (Technically, SIS comes under the FO). SIS briefed Greene before his trip to China earlier that year, with a shopping list of things to report on, although he was unable to gather the intelligence they required. In 1962, he mentioned an invitation to Poland, "this time paid for by F.O." Greene biographer Michael Shelden provides evidence that he undertook intelligence work in Vietnam in the early 1950s. His liaison was deputy head of SIS regional headquarters in Singapore Maurice Oldfield, responsible for running British-controlled agents in Southeast Asia. A bespectacled outsider in the elitist Oxbridge-dominated intelligence services, Oldfield was

Greene's main SIS contact through the decades, rising through the ranks to become head of SIS in 1973.[36]

Whether Greene performed intelligence work during his trip to Cuba in November 1957 is an open question. It appears likely, given the previously-mentioned meeting with an FO man two months before-hand. The timing of his visit to the island in the midst of the Castro-led insurrection against Batista certainly raises suspicions. The twin pur-poses for many of his journeys abroad, therefore, were to gather mate-rial for novels, films, and journalistic articles, but also to sniff out intelligence for SIS. Yvonne Cloetta, his mistress during the final three decades of his life, affirmed in her memoir of their long relationship that Greene worked for the intelligence services until his dying days.[37]

MIGRATIONS EAST AND SOUTH

After Britain declared an emergency in Malaya, due to a communist-inspired revolt and the murder of European rubber planters, Greene's brother Hugh received a posting to the colony as a psychological warfare expert. The British strengthened their garrison in order to counter local communist guerrillas, most of them ethnic Chinese operating a hit-and-run terror campaign from the jungle against planters and the civilian population.

Hugh's brief was to undermine communist morale and in doing so improve civilian morale. Soon after his brother's arrival there, *Life* offered Greene a lucrative sum of $2,500 ($25,000) to travel and report on the Malayan Emergency. Once on the ground in late 1950, he accepted an invitation from a Gurkha regiment to undertake a jungle patrol to seek out "bandits." It was a hard, physical slog for a writer unaccustomed to strenuous exertion and challenging conditions. The fourteen-strong Gurkha platoon tackled the steep, muddy jungle ter-rain "as the crow flies," covering nine miles in two and a half days, their steel blades hacking through the dense foliage. Greene succumbed to exhaustion and the jungle's blood-sucking leeches. His patrol located two abandoned camps but no communist commandos. In this war of attrition and battle for minds, Greene judged that military force counted for little and it was difficult to fathom successes for either side.[38]

Conflict in the French colony of Indochina was of a different order. Unlike the British colony of Malaya, this corner of Southeast Asia seduced Greene. After an initial two-week visit on his return journey from Malaya, he traveled to Indochina during the next four successive winters like a migratory bird. With the world's gaze fixed on a larger conflagration in Korea, this more conventional conflict exerted a stronger pull. Since 1946, the French had been battling to defend their colony against local communists and nationalists. His most political novel yet emerged out of these experiences—*The Quiet American* (1955).

Greene's main contact in Hanoi was British consul Trevor Wilson. They had worked alongside each other in SIS's Section V during the war. Wilson continued to work for the intelligence services in Southeast Asia under the cover of the consular service. However, due to his association with Greene and a trip by the writer within Vietnam that displeased the French general Jean de Lattre, he declared Wilson persona non grata and the Foreign Office recalled him from Hanoi. On the commander in chief's last night in Hanoi, he also accused Greene of being a spy.[39]

The beauty of Vietnamese women was a strong attraction, as was the "exhilaration which a measure of danger brings." He also acquired a taste for opium. His minor habit induced him to smoke about ten pipes three times a week in local *fumeries*. Opium, he said, made him garrulous, sleepy, and hazy about elapsed time.[40]

Greene flew on French bombing raids and traveled to the front line outside Phat Diem. There he saw ditches full of floating dead Vietnamese, a horrific visual spectacle he likened to an Irish stew. During his last visit in 1955, he interviewed communist Viet Minh leader Ho Chi Minh over tea.[41] By this time, a cease-fire and Geneva peace accord had divided Vietnam along the seventeenth parallel into a communist-controlled north and a nationalist-controlled south. French and Viet Minh forces agreed to withdraw from North and South Vietnam, respectively.[42]

It was an American attached to an economic aid mission, probably working for the CIA, who lectured Greene on the need to find a "third force in Vietnam" during a long drive back through the delta to Saigon. The author ascribed this ideal of a third force to CIA agent Alden Pyle—the eponymous quiet American in his novel. Pyle believes a proxy third force can execute the unpalatable work of the French army and local communist insurgents. Edward Said, a renowned expert on cultural imperialism, described Greene's "merciless accuracy" in drawing Pyle's character and his naïve world outlook.[43] Some U.S. reviews of the novel tore into the author for what they considered his unflattering and caricatured depiction of their national character through Pyle.[44]

Meanwhile, veteran British newspaper correspondent Fowler gives voice in the novel to the reportage that its author had already written and published in *Paris Match*, *The Sunday Times*, *The Spectator*, and *The Tablet*. These journalistic commissions—and SIS—financed his annual visits over four consecutive winters from 1951 to 1955.

As with Malaya, he expressed sympathy for both adversaries. In Indochina these were the eventual local victors on one side and the defeated colonial masters on the other. Yet he had no sympathy for the meddling Americans, especially CIA operatives. He was adamant they were responsible for a large bomb in Saigon's main square, where a *Life* photographer was conveniently on hand to take a graphic picture of an atrocity attributed to a third party. Even so, as one of few reporters to make it to the front line, Greene judged, "The nearer you are to war, the less you know what is happening."[45]

If this experience was not sufficient, Greene traveled to Kenya in 1953 to report on the Mau Mau rebellion for the *Sunday Times*. In this corner of Africa, the secret guerrilla group had begun a violent campaign a year earlier against white settlers. The Mau Mau belonged to the Kikuyu, Kenya's largest tribal group. According to the government, 90 percent of the tribe were converts who had sworn an oath of loyalty to the secretive organization.[46] During the rebellion, both the Mau Mau and the British army committed atrocities, including torture in the army's case. In Greene's opinion, the insurgency in Kenya was more comparable to that in Malaya than in Indochina, due to the more ubiquitous presence of white settlers. Unlike settlers in Malaya, however, most of those in Britain's African crown colony were there for life, and it was more "like a revolt of the domestic staff." Also unlike Malaya, they feared death from a blade rather than from bullets, at home and in the dead of night.[47]

In the first half of the 1950s, therefore, Greene had experienced local armed insurgencies in Malaya, Indochina, and Kenya. He had witnessed firsthand local colonial rulers' and their armies' attempts to combat guerrillas employing conventional weapons and hit-and-run tactics against them.

THE SPYING GAME

At the same time that various conflicts flared up in pockets of the colonial and rapidly decolonizing Third World—countries trapped in the conflict between the capitalism of the First World and the communism of the Second World—another battle raged. While in essence the Cold War was an ideological battle, the superpower geopolitical rivalry between the United States and the USSR induced a competitive technological race to create increasingly sophisticated nuclear weaponry. Its most obvious and ominous manifestation was research and testing of the hydrogen bomb, or H-bomb, far more powerful in its potential destruction than the atomic bomb deployed to end the Second World War. This East-West technological rivalry later grew into a race into space and eventually to the moon.

Wartime Anglo-American military cooperation, renewed during the Berlin airlift, also continued in the field of shared intelligence. Confronting a mutual adversary, the British Secret Intelligence Service cooperated with the U.S. Central Intelligence Agency in espionage and counterespionage against their Soviet counterpart the KGB. The United States considered Britain its most dependable intelligence ally.

Dependable they might have been, but secure they were not. Unbeknownst to the British, several Soviet moles were working deep inside their intelligence services. Before their discovery, however, a number of atomic scientists were discovered supplying secrets to the Russians. The first big espionage fish caught in the net was German-born nuclear physicist Klaus Fuchs, who had escaped Nazi persecution in 1933 to become one of Britain's top atomic scientists. Between 1944 and 1946, he worked in the American Theoretical Physics Department at Los Alamos, New Mexico, and passed vital plans for the first atomic bomb to Soviet intelligence in 1945.

In 1951, the defection of two British diplomats to the Soviet Union shook the intelligence relationship between the United States and Britain to its core. Only decades later came the revelation that five "Cambridge spies" had been working for the Soviets in British intelligence. The first two, Donald Maclean and Guy Burgess, had both worked at the British embassy in Washington during periods leading up to their exposure. The discovery came about after American cryptographers were able to crack a Soviet code and discover that somebody with the nom de guerre "Homer" was leaking messages from within the British embassy.[48] This could have been anybody among its many staff, from the cleaning woman to the ambassador himself. British investigations uncovered the fact that "Homer" was Donald Maclean. Kim Philby tipped off Maclean in London about his imminent unmasking. By the time Maclean fled to the Soviet Union, he was head of the British Foreign Office's American Department, overseeing all its work in the Americas. His employers declared weakly that he had only worked on Latin American affairs. The truth of the matter was that he had seen practically everything of importance related to the Korean War. Even more worryingly, while head of chancery in Washington, he had been involved with atomic energy matters, with a pass that permitted him to wander unescorted wherever he desired in U.S. Atomic Energy Commission headquarters.[49]

At this time, Philby was working as liaison officer between SIS and the CIA at the Washington embassy. Guy Burgess had been posted there a year earlier in 1950, but the Foreign Office ordered him home after a series of embarrassing indiscretions fueled by drink, including indiscreet homosexual advances. Philby instructed him to warn Maclean and their Soviet handler about the discovery of Homer's identity and to tell Maclean to escape to the Soviet Union before they interrogated him. To Philby's consternation, Burgess accompanied Maclean when he fled England. Burgess had been living in Philby's house in Washington, and suspicions were sure to arise about this and other close associations, including their time together at Cambridge.[50] Although Philby did not know it at the time, the Soviets had tricked Burgess into traveling with Maclean, fearful that he would compromise their whole espionage operation. For the U.S. government, meanwhile, the revelation that two former incumbents of the British embassy in Washington had been working for the Soviets further dented their confidence in their transatlantic allies and their ongoing intelligence sharing.

Greene's *Our Man in Havana* alludes to this and other British intelligence lapses during a scene at SIS headquarters in London when the permanent undersecretary raises with C the issue of Wormold's constructions in the mountains:

> "The P.M. [prime minister] is pressing us to inform the Yankees
>   and ask their help."
> "You mustn't let him. You can't depend on their security."[51]

C's rebuff is risible considering the major breaches in British intelligence security that preceded the novel's publication.

Just weeks before news broke about the disappearance of two British diplomats, the U.S. public was rocked by the news that an American married couple had been found guilty of passing secrets from the atom research center in Los Alamos to the Soviets. Julius and Ethel Rosenberg received the death sentence for their betrayal in April 1951. They died on the electric chair two years later, in June 1953.

Prosecution of the Rosenbergs added fuel to the flames of Senator Joe McCarthy's crusade to root out communists in the United States. His paranoiac campaign followed and later ran in tandem with that of the House of Representatives' Un-American Activities Committee (HUAC). In 1947, the committee embarked on a high-profile investigation to weed out communists in the U.S. entertainment industry. Their actions blacklisted hundreds of Hollywood writers and directors who refused to answer questions, and even imprisoned a few. In a 1950 speech, McCarthy claimed to have the names of 205 "card-carrying Communists" in the State Department, a number he soon scaled down to fifty-seven. He ultimately named only four of them. His critics accused him of conducting "witch-hunts," compromising and even destroying the careers of individuals through his intimidation of them in inquisitorial private hearings, often with only spurious evidence.

McCarthy's fierce anticommunist doctrine partly explains Greene's immigration clashes with the United States from this period, adding further fuel to the fire of his anti-Americanism. He sought to take advantage of any opportunity to highlight what he considered Washington's naïve outlook on the world. Through pen and ink, he liked to poke his "feeble twig in the spokes of American foreign policy."[52] The 1950 Internal Security Act, also known as the McCarran Act, particularly incensed him. It was the result of many anticommunist bills circulated and approved by both houses of Congress under the direction of Nevada's rabid anticommunist senator Pat McCarran. The act gave the government unprecedented authority to restrict civil liberties, including the exclusion from the United States of "aliens who, at any time, shall or shall have been members" of a list of dangerous undesirables, "anarchists" or "members" of or anybody "affiliated with" the Communist Party, either in the United States or abroad.[53] Many Americans and non-Americans recognized that the McCarran Act arose from exaggerated and irrational fears of communism engendered by the actions of the HUAC and McCarthy.

Greene spoke to a Brussels-based U.S. diplomat who told him how the State Department were keen to highlight the absurdity of the McCarran Act and the bizarre restrictions it imposed on innocent people's freedom to travel. The writer offered himself up as a willing guinea pig when he revealed in a *Time* magazine cover story that he had been a short-lived member of the Communist Party while a student at Oxford. Following his October 1951 article, the U.S. authorities denied him his usual twelve-month visa to visit the United States in 1952, issuing the writer a three-month visa instead.[54]

AUSTERITY BRITAIN

In 1953, Britons celebrated Elizabeth II's coronation as their new monarch. Economically and on the world stage, however, there was less reason to rejoice. While the country had ended the Second World War on the winning side, it did not feel like it in debt-ridden Britain. Many saw India's independence in 1947, for example, as symptomatic of the country's decline. The loss of this great colony significantly reduced the breadth of the British Empire.

In the same year as the new queen's coronation, former naval intelligence officer Ian Fleming published the first in a series of highly successful novels. Their main protagonist soon became a household name. Yet unlike his creator's experience in the Second World War, secret agent James Bond inhabited a fantasy world. In his gadget-ridden world of disfigured foreigners and exotic women, no-nonsense 007 did not involve himself in anything akin to real intelligence gathering. Fleming's distancing of Bond from reality was deliberate. His intention was not to remind British readers of their austere existence but rather to offer a mental escape from it. While Britain's empire and position on the world stage were patently diminishing, his Bond novels promoted the delusion that the country still punched above its weight. His licensed-to-kill agent's milieu of fast cars, casinos, and shaken-not-stirred martinis made 007 an aspirational figure.[55]

Greene took a very different approach when inventing his agent James Wormold—codename 59200/5—a few years later. Far from disguising the reality of Britain's compromised global power status, he highlighted British attempts to paper over the cracks. When he began to write *Our Man in Havana* in November 1957, the debacle of the previous autumn's Suez Crisis was still fresh in people's minds. Prime Minister Anthony Eden's temperament and political judgment were not helped by the powerful amphetamine and barbiturate Drinamyl he had been prescribed to reduce excruciating pain. Three years before Suez, a botched surgical operation on Eden's gall bladder had severed his bile duct and seriously debilitated his health.[56]

For all the talk of the Anglo-American "Special Relationship," when push came to shove in the Middle East, U.S. president Dwight Eisenhower pulled rank on Eden and forced Britain into a humiliating military withdrawal from the Suez Canal Zone. Eisenhower was doubly furious because the British intervention diverted people's attention from the brutal Soviet suppression of an anticommunist uprising in Hungary in late October 1956. The Suez fiasco left a good deal of egg on Eden's face, not to mention his double-breasted suit. He had first colluded with France to engineer an excuse for the invasion, and then hid his intrigue from most cabinet colleagues. Eden later lied when questioned in Parliament about the ill-conceived military campaign. The prime minister resigned two months later, a physically and politically broken man.

As opposed to Fleming then, Greene chose to satirize rather than glamorize what he considered the disturbing Cold War binary of East versus West rivalry. Instead of exaggerating Britain's ingenuity, he ridiculed its bungling officialdom. Like Orwell before him, who had coined the term, he was more concerned about individual freedoms in this ideological and technological cold war. He appeared to prioritize loyalty to people over countries or causes. James Wormold reasons with himself that he will kill his rival Carter only because Carter killed his friend Dr. Hasselbacher. But he will not kill for his country, "for capitalism or Communism or social democracy." Nor for "patriotism or the preference for one economic system over another." Wormold concludes he "will not be 59200/5 in anyone's global war."[57] Greene's fictional portrayal of human fallibilities and Cold War delusions would prove both accurate and prophetic.

5

HAVANA VICE

With his penchant for risqué locations, it is odd that Greene did not visit Havana earlier, excepting an all-too-brief glimpse of the Caribbean's largest city in 1938. For decades, Cuba had appeared in tourist-industry publicity as a pleasure island, an uninhibited tropical paradise. Perhaps the writer was aware but wary of a destination where American tourists and the U.S. dollar held sway, and this infamy diminished his curiosity. Nevertheless, when he did properly discover the sinful city in 1954, his predominant reaction was wonderment.

Prohibition against the production and sale of alcoholic beverages in the United States had first boosted Cuba as a mass tourist destination. Dry-throated U.S. citizens, keen to shun puritanical legislation that outlawed such immorality during the 1920s and 1930s, traveled in increasing numbers to the exotic island to get soaking wet. Meanwhile, rum-running between Cuba and the U.S. coastline proved a highly profitable enterprise in this period for organized crime in the United States.

After Prohibition ended in 1933, Havana still competed for U.S. visitors with money to burn in casinos, businesses often facilitated by Cuban politicians amenable to a slice in proceeds. The mafia, some with dual Italian American nationality, were prominent in the gambling world. In fact, many ran less risk and accrued more profit from Havana's slot machines and gaming tables than in rival U.S. cities.

Foremost among these was the neon oasis of Las Vegas in Nevada's Mojave Desert.

At various times, mafia names like Charles "Lucky" Luciano, Meyer Lansky, and Santo Trafficante Jr. ran—or received bans from operating—gambling and/or drug rackets on both sides of the Florida Straits.[1] In 1946, some of the biggest mafia bosses held a meeting to iron out difficulties and divide spoils at the Hotel Nacional, then Havana's most luxurious and prestigious hotel. Film director Francis Ford Coppola's *The Godfather, Part II* (1974) later portrayed this meeting in celluloid. One scene in the Academy Award Best Picture–winning movie portrays a sunny Havana rooftop terrace in 1958, where mobsters—including Michael Corleone, played by actor Al Pacino—slice up a birthday cake with an icing imprint of Cuba, a metaphor for their division of the island's best pickings.

Cuba's excesses and inequalities staggered some British visitors. In 1951, an Export Credits Guarantee Department official traveled there to discuss a contract for the sale of Leyland Motors buses. His cynical yet droll synopsis of the island's political culture and American visitors was a jewel of British condescension:

> Havana is a city with an equable climate and a warming sun, frozen daiquiris, vulgar tourists—chiefly from the East End of New York at this time of year—breathtaking prices, a tendency to put off till tomorrow anything your friend cannot do for you to-day, and politicians who hope to clear the till at the end of their term of office and settle in Miami.[2]

In the twilight of a thirty-four-year diplomatic career and on the point of sailing into retirement with his wife and their beloved dachshund, Adrian Holman sent a valedictory dispatch from the British embassy in April 1954 that portrayed Cuba's "setting of luxury and make-believe" as he ended his five-year term as Her Majesty's ambassador in Havana:

Much of what has been reported from this post may appear to have been exaggerated or verging on the ridiculous. It may have given rise to suspicious smiles and scepticism. But Cuba is indeed a country of a particular musical comedy variety, where frivolous intrigues and plots abound and so often change into ghastly tragedies over night.[3]

Greene would soon discover this backdrop "where frivolous intrigues and plots abound" and recognize it as the perfect setting for a satire about British intelligence activities in the tropics.

Sugar, the principal source of Cuba's abundant economic wealth, fueled most of the gaiety. Blessed with fertile soil and a propitious climate, the island enjoyed almost perfect conditions for sugarcane cultivation. This providence extended to the proximity of the United States, the world's largest export market for the agricultural commodity. In fact, Cuba's northern neighbor provided most of the investment for the island's sugar industry in the decades following the country's nominal independence in 1902. American dollars converted vast swaths of land into plantations for growing sugarcane and financed an island-wide network of railways and sugar mills to transport and process the harvested cane and its derivatives.

The ambassador's wife, Betty Holman, noted how their miserly spending allowance stood in stark contrast to the opulence of the parties they attended. As with Greene's foreign travel, the British government's need to conserve sterling extended even to diplomats. The Holmans' hosts from the island's affluent sugarocracy had no such issues and flew in pâté de foie gras and caviar from the United States for their guests.[4]

For the island's wider population, a bittersweet reality of enormous sugar wealth in Cuba was extreme inequality in its distribution. The sugar baron elite's extravagance and ostentation conflicted with an infinitely harsher existence for hundreds of thousands of agricultural workers who toiled with machetes under a perpendicular sun. They enjoyed regular employment only during the three-month-long sugar harvest season. A significant social divide also existed between urban and rural Cuba, where there were comparatively few amenities and high rates of illiteracy. Furthermore, the land tenure system in the countryside was dreadful. Even in Havana, many lived in slums on the city's periphery, and thousands of beggars struggled to survive on the capital's streets, including homeless women with children.[5]

Another foreign visitor to Cuba in 1954 was U.S. photographer Eve Arnold, on assignment to provide pictures for an *Esquire* article by Helen Lawrenson. "The Sexiest City in the World" objectified the city, focusing on Cuban women—particularly prostitutes—and the experience of the male foreign traveler. The article judged there was "something in the air of Havana which has a curious chemical effect on Anglo-Saxons, dissolving their inhibitions and intensifying their libidos." "The accent on sex is everywhere," she affirmed. Arnold's accomplished black-and-white photographs showed a grittier reality, including her iconic and melancholic "Bar Girl in a Brothel in the Red Light District, Havana, 1954." She later described a ten p.m. curfew enforced by tanks, and down-at-the-heels brothels frequented by sexually aroused U.S. sailors.[6]

Lawrenson's article outraged columnists in the Cuban press. Her "Latin Lovers Are Lousy" article in the same magazine, a send-up of Latin and specifically Cuban machismo, had provoked an earlier sensation in 1936. Ulises Carbó in *Prensa Libre* outlined her portrayal of their metropolis as a center of international corruption and unprecedented sexual debauchery. The $5.5 million ($51 million) film adaptation of musical *Guys and Dolls* with Marlon Brando further exacerbated local feelings at the end of 1955 with its representation of Havana as a vice mecca. Carbó concluded that his fellow compatriots must possess something unique if North American movie producers always included them in their most libidinous storylines. His column observed that Hollywood films always portrayed Cuban men as sinister drug-peddling types, sweating in a setting of banana and coconut trees.[7]

Cuban newspapers also took aim that year at a *Chicago Tribune Magazine* article about Havana. "Police Wink at Vice, and Legalized Gambling Helps to Support the Government," its headline proclaimed. Apparently, "Wide-open Town" Havana could satisfy— "for a price"—whatever "penchant for pleasure" a man desired. Particularly the city's taxi drivers and street hawkers, who obliged pleasure-seekers desiring introductions to beautiful cubanas of all shades, with "flashing eyes and peppery personalities." It cited the $55 million ($504 million) spent in Cuba by 234,200 tourists in 1954, 95 percent of them Americans.[8]

Under the banner "How they see us in the United States," the *Diario Nacional* lamented the irritating regularity of defamatory reports like this that damaged Cuba's reputation. The article insisted it was time to take action, however, when they appeared not only in the sensationalist press but in prestigious and widely read publications like the *Chicago Tribune*.[9]

DEPORTED TO HAVANA

When Graham Greene made an initial one-night visit to Havana en route to Haiti in August 1954, the city left him underwhelmed. However, an unplanned two-night stay in the city ten days later was the catalyst for all his subsequent visits. It would lead him to revive and relocate an earlier abandoned idea for a satirical espionage story.

Greene's first 1954 journey to Cuba was long and exhausting, although Dutch airline KLM did supply "lots and lots of free drink" on the thirty-hour journey via Amsterdam, Glasgow (Prestwick), Gander (in Newfoundland), and Montreal. The author's keen eye spotted American dancer Katherine Dunham among his fellow passengers to Havana. Yet his first of three visits to Cuba's capital city that year mostly escaped Greene's memory. Concrete references to it exist in a letter and two postcards he wrote to Catherine Walston from Haiti on August 23, 1954. He declared in his letter, "I didn't like Havana at all & shall try to avoid it returning." After just one night in the Hispanic-Moorish luxury of the Hotel Sevilla-Biltmore, where he temporarily mislaid his travelers' checks, he caught a 9:45 flight the next morning to Miami, another disappointing experience. A fuss at airport immigration gave the author a premonition of trouble.[10] Problems did indeed lie ahead, during his return journey from Haiti, but Greene himself fomented the trouble by responding too honestly to a routine question from a U.S. immigration official.

Greene had arranged to spend some ten days in Haiti with theater director Peter Brook and his wife, the actress Natasha Brook. In a depressive but playful mood, he bathed in the pouring rain on day 1 of his Caribbean break, drank lots of rum, took an afternoon siesta, and visited a bordello. He shared a hotel room with U.S. writer Truman Capote, whom Greene described as "an extraordinary little fat babyish figure, a fairy to end all fairies, but rather endearing & very funny." Brook was directing the Capote musical *House of Flowers* in New York. Its action takes place on a West Indian island during Mardi Gras weekend where each of the girls at Madame Fleur's brothel is named after a flower.[11]

During the next eight days in Haiti, Greene attended a "fascinating . . . but then boring, & finally rather nauseating" cockfight, experienced several power cuts, rode horses with the Brooks up the Citadelle, and witnessed a voodoo ceremony. Natasha Brook's charm managed to lighten his mood on one morose evening when he drank a good deal. While loud American tourists interrupted his sleep, Haiti's magic pleased him, the author describing its "palms & flowers & foliage, drums beating, & the lights of brothels broken by the leaves." On Monday, August 30, he saw the Brooks and Capote off on a flight to Kingston, Jamaica, and spent the rest of a tiring day cashing money and fussing over a return flight. He eventually flew to San Juan in Puerto Rico, where the trouble he had portended began.[12]

U.S. authorities had first become aware of Greene's short-term student membership of the Communist Party when he deliberately let slip the information to a *Time* reporter in Vietnam in 1951.[13] He hoped to highlight the absurdity of the Congress-approved McCarran Act that prohibited any former foreign member of the Communist Party from entering the United States. In Greene's eyes, the restriction was symptomatic of extreme U.S. sensitivity and para-noia over communism, at which the novelist liked to poke fun. While what Winston Churchill had described as an Iron Curtain separated the ideological chasm between East and West, what Greene defined as a "cellophane curtain" hung over any of his subsequent attempts to obtain a U.S. visa. The expression encapsulated his views on the superficiality and artificiality of the country's political outlook and its consumer society. On the temporary visas the writer did manage to obtain, odd numbers and symbols appeared that were intelligible only to immigration officials, frequently hindering his smooth entry into the United States. On a positive note, the travel restriction gave him a plausible excuse to refuse tiresome invitations from his U.S. publisher.[14]

Greene had organized a return itinerary that took him from Puerto Rico to New York on Pan American and thence on a transatlantic British Overseas Airways Corporation (BOAC) flight to London. He was due to arrive early morning on the East Coast and catch an onward four p.m. flight. He had arranged to meet his agent Mary Pritchett during this stopover for lunch, and "the strange Truman" had tried to set him up with an American girl who he swore was "a mutual fate." The psychic Capote reportedly had "no doubt" they need only take "one look at each other" and could already predict what drinks she would "choose from a strange menu." Greene did not believe it, assuming the girl would be very odd if she did present herself at the airport for lunch.[15]

The rendezvous never took place. His careful travel and lunch arrangement came unstuck at the first transit point in San Juan, where he arrived on Delta from Port-au-Prince on a Monday evening at 8:55 p.m. A large U.S. immigration official in a khaki uniform examined the author's passport and asked him, "Ever been a member of the Communist Party?"

In a mischievous mood, Greene responded, "Yes, for four weeks at the age of nineteen."

Only with the utmost optimism could the author have expected the official to wave him through immigration control. Instead, the surly official asked him in an unfriendly tone to step aside. As the author told a reporter two days later in Havana, they would probably have allowed him to proceed if he had lied. However, it was necessary to "fight an ideology with an ideology"—his Catholic belief in "the liberty of the human spirit" versus "the methods of the police state." He defined the McCarran Act in such terms and declared himself unhesitant "in criticizing it or attacking it at every opportunity."[16]

In the farcical situation in which the British writer found himself, and with a confessed "sense of exhilaration," he sat down to read one of the five P. G. Wodehouse novels among his holiday reading. One wonders which of the following Jeeves and Bertie Wooster adventures he perused during the two hours before U.S. Immigration called him into a small airport office: *Summer Lightning* (1929), *Blandings Castle and Elsewhere* (1935), *The Luck of the Bodkins* (1935), *Uncle Fred in the Springtime* (1939), or *Quick Service* (1940).

A subsequent letter to the Brooks in New York described what had ensued after the couple's departure, starting with a good cop/bad cop scene with the two immigration officials. Greene had suggested they allow him to spend the night merrily in an airport bar, but the surly of the two men turned down this idea flat: "For you this is a dry Airport." Two plainclothes Cuban officers then chaperoned the writer to his hotel and around the town at Uncle Sam's expense until two a.m. After some hours in a bedroom plagued by mosquitoes, they accompanied Greene to San Juan Airport early that morning.[17]

Here again there was a squabble, now between U.S. Immigration and Delta, as they decided what to do with the troublesome author. Unlike dim-witted English gent Bertie Wooster, Greene could not depend on a quick-thinking valet to extricate him from such a bothersome bind. Instead, while American officials squabbled, he made his own luck by slipping away to cable Reuters. Press reports about his contretemps soon appeared in national newspapers on both sides of the Atlantic. On discovering the officials were about to deport him to Haiti, he played his trump card. Feeling like a parcel at their whim, he declared he did not possess a valid visa to return to Haiti. They returned him there nevertheless.[18]

Hours later, another scene played out on the tarmac at the Port-au-Prince airport. Delta's "disagreeable" local manager, a quiet southerner, had gone to some trouble to secure a visa for Greene to enable him to stay in Haiti for a further three days and thence fly on to Jamaica. Greene turned stubborn, and the Delta manager struggled to make his point. Haitians in the adjacent transit bar and gift shop wondered about the reason for the quarrel. Then the Delta pilot of the Super Convair 340 plane, a "very good-looking" former Hollywood actor and communist who had suffered his own run-ins with overzealous officialdom, intervened to arbitrate the airside dispute. He overruled the local Delta manager's order that Greene stay in Haiti, declaring he would fly the author to Havana on his New Orleans–bound flight instead.[19]

It was this series of incidents, therefore, that led to Greene's unplanned second visit to Havana in 1954, just ten days after a one-night stay—although even now, his mischievous tendency to flout officialdom led him to contravene local immigration regulations again. When air hostesses distributed transit cards to passengers destined for Florida, the author took one to cover all eventualities. As the blue-rinsed Miami-bound women passengers streamed through transit at Havana's Rancho Boyeros Airport, he followed them and avoided an entry stamp in his passport. Once through Cuban immigration unhindered, he asked a taxi driver to take him to the Hotel

Sevilla-Biltmore in the old city. Following a tiring and harassing twenty-four hours, he took a hot bath and fell asleep. Then the telephone woke him. A *New York Times* reporter in receipt of the Reuters cable had phoned around Havana's hotels to track him down. It soon rang again, this time with the *Daily Telegraph*'s local correspondent on the line.[20]

Greene provided the reporter with more detail about his probationary membership of the Communist Party at Oxford, his two-shilling subscription to party funds at the rate of six pennies a week. He described to him the "rather boisterous" behavior of "junior" immigration officials at San Juan Airport, as opposed to the "most polite" treatment by the head of immigration, Mr. John Glover, who had tried to find a "loophole" to admit him. Nevertheless, he told the reporter "a very awkward situation" had ensued.[21]

"Perhaps I ought to warn you," the journalist told him.

"What about?"

"I spoke to Immigration authorities here when I was trying to trace you. They were quite surprised. They say you never passed Immigration. They are looking for you everywhere."

Greene added in *Ways of Escape*, "They never found me. The police were not very efficient in the days of Batista."[22]

BATISTA'S CUBA

Many visitors to Cuba have tried to encapsulate its unique exoticism, often objectifying the country and Cubans with clichéd stereotypes. Travel writers, photographers, and the occasional novelist have journeyed there to soak up the island's cocktail of Afro-Hispanic cultures, blended with U.S. influence, and set in a tropical climate to a rhythmic beat. Ernest Hemingway, for example, so enjoyed his first experiences that he returned to reside there on an extended basis. Additional tempting fruits such as licentiousness, and on subsequent visits risk, attracted the manic-depressive Greene. Like Wormold, who had first fallen in love in Havana, "he was held to it as though to the scene of a disaster." The author would travel there ten times between 1954 and 1966.[23]

Another ingredient to add to this cocktail was Cuba's historical struggle for emancipation from foreign domination and indirect control. Only several decades after mainland Spanish American colonies freed themselves from Madrid's rule did Cuba finally achieve its independence at the turn of the twentieth century. However, the trouble did not end there. A snippet of dialogue in Greene's screenplay for *Our Man in Havana* adroitly encapsulates the first six decades of twentieth-century Cuban history. In an early scene, SIS Caribbean Station Chief Henry Hawthorne encounters Wormold in his vacuum cleaner shop and inquires about business:

HAWTHORNE: Do you do pretty well?
WORMOLD: Yes, but there's not much electric power since the
    troubles began.
HAWTHORNE: When was that?
WORMOLD: Oh, about the time Queen Victoria died.[24]

Two Fidel Castro–led rebel actions, first in July 1953 at the Moncada Barracks in Santiago de Cuba, and later the *Granma* landing in eastern Cuba in December 1956, would suggest the logical link between prerevolutionary Cuban and contemporary British history to be Elizabeth II's coronation (June 1953) or the Suez Crisis (July to November 1956), respectively. Instead, the historically and politically astute Greene refers us back to 1901, to the period of U.S. military intervention and occupation (1898–1902).

The United States fully involved itself in Cuba's affairs in 1898. Three years into the second Cuban war of independence against Spanish colonial rule, a mysterious explosion in Havana harbor killed 266 sailors on board the USS *Maine*, a battleship undertaking a peaceful mission to the island in February 1898. A clamor of sen-sationalist news stories in the United States had already denounced Spanish cruelty against Cubans and its own citizens. The new alleged act of Spanish treachery fueled a mass circulation war between New York newspapers owned by William Randolph Hearst and Joseph Pulitzer. Jingoism, lobbying by a Cuban junta in exile, and yellow journalism were all factors that forced U.S. president William McKin-ley's hand and led the U.S. military to intervene at the eleventh hour and break the stalemate between Cuban and Spanish adversaries.[25]

Following Spain's defeat and a four-year military occupation, the United States withdrew its forces and Cuba declared independence in May 1902. The island's sugar industry boomed, but nominally independent Cuba became a virtual protectorate under Washington's tutelage. Close U.S.-Cuban relations brought undoubted economic benefits to the island's economy, particularly its sugar baron elite. However, the denial of full political independence left a sour taste against Uncle Sam's overbearing and ongoing interference in Cuban affairs. For example, the 1901 Platt Amendment gave Washington the right to intervene "for the preservation of Cuban independence," and the 1903 Reciprocity Treaty bound the countries' economies together, for good and for bad.

The situation changed after the Wall Street crash of 1929 pro-voked a dramatic decline in Cuba's sugar export earnings to its largest market in the United States. A short-lived but ultimately frus-trated revolution ensued in 1933, when the little-known mixed-race army sergeant Fulgencio Batista burst onto the political scene. The former rail worker and army stenographer from Banes in Oriente province would dominate Cuban politics for most of the period from 1934 to 1958.

In January 1934, a new president sanctioned by Washington assumed power, though as newly promoted chief of the armed forces, Batista held the real power behind a series of puppet presidents for the rest of the decade. In 1940, he exchanged his military uniform for a white linen suit to win presidential elections. U.S. political and economic interests were amenable to his wartime rule.

Batista departed Cuba to live in Daytona Beach, Florida, in 1944, but returned to stand as a senator on the island in 1948. During this time, the two presidencies of Ramón Grau (1944–48) and Carlos Prío (1948–52) proved to be the most corrupt in Cuban history. Political violence, with the participation of university students, was rife. While campaigning for the 1952 elections, Grau made accusations of electoral fraud and withdrew his candidacy. Batista and subordinates in the army made their move and enacted an almost bloodless military coup, abruptly ending democracy in Cuba. Batista thence ruled as an out-and-out military dictator, deprived of the political legitimacy he had enjoyed during the Second World War.

A year before Greene's first visit in 1954, a daring and ambitious assault on the Moncada military barracks in Santiago de Cuba in eastern Cuba attempted to stoke a revolution and overthrow Batista. A group of mostly middle-class activists under the leadership of former Havana university student and lawyer Fidel Castro carried out the raid, timed to coincide with carnival celebrations in the island's second largest city. Despite its failure, the date July 26, 1953, gave a new revolutionary movement its name: 26 de Julio.

Batista's forces captured, tortured, and killed many of the surviving young rebels. Fidel Castro was fortunate due to the arrest of his small group outside the city by a lenient army lieutenant and the archbishop of Santiago's involvement. The archbishop ensured their delivery to Santiago's prison rather than the Moncada Barracks, where torture and death probably awaited. At his subsequent court tribunal, Castro, a trained lawyer, offered his own defense. In a rousing speech, the talented orator painted a grim social picture of his country. He described a fertile island with iniquitous land distribution, where many impoverished Cubans lived without proper housing and only limited access to healthcare and education.[26] Twenty-seven-year-old Castro's speech ended with a flourish since immortalized in Cuban history: "Condemn me. It does not matter. History will absolve me." The judge condemned him with a fifteen-year prison sentence.

HAVANA VICE

Greene was unaware of these events during his short visits to the island in 1954. As he wrote later, "I never stayed long enough to be aware of the sad political background of arbitrary imprisonment and torture."[27]

Batista's sudden ending of democracy in Cuba led students and those in the middle class to organize against his dictatorship. In an attempt to maintain an iron grip on power, Batista employed a clique of thuggish police and armed forces to repress opposition. In 1956, the British embassy described chief of police Rafael Cañizares as "a gross, corrupt and sadistic brute" akin to Nazi prototype Heinrich Himmler. He died later that year after violating the diplomatic immunity of the Haitian embassy to arrest ten revolutionaries. One shot him, and he died two days later. Despite the fact that six of the revolutionaries possessed promises of safe conduct from the Cuban government, all ten were killed during the incident itself or in the following days.

Heading the police's Anti-Communist and Anti-Subversive Unit was another notorious figure, Lieutenant Colonel Esteban Ventura, a character Greene exploited to draw Captain Segura in *Our Man in Havana*. Ventura operated in Havana's fifth and ninth precincts, wore a white linen or English muslin suit, and supervised novel methods of torture. As the British embassy affirmed, the dictatorship's repressive methods increasingly alienated the general population and forfeited their support.[28]

On the day after the author's unplanned arrival from Puerto Rico, the front page of the local English-language daily *Havana*

Post reported, "Graham Greene arrived in Havana yesterday and is staying at the Hotel Sevilla. He will seek a route back to England which will avoid his having to stop at a United States port." Other front-page stories highlighted protests in Cyprus against British rule, radiation sickness suffered by Japanese fishermen after hydrogen bomb testing in the Pacific archipelago of Bikini, and a new round of U.S. Senate hearings into the conduct of Senator Joseph McCarthy.[29] Greene was preoccupied with writing a novel based on his experiences in Indochina and still three years away from commencing *Our Man in Havana*.

Economically, Cuba continued to benefit from lucrative sales of its chief export. The Korean War in 1950, like the preceding First and the Second World Wars, had been good for business. When world markets and rival producers suffered disruption, Cuban sugar profited. Despite a dip in 1952, sugar continued to bring massive economic benefits to the island, even if this wealth was unevenly distributed among the population.

Elsewhere in the Cuban economy, Hotel Law 2074 provided tax exemptions to any hotel providing tourist accommodation and guaranteed government financing from the newly created Banco de Desarrollo Económico y Social. The new law encouraged a period of rampant hotel/casino construction in Havana that boosted its credentials as a tourist destination. The Caribbean's largest city was much closer to free-spending East Coast U.S. residents than Las Vegas. In 1952, it possessed twenty-nine hotels with 3,180 rooms, but new construction boosted capacity to provide Havana with forty-two hotels with 5,438 rooms by 1958.[30]

Indeed, the city's skyline transformed between Greene's visits in 1954 and his writing of *Our Man in Havana* from November 1957 to June 1958. The district of Vedado came to boast three new towering modernist hotels. In fact, they all celebrated their inaugurations during the period that Greene wrote and polished his manuscript: the *Capri* (November 30, 1957), the *Habana Riviera* (December 10,

1957), and the *Habana Hilton* (March 19, 1958). The Capri and the Habana Hilton hotels would make brief appearances in his forthcoming novel.

Greene's decision to stay at the more traditional Sevilla-Biltmore for a second time reflected well on the establishment. Located on the edge of Old Havana, just a block from the Presidential Palace, it was the second most prestigious hotel in Havana after the Hotel Nacional. It had been remodeled in 1923 by Schultze & Weaver, the same U.S. company that built the Waldorf-Astoria in New York. One of its most alluring features was the spacious but dark Andalusian-tiled lobby with an interior patio featuring a water fountain open to the sky.[31]

The author soon developed a strong aversion to a gossip columnist for the local English-language newspaper, *The Havana Post*, who lived in a top-floor suite at the hotel. Greene would later describe Edward Scott as "a fat unattractive little New Zealander with an American accent."[32] The journalist was a familiar foreign figure in Havana, smoking H. Upmann No. 4 cigars and stalking the city's casinos and clubs by night in his DeSoto Firedome V-8 to gather intelligence for his daily newspaper column.[33]

New Zealand–born Scott, otherwise known as Ed or Ted, had a colorful past. He began as a cub reporter in New York for the *Evening Post*, covering boxing and shipping news. An accomplished lightweight boxer himself, he later became a boxing manager. Professional highlights of his journalistic career included reporting the Lindbergh baby kidnapping in 1932. Not for the last time in Scott's career, he was deported from a Latin American country when his newspaper column in *The Panama American* criticized the Panamanian president's pro-Axis and anti-American stance. Later in 1941, he interviewed Prime Minister Winston Churchill on a train in the United States.[34]

During the Second World War, he worked under William Stephenson, a Canadian-born industrialist and veteran pilot of the First

World War (and, according to Ian Fleming, an important inspiration for his fictional James Bond). Stephenson led the British Security Coordination (BSC) Office, the operational and liaison arm of British intelligence in the United States. Scott was a BSC contact in both Panama and New York. His wartime work in New York countered German spying activities and helped protect British shipping from Nazi submarine packs in the Atlantic. At the end of the war, Stephenson received a knighthood and returned to the business world. He lived most of the year in Jamaica, where Fleming was a part-time resident and friend. Scott received an inscribed watch from King George VI in recognition of his contribution to the war effort.[35]

Like Greene, the well-known British travel writer Norman Lewis also traveled to pre-revolutionary Cuba in the 1950s. His travel accounts are stylish and entertaining but not completely reliable as factual accounts.[36] According to "A Mission to Havana," Bond author and *Sunday Times* foreign manager Ian Fleming sent Lewis on an assignment to Cuba in late 1957. His mission was to make contact with long-term Havana resident Ernest Hemingway through Edward Scott and fathom the true progress of Castro's anti-Batista insurrection. Lewis stayed at the Sevilla-Biltmore, where Scott lived, and they met in the hotel's dark American bar, where Lewis described the roving reporter as "short, pink and rotund with a certain babyish innocence of expression that was wholly misleading." According to Lewis, Fleming told him the colorful correspondent was also an inspiration for James Bond, minus his physical appearance. The English travel writer eventually met Hemingway at his home, Finca Vigia, where Papa greeted him "in wretched physical shape," drinking heavily and unwilling to proffer an opinion on the insurrection.[37]

When Greene visited Cuba in 1954, Scott had recently fallen out with Hemingway, the first of two public rows with that year's winner of the Nobel Prize for Literature. The trouble first arose at a diplomatic party when the author's wife, Mary Hemingway, extolled the tastiness of lion meat. Scott spoke out of turn, as was his custom, and declared he was averse to eating the meat of a carnivore. She defined him as "stupid and prejudiced just like all the rest of the British colonials." The matter would probably have ended there had Scott not published his version of events in his "Interesting *if* True" gossip column. This evidently riled the Hemingways and elicited a long letter from Ernest, despite his absence from the party, in which he praised bushmeat from puma to gazelle and every animal in between. He accused Scott of "behaving very oddly at the party" and then writing a "screwy column" about it.[38]

Ernest and Mary Hemingway were not feeling their best following injuries suffered in two successive plane crashes in East Africa earlier that year. But less than a month after the diplomatic party, Scott added further insult to lingering physical injury by writing in his column that women "temporarily" married to famous men often acquired "the worst characteristics of their husbands." This was a direct reference to a visit to Havana by actress Ava Gardner and her husband Frank Sinatra, but the Hemingways recognized an allusion to themselves. Ernest Hemingway angrily accused Scott of writing "dirtily, snidely and insultingly" about his wife, and identified in him several defects including "an inferiority complex" and "a very bad conscience." The matter did not end there—the exaggerated machismo on display then extended to Scott challenging Hemingway to an armed duel. Suffice to say, the two expatriate Havana residents did not draw pistols at twenty paces, but it took the intervention of a Cuban radiologist acquaintance to mediate and defuse the mutually perceived affronts to wounded honor.[39]

As for the British author's unplanned arrival in the Cuban capital, Scott described a "decidedly irritated" and "browned off" Greene in his daily gossip column. Long-distance calls bombarded Havana newspaper offices to inquire about Greene's presence in the city. Scott reported that when Johnny Young of the *Havana Post* and London's *Daily Mirror* talked to the novelist, "Greene was so hot Johnny had to talk to him through a Geiger counter. Then he cooled off until he was only white hot. He was still boiling when I saw him." Greene told the New Zealander that he had joined the Communist Party alongside four or five other students in 1923 [sic], in the hope of wangling a free trip to Moscow. However, "a big husky Australian, who was a real commie," rumbled their scheme and broke it up.[40]

Two photos from this time show Greene in white Oxford bags and espadrilles in the internal patio of the Sevilla-Biltmore. In one, he is perspiring and appears angry. The other shows a grinning Greene in the company of two foreign journalists (including Young), holding a number of items, including his British passport.

The journal Greene kept during his summer holidays reveals some of the author's activities in Havana. Tuesday, August 31, was an action-packed day. After an early start and travails in San Juan and Port-au-Prince, his journal noted:

> The louche city. Cocaine & marijuana offered. Two girls & boy. Picked up nice car driver & went around with him in evening. To public blue film—seats 1.20. Pornographic book shop in lobby. To bed v[ery]. tired, after efforts to get passage. Nothing till next week.[41]

His taxi driver Rocky was a fortuitous discovery, a guide he used many times over, even seeing him after the Cuban Revolution when his vehicle fell apart. Unlike his first one-night visit, what he found in Havana during this second two-day stay astounded Greene. He recounted his adventures on a glittery postcard to Catherine Walston, adding: "I've changed my mind about Havana. It's a fascinating place—the most vicious I've ever been in. . . . I expect you've heard how I hit the front page in my war against U.S.!"

He suggested they meet in Cuba on his next visit to see Catherine in the Caribbean in November.[42] He had previously employed the word *vicious* to describe Paddington's hotels in his 1939 Mexico travelogue *The Lawless Roads*. His reference in both cases was to vice rather than violence, referring to each location's surfeit of prostitutes.[43]

The effusive author added in an otherwise identical message to Peter and Natasha Brook: "I had hardly left my hotel door before I was offered cocaine, marijuana and various varieties of two girls and a boy, two boys and a girl, etc." He told them he tried his first ever marijuana cigarette.[44]

Greene, as we know, was not averse to sampling drugs during his hedonistic trips around the globe. He craved temporary highs to alleviate manic-depressive lows. A magnetic attraction to seediness was another a notable trait in the dissolute author. On this occasion, therefore, U.S. Immigration had initiated a fortuitous train of events. They had initially interrupted a mundane journey home, gifting him the chance to prove a political point and give vent to anti-American feeling. His landing in Havana had then injected both a heavy dose of seediness and the offer of illicit drugs.

On his first full day in the city, Greene remarked on the "constant press attention" since his arrival. He obtained a passage on KLM flight 655 to Amsterdam via Montreal for September 2, a reversal of his outward journey, but bad weather delayed the post-midnight journey by twenty-four hours. This was also fortunate because it enabled him to discover a Havana establishment he would henceforth visit at every opportunity. His journal first noted a phone call from Desmond Pakenham, the first secretary and consul at the British embassy in Havana and a former SIS colleague. Before meeting up with Pakenham and his wife for dinner, Greene described "marijuana & show with three girls" in the afternoon. This probably explains his recollection years later about "how deftly the 'Emperor's Crown' used to be performed by three girls at once in a brothel in Batista's Havana." Following dinner, he attended a "terrible ballet" and left at intermission. He then sampled more of Havana's exotic delights with visits to the Montmartre and the Tropicana, the latter described as "fantastic."[45] Greene did not employ superlatives freely. He was storing these experiences in his journal, and many of them surfaced again when he began *Our Man in Havana* three years later.

The Montmartre and the Tropicana were two of the capital's principal nightclubs. The Montmartre was a casino and cabaret a few blocks from the Hotel Nacional in Vedado. The Tropicana, inaugurated in 1931, was the island's premier cabaret venue, a self-declared "Paradise Under the Stars." The three-part show that Greene savored that evening consisted of Ritmo en Fantasía (Rhythm in Fantasy), Polynesia, and Canciones de Ayer (Songs of Yesterday).[46] He sets the exotic scene in a draft of his novel, when Wormold chooses the venue for Milly's seventeenth birthday party:

> [I]t was a more innocent establishment than the Nacional in spite of the roulette rooms through which visitors passed before they reached the huge metal arch, like a hangar's of the cabaret. Beyond, the stage and dance floor were open to the sky. Chorus girls paraded twenty feet up along a plank among the palm trees. Pink and mauve searchlights swept the floor. A man in bright blue evening clothes sang in American about Paris and then the piano was wheeled away into the undergrowth and the dancers came stepping down like awkward birds among the branches while an orchestra rose into sight among the shadows of the palm flans.[47]

The public cinema with blue films was the Shanghai Theater, a regular Greene haunt on his pre-revolutionary visits to Havana. For somebody who considered himself a cognoscente of nude entertainment, the Shanghai was a revelation. In London, he liked to frequent the Windmill Theatre, "a particular blend of tattiness and glamour, sweat and eau de cologne." In order to avoid strict British censorship laws against obscenity, the venue exploited a loophole: its female models could pose naked, but only if they remained motionless. Thus from 1931 to 1964, the Windmill's Revudeville titillated audiences with a *tableau vivant* of statuesque nudes.[48] Malcolm Muggeridge accompanied him to the Soho venue one evening and observed how the spectacle's "tattiness and seediness" appealed to his companion.[49]

In an interview two decades later, Greene evoked the infinitely more sordid Havana venue:

> [T]he old Chinese theatre provided a wonderful show for 2 dollars [$18] consisting of two stage performances containing everything, with free blue films in the intervals. There was also a pornographic bookshop in the foyer and the young Cubans would buy their pornographic picture book in the foyer and look at that during the stage performance, and lay it on one side when the film came on.[50]

Located in Chinatown on Zanja, a long street that also dissects Central Havana along the route of the old Royal Ditch, this legitimate theater from the 1930s had since gained a more insalubrious reputation.[51] Greene's screenplay for the film *Our Man in Havana* describes the Shanghai auditorium:

> There is a catwalk running between the stalls, and three girls are parading down it now in the first stages of a strip tease. The old and rather dirty building is by no means full. What audience there is is Cuban (except for a few blacks) and entirely masculine. They express their satisfaction with whistles. On either side of the stage hang posters advertising in English clubs where beautiful girls can be found. A notice in Spanish and bad English forbids the audience to molest the girls.[52]

On discovering the venue, Greene affirmed that "nowhere else in the world" did such a place exist.[53] As far as he was concerned, it was the apogee of seediness, its crowning glory. Carlos Franqui, a journalist who set up 26 de Julio radio station Radio Rebelde and later edited Cuba's national newspaper, described the Shanghai as "a place right out of Fellini."[54]

On the day of his departure, Greene took another stroll around Old Havana. Rather than its architecture, a mix of sixteenth- to twentieth-century buildings in Rococo, Baroque, and Neoclassical styles, he fixed his gaze on a corner where a black vendor sold photos and books, most of them shoddy Italian romantic literature. A jukebox in a dark bar—probably the bar of Greene's hotel—played "From Here to Eternity," while an American couple proceeded from silence, and her tears, to an embrace. A tourist guide entered with a family and their "awful boy," and Greene noted in his travel journal the "outrageous" price of ginger ale and lemonade.

Out on the streets again, a "big tourist policeman" stopped Greene and the following conversation ensued:

> "Is this your first time in Havana?"
> "Yes."
> "You do not tell the truth."
> "Oh, yes, I do."
> "Your name is Strippling."
> "No, it's Greene."
> "You are German?"
> "No, I'm English."

Greene commented in his journal, "I felt on verge of more trouble."[55]

He used the incident four years later for an early street scene in *Our Man in Havana*'s screenplay. In Carol Reed's film, a burly policeman approaches expatriate German doctor Hasselbacher to ask his name, occupation, and nationality, then demands to see his identity papers.

Hours after the real street encounter, Greene finally caught his post-midnight Douglas DC-6B KLM flight to Amsterdam via Canada, seated beside a sociable Cuban widow.[56] Members of the press awaited his arrival in Montreal. A *Daily Express* reporter described Greene in a crumpled brown suit, yawning his way out of the plane and talking freely about his latest row.[57] A local newspaper quoted Greene's description of "misguided and unstable American immigration laws" and the country's "cellophane curtain."[58] Indeed, the author thanked the United States for helping him publicize his views on the "hysterical outlook" of U.S. immigration policy. To drive home his point, he asserted, "I am certainly glad Canada has no such laws." It was his third dispute with U.S. immigration authorities since 1952, when he had first confessed his short-lived membership in the Communist Party.[59]

The author continued his journey on the same plane to Amsterdam on September 3, the widow in the neighboring seat now hungover and hence quieter. On changing planes in the Netherlands, Greene was in a more humorous mood. During his half-hour stopover before an onward late-night flight to London, he told journalists as he sipped a whisky on the rocks that "the joke is always on our side," and he would not be going to New York for the Broadway premiere of his play *The Living Room*. Sticking the knife in further he added, "There are too many countries I prefer to visit and can visit without any difficulties."[60]

Greene was keen to repeat his experiences in Havana and urged Catherine Walston to join him on his next visit before the end of the year. He was already planning a trip to Jamaica at the end of October to include perhaps a few more days in Haiti.[61] He reminded her of a previous visit together when they ate sandwiches, drank as they listened to calypsos, and frolicked in a swimming pool.[62]

Immigration stamps in a new passport issued to Greene in September 1954 indicate a third short visit to Cuba in 1954. Evidence includes a Haitian exit visa on November 22 that predates a Havana entry stamp on November 24, 1954. The Spanish consulate in Havana issued a transit visa for Spain on November 27, stamped the next day in Madrid's Barajas Airport, proving a visit to Cuba after

Jamaica and Haiti, and Greene's return to Europe through Madrid. The second half of 1954, therefore, had seen a cumulative sequence of an initial one-night stopover, followed by a second two-night stay, and finally a three-night visit to Cuba in late November.[63]

Ways of Escape provides detail on this third 1954 visit with an unnamed "friend," including their last afternoon when Greene's trusty taxi driver led them on a city tour. At the Shanghai they watched the legendary sex artist Superman perform like a "dutiful husband" with a girl, played a little roulette, ate at the Floridita, smoked marijuana, and saw a lesbian perform at the Blue Moon. They hoped to indulge even further and asked their driver to procure them cocaine. But the powder easily obtained at a newsagent for five shillings had little effect when they snorted it on their bed.[64] To Natasha Brook he wrote gleefully, "In Havana we found much better blue films than I had and we tried something which was called cocaine but which I suspect was boracic powder. Anyway it had no effect except giving me a hangover next day."[65]

Superman was an itinerant sex artist in Havana, said to possess a penis of enormous dimensions.[66] Like the Shanghai Theater, its priapic star performer held a particular fascination for hedonistic Greene. His name entered Greene's novel, along with twelve mentions of the Shanghai Theater. Superman's sizable legend even reached as far as Hollywood. Francis Ford Coppola included a scene in *The Godfather, Part II* where treacherous Fredo takes his brother Michael to see Superman perform in Havana on New Year's Eve 1958. Seeing is believing, but an accompanying U.S. senator struggles to believe Superman's appendage is real. On the eve of revolution, Michael Corleone is too preoccupied with mafia rival Hyman Roth's intrigues and Fredo's ultimate betrayal to care.[67]

The unnamed "friend" who accompanied Greene to Havana's haunts was Catherine Walston.[68] The Shanghai's seediness had so enthralled Greene that he appeared eager to share the experience with her. A spectacle for Cubans at the venue that afternoon therefore was this outwardly respectable foreign couple sat amid the setting of depravity. Greene later included an episode in *Our Man in Havana* (both novel and film) where Wormold rushes to the Shanghai with SIS secretary Beatrice Severn to rescue his subagent, the burlesque dancer Teresa. The author surely based the fictional scene on his real visit with Catherine.

At no point during his three 1954 visits to Cuba had Greene ventured outside the capital city, and his only local acquaintance was his taxi driver, who had purveyed him bogus drugs. Greene had sampled some of the more hedonistic delights of Cuba under Batista's dictatorship, yet unlike in Vietnam, Malaysia, or Kenya earlier in the decade, he had made little if any effort to learn about the politics of the country.

He had also visited the Floridita for the first time, an old-fashioned bar/restaurant at the corner of Obispo and Montserrate, with a long mahogany bar, ceiling fans, and Regency-style décor. It was his favorite spot to meditate on a cocktail and eavesdrop on customers' conversations.[69] Famously, the Floridita advertised itself as the cradle of the daiquiri, the refreshing blended ice and rum cocktail perfected by barman Constantino Ribalaigua. Greene made a habit of lunchtime visits to the establishment. It afforded him refuge from Havana's oppressive heat, fine cuisine—at least prior to the Revolution—and a very dry martini to collect his thoughts. During all his visits, the Floridita's most famous barfly, Ernest Hemingway, was conspicuous by his absence.

The author next landed in Cuba in late November 1956. His visit coincided with Anthony Eden's stay from November 23 to December 14 at the Goldeneye winter residence of Ian Fleming in neighboring Jamaica. The overwrought prime minister had suffered a physical breakdown during the Suez Crisis, and his doctors ordered him to convalesce. Noël Coward was another part-time resident of the British colony at nearby Blue Harbour. The renowned British actor and playwright welcomed Mr. and Mrs. Eden with gifts of caviar and champagne to assuage the frugality at Fleming's home.[70] Two days later, Coward wrote in his diary:

> Apparent peace broods over the "paradise of the Caribbean," but alas it is only apparent, for lurking behind the quiet trees and scampering through the banana plantations are rumours, tensions and wild surmises.[71]

Eden's physical though not political revival in Jamaica coincided with the presentation of credentials by Britain's new ambassador to Havana. The prime minister's Caribbean stay also overlapped with the landing in eastern Cuba of a motorized leisure yacht carrying eighty-one men under Fidel Castro's command. Their plan was to overthrow the island's Washington-backed dictator.

6

DOWN IN HAVANA

The writing of *Our Man in Havana* would suffer a delayed start, two false beginnings, and the absence of Greene's most cherished writing companion, Catherine Walston. He definitively began the novel alone and in Havana itself, inspired by the city's streets and wider global events, yet afflicted by the highs and lows of his manic depression.

He first resurrected his abandoned spy story in 1956. Greene informed Catherine in August how he planned to change the spy story's setting—containing "imaginary agents" and a wife with "imaginary lovers"—from Estonia to Portugal. The result would have been *Our Man in Lisbon*, harking back to his wartime intelligence reports on mendacious spies in the Portuguese capital.[1] Indeed, his conception of the new writing project wavered over two years between novelette, stand-alone film, and novel.[2]

After telling another correspondent in October that he had a new novel underway, entry stamps in Catherine's and Greene's passports reveal they both traveled from Haiti to Havana on November 25, 1956. They spent three nights on the island before traveling through Jamaica.[3] Their arrival in Cuba coincided with the sailing of *Granma* from Tuxpan, a Mexican port city a few kilometers upstream from the Gulf of Mexico. The eighty-two men aboard the yacht landed in eastern Cuba two days late and in the wrong place. This forced them to wade for hours through a difficult-to-penetrate mangrove swamp.

It was an inauspicious start to what became a twenty-five-month-long insurrection against Fulgencio Batista's dictatorship.

The main triggers for Greene's manic-depression in the 1950s were crises in his private life. When he came to write *Our Man in Havana*, he was an emotional mess. Notwithstanding his ongoing affair with Catherine Walston, he had fallen in love with Swedish actress Anita Björk in December 1955, whose husband had committed suicide the year before. Catherine became aware of this rival for Greene's extra-marital attentions when he informed her about Anita a year after the affair began. Between late 1955 and 1957, therefore, the relationships with his two mistresses overlapped. Combining professional writing commitments and assignations with both women in different parts of the globe presented a practical challenge. And while two concurrent love affairs provided physical rewards, and financial benefit to Anita when the successful writer bought her a house, juggling his own and their emotions to all their satisfaction proved an impossibility. The personal torment his tumultuous personal affairs caused him was acute.

This partly explains the particular extent of Greene's long-haul traveling that year. By his own estimation he flew forty-four thousand miles in 1957,[4] making him a frequent flyer and air miles king before such terms existed. The year began in New York. During 1957 he twice visited Russia. He also flew to China, Martinique, St. Kitts, Guadeloupe, and Cuba (with another stay in New York on the way). In between, he made other short trips within Europe, to Sweden, Italy (including his second home in Capri), and France. He spent several weeks at his daughter's ranch in Canada toward the end of the year, before flying from Montreal to Copenhagen (via New York again) and onto Sweden between Christmas 1957 and the New Year.

As soon as Greene returned from his 1956 visit with Catherine to Cuba, he begged her to accompany him there the following May or June so he could write his "story." "We'd have a car & we wouldn't stay long in Havana, but find somewhere with a beach, & I'd write it like I wrote *The Third Man*," he explained. He then contemplated a lone visit in February or March—"A bit of opium & debauchery might be good for me!" These would certainly provide a welcome distraction from his tormented self. Greene's idea then turned to the summer, to write "the novelette" while Catherine lay in bed (again, the way he had written *The Third Man*). He reminded her how "fruitful" those years had been—"2 films, 2 plays, 2 novels."[5] Yet the season came and went without her agreement to accompany him and act as a sounding board for his literary creation.

Financial pressure to publish a new book made him determined to visit in the autumn. He reminded her, "Cuba could be fun & peaceful—it's not all Havana & blue films. It's also sea & Santiago & fish restaurants & villages."[6] Despite his persistence, he failed to persuade Catherine. She would never accompany him to the island again, although she did travel there with husband Harry Walston in 1968.

In the absence of Catherine, Greene made do with his other mistress, Anita. But he was bored in her company. "I'm alive with you, but I'm pretending to be alive with Anita," he had told Catherine in February 1957.[7] Unable to breach Catherine's resistance, he made a summer trip with Anita to Martinique in the French Caribbean to begin *Our Man in Havana*. Compared to Catherine, however, she proved an inferior writing companion. Her company made him restless and bored again, and not his productive self. He "carpentered" a new beginning onto something old and shaved off eight thousand words.[8] But try as he might, his handiwork proved a disappointment.

He abandoned this first attempt at his spy story to try again later in Havana. Yet apart from trusty taxi driver Rocky, Greene had no Cuban contacts in the island. He therefore cultivated Batista's man in London, the Cuban ambassador Roberto González de Mendoza, married to Ofelia de Mendoza y de la Torre, a dazzling beauty on London's diplomatic circuit. Greene wrote to the diplomat shortly after meeting him at Stonor Park, an ancient house near

Henley-on-Thames belonging to one of Britain's great Catholic families.[9] Greene told Mendoza he planned a three-week visit to work on "a long short story." The writer at first envisaged renting a house and requested recommendations. He also asked for local introductions, "useful . . . from the point of a friendly roof and good wine!"[10] The ambassador contacted his older brother, Nicolas G. Mendoza, a fifty-seven-year-old lawyer, real estate owner, and merchant resident of Havana. Batista's man in London told Greene his brother would "arrange" for him to meet the people he was interested to see.[11] The author kept his own counsel about one Cuban he hoped to meet, the rebel leader Fidel Castro.

His accommodation requirements in Havana suddenly changed when a bombshell landed: Catherine dumped him. In a subsequent letter to Gillian Sutro, he explained what had transpired. After a dinner with Gillian, Catherine had simply telephoned to end the affair. It was for his benefit, apparently. He was being "too torn in two & was getting burnt up by it."[12] Catherine might have been jealous, genuinely concerned for his well-being, or a combination of the two. Whatever it was, six years after his novel *The End of the Affair*, the affair with Catherine appeared to have ended.

A NOVEL BEGINNING

Ongoing relationship problems triggered a melancholic episode as Greene flew alone to Havana by way of New York. Four sheets of minuscule handwriting on lined foolscap detail his trip's first six days. Greene's "Havana Journal" commences at Manhattan's Airlines Terminal at 42nd Street and Park Avenue, where he checked in before boarding a bus out to Idlewild Airport. Despite the terminal's bookshops, bar, and souvenir shop, he only acknowledged its "dreariness." He consumed three whiskies on the plane down to Cuba, and a conversation with a fellow passenger about gun collecting took him "at last away" from himself and his "chaos & loss." He welcomed the distraction, and in a state of mild intoxication began to imagine a new life for himself, buying old pistols in Paris and selling them at great profit in the United States.[13]

"Uproar" greeted him at Havana's air terminal. Customs officials refused to expedite his luggage without a tip; Greene wondered what would happen if he merely called their bluff and waited. Finally installed at the Sevilla-Biltmore again, he felt "tired & flat" with "depression back round the corner." This was his mood just a day before writing the first words of *Our Man in Havana*.

Greene's only company in the hotel was a toy radio no larger than a cigarette packet that only emitted Spanish radio. He went to the hotel's dark bar and ordered a rum drink. Rather than linger in the hotel's cool interior patio of Andalusian tiles, a trickling fountain, and statuette nymphs and goddesses, he left to stroll around the block. There he noticed "more tarts than ever, & lovely ones too." Their wolf whistles and insistent taxi drivers pursued him, so he sought peace on the Paseo del Prado, where the bootblacks pestered. Linking the center of the city to the Malecón, Spanish laurel trees line and cast shadows along the Prado's ornate pedestrian walkway.[14] In Greene's novel, the whistles echo around Wormold's teenage daughter Milly as she strolls Havana's streets impervious to the baying wolves.[15]

The following day—Friday, November 8, 1957—was pivotal for both Greene's mood and his nascent novel. In the Hotel Sevilla-Biltmore, he "wrote out" some of his "loneliness & despair" in a letter to Catherine.[16] She was the only person he could write to "about anything funny or sad or work or a man [. . .] in the street." He confessed to missing her terribly and being "afraid." His new story had started to grow in his mind into "something good—funny & sad & exciting" a few days previously in New York, but the feeling had slipped away. He described to her his inflight conversation with the gun collector and the new toy radio. It would have been remiss not to mention Anita. He had arrived in New York from Paris, where he had spent a "so-so" time with the actress. Her choice of reading left him unimpressed, she raised "stupid questions," and they suffered a pregnancy scare.[17]

Greene lamented:

> This place is no fun without you. I suppose I'll go to the Chinese Theatre, but what's the point without you to come home to? [. . .]

> I've got 26 books with me, but again there's no you to say I like this or I don't like that, do read this, don't you think this metaphor's good. [. . .]

> Now I must get up & wander round & tomorrow I must try to begin "Our Man in Havana." It won't come as easily & happily as *The Third Man*. I have an awful fear that it won't work without you—what I did in Martinique was useless.

Writing to her awakened his creative spirit and stimulated him to compose the opening of his new novel. On the flap of the sealed envelope addressed to Catherine, he annotated, "Encouraged by writing to you. I've got out some clear foolscap & done the first sentence of *Our Man in Havana*—no, a whole paragraph as though you were in the room. A good opening paragraph."[18] After several false starts, Greene had definitively begun his spy fiction satire.

He did indeed leave the hotel to "wander round," entering an American bank to deposit a check from his U.S. publisher Viking. He actually included such a scene in the novel, later to appear in the cinematic version, filmed in a bank in Calle Obispo. The check-clearing process felt terribly slow to him, served not by a clerk but by an executive, who conversed on the phone to a client on first-name terms about a $150,000 ($1.3 million) loan.[19] In his novel, the client's name is Henry, and a similar overheard phone conversation brings home to Wormold his straitened financial circumstances, a motivation for him to invent intelligence reports and increase his remuneration from London.

Greene returned to the vicinity of his hotel, visiting the British embassy a few blocks away in the direction of the capital's seafront avenue the Malecón. The embassy occupied the top three floors of the Edificio Bolívar, a drab nine-story building on Capdevila, close to Havana's harbor entrance.[20] Diplomatic staff described to him the spectacle they had witnessed eight months earlier of an armed assault against the nearby Presidential Palace, on March 13, 1957. A rival group to Fidel Castro's 26 de Julio rebels, the Directorio Revolucionario, had stormed the palace in an attempt to assassinate military dictator Fulgencio Batista. They reached his study but failed to breach its door. Rebel snipers had occupied tall buildings in the vicinity, including the Hotel Sevilla-Biltmore, from where they targeted guards defending the palace.

The dictator's men soon gained the upper hand, strengthened by police, army, and navy reinforcements. They fired back with machine guns, hitting the British embassy some two hundred yards away as viewing diplomats huddled around the typist room window. *New York Times* correspondent Ruby Hart Phillips described how two .20mm shells from Batista's defending forces penetrated the walls of Ted Scott's room on a corner of the Hotel Sevilla-Biltmore. One tore a hole in his wardrobe and suits inside, and the other his bookcase.[21]

Another indiscriminate burst struck an unfortunate American tourist from New Jersey on a balcony of the nearby Hotel Regis. He later died of his injuries. Greene adapted the tragic event for an early passage in his novel: "one tourist had recently been killed by a stray bullet while he was taking a photograph of a picturesque beggar under a balcony near the palace." His smashed $500 ($4,500) Leica perturbs his foreign companions more than his death and reduces general tourist interest in the "all-in-tour."[22] The incident is a rare rebuke in the novel for U.S. materialism and tourism from an author who rarely suppressed admonitions like these. Furthermore, Greene gave the risible name Mr. Humpelnicker to one of the dead tourist's acquaintances.

On Wednesday, November 13, the British ambassadorial residence in Vedado hosted Greene as a lunch guest of honor.[23] Diplomats warned the writer that in Santiago de Cuba, the seat of the Castro-led insurrection in the Oriente province, he should "not go out after dark."[24] Eight months earlier, following the armed assault on the Presidential Palace, the embassy had identified an increase in Batista's "ruthless oppression," but also his increasing isolation.[25] An indication of Greene's still limited knowledge of Cuban politics in 1957, meanwhile, was his journal's repeated misspelling of Batista as Bautista.[26]

Following his busy morning, Greene rewarded himself with a lunch at the Floridita of stuffed crayfish and coconut ice cream in a shell. For him to remark that it was "surely one of the best restaurants in the world" was praise indeed from a fastidious client who traveled widely and ate in many of the world's finest establishments.

He proved less complimentary about the Floridita's foreign clientele. These barbs entered his "Havana Journal," but not his emerging novel. One woman at the bar appeared "like a mature whore, with huge protruding buttocks." The male member of a noisy American couple was "rolling his middle-aged arse" to the lavatory just like his female partner. His observations continued in the separate restaurant section, where another American was ignoring the menu and requesting a Welsh rarebit. Greene contemplated the faded beauty of the man's female companion, her "face stamped with dissatisfaction." "Why must the rich be so unhappy?" he asked. Maybe she had married him for money and lacked the "social courage to take a lover," a revealing comment given the mess in Greene's own private life. He noticed a government regulation that prohibited the selling of cattle meat on Fridays and surmised correctly that this was "Catholic interference." It was Holy Friday for Catholics, but pork chops remained on the day's menu.[27]

No... 1...

THE COMMUNIST PARTY
OF GREAT BRITAIN

16 KING STREET
COVENT GARDEN
LONDON : W C 2

:: **This is to Certify that** ::

Graham Greene

of *School House*

Berkhamstead

is a Member of the Communist Party

Oxford City Local

Fredk. J. March Secretary

LOCAL CONTRIBUTIONS, 1925.

	JANUARY					JULY			
					4	11	18	25	
	FEBRUARY					AUGUST			Special International levy
7	14	21	28		1	8	15	22	29
	MARCH					SEPTEMBER			
7	14	21	28		5	12	19	26	
	APRIL					OCTOBER			Special International levy
4	11	18	25		3	10	17	24	31
	MAY		Special International levy			NOVEMBER			
2	9	16	23	30	7	14	21	28	
	JUNE					DECEMBER			
6	13	20	27		5	12	19	26	

The subscriptions of all members of the Party (full members and probationary members) must be acknowledged on the card by the use of stamps issued from headquarters for these purposes.

Communist Party membership card belonging to Graham Greene.
Graham Greene–Catherine Walston collection GTMGamms168, Georgetown University Library Booth Family Center for Special Collections, Washington, D.C.

Herbert Greene *(second from left)* en route to the Spanish Civil War in 1937.
*Photograph from Secret Agent in Spain (1938), by courtesy of
The University of Liverpool Library.*

СОВЕТСКИЙ РАЗВЕДЧИК

КИМ ФИЛБИ
1912—1988
5 к ПОЧТА СССР 1990

Harold "Kim" Philby: Stalin's
deep penetration agent/British
Intelligence traitor.
Wikimedia Commoms.

Juan Pujol García (alias GARBO):
Second World War double agent
for MI6 and MI5 against Nazi
Germany. *Wikimedia Commoms.*

Graham Greene with his mistress Catherine Walston. *Graham Greene–Catherine Walston collection GTMGamms168, Georgetown University Library Booth Family Center for Special Collections, Washington, D.C. Reproduced by permission of the Greene Estate.*

Fulgencio Batista (*right*) speaking to journalists, including Ted Scott (*facing in dark suit, taking notes*), Ruby Hart Phillips (*left*), ca. 1958. *Personal collection of Bernard Diederich.*

Nicolas G. Mendoza: Havana businessman, brother of Cuban ambassador to London, and local Greene guide. *Photograph courtesy of Nicole Mendoza.*

Calle Virtudes, Havana, during its capitalist apogee prior to the Cuban Revolution. *Photograph courtesy of Fototeca del Archivo Nacional de la República de Cuba.*

Jay Mallin Sr. (*right, in glasses*) listening to Fidel Castro in 1959. *Photograph courtesy of Jay Mallin Jr.*

Nydia Sarabia: accompanied Greene incognito to Santiago de Cuba, and whose name he never knew. *Photograph courtesy of Carlos Sarabia.*

Police file image of Haydée Santamaría, who Greene first met in the Santiago safe-house in November 1957. *Photograph courtesy of Casa de las Américas.*

26 de Julio rebels in the Sierra Maestra hills of eastern Cuba during the anti-Batista insurrection, February 1957. *From left to right*: Ciro Redondo, Vilma Espín, Fidel Castro, Haydée Santamaría, Celia Sánchez.
Photograph courtesy of Casa de las Américas.

Armando Hart (*right*) with his wife Haydée Santamaría in early January 1959. *Photograph courtesy of Cuban Revolution Collection (MS 650). Manuscripts and Archives, Yale University Library.*

The 26 de Julio safe-house (*first building on the left*) in Calle San Francisco, Santiago de Cuba, visited by Greene in November 1957. The bell tower of the San Francisco Church is in the distance. *Photograph by the author.*

ABOVE: One-armed bandits in the first hours of the Cuban Revolution, January 1, 1959.
Photograph courtesy of Fototeca del Archivo Nacional de la República de Cuba.
BELOW: Fidel Castro breezes past British Comet tanks lined up on Havana's seafront
avenue the Malecón on July 26, 1959. *Photograph © Bob Henriques/Magnum.*

Rebel supporters trash casinos following the triumph of the Cuban Revolution.
Photograph courtesy of Fototeca del Archivo Nacional de la República de Cuba.

Guillermo Cabrera Infante interviews Graham Greene in the lobby of the Hotel Capri, April 1959. *Carteles* magazine, Havana, June 1959.

Dr Hasselbacher (*left*, played by Burl Ives) and Wormold (*middle*, Alec Guinness) celebrate Milly's (*right*, Jo Morrow) seventeenth birthday at the Tropicana nightclub. *Photograph from Alamy.*

ABOVE: Captain Segura (*left*, played by U.S. comedian Ernie Kovacs) and Wormold (Alec Guinness) play checkers using whisky and bourbon miniatures. Wormold later borrows the inebriated police captain's pistol to kill rival agent Carter.
BELOW: Carter (Paul Rogers) returns Wormold's fire as a prostitute (Rachel Roberts) looks on. *Photographs from Alamy.*

The Andalusian-style
lobby of the Hotel
Sevilla-Biltmore (now
Sevilla), where Greene
began to write *Our
Man in Havana*.
*Photograph by James
Clifford Kent.*

El Floridita: a view from
bar to restaurant where
dry martinis induced
the manic depressive
writer to flights of fancy.
*Photograph by James
Clifford Kent.*

ABOVE: Film director Carol Reed (*scratching neck*) during filming of *Our Man in Havana* with a Cuban bootblack (*partially hidden in hat*), April 1959. BELOW: Noël Coward (*in center, dark suit*) strides across the Plaza del Cristo in Old Havana, with the ivy-covered Santo Cristo Church in background. *Photographs courtesy of John J. Burns Library, Boston College, reproduced by permission of the Greene Estate.*

Shanghai Theater closed down and moldering following the Cuban Revolution, ca. 1960. *Photograph courtesy of Fototeca del Archivo Nacional de la República de Cuba.*

ABOVE: A Sea Fury fighter-bomber sold to Batista in late 1958, now at the Museo de la Revolución, Havana. *Photograph by James Clifford Kent.* BELOW: British ambassador to Cuba Herbert Marchant at his ambassadorial residence with Fidel Castro, Vedado, Havana, ca. 1961. *Personal collection of Michael Brown.*

ABOVE: Greene and Cuban military personnel overlook the U.S. military base at Guantanamo Bay, Sept. 10, 1966. LEFT: Greene views U.S. Guantanamo military base through binoculars. *Photographs © Ernesto Fernández Nogueras.*

Baseball game in Santa Clara, Sept. 4, 1966: (*left to right*) Minister of Education José Llanusa, unidentified man, Greene, Lisandro Otero.
Photograph © Ernesto Fernández Nogueras.

Touring the Cuban countryside: (*from left to right*) Fidel Castro,
British Ambassador Dick Slater, Lord Walston, Comandante René Vallejo
(Castro's personal physician and interpreter), December 1966.
Photograph reproduced by permission of Oliver Walston.

Distraction through fascination with the human posterior continued in other written annotations to himself in a novel he was
reading. Primed by the gin and vermouth of a dry martini, he mused
and was "bemused [that] buttocks are so emphasised in tarts & man."
He pondered the abandonment of nude art "in the better houses,"
which in Greene's argot meant upmarket brothels.[28] In his novel, as
Wormold strolls along the landward side of the Malecón, "Lovely
faces looked out of dim interiors, brown eyes, dark hair, Spanish and
high yellow: beautiful buttocks leant against the bars, waiting for
any life to come along the seawet street. To live in Havana was to
live in a factory that turned out human beauty on a conveyor-belt."[29]
Unlike his impression of foreign visitors, Cuban charms attracted
him.

Greene took a siesta from flights of fancy. He then consumed "a
long train of daiquiris" in the Sevilla-Biltmore with Ted Scott of *The
Havana Post*. Irritability, another symptom of his manic depression,
had returned. The gossip columnist "talked all the time of Havana
as a sex centre—the availability of girls." He then conversed with
the hotel's lawyer, Mr. DeVo, who spoke "as interminably about the
sexual wisdom of a new novel by James Gould Cozzens," presumably
By Love Possessed (1957). Our Englishman in Havana sought distraction again and wrote to himself, "Havana as a sex factory makes
one's sex die. I took mine to the Shanghai Theater to see whether it
would revive, but it didn't." At his favorite haunt in Havana, he sat
through the "usual long incomprehensible funny sketch," where a
gardener undressed girls in turn and made an unsuccessful attempt
to kiss their parts, until one finally acquiesced to rub "his face in
her fur." A true cognoscente of the Shanghai and its erotic offering,
Greene then anatomized three blue films, the first and best of a satyr
he had seen before. On leaving, he again noticed dirty postcards for
sale in the foyer.[30]

SEEKING ROCKY

He remembered the next occurrence well, because he included it in *Ways of Escape*. For the first time since 1954, Greene bumped into his "old taxi driver." He omitted the detail about asking Rocky to find him opium.[31] Consumption of alcohol followed by a search for this narcotic demonstrated ongoing self-medication of his manic-depressive episode. The sudden craving for his nonprescription drug of choice was a throwback to his multiple visits to Vietnamese opium dens in the early 1950s. It is not clear in his journal if he found what he sought, but in a later reminiscence about Havana, he declared "one could obtain anything at will, whether drugs, women or goats,"[32] so we can presume that he did.

In *Ways of Escape*, Greene makes his search for Rocky sound interminable. In truth, he bumped into him on day 1 as he left the Shanghai Theater. The man he remembered, he wrote, was "a good guide to the shadier parts of Havana, and I had no desire for a dull and honest man." Rocky returned to him the five shillings swindled three years earlier when he had procured Greene and Catherine boracic powder instead of cocaine.[33] After this long and event-filled day, Greene noted that he retired to bed "undisturbed."[34]

As was his custom while in writing mode, he added another six hundred words the next morning to his new foolscap manuscript. Meanwhile, he heard "a noise like a hundred air raid alarms let off simultaneously" from the Sevilla-Biltmore and asked the liftman what it was. The answer came, "I expect the President is going by." Greene might have heard Batista, but he never saw him, though the Presidential Palace was just one block from the hotel.[35]

After taking some photos in the old city, Greene lunched for a second time at the Floridita. Again, he could not walk the streets unmolested. Bootblacks with "non-existent promises" were in "constant pursuit." A middle-aged man approached: "I guess I can be of help to you." Greene concluded, "Every inhabitant seems to possess the service of some girls."[36] Chapter 4 of *Our Man in Havana* begins:

> At every corner there were men who called "Taxi" at him as though he were a stranger, and all down the Paseo, at intervals of a few yards, the pimps accosted him automatically without any real hope. "Can I be of service, sir?" "I know all the pretty girls." "You desire a beautiful woman."[37]

In the novel's film version, a middle-aged bootblack approaches Hawthorne in an early street scene and inquires, "Shoeshine? Pretty girl? Dirty movie? Palace of Art?"[38] The only Cubans the writer had met thus far were those who worked the city's streets. Indeed, his impression of Havana had still not progressed beyond his 1938 observation that the city was replete with touts.

Greene again took in a very dry martini and he fixated on the "moment of illumination" it provided. "One notices everything—the men at the bar, the phrase of a conversation, significance is just round the corner. At the second one only complains that it is not dry enough. The moment has passed."[39] Consumption of alcohol appeared to raise his mood, at least temporarily. The alchemy of gin and vermouth made him wistful again about his fellow customers, as he studied how the "softness of the young Cuban" disappears into the "exaggerated masculinity of middle age." Still in a heightened state of post-cocktail consciousness, he then compared the "sacred" French ketchup with its "false" American rival.[40]

He declared himself depressed the next morning and questioned whether his additional seven hundred crafted words were "of comedy?" In such a way, the light entertainment of the emerging novel continued to contrast with the still gloomy bearing of its creator. What followed was his most extensive exploration yet of Havana's old city and a pivotal moment in the creative process. He walked down O'Reilly, the city's street of banks and sugar financing, and came across a Catholic Mass on Compostela. There he spotted a "honey coloured girl with a pony tail" who gave him "a clue to Wormold's daughter." In the novel Milly "had hair the color of pale honey, dark eyebrows, and her pony-trim was shaped by the best barber in town."[41] There are two Catholic churches on Compostela: the Santa Teresa Church and Convent very close to O'Reilly, and the Santo Angel Convent five blocks away.[42]

Greene now wandered in the direction of the harbor, down to the "Jefatura" (police headquarters), infamous as the detention center of Batista's repressive police force. His novel noted, "There had always been unpleasant doings out of sight, in the inner rooms of the Jefatura." In the novel's film version, Wormold and Beatrice emerge from the building after questioning by Captain Segura. From the harbor, Greene returned along the parallel Obispo, a street of bookshops, and lunched for the third consecutive day at the Floridita. A dry martini inspired his thoughts again:

> Couldn't one write a book on Confessions of a Martini Drinker? The tiny rest from reality which no other cocktail will give: the nearest approach perhaps to opium. One can only write about it under its influence. The intensity of the experience lies in one's knowledge of its brevity—one is never deceived: one knows the clarity & the interest in everything one sees or hears is false, but for five minutes why not be false?

He weighed the qualities of rival London dry gins: Gordon's versus Booth's. Overall, he preferred the superior appearance of Gordon's.[43] In such a way, the alcoholic spirit and other stimulants helped take the depressed author away from himself.

Rocky appeared to be stalking him—or working on a tip-off from fellow taxi drivers—because they ran into each other after lunch. Greene asked him for opium again, and a meeting was arranged. He also planned a car trip to Cienfuegos and Trinidad on Cuba's southern coast. Companionship and talking to Rocky helped lift Greene's depression a little more. He later consumed drinks but no dinner—his evening regimen since arriving in Havana—suffered sad dreams about Catherine, and took a sleeping pill.[44]

Clustered symptoms to indicate an ongoing melancholic episode were abundant: lack of appetite, disturbed sleep and dreams, a search for drugs and sexual titillation, albeit mitigated by deficient libido. He had also indulged in whimsical thoughts under the influence of dry martinis and turned irritable toward American tourists.[45]

Despite this, the completion of nine hundred more words the next morning aided his reviving spirits and he became more expansive as mania flirted with melancholia. Milly's character had come "unexpectedly alive" after seeing her model at Mass the previous day. His optimism continued throughout the day, raised by breaking waves over the sweeping Malecón. In *Our Man in Havana*, "rollers came in from the Atlantic and smashed over the sea-wall. The spray drove across the road, over the four traffic-lanes, and beat like rain under the pockmarked pillars." After a drive to Vedado, Greene booked air passage to Santiago, a trip on his mind since arrival, and took photographs of the fictional Milly's school. Considering Catherine's absence and his state of mind, it is striking that Greene carried with him *On Love* by French writer Stendhal: a classic early-nineteenth-century treatise about love, the stages of love, and its psychological effects. While in Havana, he undoubtedly pined in the absence of his mistress—now ex-mistress —with whom he was still very much in love. Reading Stendhal probably informed his fatalistic assertion to her on November 8 that "I don't use love in quite the same sense as you. So I can say I love only you & shall only love you—you are the last attachment." Pencil annotations on its inside back cover show that *On Love* accompanied him during daily lunches at the Floridita, where on this occasion he consumed crawfish au gratin containing white truffles, asparagus, and small peas.[46]

Again, the author scrutinized fellow patrons in the Floridita, not this time their conspicuous buttocks but the conversation between a loud, "high powered" American and a "sad-faced" young Spaniard, who failed to comprehend a proposed business deal because his counterpart spoke too quickly: "Do you understand me? Do you understand me? You trust me not to take off 5 cents?" Somehow, the Spaniard spotted the writer eavesdropping on their conversation and led the American away. Meanwhile, other Spanish businessmen filling the bar managed to enjoy the pleasures of drink, food, and gossip while ignoring the clock. In nearby streets, Greene observed and described in light pencil inside Stendhal's book "the little church covered with ivy in Villegas," buses coming up Lamparilla with its "white dome at the end," and the blue-and-white Escuela Parroquial del Santo Cristo. He spoke again with Rocky, and they fixed their trip to Cienfuegos and Trinidad.[47]

He finally spent time with a Cuban other than his taxi driver on the evening of his fourth day. This was Nicolas Mendoza, the Cuban ambassador to London's older brother, accompanied by "his incongruous little American mistress." Nick Mendoza was a well-connected and sociable man, with a house by the sea in Miramar. It was half-hidden and an ideal location for political meetings, including those by members of the Directorio Revolucionario and the 26 de Julio movement.[48] They fetched the daughter of Mendoza's first cousin, Natalia Bolívar, whose lover had been killed earlier in the insurrection. Over dinner, they discussed Greene's planned trip to meet the rebels.[49] Bolívar was an active member of the Directorio Revolucionario movement and belonged to an upper-class Camagüey family, descended from Latin American independence hero Simón Bolívar. Furthermore, family descendants had fought alongside "Bronze Titan" Antonio Maceo in the nineteenth-century Cuban-Spanish wars of independence. Another descendent, the banker Pablo González de Mendoza, built the large mansion on a corner of Paseo that became the British ambassador's residence in the mid-1950s. The building later acquired the first indoor swimming pool in Cuba.[50]

Back in his hotel, Greene had suffered a bad sleepless night, not helped by a terrible itch.[51] On a colorful postcard of the Prado that he posted to confidants John and Gillian Sutro the next day, he expressed gloom about his failed relationship with Catherine. Havana alone was "boring," he told them, and he wondered if his "disinclination for debauchery" was simply due to old age or the complications of life. He also mentioned the beginnings of a "mix-up" of a nonsexual type.[52] This comedy of errors began in Havana and continued in Santiago.

That morning produced another six hundred words for his new novel, a third less than the previous day. He walked to the cathedral in the heart of Old Havana and visited Miramar Yacht Club at the invitation of club member and *Time* magazine local correspondent Jay Mallin. Over lunch Mallin gave Greene "a lot of background material," but not for his story. He told his guest how sixty bombs had exploded the previous Friday between nine and nine fifteen p.m., provoking fear of an aerial bombardment. This was all news to Greene. On Friday evening, he had been absorbed in an erotic gardener sketch at the raucous Shanghai Theater.[53]

EAST TO REBEL TERRITORY

In February 1957, veteran *New York Times* journalist Herbert Matthews had breached Batista's army security cordon to interview Fidel Castro at his rebel base high in the Sierra Maestra hills. Headline articles in the U.S. newspaper over three consecutive days revealed to the world the bearded guerrillas' Robin Hood existence in the Oriente province and proved wrong the dictator's claims that Castro was dead. Ruby Hart Phillips, Havana correspondent for the same newspaper, had turned down this assignment due to justified fears it

would compromise her long-standing position in Cuba. Ted Scott of
NBC and *The Havana Post* shared Ruby's office on the second floor
of 106 Refugio Street near the Presidential Palace. He also refused
the assignment, and for the same reason. It would risk their expulsion from the island.[54]

November 1957 was practically the midpoint of the insurrection,
which lasted from December 2, 1956, to December 31, 1958. Greene
explains in his autobiography that while planning his "fantastic
comedy," he learned for the first time about the realities of Batista's Cuba. He had "hitherto met no Cubans," ignoring of course his
earnest taxi driver, and had never traveled into the interior. Yet now,
"while the story was emerging," he set about "curing" some of his
ignorance. He relates how he traveled to Trinidad and Cienfuegos,
and when his taxi ran over and killed a chicken, the superstitious
driver (i.e., Rocky) bought a lottery number corresponding to the
feathered fowl.[55]

The local lottery fascinated Greene more than casino gambling
in the island, and both forms of betting would enter his emerging
spy story. An official state lottery had existed since Cuba's colonial
period, with weekly draw numbers chanted over the radio every Saturday afternoon by orphaned and abandoned children. While some
charitable organizations benefitted from the lottery, it was also a
massive source of corruption. But it was the less expensive, illegal
spin-off *la bolita*, played by the island's poor, which particularly fascinated Greene. A whole mythology and folklore had grown around
la bolita, with numbers acquiring names and symbols (e.g., a cock-
erel was number 11). People's dreams were another factor in their
choice of numbers and aspirations to win big and improve their lot.[56]

Cienfuegos on the island's southern coast was the site of a naval
base. Just two months earlier, Batista's forces had crushed an armed
rebellion there by young naval officers, political militants, and 26 de
Julio rebels. In a passage edited out of the draft for his 1963 introduction to the novel, Greene describes how Rocky "had the air of a

conqueror" as they entered the port city, a visitor from Havana who planned to seduce a girl the first night and take her to bed on the second. Events that evening did not go as planned. Instead, Rocky and Greene accompanied each other to see a film. Akin to the Shanghai's clientele, the cinema-going audience laughed and bawled at Marilyn Monroe's "close-skirted bottom" on screen alongside Laurence Olivier in that year's release *The Prince and the Showgirl*. On day 2 of their trip, the less glamorous pairing of the author and the taxi driver hit the road again.[57]

During his dinner with Nick Mendoza and Natalia Bolívar, Greene had expressed a wish to visit the rebels in the mountains. Fidel Castro's 26 de Julio movement was not the only show in town, however, and the Sierra Maestra were not Cuba's only mountains. Bolívar made contact with her fellow members in the Directorio Revolucionario, but the organization had internal problems. The DR's chief in Havana, Eloy Gutiérrez Menoyo, had recently traveled to Miami to meet with other Directorio leaders and discuss changes to the organization's strategy. Hitherto they had aimed to strike at the top of Batista's dictatorship, hence their March 1957 attack on Batista's Presidential Palace. Like the 26 de Julio rebels, they now decided to open a guerrilla front, this time in the southern Escambray Mountains adjacent to Trinidad. Gutiérrez Menoyo inspected the area and set up the front in October 1957, and the DR declared this a second national front against Batista's regime on November 10. Naturally, Bolívar's superiors in the Directorio were not amenable to Greene visiting their only recently established guerrilla front.[58]

Bolívar therefore contacted an acquaintance from Santiago de Cuba, Nydia Sarabia, a member of the clandestine 26 de Julio movement. Their guerrilla operations base was in Oriente province. Sarabia, a journalist by profession, had just returned from accompanying a group of tourists to Mexico. She belonged to a 26 de Julio propaganda cell, headed by Jacinto Pérez, the nom de guerre of Armando Hart, a well-known figure in the organization and later a minister in Castro's new revolutionary government. Nick Mendoza drove Bolívar and Greene to Sarabia's student residence in Vedado. Sarabia climbed into the rear of Mendoza's sports car and was astonished to see the blue-eyed and sunburnt fifty-three-year-old British author of *The Power and the Glory*, a novel she had only just read. The four of them arranged to dine later that day at the Chico de Wajay restaurant on the outskirts of the city.[59]

That evening Nick Mendoza dropped the roof of his convertible Mercedes-Benz and drove them all at breakneck speed to Wajay near Rancho Boyeros Airport to discuss Greene's trip to Santiago de Cuba. They chose the Chico restaurant for its quiet location, a dimly lit locale safe from the prying eyes and ears of Batista's police and informers. With the cooler winter months approaching, Sarabia asked Greene to carry half a dozen long-sleeved sweatshirts and two leather jackets (one intended for Fidel) in his suitcase for the rebels in the mountains. The writer remembered the cargo in *Ways of Escape* as a few sweaters and thick socks.[60]

Earlier in the year, the new U.S. ambassador had visited Santiago de Cuba at a particularly unpropitious moment, also described in Greene's *Ways of Escape*.[61] The U.S. State Department had replaced noncareer ambassadors with a new set of political appointees in June 1957, and the notably pro-Batista Arthur Gardner retired. His replacement, Earl T. Smith, had no diplomatic experience, which soon became evident. He was a wealthy investment broker and a prominent Florida Republican with minimal knowledge of government administration. Cuba at this time was not a matter of overriding concern in Washington. Its attention focused instead on events in the Middle East and the launch of the Eisenhower Doctrine to establish greater U.S. presence there.[62]

Smith soon underwent a severe test in an early visit to Santiago de Cuba. On July 30, just a day before his arrival in the city, police gunned down Frank País, the chief urban leader of the 26 de Julio movement.[63] The ambassador and his entourage were onlookers to the funeral cortege for the slain rebel and a mass demonstration. Police wielding truncheons and fire hoses lashed out at the protestors. At a press conference later in the day, Smith described the "excessive police action" as "abhorrent." The events and Smith's condemnation sparked outrage, from both rebels, who instigated a fresh wave of armed activity across the island, and Batista's officials, who lambasted the diplomat for meddling in Cuba's internal affairs. There were rumors that Washington would recall their inexperienced new ambassador.[64]

Greene picks up the story in *Ways of Escape*, praising the actions of Ambassador Smith, who witnessed the repression from the town hall balcony and, "to his honour, broke up the party." At a diplomatic cocktail party in Havana, Greene says he discussed the episode with the Spanish ambassador:

> "It was most undiplomatic," the envoy exclaimed.
> "What would you have done?" Greene asked.
> "I would have turned my back," came the reply.[65]

Spain's ambassador in Cuba (1952–60) was a Basque, the Marquis of Vellisca Juan Pablo de Lojendio, who got his title of grandee through his attractive and much younger wife. A British diplomatic profile of him was less than complimentary: "Apart from his good looks he is certainly arrogant, possibly tactless and already seems to be throwing his weight about a little too much in a country where Spanish domination has not yet wholly been forgotten."[66]

Spanish dictator Francisco Franco's man in Havana got his comeuppance after Fidel Castro criticized his country's diplomacy during a live television broadcast in January 1960. The short-fused diplomat raced to the venue and stormed in to defend Spanish honor in a face-to-face confrontation with the revolutionary leader, the incident transmitted live on Cuban TV. As opposed to Batista's lenient treatment of U.S. ambassador Earl T. Smith, Castro declared Lojendio persona non grata. He left his post within a few days, a victim of his own undiplomatic behavior.[67]

"A COMEDY OF ERRORS"

All arrangements were in place for Greene's visit to Santiago de Cuba. Unfortunately, however, his "Havana Journal" runs dry at the end of his fifth full day in Cuba. It is likely he feared his diary notes falling into the hands of Batista's Servicio de Inteligencia Militar (SIM) agents in Santiago. After November 12, therefore, we have to rely on his account from *Ways of Escape*, first written six years after the event. We also benefit from the firsthand accounts of his two guides to the eastern city.

The island's second largest city—and the Oriente province in which it was located—had a long insurrectionary tradition, dating from nineteenth-century resistance to Spanish colonial rule. This history included two Cuban wars of independence against Spain in Oriente, the first lasting ten years from 1868. Three years into the second war of independence and at the point of stalemate, the U.S. military intervention commenced with landings at beaches near Santiago in June 1898. The U.S. army suffered the ravages of mosquitoes and tropical diseases, while the U.S. navy annihilated Spain's inferior squadron as it attempted to flee with honor intact from Santiago's natural harbor. Madrid had no choice but to relinquish its remaining colonies in Puerto Rico and Cuba some sixty to eighty years after mainland Spanish American colonies had achieved their independence.

Fidel Castro's 26 de Julio guerrillas thus replicated the actions of nineteenth-century rebels when they began their insurrection against Batista in Oriente province on December 2, 1956. Unfortunately, the second half of November 1957 proved a most inauspicious moment for Greene to visit. He flew into the city with a plan to visit the rebel stronghold in the nearby Sierra Maestra hills just as the first anniversary of the *Granma* landing approached. Yet Batista's army had set about crushing increased guerrilla activity with brutal suppression. While rebels targeted energy supply infrastructure and army posts in and around Santiago, secret police and marauding soldiers rounded up suspects, often to torture them or dump their bodies on the city's streets. Indeed, as the prominent female revolutionary Vilma Espín later remarked, to work clandestinely for the rebel movement in the city was to live "like a hunted animal." In the hills, they could at least die in open fighting. A virtual curfew existed at night when Santiago's population, most of them sympathetic to Castro's cause, closed their shutters and remained indoors.[68]

In *Ways of Escape*, Greene defines his November 1957 trip to Santiago de Cuba as "a comedy of errors," "as absurd" as anything he later described in *Our Man in Havana*. The comedy in the midst of terror stemmed from the fact that both *Time* correspondent Jay Mallin and Nydia Sarabia accompanied Greene to Santiago with the same purpose: to arrange a trip by Greene to the Sierra Maestra mountains and an interview with Fidel Castro. It is just that neither of them knew they were working to the same end, with Greene unable to enlighten them. Furthermore, Sarabia suspected that Mallin was an FBI agent. While she knew about his presence, he had no idea that another guide was accompanying the author on this trip east. These facts and the air of fear and suspicion in Santiago de Cuba added intrigue to the comedic episode.

There are naturally discrepancies between the three participants' recollections of events. Sarabia wrote fourteen months after the Santiago trip that they had arranged to sit apart on the plane, and for Greene to phone her from his hotel the morning after their arrival. She gave him a letter of introduction to the rebel movement, but Greene only knew her as Lidia Hernández, an approximation of her first name plus her second surname. When she arrived at Rancho

Boyeros Airport outside Havana, she was horrified to see the *Time* correspondent, whose name she later remembered as Allen as opposed to Mallin.[69]

After making his arrangement with Sarabia, Greene says that *Time* instructed Mallin to accompany him to Santiago. Yet it was too late to warn her, and neither Greene nor his host (Mendoza) had even her name or address. Greene lingered in the airport bar while Nick Mendoza waited for her arrival, whence they arranged that she would telephone Greene at his hotel.[70] The diminutive Sarabia sat several rows behind six-foot-two Greene on the same Vickers Viscount plane to Santiago. The authorities did not normally search the luggage of foreign passengers, and Greene, "blue-eyed, tall, and slim" and carrying warm clothing for the rebels in the hills, passed through Santiago's airport unchecked.[71]

Greene and Mallin stayed at the Casa Granda hotel, adjacent to the city's cathedral on a neighboring corner of Parque Céspedes in central Santiago de Cuba. The Casa Granda stands on the site of a former house owned by Don Manuel de Granda in the nineteenth century, where the four-story hotel was constructed in 1913. Ten wide stone steps connect street level with the first-floor cafeteria/bar terrace and the adjacent lobby with its tiny elevator. Arriving just before the unofficial curfew, Greene contemplated a seated man in soiled white cotton rocking to and fro to create a draft and evade mosquitoes. This made him recall the oppressive and menacing Mexican town of Villahermosa two decades earlier. Both locales belonged to so-called Greeneland, the milieu in which the writer thrived and set his novels.[72]

Our Man in Havana contains a scene where Wormold makes an annual visit to vacuum cleaner retailers in the provinces, including Santiago. His Hillman breaks down in Santa Clara to "lay down beneath him like a tired mule." The description evokes the writer's 1938 trip to Mexico, when a plane failed him in Chiapas and he traveled overland by mule. Wormold arrives in Santiago at the menacing curfew hour, which mimics the writer's real visit to the city in November 1957. His novel would describe a "hotel of real spies, real police-informers and real rebel agents."[73]

Indeed, *Ways of Escape* also describes the Casa Granda and the city as "full of Batista's spies."[74] Both he and Sarabia knew that the dictator's SIM agents regularly tapped the hotel's phones. She wrote in 1959 that Greene had not taken the precaution of giving a false name to the hotel reception, which informed Mallin of the writer's nine a.m. phone call to her.[75] Greene recalled that as he breakfasted in his room, the *Time* correspondent knocked on his bedroom door, accompanied by "a middle-aged man in a smart gabardine suit with a businessman's smile." While they talked, the telephone rang and Greene asked them to leave while he took the call. It was "the girl" (Sarabia) with the number of the house he should visit in Calle San Francisco. An argument ensued when the men returned. "Castro's public relations man in Santiago," as the author dubbed him, accused Greene of contact with a Batista agent.[76] Plainly, Greene could not confess to either man or to Sarabia that they were both facilitating his meeting with the rebel underground in Santiago. This was the nub of the comedy of errors.

Mallin explained decades later that his companion that day was Fernando Ojeda, a dapper businessman with a penchant for Dewar's whisky and a main figure in the Movimiento de Resistencia Cívica. The professional, commercial, and industrial sectors had set up the Civic Resistance Movement to oppose Batista through financial and moral support for the 26 de Julio movement. Mallin does not recall the row in the hotel and doubts that Ojeda, "very much the gentleman," would have argued with Greene. Furthermore, he says that anyone designated "Castro's public relations man in Santiago" would have been shot on sight.[77]

Greene then describes leaving the hotel and stepping straight into a taxi in Céspedes Park, where "a Negro, flashily dressed" took the seat beside him and offered his services as unofficial guide. Greene thought that if anyone was a Batista spy, it was this man. They took in the sights of Santiago: the port, and San Juan Hill, made famous by future U.S. president Theodore Roosevelt when he charged Spanish defensive positions with his volunteer cavalry regiment of Rough Riders during the U.S. military intervention in 1898. Greene had to lose his unsolicited guide and suspected Batista informant, so he thought quickly. He asked them to drop him off at the San Francisco church for prayer, assuming correctly that the street where he needed to go had a church of the same name. Batista's police had identified and killed Frank País just four months earlier in a street behind the church. After some prayers, Greene walked up the interminable Calle San Francisco, later recalling a house at its far end and an oppressive midday sun.[78] In fact, the house was only six blocks and a five-minute stroll from the church, and if he had known the route, only eight blocks from his hotel.

The house stood in the historic quarter of Santiago de Cuba, in streets where safe houses had first offered refuge to rebels after the Moncada assault in 1953. They performed the same function after the uprising at the end of November 1956 and during the whole period of the insurrection until the end of 1958. The colonial houses in Calle San Francisco do not appear outwardly large. Yet they have ample interiors, often with a patio and a *zaguán* (originally an entranceway to accommodate a horse carriage), many of them occupied in this period by the city's middle classes, including prominent physicians. This particular house belonged to Dr. Enrique Ortega and his wife, Eva Maggi, an English teacher and third-in-command of the Resistencia Cívica. According to Sarabia, Haydée Santamaría and her husband, Jacinto Pérez (Armando Hart), were also present.[79] They were leading figures in the 26 de Julio national directorate, with Hart the national chief for organization, responsible for the movement underground and abroad, and Santamaría in charge of fundraising.[80] It was they, according to Sarabia, who decided which people traveled to the Sierra Maestra.[81]

Sarabia says she waited at the house in San Francisco for half an hour. Allen (Mallin) arrived first, accompanied by a member of the Resistencia Cívica (Ojeda, according to Mallin). Greene knocked on the door next, having removed his loose English-tailored jacket. He was sweating profusely. Although he was surprised to see the *Time* correspondent, she recalled, he maintained his "English phlegm," and both Sarabia and Greene evaded Mallin's inquiry about who had facilitated the writer's arrival there.[82]

Greene recalls that Mallin and his companion pulled up in a car as he walked up Calle San Francisco. They had been looking for Greene throughout the city after discovering his contact with the businessman Ojeda's movement through other means, and therefore arrived at the house in their car. According to Greene, the courier (Sarabia) was there along with her mother (Sarabia denies this), plus a priest and a man dyeing his hair. This was Armando Hart, who was disguising himself following a daring escape from a lavatory window during a recent court trial.[83] Batista's army captured Hart again in January 1958 as he returned from a rendezvous with Fidel Castro in the Sierra Maestra hills, and he spent the rest of the insurrection in prison.

A SECRET MOTIVE

Alas, Greene did not make it to the Sierra Maestra. The fact is that between May and December 1957, the rebel movement did not allow any outsiders to travel up to their guerrilla base in the hills.[84] Our peripatetic writer had a habit of being in the right place at the right time. He had survived the London Blitz, a series of annual visits to Indochina during its long colonial war, an onerous trip to British Malaya during its "Emergency," and Kenya during the Mau Mau uprising. On this occasion, however, he was in the right place at the wrong time. Like the rival Directorio Revolucionario, the 26 de Julio movement was passing through a difficult and transitional phase. The head of its urban underground, Frank País, had been killed on the streets of Santiago in July, and his brother Josué a month earlier. There were disagreements over strategy and direction between the Fidel Castro–led rebels fighting in the *sierra* (mountains) and the leaders in the *llano* (plains, including towns and cities). The *llano* leaders supplied essential equipment including weapons, ammunition, and clothing, as well as local and international fundraising/ finance and propaganda. Furthermore, fighting between the rebels and Batista's army in the foothills of the Sierra Maestra near Santiago had intensified in November 1957. The dictator's planes were regularly strafing rebel approach routes and hideouts.[85]

Conversation even got down to the boots Greene required for hiking into the mountains, according to Mallin. When informed in the doctor's house that he would need to wait at least a week to make the journey, the writer made his excuses. He told Mallin he had to be in New York for the opening of a new play. Sarabia says he needed to be in London, and in Kenya to report on the Mau Mau rebellion again.[86] As Antipholus of Syracuse declares in Shakespeare's *The Comedy of Errors*, 'twas time "to trudge, pack and be gone."[87]

The most conspicuous discrepancy between the accounts by Greene, Sarabia, and Mallin is the stated motive for his journey. According to Greene, his journeys into the interior were for "curing a little of [his] ignorance," but both his guides are adamant his main reason for traveling to Oriente was to interview Fidel Castro. Also conspicuous by their absence in Greene's account are the names of his facilitators in Cuba: Mendoza, the middle-class Cuban who would leave the island in 1960; Sarabia, the "courier for Fidel" whose real name he never actually knew; and Mallin, the *Time* correspondent who—like Mendoza—left Cuba early in the Revolution for political reasons. By the time Greene wrote a new introduction to his novel in 1963, Cuba had become a hot political potato at the height of the Cold War. Following the Castro-led Revolution, the island quickly transformed from a capitalist playground into a Soviet satellite, a reality highlighted by the Cuban Missile Crisis in October 1962. Evidently, Greene did not want to embarrass his hosts or himself by revealing their assistance to his ambition to visit Fidel Castro in the Sierra Maestra hills just a few years earlier.

Greene's views on the rebel movement and the insurrection in the mountains would have been informed and insightful, given his rich prior experience of conflicts around the globe. Indeed, Sarabia laments that the author's trip to the mountains did not take place: "If Graham Greene had stayed a week, his interview would have been as famous as Herbert Matthews's."[88] It was not to be. Nevertheless, he would directly involve himself with the rebels' cause in a very practical way in late 1958, a crucial phase of the insurrection that coincided with the publication of *Our Man in Havana*.

1

OUR ARMS IN HAVANA

reene flew on Cubana Airlines to New York on November 21, 1957, and then traveled on to his daughter and son-in-law's ranch in Alberta, Canada. For several weeks, he ate a lot and drank nothing alcoholic in the "sunlight & mountain air" of the Rockies. But Anita was not a letter writer, and he felt "a bit alone." He confided in a letter to Gillian Sutro how his Swedish girlfriend was "a sweet girl to sleep with, but she's not, alas, Catherine!" He continued to toil "not very satisfactorily but steadily" on his "second-rate" entertainment, completing fourteen thousand words of *Our Man in Havana* by December 7. He added another ten thousand words in the following two weeks but worried his burgeoning novel might "irritate" his "F.O. friends"—i.e., his colleagues in SIS. He then put the manuscript aside to concentrate on completing a play.[1]

The Complaisant Lover opened in London in June 1959 to critical acclaim. It would enjoy a successful one-year run in the West End. Partially mirroring his own private life, the comedy involves a love triangle with a cuckolded husband (a dentist with a love of practical jokes), his adulterous wife, and her lover—an antiquarian bookseller. Not by coincidence, Greene always considered second-hand bookselling a default profession should his writing career fail to flourish. Ironically, and pertinent to his own situation, the play's male interloper eventually loses out and becomes complaisant.

Back in England, Greene returned to his "Cuba story" in the New Year, rising at seven thirty each morning to write his daily word quota before breakfast. On one morning, he managed to complete four hundred words in bed, despite "suffering from severe alcoholism" after an unexpected evening visit from a friend. They had each consumed four of Greene's dry martinis, three pink gins in a pub, and shared a bottle and a half of wine at the Lyric Theatre.[2]

He visited girlfriend Anita Björk in February, one of several trips to Sweden in 1958. They broke up, but their relationship soon restarted, only to stall again in July.[3] By the time of a research trip to the Belgian Congo for a new novel early the following year, their on-off relationship was definitively over.

On returning to his Mayfair flat in late February, he felt "filleted," living on "drink & sleeping pills," and had lost three pounds in weight. He was "working well," with forty thousand words completed by the end of the month, just three thousand behind schedule, when his "fuse blew." He wrote to Catherine Walston from a snowy London, wishing they were drinking fresh lime together in Jamaica by Noël Coward's swimming pool. At the same time, Greene was planning a visit to Geneva with his publisher friend Max Reinhardt to negotiate with Charlie Chaplin. They wanted the former giant of silent film to publish his forthcoming autobiography with their company, the Bodley Head.[4]

In late 1957, Greene's son, Francis, had been called up to national service, and these initial career steps influenced some practical details in *Our Man in Havana*. Francis Greene wrote to his father from Catterick Garrison in North Yorkshire following an interview for a research post at the Atomic Weapons Research Establishment at Aldermaston. Another interview for a Foreign Office job was unsuccessful, despite his father's close and continuing connections to the government department. Greene sought his son's advice about microphotography, wanting his fictional spy Wormold to reduce a document down to the size of dot. Francis replied it would indeed be possible for an amateur to produce a square, full-stop-sized micro-photograph with the aid of a box camera and a microscope.[5] In the novel, SIS secretary Beatrice explains to Wormold how they can send his intelligence to London on a microphotograph affixed to the back of a postage stamp.[6]

During the first five months that Greene worked on his novel, Batista appeared in firm control of Cuba. The first sign of a reduction in Washington's full support only came with its embargo on arms sales to his regime in late March 1958. Yet even then, the U.S. State and Defense Departments disagreed over policy. When Greene wrote about "strange machinery in transport" and "big military instal-lations under construction" in Oriente Province, his tale appeared far-fetched to the point of preposterous. Enjoying long-standing and mutually beneficial close relations with the United States, no poten-tial foreign aggressor lurked on the Caribbean horizon. Yet fast-forward to summer/fall 1962, and the fictional scenario turned very real. In the intervening period, the U.S.-backed Caribbean island pre-cipitously entered the Soviet sphere. The buildup to the Cuban Mis-sile Crisis, the Cold War's most perilous episode, would demonstrate just how prophetic his story was.

The handwritten manuscript and later typed drafts of the novel underwent various minor revisions during the writing process, some of them to reflect contemporaneous events. For example, the only once mentioned Bulgarin became Khrushchev to reflect change at the top of the Soviet political structure in March 1958. Engineer Gherado mutated into Engineer Cifuentes, a change probably inspired by an event at the Habana Gran Prix in February 1958, when the Ferrari 500 Testa Rossa piloted by twenty-six-year-old Cuban driver Armando García Cifuentes hit an oil patch and plowed into the crowd lining the Malecón during lap 5. Seven spectators perished in the accident, in a period when only old tires and straw bales provided protection for the race-going public.[7] (In the novel, of course, a car accident on the airport road kills Cubana Airlines pilot Raul Dominguez.) Castro's 26 de Julio movement kidnapped Argentine racing-car champion Juan Manuel Fangio from the lobby of the Lincoln Hotel before the Habana Gran Prix and only released him after it, creating worldwide publicity for their cause.

Early drafts of his manuscript show that Wormold's Cuban vacuum cleaner shop assistant started life as Miguel before mutating into Lopez. Captain Segura's original sobriquet was the Red Devil before becoming the Red Vulture. The location of Wormold's vacuum cleaner outlet moved from its original location in O'Reilly Street to the parallel Lamparilla Street three blocks away. "They don't have G-strings at the Shanghai" truly reflected the dance troupe's lack of attire at the seedy establishment but was perhaps too risqué for a 1950s readership and did not make the manuscript's final draft. Hawthorne originally instructed Wormold to meet him at six p.m. in the Sevilla-Biltmore to explain the espionage game to him, but the time later reverted to ten in the evening.[8]

A few mistakes and oversights also entered Greene's published novel. It twice refers to the Avenida de Maceo, although the commonly used name for the seafront avenue over which waves break spectacularly is the Malecón. The misspelling Virdudes persists instead of Virtudes (Virtues) for the Wonder Bar's location, an ironic street name given its location in the heart of Havana's red-light district.

Most intriguingly, only in final edits does Greene have Hawthorne leaving Wormold his key for room 501 at the Sevilla-Biltmore instead of room 510. Unfortunately, the author and his editors only partially implemented this late change in the final typed manuscript and both room 501 and room 510 appear at different points in the first William Heinemann edition of the published novel.[9] After receiving a signed copy of Our Man in Havana from Greene, his wartime boss at SIS, Felix Cowgill, wrote to his former intelligence subordinate to praise his novel but lightheartedly admonish his error on this important point of detail.[10]

One wonders why Greene changed his mind so late. The inspiration for choosing the room number arose from his work in Security Room 51 of a discreet SIS building in London's St. James's under Kim Philby's supervision during the Second World War. Coincidentally, long-term Havana resident Ernest Hemingway wrote some of his novels in room 511 of the Ambos Mundos Hotel in Old Havana. It is not far-fetched, therefore, to suppose that Greene discovered this fact late in the writing process and decided to amend 510 to 501 because his original choice paid inadvertent and undesired homage to his American literary rival.[11] It is less likely that Greene sought affinity with room 101, a basement torture chamber in Orwell's *Nineteen Eighty-Four*.

The most significant factual edit in the writing process removed Batista's name and added "dangerously" (after *creaking*) to the sentence, "President Batista's regime was creaking towards its end," when explaining a dearth of tourists at Sloppy Joe's bar.[12] A likely explanation for this change was that it reduced the possibility that Batista would veto permission to film a cinematic version of the novel in Havana. Suffice it to say the question did not arise. His dictatorship imploded some twelve weeks after the novel's publication.

Greene finished revisions for the typescript of *Our Man in Havana* on June 2, 1958, seven months after writing its first paragraph in the Hotel Sevilla-Biltmore. Negotiations about a film version of the novel had already begun in May. His novels had an impressive record of successful adaptation to the big screen, and he had conceived this story originally as a film treatment anyway, set in prewar Estonia. Unfortunately, he detested the most recent film adaptation of one of his novels, *The Quiet American*, by Joseph L. Mankiewicz in 1958. Greene judged it a travesty because the American director changed the controversial anti-American ending to his story. According to a close friend, the episode hence made him "very tiresome" concerning script and cast approval for future film adaptations, despite the fact he often relinquished such rights when chasing the highest possible sum. The sale of rights for *The Quiet American* enabled his daughter to buy a ranch in Alberta, Canada.[13]

The author's literary agents on both sides of the Atlantic proceeded with negotiations for a film version of *Our Man in Havana*, but he was adamant about one thing: Alfred Hitchcock would not direct it. As a regular film critic for the *Spectator* in the 1930s, Greene did not share many people's admiration for the recognized master of suspense. On learning that his U.S. agent Monica McCall was attempting to sell it to Hitchcock for $50,000 ($430,000), Greene blew his top and demanded to see all bids as they arrived. Carol Reed read a proof of the novel and immediately contacted the author, with whom he had already completed two successful films, *The Fallen Idol* (1948) and *The Third Man* (1949). He was more than keen to renew their director/screenwriter collaboration.[14]

Greene described to Catherine Walston the clamor of film companies as they sought to secure rights for his next film. Alexander Mackendrick, director of the Ealing Studios comedy *Whisky Galore* (1949) and his Hollywood debut, *Sweet Smell of Success* (1957), was enthusiastic, and actor Cary Grant was reading a proof. There was talk of Greene traveling to Havana with Mackendrick, so he suggested to Catherine that she join them. They could visit "lovely little" Trinidad, taste "coconut ice & dry martinis at the Floridita, & look in once in a while at the Shanghai." Neither part of the plan materialized, however. Greene instead joined Carol Reed in Paris for two days in August, and all boded well for their third screenwriter/director collaboration.[15] Reed's company Kingsmead Productions backed by Columbia Studios offered $100,000 ($900,000) for the film. Greene also gained an assignment to write the script and earn him another £6,000 (£133,000). Reed therefore elbowed Hitchcock out of the discussion.[16]

After formal agreement to work together again, Reed and Greene traveled to Havana in October 1958 to reconnoiter possible film locations and talk with local authorities about shooting the film.

They took a "dreary" and delayed flight on a ten-year-old BOAC De Luxe Monarch Boeing 377 Stratocruiser to New York that "bumbled along like an old bus." Nevertheless, "a very mysterious & pretty" twenty-five-year-old English passenger—with mink and sable coats and "no profession except travelling"—piqued the author's interest. She happened to be reading his recently published *Our Man in Havana* in the plane's lower-deck bar lounge, connected to the upper-deck cabins by a spiral staircase. She wrote to Greene on the flyleaf of his novel, "Is Superman worth seeing?" He responded by writing, "Better for you than me."[17]

After making the chance mile-high acquaintance, Greene discovered his mysterious fellow passenger was "passionately fond of Havana, blue films & brothels." She described to Greene the foot fetish of a Havana landlord who liked to wash her feet in champagne and Curaçao and then lick them off. He would have gone further, had she not kept him on the floor below knee level. She had been in love with another man in the city, but he had a "kink." He was into humiliation and wanted to watch her perform in a brothel with the first six paying customers, at least one of them a black man. In a letter to Catherine Walston from New York, with whom he liked to share such titillating experiences, he described how "the bar can never have heard such concentrated & realistic sexual conversation."[18]

A new Rolls-Royce and a chauffeur awaited Greene's new acquaintance at New York's Idlewild Airport, where the plane touched down seven hours late (at three p.m. instead of eight a.m.). They later met for a drink at the Algonquin Hotel in Manhattan and shared a Benzedrine, which reportedly made his dinner with Reed and a Columbia Pictures executive more bearable.[19]

Greene related in his letter to Catherine that the young woman was "called—dubiously—Patricia Marlowe." This was not, as he suspected, her real name. His fine-tuned intuition was working impeccably. While known as a "'golden girl' of the Mayfair set," her origins were far humbler. She was in fact Anita Wimble, daughter of a car-hire proprietor from Chatham. A former waitress and switchboard operator, the part-time actress was found dead in her Mayfair flat four years later, in August 1962, next to empty pill bottles and her fifteen-month-old son. A Westminster coroner judged she had died from acute barbiturate and promethazine poisoning. Newspapers reported her champagne lifestyle and show business friends, her three mink coats, her twenty-three visits to the United States, plus trips to Monte Carlo for gambling and Cannes for sunbathing. According to friends, she was sad and depressed at Hollywood star Marilyn Monroe's death just a few days earlier in similar circumstances. Many years after Pat Marlowe's death, it emerged that entertainer Max Bygraves was the father of her illegitimate child.[20]

Following the chance meeting with Marlowe, Greene saw his good fortune continue on arrival in Havana, as he fully indulged in Batista's bawdy city once again. On a postcard advertising the Tropicana nightclub, he was thrilled to tell Catherine how a slot machine had spilled seventy dollars ($608) from a single twenty-five-cent piece ($2). "You've never seen such a jackpot!" he exclaimed.[21] Reed described how they hung out in Havana's cafés and streets, discussed *Our Man in Havana* and its characters, and visited locations described in the novel.[22] If we consider that during "research" for *The Third Man* in Vienna they made many early-morning visits to Maxim's, the Casanova, and the Oriental, surely we can assume that in Havana their research also involved taxing nocturnal visits to the Shanghai Theater, the Blue Moon, and the Sans Souci.

The two resided at the Sevilla-Biltmore, where an encounter with Ted Scott on the hotel's steps reversed his gambling fortune. Like Patricia Marlowe, the gossip columnist had already devoured and dissected Greene's newly published *Our Man in Havana*, and with innate sarcasm, his "Interesting *if* True" column questioned the author's disclaimer of "any connection between [his] characters and any living people." Regarding locations, despite several references to the Shanghai Theater, Scott guaranteed that "all the Queen's horses and all the Queen's men could not drag [Greene] into such an establishment, [. . .] that flea-bitten dive." Scott noticed the author was particularly reticent in his company. If the penny had not already dropped, it did now. Scott lamented, "I am sitting here crying my eyes out because the conviction has taken hold of me that I am not quite his cup of tea."[23] It was the understatement of 1958.

Cuban cinema critic Guillermo Cabrera Infante tracked down Reed for an interview in *Carteles* magazine. He asked *The Third Man* director if he would depict Havana like Vienna, with its leaden atmosphere of violence and intrigue. Reed's answer indicated there was no plan to portray the violence of Batista's dictatorship. Instead, Reed and Greene envisaged a becalmed Havana replete with contrasts and local idiosyncrasies such as the local lottery. They were interested in Old Havana, but also the beautiful new sections of the city with modern skyscrapers and hotels.[24] Whereas physical aspects of Vienna had changed when Reed and Greene returned to shoot *The Third Man* in November 1948 after their earlier research trips to the city, what would change between planning *Our Man in Havana* in October 1958 and shooting the film six months later were Cuba's rulers and its moral climate.

On arriving back in Britain, Greene and Reed took a suite at the Hotel Metropole in Brighton. They adopted their customary working routine and wrote the film script in separate rooms. Greene woke early to complete his daily screenplay quota; a secretary typed up the pages in a middle sitting room and then handed them to Reed in bed. The screenwriter and director discussed progress and ideas over lunch, amused themselves together in the evening, and avoided outside distractions as best they could.[25]

They then traveled to Spain to scout locations in Seville and Cadiz in case Batista's regime denied them permission to shoot in Cuba. The logic was that both Andalusian cities shared architecture similar

to Havana should their film production require a plan B. Greene
wrote to Catherine at the end of their trip:

> My news is only work & liver & liver & work. I hate Spain.
> Seville was cold & bad food, & Cadiz was worse cold & worse
> food. After deciding that if it was really necessary we could shoot
> some scenes here, we flew straight back at the week-end.[26]

As opposed to the euphoric distraction of a casual mile-high
encounter with Patricia Marlowe followed by a big gambling win
in Havana, his irritability, recourse to alcohol, and general fastidi-
ousness about Spanish food and surroundings were all symptoms of
another melancholic low.

AMORAL BUSINESS

His experiences of military conflict during the Second World War
and in Vietnam provided the context for Greene's strong feelings
about British arms sales to Batista in the final period of his dictatorship. During the Luftwaffe blitzkrieg on London in the early part of
the war, he had been an air raid warden in the Gower Street area of
Central London. There he witnessed at close quarters the destruction and human horror caused by bombs and incendiary devices, of
people severely cut and bleeding from shattered glass.

Ways of Escape contains a journal he kept during the Blitz. In it,
Greene recounts how he saw the first dead body of his life among
the gray rubble of a collapsed building. He viewed another in Tottenham Court Road, passed over by three fire engines. A fellow
warden placed a fur coat purloined from a broken shop window
over one bleeding man who lay on a door in the road. Later, a thief
rifled through the prone man's pockets. Greene struggled to carry an
injured woman down the stairs of a club destroyed by a parachute

bomb, where 350 Canadian soldiers had been sleeping. She apologized for being overweight. The "purgatorial throng of men and women in dirty torn pyjamas with little blood splashes standing in doorways" stayed with him for the rest of his life. Indeed, memories of bombs and a nightmare about Nazi invasion later appeared in his "Dream Diaries."[27]

He portrayed the casual killing of fellow humans in *The Third Man* through the character of criminal arch-cynic Harry Lime. The film's most emblematic scene takes place in the cabin of a Ferris wheel, which represents the cycle of life and death. Holly Martins is perturbed to discover his "friend" Harry involved in a black market racket that wreaks enormous harm and death on hospitalized children treated with watered-down penicillin. Amoral Harry defends his actions to Holly as their cabin slowly gyrates far above the heads of people who scurry like ants on the ground below them:

> Would you really feel any pity if one of those dots stopped moving—forever? If I said you could have twenty thousand pounds for every dot that stops, would you really, old man, tell me to keep my money . . . without hesitation? Or would you calculate how many dots you could afford to spare? Free of income tax, old man. Free of income tax.

Was Harry Lime's cynicism not justified, given the death of millions in the recent world war, and deployment of atom bombs against Hiroshima and Nagasaki? Governments taxed their own citizens, led them into devastating wars, and developed increasingly destructive nuclear weaponry. Lime was only looking after himself. If politicians and governments only cared about themselves, why shouldn't he?

In 1952, during one of several visits to Indochina, a French B26 pilot invited Greene to accompany him on a "vertical raid" against Vietnamese insurgents near the Chinese border. Sat cramped on a small metal plate with his knees pressed against the navigator's back, the plane dive-bombed some fourteen times from three thousand feet to repeatedly strafe a village. As the bomber returned from the forty-minute patrol along the Red River valley above untended rice fields, the pilot spotted a flat boat:

> The gun gave a single burst of tracer, and the sampan blew apart in a shower of sparks. We didn't even wait to see our victims struggling to survive, but climbed and made for home. I thought again, as I had thought when I saw a dead child in a ditch at Phat Diem, "I hate war." There had been something so shocking in our fortuitous choice of prey—we just happened to be passing, one burst only was required, there was no one to return our fire, we were gone again, adding our little quota to the world's dead.[28]

Presumably, both the French pilot and Harry Lime were able to distance themselves morally as well as physically from their victims. Greene could not. He had survived the Russian roulette of Hitler's bombs and flying rockets raining down on London during the war, and he had now seen Vietnamese peasants targeted from the air. Thus when the author learned in 1958 that the British government was prepared to approve arms exports to Batista's repressive dictatorship for use against Castro's rebels and followers in the Sierra Maestra hills, it pricked his conscience. He knew how government bureaucracies functioned because he had worked for a few of them, so he decided to do something about it.

✳

Cuba's traditional supplier of arms was the United States under the Military Assistance Program (MAP), a wide-ranging agreement maintained with various Latin American governments. The program's terms, agreed with Cuba in 1952, prohibited employing U.S. military equipment for internal security. It became obvious during

1957 that Batista was contravening that agreement.[29] As the Castro-led guerrilla insurrection grew in strength, and Batista's forces became increasingly repressive, the United States started to question the dictatorship's employment of arms supplied to Cuba under the program. During the course of 1957 and the first months of 1958, Cuban exile groups and others pressured the Eisenhower government to cease arms exports to Batista's dictatorship.

When Washington deferred a decision on supplying eight medium tanks to Batista's government in May 1957, he canceled the order and made tentative inquiries elsewhere, contacting Britain about the purchase of helicopters in July, for example.[30]

In *Our Man in Havana*, meanwhile, one of Wormold's invented subagents is the oft-drunken Spanish pilot of Cubana Airlines Raul Dominguez, who lost his wife in the Spanish Civil War. His fictitious mission is to fly over and obtain photographic evidence of the "mysterious constructions in the mountains of Oriente province." In reality, in October 1957, the local representative of UK arms manufacturer Westlands & De Havilland was Captain Gregorio de los Reyes, chief pilot for Cubana Airlines. In that month he requested quotes via the British embassy in Havana for automatic rifles, light tanks, reconnaissance cars, hand grenades, and military aircraft. The embassy's first secretary Peter Oliver advised London to keep the inquiry confidential, given that the United States had hitherto supplied all Cuban armaments.[31]

In Washington, human rights abuses on the island and the dictator's growing domestic unpopularity led State Department officials to question U.S. policy toward Cuba, and particularly their military relations with the island. Public and congressional opinion against the sale of arms to a dictatorship was strong.[32] Yet the arms question still split U.S. government opinion. The Department of Defense supported Batista's close relations with the United States and his stand against communism, while the more liberal State Department was keen to avoid an escalation of the conflict in Cuba that could threaten the totality of U.S. military and economic interests.[33]

Batista's position weakened further on March 10, 1958, after Raúl Castro opened a second front in the north of the Oriente province, and a radio manifesto by Fidel Castro on the same day called for a general strike. Two days later Batista suspended constitutional guarantees and imposed press censorship, prompting U.S. secretary of state Christian Herter to suspend export licenses for arms. He informed the U.S. embassy in Havana: "In taking this action [the] Department considered [the] failure of [the] G[overnment] O[f] C[uba] to create conditions for fair elections and [the] deteriorating political situation."[34]

It was at this juncture that Greene first encouraged his Labour Party member of parliament (MP) friend Hugh Delargy to ask the Conservative government a parliamentary question in the House of Commons about possible British arms sales to Batista. Subsequently, he sent a cutting from *Hansard* (the transcript of parliamentary debates) to his "friends in Cuba," trusting they would "be encouraged that something was said in the House of Commons."[35] There were no British arms exports at this time. But Greene would raise the issue again a few hours after returning from a visit to the island with Carol Reed in October 1958.

The arms embargo imposed by Washington in March 1958 was not a complete victory for the State Department, because the Pentagon still maintained its military missions in Havana. Batista was in no mood for coercion, however, and again made contact with other foreign arms suppliers. One of these was Britain, and the new inquiry stimulated a sizable debate in the Foreign Office about the propriety of supplying arms to a traditional U.S. market. This reflected on one hand the recent harmonization in Anglo-American relations following the debacle of the Suez Crisis. On the other hand, British officials were loath to turn down this gift of a dollar-earning export opportunity given the international competition for new markets, and the country's postwar economic weakness relative to other competing nations. The debate also echoed a falling off in the postwar arms sales boom, and the penetration of traditionally British markets by U.S. arms exporters.[36]

During discussions between British diplomats and State Department officials in December 1957, it transpired that there was no U.S. objection to Britain selling arms to Cuba. Washington did advise the British to be cautious, however, given that "Batista might find it increasingly difficult to keep himself in the saddle." Furthermore, U.S. officials stated their aversion to the "supply of tanks and aircraft" to his flagging regime.[37] This dilemma grew during the course of 1958, particularly from the point that Britain first supplied arms to Batista's government that summer. Cuban Airlines captain Gregorio de los Reyes, a close friend of Batista and army chief of staff General Francisco Tabernilla, acted as intermediary between the Cuban and British governments during these arms sales.[38]

During their deliberations over selling arms during 1958, the Foreign Office relied almost solely on its embassy in Havana for analysis of the fluid political situation on the island. Stanley Fordham headed the embassy at this time, the ambassador having presented his credentials to Batista just a few weeks before the *Granma* landing in December 1956. Fordham had spent most of his foreign service in the Americas, mostly Latin America, and had a Peruvian wife. From 1949 to 1950 he had been counsellor (head) of the American Department in the Foreign Office, until illness forced his replacement by Donald Maclean, one of the "Cambridge spies" uncovered as a KGB mole in 1951.[39]

Based in Havana, the ambassador was isolated from the civil conflict between the Cuban government's armed forces and Castro's rebels, as most conflict took place on the east side of the island. He had limited contacts outside his diplomatic circle and relied on reports about the provinces from contacts in the area—for example, the general manager of the Royal Bank of Canada. Colleagues in London, meanwhile, were reading newspaper articles like those by *New York Times* journalist Herbert Matthews, who had breached the Batista army's security cordon to interview Castro in the Sierra Maestra hills in February 1957.

London-based diplomats judged Fordham's view of the situation "more sanguine than many." The British ambassador normally received reports about Oriente, the rebels' stronghold, from the British vice-consul in provincial capital Santiago de Cuba. Unfortunately, again, not only was there no secure line of communication between Oriente and Havana, but Neil Hone, a former sugar planter and long-term consular official, was convalescing at the U.S. naval base at Guantánamo during a vital three-month period in 1958. Batista's fortunes were in decline and the rebels were gaining strength, but Fordham was not receiving an accurate and up-to-date picture of Oriente province. Furthermore, Batista imposed press censorship within Cuba during the guerrilla insurgency, further limiting sources of news from the more troubled interior provinces.[40] Fordham's confidence in the dictator's hold on power fluctuated during 1958 but actually strengthened as the year progressed. In April, he was most noncommittal, writing, "No one can guess as to what will happen in the next few days, let alone months. For what it is worth my guess is that that Batista will survive. But I shall not be much surprised if I am proved wrong."[41]

The failure of the 1958 general strike called by Castro is essential to understanding the British decision to arm Batista. April 9, 1958, was not the start of what the guerrilla leader termed a "total implacable war," or the commencement of a "final stage."[42] It was in fact a complete failure. In Fordham's opinion there was no doubt that the episode dealt Fidel Castro a very severe blow.[43] The Foreign Office saw this as a signal that Castro and his rebel army were a spent force. Events in the coming weeks, however, would prove Batista's forces the weaker of the two adversaries.

In the following month, Fordham stuck his neck out and judged an overthrow of Batista unlikely.[44] He also considered that the value of future arms orders, plus the long-term advantage in gaining a foothold in this new market, outweighed the risks involved.[45] The Cuban air force asked British manufacturer Hawker Siddeley for a quote on twenty-five Sea Fury fighter aircraft and the Arms Working Party, a cross-governmental department group that recommended sales and issued export licenses, approved the deal in principle. Meanwhile, Batista's forces soon matched Castro's failed offensive when they were unable to press home their advantage in numbers and arms. The dictator launched a "summer operation," during which his soldiers managed to surround Castro's guerrillas in the Sierra Maestra hills, but they were unable to gain the upper hand. *The London Times* published a leading article on July 4 that clearly described a "civil war" in Cuba.[46]

In July 1958, the Ministry of Supply in London offered surplus and reduced-price Comet tanks to the Cuban government via the British embassy in Havana, but without going through the normal approval channels of the Arms Working Party. A swift reply from Batista's government expressed an interest in the immediate supply of fully armed tanks.[47] Well aware of the failure of Castro's general strike, the Foreign Office appeared less informed about the failure of Batista's summer offensive against the rebels. Judging that the rebellion had lost most of its momentum, a Foreign Office memorandum ventured that Castro coming to power was now a remote possibility and recommended the sale.[48] A signed contract to purchase seventeen Sea Fury fighter aircraft followed in late August.

In the first half of October, a two-month-old U.S. intelligence report indicated to the Foreign Office that the rebels were better equipped and organized, and enjoyed higher morale and support from Cubans than they had ever realized. A CX report received in mid-October (with information from the UK Joint Intelligence Committee) stated that rebel forces were now in control of most rural areas in the Oriente and Camagüey provinces and had recently moved into Las Villas.[49]

In the second half of October, vociferous telegram protests reached the British prime minister's office and Buckingham Palace from irate Cuban exiles in the United States. One message to Her Majesty Elizabeth II from a 26 de Julio supporter in Miami pleaded, "DO NOT SELL WAR PLANES TO DICTATOR BATISTA HE WILL BOMB LIBERTY LOVING CUBAN POPULATION LIKE HITLER DID WITH ENGLAND."[50] Radio Rebelde, the shortwave voice of Castro's guerrillas, set up by Carlos Franqui in the Sierra Maestra, broadcast denunciations of the British government for permitting arms sales to Batista. The BBC Monitoring Service picked up the following broadcast on October 19, 1958:

> England is not strong enough to scorn the sentiments of a heroic people destined to be massacred by the planes it is selling to Batista. England is betraying the memory of the bombings of Coventry and is forgetting the lessons of its own people that no power is strong enough to conquer patriotism and human dignity.[51]

The Foreign Office and the British government suffered a veritable barrage of criticism from 26 de Julio supporters. The rebel movement announced "Law No. 4 of the Sierra Maestra," urging Cuban citizens to boycott *productos ingleses*, including whisky, Dog's Head beer, Gordon's gin, cars, Glaxo pharmaceuticals, cloth, Irish linen, insurance company policies, and all products (including gasoline) sold by the Shell Oil Company.[52] Timing for the Anglo-Dutch oil company could not have been worse. It had inaugurated its new $25 million ($223 million) refinery in Havana's harbor just eighteen months earlier. In the meantime, Foreign Office officials in London advised the suspension of further arms deliveries until the forthcoming November elections in Cuba.[53]

Our Man in Havana appeared in bookshops on October 6, 1958. Only two hours after returning from his film location reconnaissance

trip to Cuba with Carol Reed on October 24, Greene wrote to MP
Hugh Delargy. The change in conditions since his visit the previous
November was "very striking." Castro's guerrillas had now cut communications within the island to a minimum. In late 1957, Greene
had been able to travel by car to Cienfuegos and Trinidad, but now
no driver would take him more than a few miles outside Havana.
"Under the circumstances," he wrote, "if only to prevent anti-British
feeling on the part of the man who is likely to be the next ruler of
Cuba, cannot you raise some opposition to the sale of these planes in
the House of Commons?"[54]

Here was concrete evidence of his support for the rebel cause.
Greene's letter to a sympathetic Labour MP was instrumental in ini-
tiating parliamentary opposition to the Conservative government's
arms sales. Nevertheless, in the Foreign Office just eleven days after
Greene's letter, head of the American Department Henry Hankey
wrote, "There is very little reason to suppose that Fidel Castro will
come to power in the foreseeable future."[55] Underlying Hankey's
point of view was its confidence that when push came to shove,
Washington would go to considerable lengths to avoid the suspected
radical Castro from reaching power, and Britain's risky arms sales
policy could shelter with confidence behind the U.S. position.[56]

Direct pressure from Cuba arrived in London on November 12
in the figure of 26 de Julio official emissary Dr. Manuel Piedra. He
came with instructions to seek a suspension of further arms supplies
and, failing that, to contact Labour Party leaders and trades unions
to stir up agitation. The Royal Ballet's prima ballerina Dame Margot
Fonteyn arranged a meeting between Piedra and opposition Labour
Party leader Hugh Gaitskell at the House of Commons.[57] Liberal-
leaning Fonteyn and her husband, Roberto Arias, a diplomat and
son of Panama's former president, were involved in an amateurish
and unsuccessful plot to overthrow Panama's authoritarian government in a coup d'état just six months later. They doubtless gained
some inspiration from what would soon be Castro's rebel victory.

Delargy tabled his parliamentary question on November 19. He asked the foreign secretary why the British government had supplied Cuba with "jet aeroplanes and tanks," and if his government knew that "civil war is raging in Cuba?" The aircraft were in fact "piston-engined." Selwyn Lloyd acknowledged the situation on the island had "rather changed since these orders were given," and "future requests" for arms would need careful examination.[58] Greene wrote to Jay Mallin in Havana, a figure "trusted by the Castroites," according to the author, enclosing a cutting of the parliamentary proceedings and adding that it would interest "some of our friends," namely the 26 de Julio movement.[59]

At the same time, the Foreign Office began to recognize the seriousness of the insurrection in Cuba and the inherent risk to Britain's arms policy. Henry Hankey, the arbiter of Foreign Office policy toward Cuba, now described Castro's movement as "a group of twelve men" that had expanded "to an army of over 10,000" within two years. In a mournful tone, Ambassador Fordham sent a personal handwritten letter to Hankey, remarking on the multitude of rumors and the scarcity of reliable news in Havana. He told the head of the American Department how it was extraordinarily difficult to evaluate the situation on the ground. Many Cubans and U.S. citizens were blaming Washington for the current situation. The Cuban government had provided him with many guards, due to the risk of kidnapping, but he had little faith in their ability to protect him.[60]

By mid-December the arms sales question had grown even more contentious. The opposition Labour Party learned that the cargo ship SS *Sarmiento* was about to sail for Havana with a load of "100 tons of rockets." In fact, the SS *Sarmiento* was about to transport five of the Sea Furies, plus some armaments and aircraft spares. Four of the fighter-bombers had left London on the SS *Santander* on September 12 and another four on the SS *Cotopace* on October 10 for their two- to three-week journey across the Atlantic. Such was the fear of sabotage by Havana dockworkers with pro-Castro sympathies that they worked under instructions to unload the unmarked aircraft boxes attired in only shorts and shoes. *New York Times* correspondent Ruby Hart Phillips also described the enormous armed escort that accompanied the Sea Furies to their assembly point at military Camp Columbia.[61]

An ocean away from insurrection in the Sierra Maestra of eastern Cuba, British MPs convened to debate the arms-to-Batista issue in the House of Commons. Fine Habana cigars were perhaps the only item that bearded Cuban guerrillas in olive-green fatigues under Fidel Castro's command and politicians in pinstripes in Harold Macmillan's ruling Conservative government—many of them members of exclusive gentlemen's clubs—had in common. During a lengthy and rowdy parliamentary debate on December 15, 1958, Hugh Delargy accused the government of engaging in a "sad and sordid traffic in arms" and doing a "dirty deal . . . behind the backs of the British people and of Parliament." Despite stonewalling replies from minister for foreign affairs commander Allan Noble, combative Labour MPs including Aneurin Bevan insisted on debating the "wicked deed" there and then for fear of a postponement until January. After a raucous session, the embattled minister finally pledged that "no further weapons of any sort" would leave Britain without first informing Parliament.[62] His commitment created a degree of unease in the Foreign Office, as an outstanding order of five aircraft remained unshipped.

Meanwhile, the arms intermediary Captain de los Reyes pestered the British embassy in Havana for his sales commission. First secretary Peter Oliver detailed to the Ministry of Supply in London the pilot's prominent role in the deal and the fact that "internal accountancy methods" in Latin America did not preclude "a certain amount of marginal profit here and there for people who are responsible for negotiating purchases." The effective price paid for each Sea Fury aircraft had increased from £14,750 (£328,000) to £19,000 (£422,000) to take into account "the usual 'contingencies.'" The Ministry of

Supply blamed the Havana embassy for the misunderstanding and denied Captain de los Reyes his "division of the cake."[63] Had it materialized, his commission would presumably have come free of income tax, in the manner of Harry Lime.

In a strategy reminiscent of *The Quiet American*, meanwhile, Washington made a last throw of the dice in December with a mission to Havana that sought to install a "third force" as an alternative to repressive Batista and radical Castro. But Florida businessman William Pawley, whose company first brought Leyland buses to Havana and later helped organize the Bay of Pigs invasion, failed to convince the dictator to step aside and retire in Florida.[64]

Only on December 12 did the Foreign Office acknowledge a state of civil war in Cuba.[65] Three days after the minister's parliamentary undertaking, the Foreign Office instructed its Washington embassy to convey the following message to their host government:

> [I]nform them that, like them, we are seriously disturbed by the trend of events in Cuba, that we still suspect the best course might have been to enable the Government to crush the rebels finally before they virtually got out of control.[66]

They appeared to lay blame for the situation at Washington's door. The British government's underlying assumption throughout was that weightier U.S. strategic and economic interests in Cuba would ensure a robust policy against Castro's forces and mean they never came to power.[67]

Greene wrote to Delargy on receipt of the December 15 House of Commons proceedings, and evidence of the MP's efforts alongside Labour colleagues Aneurin Bevan and Leslie Hale, "I think the three of you did wonders."[68] Just hours before the final implosion of the old order under Batista and the triumph of Castro's rebels, Fordham reported "a sudden deterioration in the military-political situation" on New Year's Eve. He added, "I doubt however if it is quite so desperate as one would gather from listening to the B.B.C. which seems to get its news of Cuba entirely from American agencies which in turn base their reports largely on the rebel broadcasts." He was candid in explaining, "We diplomats—including even the Americans and Spaniards who, for different reasons, ought to be well informed—are certainly very much in the dark about what is happening."[69] His final assertion soon proved correct.

At 2:40 a.m. on January 1, 1959, Fulgencio Batista took advantage of subdued New Year revelries to board a DC-4 plane for the Dominican Republic, never to set foot in Cuba again.[70] On the other side of the Atlantic, meanwhile, Macmillan's government and the Foreign Office immediately faced embarrassing questions about their recent arms sales to the now-deposed dictator.

PART II

AFTER THE CUBAN REVOLUTION

8

SHOOTING *OUR MAN IN HAVANA*

As Fidel Castro descended from the Sierra Maestra hills to Santiago de Cuba to proclaim victory, Greene passed New Year's Day 1959 quietly. Following a health scare, he had spent ten lonely days over Christmas waiting for X-ray results. Yet his longing to see Catherine Walston appeared to outweigh any fear about cancer, in his words, "a desired doom." He wondered when he might see her again due to Catherine's absence in the West Indies and his forthcoming trip to the Belgian Congo. After receiving the medical all-clear on what turned out to be intestinal inflammation, due "to overwork & worry, not alcohol," he took Gillian and John Sutro to the opening night of a new striptease club in London. The show was "awful except for one girl," and he longed to be elsewhere. "I wish I was in Havana now, I'm glad Castro has won," he told Catherine.[1] If he had the Shanghai Theater's more debauched cultural offering in mind, he would need to hurry. The island's new revolutionary government would soon close it down.

Greene's political involvement in Cuban affairs was hitherto unknown, but he drafted a letter to *The Times* on January 2, 1959, denouncing the Foreign Office and the British government over the arms sales. An enclosed note to the newspaper's editor, Sir William Haley, added, "Could you let me know if you feel unable to publish this letter as I would like to send it elsewhere?" It made a good story, and *The Times* had no issue with publishing it in their correspondence section. After sub-editors at the newspaper had corrected Greene's continued "Bautista" misspelling, his published letter began:

> The welcome success of Dr. Fidel Castro in overthrowing the dictatorship of Batista reminds us again of the extraordinary ignorance of Cuban affairs shown by the British Government. If it had not been for the intervention of Mr. Hugh Delargy, MP, this country would have gone on happily supplying the dictator with arms.
>
> [. . .]
>
> Any visitor to Cuba could have given her Majesty's Government more information about conditions in the island than was apparently supplied by our official representatives.[2]

In response to a January 5 article in the same newspaper, Greene wrote again to the editor three days later, "I hope you can let me have one more shot as the position does not seem to me quite as favourable to the Foreign Office as your Diplomatic Correspondent suggests." He detailed what he had seen in Cuba during his most recent October 1958 visit.[3] One can speculate as to whether Greene carried out on-the-ground reconnaissance for SIS during this visit, and if he did, whether the intelligence supplied led the Foreign Office to finally recognize the extent of the insurrection a month later. In reply to a letter from a member of the public who questioned the official explanation in *The Times*, Greene asserted, "My own impression is that the Government was at a complete loss and hardly knew of the existence of a civil war. Certainly that was the impression given by both Selwyn Lloyd and Commander Noble in the House of Commons."[4]

A *Guardian* editorial highlighted a "crowning piece of ironic Greenery." With the arms sales, it stated, "fact has not merely imitated but outrun fiction," because the opposition Labour Party had in fact saved the government's face by pushing back against the arms sales. *The Economist* asserted in a similar vein that the affair "made Whitehall look pretty silly."[5] A detailed analysis by the *Guardian*'s diplomatic correspondent highlighted yet another embarrassing blunder for the Foreign Office in 1958. A summer coup in Baghdad had left diplomats flat-footed, as had a revolt of colonels in Algiers. In the case of Cuba, however, the correspondent pointed out that Fordham—"rightly or wrongly"—was on extended leave during the vital summer months between mid-July and mid-October 1958, and that diplomats were inevitably "less well placed to gather certain types of information." As the monarch's personal representatives, people expected diplomats to behave diplomatically.[6]

Of course, such restrictions did not apply to Greene, our itinerant investigative novelist and part-time intelligence gatherer. He was able to travel relatively freely around the island in 1957, but not in October 1958. It is clear that newspaper correspondents were unaware in January 1959 that the novelist himself had instigated the parliamentary debate on the arms sales by contacting Delargy. While Greene had drawn attention to his government's poor judgment in the letter pages of *The Times*, he had also saved politicians and the Foreign Office from far more embarrassment. Officials could at least claim that British arms sales were restricted at the time of the revolution. Yet they could only make this claim because Greene had prompted Delargy to ask a parliamentary question on the matter. Under persistent Labour Party opposition questioning, the government minister had succumbed to pressure and halted further shipments of arms.

Greene had portrayed the ingenuousness and bungling of SIS handlers and military chiefs of staff in his recently published *Our Man in Havana*. The novel depicted senior officials spellbound by Wormold's sketches of military installations, based on nothing deadlier than the parts of a vacuum cleaner. In parallel, Foreign Office diplomats in Havana and London had failed to fathom real events on the ground in Cuba in 1958. They compounded their ignorance by approving the export of military planes and tanks to a waning dictatorial regime.

Also in the satirical novel, Wormold compiles his economic reports from local newspapers because he reasons it "unlikely that anyone in Kingston or London studied the daily papers of Havana." Greene had in fact underestimated official incompetence. In mid- to late 1958, no British diplomat in Havana or London appeared to take sufficient notice of what even the international newspapers were saying about the situation in Cuba. The aforementioned *Guardian* editorial continued in the same vein, pointing out that rather than relying on its embassy in Havana for news on the ground, the Foreign Office in London would have been better advised "to sit at home reading the newspapers."[7]

The Foreign Office instigated its own inquest into the affair. Passing the buck somewhat, one of its main findings was a "lack of reliable information from the Americans." For example, London only received a vital CIA report dated August 15 in mid-October. Meanwhile, a separate Parliamentary Select Committee set up to investigate the arms sales debacle concluded there had been a "serious failure to obtain timely and accurate information."[8] At the denouement of *Our Man in Havana*, the British ambassador summons Wormold to the embassy after he hears about his spreading of false information and advises him, "The correct sources for information abroad are the embassies."[9] How wrong he was.

In reality, implicated diplomats in Havana were dismayed to read Greene's "offensive" letters in *The Times*. First Secretary Peter Oliver, the embassy's chargé d'affaires during his ambassador's summer 1958 absence, lamented:

> Although Mr. Greene showed, both in his book "Our Man in
> Havana" and during this stay here, that on points of geographical
> detail he was not above suspicion, his two letters must have left

the public with a poor impression of the standard of reporting from this post.

An evidently crestfallen Fordham contradicted this assertion when he wrote to London five months later, "Members of Her Majesty's Foreign Service are expected to be right when all around them are wrong. I have been greatly concerned that I have failed in this respect and that in consequence I led you and others astray."[10] Another seven years later, Fordham's Peruvian wife wrote to Greene after the *Sunday Times* published his article describing a visit to Cuba in 1966. Either his memory failed him or he was being disingenuous when he told her that he had directed his earlier criticism at the "less than frank" foreign secretary Selwyn Lloyd and not that "admirable source of information—the embassy in Havana."[11]

The triumph of Castro's Revolution came as a surprise to Greene's contact in the Cuban embassy in Britain, the ambassador Roberto González de Mendoza. Batista's man in London cut short a skiing holiday in Germany to return to his diplomatic posting. He telephoned the Foreign Office to ask if they had any information about his position. They did not. The new revolutionary government replaced him as ambassador a few weeks later.[12]

In Havana, meanwhile, Fidel Castro gave an interview to the *Daily Telegraph* in which he affirmed that the Sea Furies and possibly the tanks had not seen any action.[13] Two days later, on January 8, 1959, a victory caravan led by Castro and other hirsute guerrillas entered Havana after traversing the length of the island in captured military equipment. They occupied the newly inaugurated Habana Hilton hotel and made it their base of operations. Photos and resonant film footage seen around the world showed the exultant but fatigued rebels riding into the capital atop jeeps and small tanks. The fifteen Comet tanks sold by the Ministry of Supply paraded behind and parked at the military base Camp Columbia. They had only been in Cuba for three weeks.

Castro sought a conciliatory gesture from the Foreign Office the next day to make amends for selling tanks and planes to Batista. Although Prime Minister Harold Macmillan considered one, it was not forthcoming.[14] The revolutionary leader spoke at the Anglo-Dutch Shell refinery in early February 1959 and lifted the unofficial boycott of British products and services.[15]

In the heady early weeks of 1959, summary military trials of Batista's alleged accomplices and executions of those judged guilty deflected attention from the ill-timed British arms sales. The pace of change was rapid, as the new revolutionary government set about resetting the established economic and political foundations of the country, particularly those that bound the island to the United States. For example, the island's new rulers soon repudiated "all types of vice, especially gambling," and closed down the island's casinos. Vengeful rebel supporters had already wrecked several of them during the first hours of revolutionary fervor. However, Castro immediately confronted protests from an industry that faced losing lucrative business and its workers their only employment. Almost as soon as they had stopped, the roulette wheels started spinning again.[16]

Cubans quickly became accustomed to frequent and lengthy speeches by Fidel Castro, lambasting more than sixty years of U.S. hegemony in the island and Batista's military dictatorship. At this early stage, the Revolution was fervently nationalist although not yet socialist in nature. The bearded leader flew to Washington on April 15 for his first post-revolutionary visit to the United States at the invitation of U.S. newspaper editors. Castro met Vice President Richard Nixon rather than President Eisenhower, who was playing golf in Augusta, Georgia, instead. Nixon noted his visitor's leadership qualities and judged he was "either incredibly naive about Communism or under Communist discipline."[17]

FILMING IN REVOLUTIONARY CUBA

An immediate concern for Carol Reed's production company following Batista's demise was the new revolutionary government's attitude toward his crew filming on the streets of Havana. In light of this, one could view Greene's denunciatory letters to *The Times* as a way to remind the revolutionary leadership about his help over the arms sales and thus secure their agreement. Columbia Pictures production executive Bill Graf achieved this objective when he traveled to the island in late January to seek assurances, fixing a definite starting date for production of April 13, 1959.

An advance guard of Kingsmead production supervisor Ray Anzarut and art director John Box landed in the Cuban capital on March 13 to set up headquarters at the swanky Hotel Capri. Built for $5 million ($45 million) and opened in November 1957, the time of Greene's main investigative and writing visit, it boasted a rooftop swimming pool with underwater windows.[18] The fact that the film production team and the main actors resided at the Capri no doubt informed the decision to change the location of room 501 from the Sevilla-Biltmore in the novel to the Hotel Capri in the film. A January 12, 1959, version of the script had actually located the book code scene between Hawthorne and Wormold in room 506 of the Hotel Riviera, a new $12 million ($107 million), twenty-story, air-conditioned hotel with four hundred rooms, inaugurated just ten days after the Capri.[19]

Geographically, the Sevilla was in Old Havana, within short walking distance of most on-location filming. The new Capri stood on a hill in the more distant Vedado district. Therefore, the Capri gained some free publicity at the expense of both the Sevilla and the Riviera, while Greene could more easily avoid his nemesis Ted Scott, a long-term resident at the Sevilla-Biltmore.

Pending the arrival of the full production crew, Anzarut and Box set about charting final backgrounds for the film and liaising with the Cuban Film Commission and unions representing local artists and technicians. The shooting schedule would last four weeks, with Oswald Morris appointed director of photography.[20] Therefore, just three and a half months after the triumph of the Cuban Revolution, the cast and full crew descended on Havana to film one-third of the movie on location in the city's streets. Forty-three British technicians came from London with their gear, including cameras and sound equipment, while electrical equipment arrived from New York.[21] An agreement with the Cuban Labor Department provided that thirty-seven local technicians worked on set, along with twenty-one Cubans in liaison jobs (chauffeurs, translators, etc.) and an estimated 1,500 local extras.[22]

Reed had assembled a multinational cast combining mostly Anglo-American actors, a few Cuban actors, and an Irish actress. Star billing went to the newly knighted Alec Guinness and to Noël Coward, both with a long list of theater and film productions to their names. Guinness had recently won a best actor Oscar for his portrayal of Lieutenant Colonel Nicholson in *The Bridge on the River Kwai*, also voted 1957's best picture. Ralph Richardson, star of the Reed/Greene collaboration *The Fallen Idol*, would play SIS chief C in London, and hence was not required for location shooting in Havana. Irish actress Maureen O'Hara took the part of SIS secretary Beatrice Severn. Cigar-smoking American TV comedian Ernie Kovacs had the role of Police Captain Segura. Burl Ives, originally a folk singer who had recently played Big Daddy in *Cat on a Hot Tin Roof* (1958) and won a best supporting actor Oscar for *The Big Country* (1958), would be Dr. Hasselbacher. In the eyes of many, however, he had besmirched his name by providing testimony against alleged communists in Hollywood at Joseph McCarthy's congressional hearings.

That just left the part of Milly, Wormold's teenage daughter. Reed gambled on the relatively inexperienced nineteen-year-old blond Texan actress Jo Morrow. She had majored in mathematics at high school, taken one drama course, and, after winning a talent contest, obtained a film contract for a very small part in *Ten North Frederick* (1958). When Twentieth Century Fox dropped her, Columbia Pictures awarded Morrow small parts in the surfing picture *Gidget* (1959) and *Juke Box Rhythm* (1959). It was on the strength of a screen test to play a twenty-six-year-old prostitute in another film and some good references that Reed awarded her Milly's role. He had a reputation for coaxing good performances from youthful actors.[23]

Greene arranged to be in Havana during the first week of film shooting, primarily to assist Carol Reed with on-the-spot script adjustments and location advice. The 26 de Julio movement was aware of the author's arms sales intervention with a Labour MP, and it was hoped that his published letters on the controversy might smooth relations with the new revolutionary authorities should the need arise.

Prior to traveling to Havana, however, Greene undertook an arduous six-week trip to research a new novel at a leper colony in the Belgian Congo. This experience mirrored the background to Joseph Conrad's *Heart of Darkness* (1899) and led to Greene's following novel, *A Burnt-Out Case* (1961). Its title referred both to a leper whose disease has run its course and to the novel's main character, a visitor who arrives as a morally and psychologically burnt-out case to work in the colony. Greene himself was an emotionally burnt-out case, and the trip helped him shake the failed relationship with Anita out of his system.[24] During a stopover in Cameroon en route back to Europe, he met the wife of a French businessman and a relationship soon developed. Unlike his previous mistresses, Yvonne Cloetta would bring stability to the long final chapter of his life.

Staid British film censors had driven Greene to a different sort of distraction for years, enforcing changes to several cinematic versions of his earlier novels. One of their early purges was against *Brighton Rock* in 1947, which Greene said was "damaged by the censor" due to an objection about the story's religious theme; main character Pinkie was a murderer, and censors cut his references to Mass because they considered them offensive toward Roman Catholics.[25]

The 1955 cinematic version of *The End of the Affair* had to tread very carefully in its portrayal of a wartime affair between middle-aged novelist Bendrix and Sarah, a senior civil servant's wife. The only hint of the sexual act was Sarah's removal and postcoital replacement of earrings in the bedroom.

In *Our Man in Havana*, the principal objects of ridicule were the bungling British intelligence services. Surely there was little if anything that could offend the revolutionary authorities in licentious Cuba, so far removed from conservative British morals. When Greene and Reed returned to Havana, they were no doubt expecting to notice some changes since their October 1958 visit six months earlier. They were probably not expecting their screenplay, on which they had worked so diligently, to be the target of censorship.

OUR THESPIANS IN HAVANA

The Kingsmead Productions team and their equipment flew direct on a chartered plane from London. Cinematographer Oswald Morris accompanied nervous flyer Reed on a Stratocruiser to New York. Their onward flight to Havana made a forced landing at Miami due to engine trouble, but a bumpier ride lay ahead in Cuba. Greene flew BOAC via New York to land in Havana at one thirty p.m. on Friday, April 10, meeting up on his first day with Sir Carol Reed, Sir Alec Guinness, and Noël Coward.[26] During the afternoon Reed introduced them all to the young and relatively inexperienced American actress Jo Morrow. Greene described the scene outside a seafront restaurant after she left: "There was a long, long silence then Noël said: 'Carol, what on earth induced you to hire that girl?'" Carol blamed her shyness at "meeting all you famous people," to which Noël exclaimed, "That little tart, shy?" "And all Alec [Guinness] did was rub his hand up and down the edge of the table, saying nothing with a look of despair on his face."[27] The exchange foretold trouble.

On Saturday evening Greene went "round the town" with his best local friend, Nick Mendoza. On Sunday he returned to his favorite lunchtime restaurant, the Floridita, and again went "round the town" with Mendoza in the evening, this time taking in Carnival. He was at the Floridita again the following day, alongside *Time* correspondent Jay Mallin. In the evening, he again toured the spots of Havana, this time with a different foreign journalist.[28] Greene appeared keen to exploit whatever the city still offered in terms of gastronomy and entertainment. The pace proved too much for Rocky. As Greene was being interviewed, he entered the Capri's lobby one morning looking pale and fretting about his mislaid camera. Cinema critic Guillermo Cabrera Infante described the smiling taxi driver rubbing his stomach after a night of overindulgence. Explaining that a doctor had advised him to cease drinking, Greene asked if he would follow the advice. "Maybe next week," replied Rocky.[29] Perhaps he knew his English client was going to depart the island by then.

The film's main actors arrived via a different route than Greene and Reed but on the same day. Noël Coward hosted Alec Guinness and his wife, Merula, at his home in Jamaica for ten days beforehand. A "biblical deluge" of rain and "lots of policemen with long hair, beards and tommy-guns" awaited them at Havana's airport. Also dampening the spirits of the British thespian guests was the glitzy Hotel Capri in Vedado, with Miami-American décor that was simply not their cup of tea. Coward described its "ornate gambling casino, freezing air-conditioning, bad service and inedible food." Guinness and his wife also found the recently opened hotel far too extravagant for their tastes. Following his wife's early departure, he swapped their "raspberry fool apartment" for a smaller suite in "nauseating blue-green." A small American boy then disturbed his peace in the lobby by swooping a model airplane at the Oscar-winning actor while shouting, "I bomb you all! Bomb! Bomb! Bomb!"[30]

On a more relaxed note, Guinness attended Mass and confession, probably at the Iglesia del Santo Cristo, one of three Catholic churches noted in his diary.[31] Unfortunately, however, he had to abandon regular swims in the Capri's rooftop pool due to persistent autograph hunters.[32] Given a choice, the British actors would surely have preferred to reside at the less American and more restrained Sevilla-Biltmore in Old Havana.

Sir Alec enjoyed—up to a point—the company of American comedian Ernie Kovacs, playing the sinister chief of police. Despite Greene's denial in the prelude to the novel's first edition, he based Captain Segura on Batista's chief henchman Esteban Ventura, who fled the island alongside the dictator in the early hours of January 1, 1959. Kovacs larked about both on set and at the Capri, where he had a room on the same floor as Guinness. On one rest day, Guinness noticed his fellow actor's door wide open, and Kovacs typing away at a desk with half a dozen fully naked girls sprawled around the bedroom.[33] The comedian liked to burn the candle at both ends.

In letters to his wife, who was now back in England, Guinness berated himself for his unassertiveness on set. Kovacs had also driven him half-mad with endless jokes, TV stories, and on-set fooling around. Meanwhile, the "frightfully slow and rather stupid and a bit near-drunk" Burl Ives and his entourage had attempted to steal scenes. "Jo Morro" [sic] had proven herself more lively than their initial meeting suggested, but she had quietened down, probably after an early word from Reed. Still, she often interjected with "loud screams of Hi! and O-Daddy-O." Guinness recognized she had "some talent," although it failed to appeal to him. Even Carol Reed had proved a pain by acting out Sir Alec's scenes before giving him the chance to conceive them himself.[34]

Lighting a black-and-white film was problematic for the director and his cinematographer, and some locations scouted with Greene six months earlier proved unsuitable for filming. Particular street corners of Old Havana were permanently in shadow because judicious colonial architects had designed narrow thoroughfares and high buildings specifically to avoid direct sunlight and overpowering heat.[35] Yet despite all the tribulations, Guinness viewed some "wonderful" early rushes and praised their "really beautiful" photography and marvelous rendition of Havana's "heat and bustle and voice."[36]

Shooting of background scenes began on Sunday, April 12, in Plaza Vieja, a cobblestoned square with chrome yellow façades, and former location for bartering and selling slaves. *The New York Times* described a band of roving musicians and assorted tropical fruits arranged neatly on a corner stand and a cart laden with colorful local flowers. It added, "Graham Greene stood under a crumbling archway, behind the camera, a Leica dangling from his neck, intently watching and occasionally recording the goings-on." Meanwhile, Carol Reed directed in a light linen open-necked Cuban guayabera hanging loosely over his trousers. SIS's man in the Caribbean Henry Hawthorne (played by Noël Coward) was dressed less fittingly for the ninety-plus-degree-Fahrenheit heat. He appeared rigid in a tight-fitting blue woolen suit and stiff white collar, topped with a homburg—the stereotypical and incongruous Englishman in the tropics, with an umbrella to boot.[37]

Coward had composed and sung the classic 1930s ditty "Mad Dogs and Englishmen," decrying those expatriates foolhardy enough to emerge under the oppressive midday sun in tropical foreign climes. Describing his work on set the next day, Coward wrote in his diary: "On Monday all I did was walk about the streets very fast watched by thousands of bewildered Cubans and surrounded, for protection only, by hirsute armed policemen."[38]

On Tuesday, April 14, the crew filmed a key scene in Sloppy Joe's at the corner of Zulueta and Ánimas. Long-term Havana resident Ernest Hemingway dropped by to witness proceedings and chat with old friend Noël Coward between takes. Jay Mallin recalls introducing Hemingway to Greene at Sloppy Joe's bar. However, despite their shared depressive natures and predilection for the world's war zones as foreign correspondents, the visiting Englishman and the Havana-residing American did not hit it off. As Mallin relates, "it was perfunctory; they didn't like each other."[39] According to Ted Scott's "Interesting *if* True" column, Hemingway wore only a "beard, shorts and sports shirt" and merely said "Howdy" to Greene. The Englishman did not attend Hemingway's cocktail party later that day at his San Francisco de Paula home.[40]

Also in Greene's absence, Coward described how a car whisked some of them off at lunchtime after shooting at Sloppy Joe's to meet "the famous Fidel Castro." After waiting for more than an hour, they gave up on their host. Coward reportedly mouthed *"mañana"* to a local official as they departed. As for the gathering at Hemingway's home, he described everybody getting "thoroughly pissed." His location shooting and five-night stay were now over, and he flew off to New York the next day feeling "very peculiar."[41]

One can speculate as to reasons for the frosty Greene/Hemingway encounter. They had a lot in common, but their personalities were so different. Both drank and chased women, but the American's all-action physicality was the polar opposite of Greene's awkward impracticality. For example, both had spent time in Africa, but Greene would never dream of hunting big game as trophies and adorning his home's walls with them. Wartime intelligence work was another experience they both shared, but again, it took a completely different form. As opposed to Greene's largely office-bound work in Sierra Leone and London, Hemingway had assembled a motley international crew—the Crook Factory—to hunt down prowling Nazi U-boats in Caribbean waters, adapting his *Pilar* fishing boat with light arms for the enterprise. Still, the two-year-long escapade, endorsed by the U.S. ambassador in Havana from late 1942, turned into a lark and achieved next to nothing.[42]

Professional jealousy could be part of the explanation for their brief meeting. Hemingway had won the Nobel Prize for Literature in 1954, while his English rival was never to receive the coveted prize. But the men supposedly had a more personal connection as well. According to an improbable story, during the Spanish Civil

War, Claud Cockburn came across a scene where Hemingway identified a tall man in glasses as an enemy spy. The man was identified as
Herbert Greene, Graham Greene's older brother. Cockburn allegedly
exclaimed, "Don't shoot him, he's my headmaster's eldest son."[43]
Still, if the story is true, it is unlikely that Greene harbored any ill
feeling toward Hemingway for threatening to kill his troublesome
brother. Had he shot Herbert, he might have saved the Greene family
a lot of later bother.

Greene possibly resented Hemingway's recent criticism of him in
an interview with George Plimpton, published by the *Paris Review* in
spring 1958. Despite Papa's reluctance to explore his inspiration for
writing during the whole interview, Plimpton pursued the question
and proposed a nameless author's idea that a writer "only deals with
one or two ideas throughout his work." After Hemingway had dis-
missed the proposition as too simplistic, the interviewer named the
source as Greene. Pressed again, Hemingway contended a good writer's most essential gift was "a built-in, shock-proof, shit detector."[44]

We can turn to well-connected American actress-turned-writer Elaine
Dundy for Hemingway's forthright take on Greene. Both she and her
husband, Kenneth Tynan, were friends with "Hem" and had indulged
a mutual interest in bullfighting alongside him in Spain. After downing
some potent double daiquiris at the Floridita in April 1959, the couple
dined at his home up in the hills, where the boorish American took aim
at fellow writers. He gave Greene both barrels, accusing the English
interloper of spending a mere ten days in Havana and writing a book
that confused the city's street names and buildings. Furthermore, the
Englishman had then tried to deflect criticism by calling *Our Man in
Havana* an "entertainment." Greene had produced some good work,
he said, "but now he's a whore with a crucifix over his bed."[45]

Papa had at least paid the guilt-ridden Catholic the tribute of
reading his Havana novel, even if he miscalculated his days spent
in the city. It is true Greene had confused a few street names, using
the formal Avenida de Maceo (instead of the informal Malecón),

misspelling Virdudes (instead of Virtudes), and even giving the same hotel room two different numbers (both 510 and 501). In Dundy's opinion, the fact that his rival's new novel was a success, with its film version then in production on Havana's streets, "may not have improved Hemingway's temper."[46]

We might have never known the reasons for Greene's reticence during his brief meeting with Hemingway, save for a diary entry from a later visit to Cuba in 1963. Pondering Sloppy Joe's, where Hawthorne recruits Wormold in *Our Man in Havana*, he scribbled to himself, "Hemingway came to see the filming—we shook hands & exchanged wry glances: I was muscling in to his territory."[47] The annotation pointed to his scorn for Hemingway's exaggerated machismo and confirmed the mutual feeling that Greene was trespassing on Papa's literary patch.

HEDONISM TO PURITANISM

When Wormold flies back from Jamaica following his urgent summons from Hawthorne, he meets fellow vacuum cleaner sales representative Carter on the plane, and they engage in small talk:

> CARTER: This is only my second trip to Cuba. Gay spot, they
>   tell me. [. . .]
> WORMOLD: It can be, if you like roulette or brothels. [. . .]
> CARTER: I didn't exactly mean . . . though I'm not a Puritan,
>   mind.[48]

In 1959, new rulers with radical ideas had assumed power in Cuba, keen to eradicate any vestiges of their neo-protectorate status under the six-decades-long tutelage of the United States. Despite the fact that Cuba and its inhabitants provided only background for Greene's and Reed's satire about British intelligence, the cinematic portrayal they were filming in Old Havana's streets soon clashed with local sensibilities.

Prime Minister Fidel Castro and minister of education Armando Hart, whom Greene had met at a Santiago de Cuba safe house in November 1957, had recently signed the first decree concerning cultural affairs and formed the Cuban Institute of Cinematographic Art and Industry (ICAIC) in March 1959. Another young activist in the urban underground, Alfredo Guevara (no relation to Che), a friend of Castro's from their student days at Havana University, headed the new institute. The decree declared cinema an art, an instrument for the creation of individual and collective consciousness and thus able to deepen revolutionary spirit and feed its creative inspiration. Among the ills that the institute and the revolutionary government wanted to rid from the island was its reputation as a gambling and sex destination. As the British embassy affirmed later in the year, "The real attraction of Havana for tourists in the old days was its reputation as a 'wicked city,' and this is an aspect which the present Government is anxious to play down."[49]

Cuba's new rulers and officials also had very fresh in their minds the abuses and cruelty of the recently defeated Batista dictatorship. Furthermore, they felt that recent North American film productions shot on location in Cuba had denigrated their country and its citizens. One recent example was the 1956 Warner Brothers action-adventure *Santiago* starring Alan Ladd, which portrayed Cuba's bloody struggle for independence from Spain in 1898 with numerous clichés. These included North Americans in heroic roles and some offensive historical inaccuracies. For example, the action involved two Cuban national heroes as characters in the film, despite the fact that José Martí and Antonio Maceo died in the independence war prior to the battle for Santiago de Cuba in 1898.

The foreign filmmakers' shooting of an early establishing scene for *Our Man in Havana* managed to upset local sensibilities on day 1. As Carol Reed told David Lewin of the *Daily Express*, "when they saw Noël Coward being pursued down a street by three musicians twanging guitars in his face they thought this might give a bad impression."[50] Dr. César Blanco from the Bureau of Public Order in the Ministry of the Interior announced that while the Ministry of Labor had approved filming and that Alfredo Guevara's ICAIC had reviewed the script, this did not rule out additional checks by his bureau. While it was not their job to censor or criticize, he explained, his bureau was determined to eliminate "the false impressions" created by the film. He made the following criticisms of the script:

* It depicted tourists besieged by hundreds of imploring shoeshine boys.
* It showed the entire Cuban population dedicated to selling maracas and dancing the rhumba.
* The only entertainment for Cubans appeared to be cabarets frequented by disreputable clients and criminals.
* The only work for Cuban people appeared to be selling lottery tickets.[51]

Additionally, producers would have to leave no doubt in viewers' minds that the depicted action occurred under the Batista regime.[52]

A front-page column in *The Times of Havana* blamed the "rosy Red idea department of Alfredo Guevara, Communist director" of the newly formed ICAIC. According to the thrice-weekly English-language newspaper, the production ignored suggested changes and Dr. César Blanco at the Ministry of the Interior would therefore "censor the script." Yet the column affirmed that rather than denigrate Cuba, the film was "a spoof of the British Intelligence service." It claimed producers would merely "say yes politely to every government restriction here and now; and then blithely proceed to film the movie following the original script once they have left the country."[53] So according to this American-owned newspaper, straightforward British pragmatism would trump an oversensitive local reaction.

Like Carter's outlook in Greene's novel and screenplay, local sensitivity to the portrayal of Havana as a sex center appeared puritanical. Greene made just this point when, mimicking Wormold's late-evening invitation to Carter at the denouement of *Our Man in Havana*, he took *Daily Express* "showbusiness" reporter David Lewin on a tour of Havana's "spots" on Monday, April 13, 1959. By midnight, they had covered "some of the darker bars" with the assistance of Greene's faithful taxi driver Rocky. They called in at the Blue Moon, the Mambo, and the Victoria, "not nearly as respectable" as its name suggested. Disappointingly, it was not the same city he had visited six months earlier. Lewin quoted Greene, who "shook his head sadly" and said, "All very changed since I was here before the revolution." "Revolutions are so puritanical, at least in their early stages. What fascinated me about Havana was its looseness and its strangeness."[54] For his tastes, the city had lost some of its essence in the intervening period.

The English theatre critic Kenneth Tynan made similar observations during his visit in these weeks, noting that nightlife under the new regime had become "furtive or vanished altogether." Castro's well-armed and battle-dressed *barbudos* now patrolled the city's clubs and bars to identify wanton behavior. "It is as if the Amish had taken over Las Vegas," he wrote. British journalist Stanley Price was another witness to Greene's quest for hedonism in a sea of puritanism. Bored with the tedious filmmaking process, Greene roped Price into a fruitless search for Superman with the aid of local taxi drivers. Their pursuit succeeded in finding well-endowed women, but not the superhero performer. They should have tried the Blue Moon a second time, because—according to Tynan—the club had escaped the ban, and voyeurs were still enjoying Superman's "legendary skills" for the right price.[55]

The New York Times described local apprehension that Greene "occasionally referred too strongly to the seamy side of Havana life." According to the newspaper and several other sources, the script underwent thirty-nine changes to obtain local approval. The Ministry of the Interior assigned an observer to the production, secretary of the Film Board Dr. Clara Martínez Junco, who also happened to be César Blanco's wife.[56] On the day that David Lewin witnessed the observer in a brown suit at the country club, her supervision was somewhat redundant. They were filming a scene between Hawthorne and Wormold set in Jamaica. Carol Reed explained to Lewin the current state of play: "What they want is to make sure that our story, which is set in the old regime under dictator Batista, shows just what a police state it was then. We are doing that anyway with odd little scenes outside police stations and references to torture of political prisoners. But most of the plot is comedy and we cannot make it too heavy. [. . .] We are just going on filming and there is no question of our having to stop because of trouble." Greene was not asked to rewrite his script and was equally diplomatic when he explained, "This sort of thing always seems to happen in a fluid situation after any revolution."[57]

New Zealander Scott gave his readers an insight into the dark British sense of humor but also lectured the British that Latin Americans reacted differently to foreign representations of "their profound tragedies." Locals were dismayed, for example, that Esteban Ventura's reputation as "a killer and a torturer of the Batista regime," as "one of the most sadistic officers of repression in the tyranny," especially against suspected insurrectionists in both the 26 de Julio and Directorio Revolucionario movements, was represented by the character Captain Segura as a "mere romantic" or a "romantic rogue."[58] Comedian Ernie Kovacs had cultivated a fortnight-old beard to portray Batista's chief torturer, but he clipped it down to a moustache within days of arriving in Havana. The revolutionary authorities could not abide his resemblance to a *barbudo*, one of Castro's bearded rebels, when Ventura was in fact a chief henchman of Batista.[59]

Such was the level of odium, in fact, that local onlookers "hissed and booed" Cuban actors wearing the hated powder blue police uniforms of Batista's day.[60] The dictatorship's recent atrocities were raw in people's minds. Indeed, Alec Guinness described the vengeful mood that hung in the air during this early Robespierrean stage of the Revolution. He likened the farm carts and trucks he witnessed to the tumbrils of the French Revolution. The Cubans confined inside their improvised chicken-wire cages were destined for interrogation and military trial, and those found guilty were executed in the Cabaña Fortress on the opposite side of Havana's harbor.[61]

Kenneth Tynan described introducing Ernest Hemingway to his heavyweight literary compatriot Tennessee Williams in the icily air-conditioned Floridita restaurant. During a pregnant pause of the awkward lunch, "a tiresome Commonwealth journalist" appeared, surely none other than Ted Scott. He breezily invited the male trio to the colonial Spanish fortress to witness a post-midnight firing squad in action. While Tynan politely declined after debating its merits with Hemingway, Williams accepted the invitation. He reasoned that writers should expose themselves to the full range of human experience, however distasteful. Unfortunately for the playwright, bad weather postponed that evening's open-air spectacle.[62]

Cuban film critic Guillermo Cabrera Infante was closely involved with the foreign production at its very beginning on April 13 and on the final evening of night shooting on May. In between, he accompanied Fidel Castro on his April 15–May 8 trip to North and Latin America, while keeping abreast of events back in Havana. In this early period of the Revolution, before a clampdown on press criticism of officialdom, his June 1959 article in *Carteles*, the country's principal cinema magazine, mainly blamed the director of public order (the unnamed César Blanco) and his wife, Clara Martínez Junco, for the censorship of *Our Man in Havana*. The article describes how Cabrera Infante and Alfredo Guevara had initially met with Sir Carol Reed merely to encourage him to portray the Revolution in a positive light, and the director and Greene had been happy to comply with a series of minor changes to their script.[63] Yet almost as soon as production began, the director of public order marched onto the set like an insolent and intransigent "pequeño César" (a little Caesar: his actual name), demanding that nobody step out of line. He then appointed his wife to supervise the cinematic production. Cabrera Infante's article affirms that before departing with Fidel Castro for the United States, the journalist tried to reason with Martínez that the full force of the state should not apply to a mass medium like film. He was unsuccessful and therefore decided with Guevara, heading the newly founded ICAIC, to defend Reed against the militant Bureau of Public Order.[64]

It was also evident that at this early juncture following Batista's demise, the island's new rulers were finding their feet. With revolutionary zeal, they acted at times impetuously, closing and renaming government ministries and reallocating their responsibilities. The situation was fluid and at times confusing. As one of the film production team explained, "It looks like a case of the left hand not knowing what the right hand has already done."[65]

Cabrera Infante enumerated four major interventions by the secretary of the Film Revision Commission. First, policemen interrupted proceedings in Plaza Vieja on day 2 of filming to confiscate the script until the director of public order could read and approve it. Then in the Casa de Beneficiencia, Martínez complained that too many black Cubans appeared in the film, alleging (very contentiously) that few of them had fought against Batista. The third incident occurred at the Shanghai Theater, where the day's filming was just ending when Martínez arrived to order that two policemen seize the footage and prevent it leaving the country. Cabrera Infante was already back on the island for the final incident, when an arrest warrant hung over Carol Reed for refusing to sign an order that he send the completed film to Cuba for approval by the Bureau of Public Order. By this time Fidel Castro, also freshly repatriated from his twenty-five-day foreign tour, had gotten wind of the proceedings. He intervened to halt extreme measures that threatened to tarnish the new Revolution's image abroad.[66]

Almost at the very end of location filming, Alfredo Guevara invited and accompanied Fidel Castro to the set in Cathedral Square on May 12, with Cabrera Infante in attendance to alleviate tensions and make introductions. During Castro's late-night, forty-five-minute visit, he chatted with Carol Reed, Maureen O'Hara, Alec Guinness, and Ray Anzarut.[67]

Graham Greene had long departed, therefore missing another opportunity to meet Castro. He began his return to London on Friday, April 17, traveling via Paris.[68] Following custom, he met a fellow passenger who piqued his interest, the twenty-eight-year-old owner of the Viking Hotel on Miami Beach. In a letter to Nick Mendoza, he described a man they had actually seen together in a Havana bar. He attracted Greene's interest because he was a "young gigolo," a "curly headed young man with a greek god face" who had prospered financially through his "prowess as a dancing instructor."[69] He sounded like a rival to Superman and his sexual proclivity in the Shanghai Theater.

In order to appease the hardline Bureau of Public Order, Carol Reed made subtle changes to his film. According to a report in *Time*, Cuban officials insisted on the inclusion of an anti-Batista atmosphere in the film—sirens and Black Marias, for example.[70] However, the script produced by Greene before Columbia production executive Graf's early January arrival in Havana contains all the scenes subsequently shot in the city and at Shepperton Studies in England. The only major concession to local sensitivities was the inclusion of the following disclaimer at the very beginning of the film: "This film is set in Cuba before the recent revolution." There were other changes, but they were minor, affecting mostly the mood of the film rather than the script.

When interviewed in England ahead of shooting scenes at Shepperton Studios, just two days after meeting Castro in Havana, Alec Guinness was diplomatic. He described differences with the Cuban authorities as "greatly exaggerated in the press back home." As for censorship, there had been "no alterations" as far as he was aware.

The authorities were merely eager for viewers to realize the story was set in Batista's time and not under the new revolutionary government. Asked for his impressions of Cuba, Sir Alec highlighted a "very alive, very stimulated" atmosphere, and Cubans' "great personal devotion" toward Castro, "a very courageous man, and a very impressive one."[71]

A Columbia Pictures spokesman was also on message when describing "widely published and grossly exaggerated" reports about "government interference." He did confess that "minor changes" came about at the Cuban government's request. Yet even with Dr. Clara Martínez Junco from the Ministry of the Interior sitting "in a ring-side seat," the "situation in Havana"—as far as the film was concerned—"could not be better." Furthermore, the Cuban technicians were "fast and efficient" and geared to working in the intense heat. Bill Graf was equally complimentary about local cooperation, describing the complete freedom given to the crew in busy downtown Havana and "streets roped off at a moment's notice."[72]

In private, however, Guinness did voice reservations. He wrote to his wife ten days before his departure from Havana: "we ran into acute censorship trouble yesterday and Carol [Reed] had to sign a statement before lawyers that he wouldn't show in the film a shot we did of chorus girls throwing stockings at a rowdy audience. And the man who staged the chorus girls was hustled away at pistol point and thrown into gaol."[73] In the finished film, the Shanghai's striptease artistes are seen gyrating and removing their outer garments on stage, but none fling their underwear into the baying audience. Sir Alec's observation demonstrates just the sort of modification that Reed made in order to circumvent censorship without substantively changing the script.

Robert Emmett Ginna flew down to Havana from New York to observe the film production for the arts magazine *Horizon*. He provides a little more detail on what transpired at the Shanghai Theater, although it appears he did not personally witness proceedings at the venue because his article confuses the censor's gender. He describes how the film production team had to search out former members of the stage chorus, due to the authorities' prompt cleaning-up of such insalubrious establishments. When dancers tossed their intimate apparel into the audience, the government censor leapt to "his" feet to decry the scene's immorality. He ordered seizure of the whole day's negatives and, after a stand-off lasting several hours, forced Reed to sign a deposition. Assistant director Gerry O'Hara told Ginna they could have reshot the whole scene back in England, "and a lot naughtier too."[74] They did not resort to this expedient.

Once back on European terra firma, Greene wrote to his son, Francis, "Havana was a little touchy for a few days, as I expect you gathered from the papers, but I think all is going well now."[75] Graf contradicted this impression when he wrote to Greene a month later, promising to update him on the "trials and tribulations" suffered by the production team following the author's departure from Havana.[76] In another apparent sign of puritanism in this period, the aforementioned chief of public order Dr. César Blanco would go on to head a campaign to raid and shut down brothels and rehabilitate prostitutes.[77]

Echoing Greene's earlier observation, British Marxist historian Eric Hobsbawm identified a "persistent affinity between revolution and puritanism," even in countries like Cuba, whose cultural tradition was "the opposite of puritan."[78] It is likely Hobsbawm had in mind the blending of native Caribbean, Hispanic, and African cultures on the island. Of course, this tradition was alien to the puritanism that stemmed from late sixteenth- and seventeenth-century English Protestants, some of whom were early settlers in England's new American colonies on the Eastern Seaboard. By the twentieth century, North Americans seeking to escape a clampdown (e.g., Prohibition) on immoral behavior in the United States flew or sailed down to Havana to indulge in hedonistic pleasures, including consumption of alcoholic drinks and sex with prostitutes.

Part of the explanation for the Cuban Revolution's hasty puritanical drive lay in the notion that foreign powers and visitors had long exploited the island. Following nearly four centuries as a Spanish colony, U.S. capital and tourists had imposed themselves on Cuba, giving it a sullied reputation as the "whorehouse of the Caribbean." In this light, the new rulers considered vice a capitalist pathology and determined that foreigners would no longer have free rein to debase Cuba and its people. Castro's revolutionaries were eager to project a new image of their country.

AN "INTERESTING FAILURE"

Two decades earlier, when Greene had reviewed *Deuxième Bureau* (1935) for the *Spectator*, he had criticized "a rather dull film, a long packed melodrama of the French and German Secret Services." He judged it began "brilliantly enough," yet:

> The film, alas, does not maintain this sinister and satiric level. Two secrets stolen from the Germans, a double-crossing agent, a motor chase, a beautiful woman spy who falls in love with the Secret Service officer she has been sent to trap, two murders and an attempted suicide: the film is too thick with drama.

Greene the film critic lamented, "It is a great pity, for what an amusing film of the Secret Service could be made if the intention was satiric and not romantic, the treatment realistic and not violent." He applied his own medicine splendidly to his 1958 novel. However, his screenplay and Reed's rendering of it for their 1959 film version contained elements and drawbacks similar to the French production twenty-four years earlier.[79]

Our Man in Havana premiered at the Odeon Leicester Square in London on December 30, 1959, but the new Reed/Greene film received lukewarm reviews. Critic Isabel Quigly put it nicely when she described "a scrappy film full of 'moments' of collector's pieces:

which added together make the film into something of a let-down, the parts being worth so much more than the whole."[80] It plods along splendidly until its midpoint, when satire turns to melodrama, and the plot becomes difficult to follow. Who is the enemy targeting Wormold? It is never clear. A telegram dispatcher is suspicious about a number-coded message and puts it aside. An anonymous man buys a copy of Lamb's *Tales of Shakespeare* in the street. Carter stammers at the Traders Lunch, and the viewer needs to make the connection with Segura's earlier tape recording of a man with a stammer telephoning Hasselbacher. When the German physician's body appears prostrate at the Wonder Bar, some reviewers were unsure if it was a case of murder or natural death. *Film Quarterly* judged that "the plot gives one the effect of too many *Cuba libres*" (i.e., rum and Cokes).[81]

Unfortunately, Reed did not allow Guinness to play the part of Wormold the way he envisaged him, "as a more clearly-defined character, an untidy, defeated sort of man." Instead, the director ordered him to avoid character acting and portray instead a nonentity, somebody invisible in the crowd, a blank surrounded by more colorful characters.[82] Sir Alec was left "in a rather 'I-told-you-so-mood'" when he read the *Daily Mail* review of his "dull" portrayal of Wormold. "I did keep telling Carol—I ought to have characterized it all more as a shopman, perhaps with a squint, a wall eye, buck teeth and a mop of ginger hair and a Manchester accent."[83] He pictured "a totally different concept of my own character—I saw him much more as a rather untidy *New Statesman and Nation* type."[84]

There are various problems with Jo Morrow as Milly. First, her American accent seems out of place, even if Greene's screenplay weakly blames it on her local convent school education. She is also physically too mature to convince as Wormold's sixteen-turned-seventeen-year-old daughter. Most important, she appears more a wholesome North American twenty-something than an acquisitive Catholic teenager. She does not convey the "invisible duenna" of the novel, and never convinces as the target of Segura's affections. Columbia Pictures, who demanded a quota of American actors to attract U.S. audiences, appear to have imposed her on Reed. His original idea for the part, Jean Seberg, was apparently contracted to play an American student in Jean-Luc Godard's *À Bout de Souffle*.[85]

Greene later recalled a quite different sequence of events, saying that he himself rejected Seberg when a Columbia Pictures executive suggested her for Milly's role during an October 1958 meeting with Greene and Reed in New York. It was on this occasion that he shared a Benzedrine with the dubiously named Patricia Marlowe, both welcome dinner distractions at Manhattan's Algonquin Hotel. Greene had seen Seberg debut in *Saint Joan* (1957), whose screenplay he had written, but judged in a 1983 interview, "she can't act." Later in the same interview, however, he appeared to blame Reed for casting Morrow but was unsure how it came about. Still, he had no doubt that she ruined "every scene she was in," and Alec Guinness's performance.[86] When Greene sent Noël Coward a copy of the novel, his dedication read, "In happy memory of Hawthorne and in memorable horror of a certain Jo Morrow."[87]

White American comedian Ernie Kovacs's portrayal of the sadistic Captain Segura is problematic because the sinister suitor to teenage Milly appears less the cruel Red Vulture of Greene's novel and more a purring pussycat. It is no wonder his comical depiction of this fictionalized Esteban Ventura offended Cubans. Of course, Greene insisted he had written a comedy and therefore made Segura "a rather light character," with only brief references to torture. His Cuban friends thought he had painted Segura too lightly, while Greene argued that a more horrible character would have ruined the comedy.[88] By naming the fictional Segura so closely to the real Ventura, and with the history of his cruelty so contemporaneous to Greene's novel and film, local offense was inevitable and profound.

The most successful acting performance of the film belonged to Noël Coward. His portrayal of SIS Caribbean station chief Henry

Hawthorne fits the bill perfectly. He encapsulates the stiff-upper-lipped Whitehall bureaucrat abroad and his obsession for professional drill. As well as looking the part from his homburg to his polished shoes and umbrella, Coward sounds the part, his "supercilious, clipped, dry voice" making the "most simple and casual remark sound like a glittering epigram."[89] His scenes are standout moments in the film, and those in London alongside Ralph Richardson as C are among its best.

In a private letter to the author, Noël Coward pointed to his own depiction of Hawthorne, a caricature of all the "hapless, bumbling bureaucrats" he had encountered during the war. Surely, he conjectured, the novelist had not needed to invent such comic figures.[90] Indeed, he had not. Greene's intelligence work during the same war had brought him into contact with several bungling models to inspire his later fictional portrayal.

Coward both gloated and squirmed after waltzing away with reviewers' plaudits under the noses of talented performers like Alec Guinness, Ralph Richardson, Maureen O'Hara, and Burl Ives. He wrote with sincerity in his diary, "Delighted as I am to have made such a spectacular success . . . my pleasure is tempered with irritation at being used as a flail against my fellow artists. This is not noble modesty on my part. I *am* very good, the picture *is* slow in parts and Alec *is* dull at moments."[91]

A real star of the film is Havana itself, with monochrome Cinema-Scope that portrays the city at its stunning best. On-location shots of Old Havana are sumptuous, evidence of how the former Spanish colony developed economically and aesthetically from the sixteenth century until 1898, with the addition of modern adornments during the first six decades of the twentieth century preceding the Revolution. Narrow colonial streets and squares—and the elaborate neon signage of businesses and services suspended over them—provide a beautiful distraction for viewers unable to follow the film's plot.

When comedy turns to melodrama in the later nocturnal scenes of the film, as Wormold pursues fictitious subagents and the duplicitous Carter, many elements are reminiscent of *The Third Man*. Like postwar Vienna, the camera shoots colonial Old Havana's buildings and streets at low angles with a tilted lens. Characters cast long shadows and scamper over glistening wet cobblestones, while footsteps echo off ornate buildings. *Our Man in Havana* the film, however, did not receive and did not deserve the plaudits of the earlier Greene/Reed picture, and it marked their final collaboration together.

Those who do not share Greene's ingrained scorn for Alfred Hitchcock's directorial talents will always wonder how the master of suspense would have conceived the intelligence satire/melodrama. Following rejection of his offer for the film, he went on to direct *North by Northwest* (1959) with Cary Grant in its starring role. In this classic suspense story, a group of foreign spies mistake an advertising executive for a government agent and pursue him around the United States. The film attracted huge critical acclaim, unlike *Our Man in Havana*.

Alas, its principal English actors and Greene largely blamed Jo Morrow's portrayal of Milly for the film's failure, despite its other shortcomings. Interviewed for the *Daily Express*, the blond American actress told its reporter, "I'm not scared of acting with such important people. They can give you so much and make you look so good. If I don't get anywhere after 'Our Man in Havana,' with all this talent around me, I'll quit."[92] Whether her fellow actors' criticism was fair, Morrow's curtailed cinematic career shows she soon heeded her own advice.

9

REALITY IMITATES FICTION

reene's novel would prove prescient in several respects. Not only did Wormold's invention of "big military installations under construction" in the mountains of eastern Cuba presage the Cuban Missile Crisis, but Greene's fictional tale, wherein a novice spy's deception leaves egg on the faces of high-ranking British officials, also preceded the real-world embarrassment heaped on the Foreign Office and Macmillan's government. The author compounded this humiliation with his aforementioned letters to *The Times*. Furthermore, he named the naïve bungler who believes Wormold's fictitious drawings (based on an Atomic Pile vacuum cleaner) Henry Hawthorne, which is either prescient or a spooky coincidence. In tandem with fictional SIS Caribbean Chief Henry Hawthorne, the American Department chief in the British Foreign Office who oversaw the ill-timed arms sales to Cuba in late 1958 was Henry Hankey, another H.H.

After Wormold and Beatrice kidnap exotic dancer Teresa and drive her away from the Shanghai Theater, a spectacle looms on Havana's horizon: "The skyscrapers of the new town stood up ahead of them like icicles in the moonlight. A great H. H. was stamped on the sky, like the monogram on Hawthorne's pocket."[1] Did the letters *H. H.* carry a significance beyond Henry Hawthorne's pajamas and advance publicity for the twenty-five-floor-high Habana Hilton?

*

Following his triumphant military procession into Havana on January 8, 1959, Fidel Castro arranged a meeting with Stanley Fordham at the ambassador's residence three days later. Cuba's revolutionary leader arrived at one a.m., a full six hours late, accompanied by a convoy of vehicles laden with guns and soldiers. Due to another pressing appointment, he asked the British ambassador to accompany him, and they discussed Anglo-Cuban relations while speeding along Havana's deserted streets.[2]

In the following month, with the arms controversy fresh in mind and amid a flux of rapid changes, Fordham professed himself "reluctant to crystal gaze."[3] By August 1959, Castro was still condemning the United States in impassioned speeches. Animosity between the Cuban revolutionary and Rafael Trujillo in the neighboring Dominican Republic also intensified. Ambassador Fordham judged that only "the fertile imagination and fluent pen of an Ian Fleming or an Eric Ambler (or even of a Graham Greene)" could do the events "full justice."[4] Yet, despite the many challenges, he avoided further controversy during the remaining year of his diplomatic posting in Havana and dispelled rumors of an early recall to London.[5]

The Macmillan government's arms to Cuba policy came under further scrutiny later in 1959, and critics again included Graham Greene. When Batista fled the island in the early hours of New Year's Day 1959, five of the seventeen Sea Fury aircraft remained undelivered. Britain decided its arms policy in the Caribbean in consultation with Washington in March. Policymakers in London acceded to the U.S. request to suspend all arms supplies to the area, owing to incipient rivalry between Castro and Trujillo, and a series of armed raids against their respective Caribbean territories.[6]

Arms suppliers were reluctant to refuse fresh export opportunities. Despite the new restrictions, competitors—including the United

States—continued to sell limited quantities of arms. The British found justification therefore in supplying Cuba with the five outstanding Sea Fury aircraft in mid-May 1959. Another quandary for Britain arose from Castro's request to exchange all the recently delivered Sea Fury aircraft for new Hawker Hunter jets. The arms manufacturer Hawker Siddeley agreed to the deal in July, but it required British government approval in order to proceed. Cuba would pay $189,000 ($1.6 million) for each Hawker Hunter jet and receive $80,000 ($700,000) for each piston-engine Sea Fury returned. Such a substantial deal was commercially very attractive, but there were a whole host of considerations, not the least of which was the fragile Caribbean arms embargo.[7]

Unlike European competitors, Britain's close relationship with the United States constrained the government's natural inclination to accede to the Cuban request.[8] Foreign Office officials highlighted pressure from industry and other government departments, and possible repercussions should foreign competitors win the business.[9] Considering London's previous arms sales to Batista, meanwhile, Fidel Castro declared he would consider the decision a "touchstone" of Britain's attitude to his new government.[10]

During the course of 1959, Foreign Office officials questioned the wisdom of Washington's policy toward Cuba and its estimations of radicalization in Castro's administration. U.S. diplomats were far quicker than their British counterparts to discern communism on the island. One official in London, for example, described Washington's tendency to define all left-wing neutralism or anti-Americanism as "communist."[11] While there was undoubted difficulty in gauging communist influence in Cuba, officials in the Foreign Office deemed U.S. fears of a communist throttlehold "much exaggerated."[12]

In October 1959, several factors exacerbated an already complex situation. The U.S. State Department first heard about Cuba's request for an aircraft exchange from a news agency report on October 12.[13]

Without consulting the British government, it called a press conference on October 16. *The Times* reported the next day:

> The United States is understood to have expressed strong
> opposition to the possible sale of British jet fighters to Cuba. A
> State Department spokesman said to-day that it was no secret
> that the United States did not like and was not happy about
> moving arms into the Caribbean area, and it had made this clear
> to Britain "in forthright language."[14]

According to British officials, Washington had commented on the
possible Hunter deal in the clumsiest possible way, giving the impression of exerting overt pressure on Britain. The indiscretion galva-
nized their debate on the aircraft exchange. It might now be wiser,
some argued, to ignore the United States and its shortsighted policy.[15]
They had now found the best justification to allow the exchange.

This prompted Greene to renew his earlier correspondence to *The
Times* on the subject of British arms sales to Cuba. He wrote to its
editor, "There will surely be little visible justice if the British Government refuses the replacement of jet fighters to Castro in time of
peace (even though an uneasy peace) when it supplied jet fighters to
Batista in the middle of a war."[16] His letter outlined the hypocrisy
of British policy toward Cuba and his early support for the revolutionary government.

Both the prime minister and his foreign secretary still intended to
approve the planes exchange, despite Washington's opposition. In a
series of high-level contacts, U.S. Secretary of State Christian Herter
highlighted to Foreign Secretary Selwyn Lloyd a deteriorating political situation in Cuba, the risk of supplying arms to Castro, and the
need to maintain the arms embargo. Cabinet changes in the Cuban
government had demoted moderates and promoted known left-
wing extremists. U.S.-Cuban relations appeared beyond the point
of no return. Importantly, Lloyd now acknowledged a worsening

outlook in Cuba, and substance in U.S. reports. He wrote in his diary on November 23, "It looks as though we dare not do it—if he were to fall just after, as Batista did last year, we should look very silly."[17]

Lloyd informed his cabinet colleagues of continuing U.S. opposition to the aircraft exchange. Balancing a negative U.S. reaction on the one hand and the size of the export order on the other, he recommended rejection of the deal. The prime minister noted Britain's flourishing trade with Cuba. Yet the chancellor of the exchequer ventured that the cost to Anglo-American relations would outweigh the economic benefits of expanded trade with Cuba. The cabinet agreed to turn down the aircraft exchange.[18] Later the same day, Lloyd described his "long wobble" in cabinet and colleagues' quiet acceptance of his finely balanced decision to decline the Hunter deal.[19]

Cuban sentiment reacted strongly to Britain's decision to reject the deal with the excuse of "tension in the Caribbean region." The daily newspaper *Revolución*, the mouthpiece of the new revolutionary government, claimed it bore the stamp "Made in the U.S.A." The article asked why the previous year's "bombing of open cities" had not been considered "tension" when selling arms to Batista. Another article proposed, "Cuba can very well do without Perfidious Albion," and that the "insignificant colony of the United States—England—obeys and obeys faithfully. It is a case of a decadent nation."[20] It was the French who had termed their cross-channel rivals *la perfide Albion* in the eighteenth century, referring to their "alleged treacherous policy towards foreigners."[21] Less than a year into the Cuban Revolution, the new regime was not slow to highlight and ridicule what it viewed as the treacherous and weakened position of Britain in its relationship with the United States following the Suez Crisis.

U.S.-CUBAN RELATIONS

The relationship between Cuba and the United States deteriorated rapidly during 1960, as the Caribbean island took an abrupt political turn to the Left. Spanish colonial rule had integrated Cuba into the world capitalist economy, but close ties to Moscow would sever these ties. Alarm bells rang loudly in Washington when Soviet First Deputy Prime Minister Anastas Mikoyan visited Havana in February. The new allies signed a trade agreement in May. When Castro asked the three large, foreign-owned refineries in Cuba to process Soviet oil, they traveled to Washington for consultations and refused his request. The Cuban government then "intervened" and nationalized the refineries. It also nationalized the new hotels inaugurated during the armed insurrection. The Habana Hilton was one example, renamed the Habana Libre in June 1960.

As the year progressed, Washington and Havana traded a series of tit-for-tat measures as their hitherto close relationship fell apart. Under mounting domestic pressure, the Eisenhower administration enacted a "get tough" foreign policy against its close neighbor. When Congress gave the president authority to severely cut the Cuban sugar quota, Castro reacted by nationalizing many established U.S. properties and companies in the island. The Soviet Union demonstrated its support for Castro's government with the announcement that it would import all the Cuban sugar not purchased by the United States.

Intolerance toward continuing criticism of the Cuban government in the local press led in the spring to further pressure on three Spanish-language daily newspapers and their closure. Titles that disappeared included the prestigious *Diario de la Marina*, the doyen of Cuban newspapers. The two English-language dailies closed in the autumn, including *The Havana Post*. Before then, its long-standing columnist Edward Scott, bête noire of Graham Greene, suffered

problems of his own. At the beginning of June 1960, Cuban authorities detained him at Havana's airport aboard a Miami-bound plane.
According to reports, they had found his name on a piece of paper
in the possession of an American pilot accused of counterrevolutionary activities. After three days in a Cuban jail alongside the pilot
and seventeen Cuban prisoners, they deported the New Zealand–
born journalist and he finally completed his journey to Florida.[22]

Unsurprisingly, his misfortune did not elicit any sympathy from
Greene, who wrote to Nick Mendoza in July 1960, "I must say I
was delighted to hear that Ted Scott had been deported. He was
really one of the nastiest pieces of work I have ever encountered."[23]
One wonders if Scott's espionage connections, first in the Second
World War through British Security Coordination in Panama and
New York, and possibly later in Cuba, fed Greene's unease about
him. Scott, meanwhile, probably knew that Greene was a former
MI6 officer who had never fully left the service. Maybe it was a case
of two part-time spooks, suspicious of each other's activities in Cuba
and wary of having their cover blown.

The Revolution's radical trajectory rankled Cuba's middle and
professional classes as they saw their privileges evaporate. Many fled
the island for the United States in 1960 and 1961, taking their social
capital—skills, education, contacts—with them. They hoped to
return just as soon as the new regime imploded or, failing that, when
Cuba's infinitely more powerful northern neighbor forced it from
power. Among those who abandoned Cuba for the United States
were two of Greene's guides in the island prior to the Revolution:
Havana businessman Nicolas Mendoza and journalist Jay Mallin.

Less than a year after their most recent correspondence, Greene
received a circular from Mendoza with a Greater St. Louis School
of Anti-Communism letterhead. Greene replied with a seven-word
message, "What on earth are you up to?!"[24] Sixty-year-old Mendoza
explained from exile in Arkansas that laws promulgated in October
1960 had convinced him his country had reached the point of no

return toward communism. In November 1960, he had abandoned his home, his farm, his shop, his law practice, and his properties and followed his burgeoning family northward. He initially found work with *Encyclopedia Britannica*, then received invitations to give talks on Cuba, before presiding over the International Organizations Committee of the Greater St. Louis School of Anti-Communism.[25] Greene's cryptic and extremely brief reply indicated both surprise and less than wholehearted support for Mendoza's political stance.

Time-Life correspondent Jay Mallin also left Cuba early in the Revolution. Among other books, he authored *Fortress Cuba: Russia's American Base*, published in 1965. In the 1980s, he became news director at Radio Martí in Washington, DC, an anti-Castro broadcaster beaming Spanish-language news and other programs into Cuba from the United States.[26]

OUR INTELLIGENCE IN HAVANA

Herbert Marchant succeeded Fordham at the British embassy in the summer of 1960. He was well qualified to describe the tumultuous events that unfolded during his three-year ambassadorship in Havana. A former assistant master at Harrow School (1928–39), he had worked at the Government Code and Cypher School (later GCHQ) at Bletchley Park during the Second World War. Marchant, who preferred the name Bill to Herbert, acted as deputy head in Hut 3, the section responsible for translating and processing German army and air force intelligence.[27] Before his appointment to Havana, he had occupied diplomatic posts in Bucharest (1948–49) and Paris (1950–52). He also held consular posts in Zagreb (1952–54), North Rhine/Westphalia (1954–55), Düsseldorf (1955–57), and San Francisco (1957–60). According to his obituary, he developed an interest in amateur dramatics at Bletchley Park and produced its Christmas pantomime.[28]

This, his diplomatic experience, and knowledge of both the Russian language and Soviet bloc politics stood him in good stead for what appeared on the Cuban horizon. Two years into his posting, the chill winds of Cold War geopolitics would barrel through the Caribbean like a cyclone and sweep tropical Cuba into the vortex of global superpower rivalry. A cool head was required.

Following rupture in U.S.-Cuban diplomatic relations at the start of 1961, the Cuban authorities acted on rumors about an armed U.S. invasion. British diplomats in Old Havana again found themselves too close to the action in January, when the military authorities mounted sandbagged machine-gun emplacements on the roof of the building whose top three floors the embassy occupied.[29] While its strategic elevated position was a drawback on this occasion, it would prove an advantage the following year.

When rumors of an imminent invasion reached a crescendo in early April 1961, just days before the actual Bay of Pigs fiasco, Marchant was unequivocal in his assessment:

> Prospect of badly organised landings planned on the assumption that internal opposition is strong enough to give decisive support continues to cause considerable concern to me and to all my European colleagues. [I]f the American assessment is based exclusively on counter-revolutionary sources it is almost certainly wrong.[30]

The Bay of Pigs was one of the Cold War's most infamous episodes. President Kennedy endorsed CIA advice and some 1,400 mercenaries and Cuban exiles, financed and trained in Central America by the CIA, launched an amphibious invasion at the Bay of Pigs on Cuba's southern coast. Their plan was to establish a beachhead and foment a mass internal uprising against the revolution. Here was a concrete case of an intelligence organization if not fabricating then at least exaggerating a plan's chances of success.

The Cuban authorities had arrested thousands of suspected counterrevolutionaries before the ill-conceived military operation. Furthermore, a preemptive attack by B26 bombers destroyed only half of Cuba's air force. At 4:45 a.m. on April 17, 1961, Fidel Castro called the San Antonio de los Baños air base to speak to his chief pilot. A jeep ferried Captain Enrique Carreras Rojas to the air control tower to communicate with the revolutionary leader. Castro informed him an invasion was taking place on Cuba's southern coast and ordered him to fly there before daybreak and sink the enemy's vessels.[31]

Piloting a Sea Fury fighter-bomber plane—sold to Batista by the British in 1958—the U.S.-trained Cuban pilot obeyed his commander in chief's orders to the letter. Rockets launched from his Sea Fury sank the *Río Escondido* and beached the *Houston*, disabling the proxy invasion force's main supply ships. This was the turning point of the CIA-sponsored fiasco, and it came the very day after Castro first declared the "socialist" nature of his revolution.[32]

The irony was clear. Graham Greene had persuaded a friendly Labour MP to protest the British export of tanks and planes plus ammunition (including rockets for the Sea Furies) in the House of Commons in late 1958. In arming the dictator Batista when his position was weakening by the day, Britain had unwittingly supplied his successor Castro with the means to sink its Cold War ally's botched invasion in the water. Furthermore, Washington had replicated Britain's ill-judged invasion against Nasser in Egypt five years earlier, an event that had ended in the Suez Crisis. When Marchant reflected on the Bay of Pigs at the end of 1961, he concluded that the U.S. military reverse had "made the Suez campaign look like a successful picnic."[33] The ambassador's verdict was a classic of British schadenfreude, and the Bay of Pigs a Cold War debacle that even Graham Greene's fertile imagination could not invent.

PRESCIENCE IN HAVANA

Soon after the American fiasco at the Bay of Pigs, Marchant estimated that neither potential counterrevolutionaries nor anyone else
could now "foresee what the future has in store for this country,
now that is has been so helplessly caught up in the whirlwind of
international politics."[34] British diplomacy's main man in Havana
continued to express concern that the distorted picture of Cuba
reaching Washington's ears—from expelled journalists and embittered refugees—was forming "a most dangerous intelligence basis
on which to plan future policy."[35]

In *Our Man in Havana*, Wormold decides to invent intelligence
on his return from a trip to the provinces. Wormold sits down with
an Atomic Pile vacuum cleaner for inspiration and sketches "big
military installations under construction in [the] mountains of Oriente Province," and scaled drawings of a "large concrete platform"
and "strange machinery in transport." His SIS chiefs in London are
impressed but perturbed by constructions that indicate weaponry
even more destructive than the hydrogen bomb.[36]

This story of invented intelligence might have seemed unlikely
on its publication in 1958. But four years later, in 1962, important
aspects of this fantastical fiction mutated into disconcerting reality.
Ambassador Bill Marchant and other British diplomatic staff were
instrumental in supplying intelligence to London and Washington
in the prelude to the Cuban Missile Crisis, in the midst of the crisis
itself, and in its aftermath. Writing from the calm that followed the
high-stakes global storm, Marchant would readily identify parallels
between the events in 1962 and Greene's spy fiction satire.

One wonders how Greene achieved his astonishing feat of pre-
science. Perhaps he had simply given expression to the tangible fear
that many citizens around the world harbored about a thermonuclear conflagration. A story about constructions in the mountains

also reflected many of the real events that took place while Greene was planning and writing his novel. In fact, inspired by newspaper reports about uranium discoveries and the development of the hydrogen bomb, Greene had traveled to the Harz Mountains in Germany in 1950 to research a proposed film treatment, *The Harz Mountains Story* (1950). Carol Reed rejected the project.[37]

Our Man in Havana was a product of its age, reflecting real fear of a Third World War involving nuclear exchange. Eight years after the aggressive U.S. deployment of atomic bombs against Japan at the end of the Second World War, the Soviet Union tested a hydrogen bomb in August 1953. Its Cold War adversary, the United States, then detonated a hydrogen bomb in the Pacific archipelago of Bikini in March 1954. The Soviets followed three months later with their first production of atomic energy at a power station. Britain carried out its first thermonuclear test in the South Pacific in May 1957. Then in October, the Soviets stunned their U.S. arms race rivals with the launch of the Sputnik satellite and its orbit of the earth. Greene began writing his novel in Havana five weeks later, on November 8, 1957, in the context of these epochal events. On this same day, Britain detonated its first true thermonuclear bomb (or H-bomb) over Christmas Island, a 1.8-megaton device codenamed Grapple X.[38]

Public concern over such fast-paced technological developments and politicians' ability to resolve international tensions without recourse to a global war led to the formation of the Campaign for Nuclear Disarmament (CND) in England. It held its inaugural march to the Atomic Weapons Research Establishment (AWRE) at Aldermaston in England in March 1958, as Greene still worked on his novel. In fact, his son, Francis, was completing his National Service at this time. He had an interview for a temporary research post at the AWRE in November 1957, where he started work a year later. In May 1958, his father picked his brains about the science of microphotography.[39]

It needs no great leap of imagination to suppose that Greene had such contemporaneous Cold War events and fears in mind as he wrote his fantastical novel. Furthermore, his multiple journeys to Cold War hotspots such as Indochina and British Malaya, as well as Russia and Czechoslovakia, afforded him considerable firsthand experience of war and Soviet bloc politics. Additionally, he had survived the Blitz in London, a dangerous yet (for him) invigorating experience.

The "father of science fiction," H. G. Wells (1866–1946), was an inspirational figure for writers of Greene's generation. The science he depicts in his novels imperils the future of the world as much as it promises to improve it. Both *The Time Machine* (1895) and *The War of the Worlds* (1898) were influential and remarkably prescient. *The World Set Free* (1914) even prophesized the atomic bomb. His later novel *The Shape of Things to Come* (1933) was both a short history of the world and an anticipatory history of the future up to the year 2106. Wells's story originates from a "dream book" bequeathed by the recently deceased League of Nations intellectual Dr. Philip Raven, envisioning the future of humanity. This novel—like his others—tapped into contemporary preoccupations and anxieties, and portrayed an at turns utopian and apocalyptic future. Some of its many predictions proved accurate, including the occurrence of a Second World War.

Books by former aeronautical engineer J. W. Dunne in the 1930s influenced Wells, as they did Greene. He acknowledged the debt in the introduction to his 1939 novel *The Confidential Agent*. In *An Experiment with Time* (1927), Dunne proposed a theory of dream-based precognition wherein dreams drew on future as well as past events. He observed that while awake, human consciousness tended to focus on time proceeding at a steady rate in approximation to the present. The mind of a sleeping person, on the other hand, could roam and view different moments of time, including both the more distant past and the future. Instead of dreams merely reflecting lived

experience, his new theory stressed premonition and reverse cau-
sality. He based this on his own experience of precognitive dreams
that were premonitions of later disasters. In practical terms, he suggested that individuals with the gift of precognition should write
down their dreams to prove his theory.[40]

Transcribing his dreams was indeed a practice that Greene
adopted during various periods of his life in "dream diaries,"
a series of detailed and fully indexed volumes. In fact, a psychia-
trist recommended he transcribe his dreams in order to assuage his
manic depression. As we know, he first recounted dreams—some of
them invented—to an amateur psychoanalyst in London during his
depressed adolescence. Several years after the Cuban Missile Crisis
an interviewer asked Greene if he suffered from nightmares. His
answer was not often, but he did recall a period when he had "a
lot of atomic war dreams, which . . . probably contained memories
of the Blitz." In them, he had envisioned the destruction of New
York, an "oppressive, dirty and nervy city" he disliked. Based on his
real experiences during the Blitz, he also dreamed about standing
on Hampstead and "seeing the total destruction of London with St.
Paul's rising up like a tooth in a mouth." He confessed the dreams
were "not frightening but interesting spectacles," due to the fact he
"was resigned about the end."[41] Of course, those of a skeptical per-
suasion would readily observe how easy it would be to manipulate
the recorded memory of a dream to correspond with a subsequent
real event.[42]

Nevertheless, details in various Greene novels do appear remarkably prescient. He was adept at producing accurate portrayals of
reality with believable characters, perhaps because he had lived
through many of the twentieth century's brutal realities himself.
Most of his trips to troubled parts of the globe were a symptom
of his manic depression and desire to escape a tormented personal
life. Perhaps a manic-depressive personality, writing talent, vivid
life experiences, and an active subconscious combined to create his

highly realistic and prophetic fiction. His stories closely mimicked reality, and almost inevitably, therefore, reality often mimicked his fiction. One could even make the case that his smoking of opium in the 1950s and beyond allowed him clearer access to his labyrinthine subconscious, rich life experiences, and a graphic imagination.

In the first draft of his screenplay for the film version of *Our Man in Havana*, Wormold's vision is even more nightmarish than in the novel. As our vacuum cleaner salesman contemplates his completed sketch for SIS, he asks himself, "Is it a rocket to the moon or some sinister new weapon which will imperil the whole human race?"[43] It was the latter that the Soviets deployed to Cuba in the summer of 1962, and which a U.S. Air Force U-2 reconnaissance plane photographed from high altitude in October that year to precipitate the Cuban Missile Crisis.

In the 1958 novel, London wants photographic evidence of the construction sites and sends out a secretary and a radio operator to assist their man in Havana with his burgeoning network of sub-agents. Wormold has to pretend to organize a flyover of the installations in the mountains by fictitious Raul Dominguez of Cubana Airlines, a pilot fond of whisky. Fiction then suddenly merges into reality: Hasselbacher invites Wormold and his new secretary Beatrice to his home for drinks and receives a phone call informing him that one of his patients has died in a car crash near the airport. His name happens to be Raul, the same as Wormold's invented pilot.[44]

THE CUBAN MISSILE CRISIS

The Cold War's most perilous episode came out of a clear blue sky. In his annual end-of-year report for 1962, Marchant lamented:

> Even with the full benefit of hind-sight I find it difficult in reviewing the local scene over these last twelve months, to piece

together a probable and coherent sequence of events which can be seen to have led up to that most improbable piece of history, the story of the Cuban missile crisis.[45]

On the face of it, there was no scenario less comic. Thermonuclear war threatened the annihilation of millions around the world. Yet the first intimations of the arrival of rockets that went beyond the realm of conventional Soviet bloc arms are akin to elements in Greene's satirical novel. For example, a telegram from Marchant in January 1961 related intelligence from a caller at the embassy, an "independent source of unknown reliability," who reported seeing "concrete rocket land sites" under construction in eastern Cuba.[46] A source in a July 1961 report described the arrival in port of tubes ten meters long and two meters in diameter, eight with Russian characters in blue, the remainder in red.

Castro's opponents in the United States and Cuba had cried wolf before, making British diplomats skeptical about such reports. The British embassy reported:

> Rumours and stories abound, but as you might imagine it is very difficult to obtain confirmation. Tales about the arrival of rockets have cropped up again, but these must be regarded with particular caution as they may well be spread by counter-revolutionaries under the impression that the establishment of rocket bases in Cuba would be a signal for American intervention.[47]

All of which led the aforementioned Henry Hankey, still head of the Foreign Office's American Department, to annotate on the report, "Mr. Graham Greene was prophetic."[48]

On a Caribbean island that had transformed from a capitalist playground to a communist showpiece within two years, it was a considerable challenge to separate rumor from fact in both fiction and reality. Aiding British diplomatic staff, however, was their embassy's providential location. It stood midway between the Presidential Palace and the seafront, in close proximity to the capital's harbor entrance. Furthermore, the embassy occupied an elevated position on the top three floors of a nine-story building, making it an ideal vantage point for observing ships entering and leaving the harbor. A new tunnel had opened in 1958, linking Havana's main seafront avenue with the coastal highway on the opposite eastern side of the harbor. The embassy directly overlooked the western entrance and exit tunnels to this main arterial route in the capital city as well as the seafront avenue the Malecón.[49]

Following the rupture in diplomatic relations between the United States and Cuba in January 1961, the British embassy acted unofficially as Washington's eyes and ears in Havana. It performed the role of a "listening post," passing on intelligence to the United States.[50] The embassy's contribution had three clear phases: before, during, and immediately following the Cuban Missile Crisis. This involved:

1. Intelligence supplied to both London and Washington during the Soviet military buildup in the summer of 1962.
2. Intelligence and analysis communicated at the height of the crisis—once the intelligence services were definitively aware of the offensive Soviet nuclear capability in the island.
3. Intelligence that detailed the military withdrawal following the gravest period of the crisis.

Like Wormold with his book code and drawings based on an Atomic Pile vacuum cleaner, there was little sophistication to British intelligence gathering in Cuba during this period. In January 1962, British embassy staff made a team effort to observe Havana's armed forces and increased adoption of Soviet equipment in their annual military parade. Diplomats reported all their findings to Washington. While the ambassador and head of chancery (with camera) sat in the stands, three staff members joined the crowds lining the route, with

two more watching television indoors to photograph on-screen proceedings. The results obtained impressed U.S. officials.[51] In March,
Marchant visited the Joint Intelligence Bureau (JIB) in London and
old associates underlined to him the importance of photographic evidence. They requested precise information on certain vehicles and
affirmed he was their "only source in Cuba."[52]

The obvious difficulty with gathering on-the-ground intelligence
like this was that the Cuban authorities would soon discover accred-
ited diplomatic staff undertaking the risky work. During this crucial
embryonic stage of the revolution, British staff maintained a twenty-
four-hour presence at the embassy. The mission possessed a Western
Union terminal, but not its own secure telegraphic line to London.
When the terminal malfunctioned, diplomats took cipher messages
by hand and sent them from a Western Union office in Obispo in Old
Havana. From London, the Foreign Office maintained its own transatlantic cable to Washington, the "direct line," via which it retrans-
mitted the vast majority of Havana-origin cables to its embassy in
the U.S. capital. The conspicuous British vehicles used by diplomatic
staff in Cuba were another handicap. These included a large green
Humber, a pale blue Morris Oxford, and a white Ford Anglia, not
to mention the black Austin Princess ambassadorial limousine.
These all stood out next to the ubiquitous American-made cars in
and around Havana.[53] For example, in April 1962, two staff driving
home from the embassy spotted an army vehicle never seen before
and "gave chase" through the tunnel under Havana harbor, tenta-
tively identifying it as a Soviet rocket launcher.[54]

Hindsight tells us that the Soviet Union's nuclear deployment
to the Caribbean island in the summer of 1962 involved forty-five
thousand arrived troops plus tactical nuclear weapons and strategic
nuclear missiles. All this equipment and personnel arrived in Cuba's
principal ports and traveled on the limited number of main roads
capable of carrying such heavy military loads. In order to foil their
Western adversaries, the KGB mounted a campaign of deception.

They fed zealous counterrevolutionary groups and press outlets with reports of a large arms buildup in Cuba. The Soviets hoped and assumed that the CIA (among others) would discount these exaggerated stories and underestimate the true picture of what was happening in the island. Their double bluff worked effectively, at least for a while.[55]

On October 22, 1962, U.S. president John F. Kennedy offered the world irrefutable evidence to the contrary. Eight days earlier, a U.S. air force reconnaissance flight had photographed the construction of offensive Soviet medium-range ballistic missiles sites on the island. The potent arsenals of the Western and Soviet camps thence stood in readiness for a nuclear conflagration, with the potential to annihilate millions in a thermonuclear war. Given the propensity of some in the United States to reach paranoiac conclusions about Soviet intentions, some in Britain—including shadow leader Hugh Gaitskell and Denis Healey of the Labour Party—questioned initial U.S. intelligence reports about Soviet missiles in Cuba.[56] Their skepticism was unfounded.

Kennedy and his advisors had no such doubts and announced a naval "quarantine" of the island, demanding that the Soviet Union remove its missiles. After a high-stakes game of international brinkmanship that endured for thirteen perilous days, Soviet premier Nikita Khrushchev blinked first and agreed to withdraw Soviet nuclear warheads from Cuba in exchange for the withdrawal of U.S. missiles from Turkey. In turn, Kennedy made a commitment that U.S. forces would not invade Cuba.

FICTION INTO FACT

In *Our Man in Havana*, Wormold leaves Havana in his "ancient Hillman" to drive to the provinces. Ostensibly, he is making his annual visit to retailers outside Havana, but the vacuum cleaner

salesman is actually on an intelligence-gathering mission. Unfortunately, his British vehicle breaks down in Santa Clara, and he must
continue his journey to Santiago de Cuba by coach.[57]

At the height of the Cuban Missile Crisis, various ranks of staff in
the British embassy engaged in such low-level intelligence gathering
in order to monitor the movements of Cuban and Soviet military
personnel and equipment. After leaving the embassy "'in the wee
small hours' of the morning after late telegram duty" on October 26,
1962, Mr. Grace and Mr. Capie spotted a large convoy of vehicles on
Fifth Avenue in Havana at 12:25 a.m. They deemed it prudent not
to follow given its heavy guard, the quietness of the streets, and their
"rather conspicuous" white Ford Anglia. Even so, they were able to
provide sketches and detail on the type and quantity of vehicles.[58]

Following the thirteen white-hot days of the crisis, British diplomatic staff in Havana and the vice-consul in Santiago de Cuba
traveled the length and breadth of the island in a determined effort to
provide intelligence on the agreed Soviet military withdrawal. While
high-level U.S. air reconnaissance provided much direct intelligence,
it could not distinguish between different models of tanks or tell
Russian from Cuban operatives.[59] The British vice-consul in Santiago
made two trips that traversed the island, traveling to Havana on
November 4 and 5, 1962, and returning to Santiago by another route
on November 8 and 9. Frustratingly for staff on the ground, tarpau-
lins often covered equipment carried on trucks, and they could make
only tentative identification based on outlines of odd-shaped loads.[60]

There was minimal sophistication to British intelligence surveil-
lance of the Soviet military withdrawal. Due to the unreliable reception in Key West, Florida, of Cuban TV broadcasts, the British again
supplied Washington with photographs of military parades taken
from television screens.[61] The embassy's close proximity to and view
over Havana's harbor again aided Marchant and his diplomatic colleagues when Washington requested reports on the movements and
exact locations of Soviet ships, their cargoes, and personnel aboard.

Foreign secretary Lord Home (later Sir Alec Douglas-Home) valued Marchant's serene reports from Cuba during the heightened atmospherics of the crisis. Not so much from the eye of the storm, but what the ambassador described as the "edge of a cyclone," where "an unnatural calm" prevailed.[62] After the political tempest had subsided, Her Majesty's man in Havana offered the following postmortem:

> Any record of the story of these first two weeks of the Cuban Crisis must necessarily read more like a wildly improbable sequel to "Our Man in Havana" than a Foreign Office dispatch. Indeed I doubt whether months ago any reputable publisher would have given a moment's consideration to a story in which Soviet Russia was to be credited with shipping some four dozen giant missiles, each one longer than a cricket pitch, across the Atlantic to Cuba, where, Russian military technicians disguised as agricultural advisers would set them up in secret on launching sites.[63]

The ambassador evidently saw a very direct connection between Greene's spy fiction and the playing out of real-life Cold War events in Cuba. It was not so much that truth was stranger than fiction but that truth had imitated fiction. Numerous experiences of war and insurgencies were ingrained in Greene's subconscious, feeding his imagination and therefore his fiction.

When Wormold insists to Hasselbacher that agent Raul was only an invention, meaning the real death of a namesake pilot was pure coincidence, the German doctor tells his English friend, "Then you invented him too well, Mr Wormold."[64] It appears that in *Our Man in Havana*, Greene also invented his fictional characters and their fantasies too well.

10

"RETURN TO CUBA"

Greene's political views on Cuba and communism were an enigma at times, like the man himself. Shortly after the Bay of Pigs debacle in April 1961, the *New Statesman* published some verse by the author titled "Lines on the Liberation of Cuba":

> Prince of Las Vegas, Cuba calls!
> Your seat's reserved on the gangster plane,
> Fruit machines back in Hilton halls
> And in the Blue Moon girls again.[1]

Criticism of the Las Vegas–Havana gambling link and American mob ownership of casinos in the island was at odds with his indulgence in such guilty pleasures during its capitalist apogee. Was Greene now eulogizing Havana in Batista's day, criticizing it, or merely censuring U.S. control of such delights?

The so-called "Prince of Las Vegas" was John F. Kennedy. The new Democratic president had inherited the CIA's Bay of Pigs plan from Dwight Eisenhower and ordered the invasion to proceed, only to see it fail in spectacular and humiliating fashion. Inspiration for Greene's nickname for the president were rumors about Kennedy love affairs with glamorous women, including Marilyn Monroe.[2] Notwithstanding travails in Greene's own personal life and journeys to pre-revolutionary Cuba, his published verse deemed Las Vegas both a rendezvous point for Kennedy's extramarital liaisons and a gambling twin to Havana in the Caribbean.

Several Cuban casinos still operated at the beginning of 1961, but the Bay of Pigs invasion finally persuaded the revolutionary government to definitively nationalize and/or shut down the remaining vestiges of capitalist influence in the island. These included gambling, a remaining bowling pin of capitalism that the revolutionary government relished knocking over. Fidel Castro declared in September 1961 that the remaining four or five functioning casinos were not compatible with a Socialist revolution. Furthermore, he advised the "parasites" who frequented them to leave the island and gamble in Miami or Las Vegas instead.[3]

In an attempt to transform Cuba and forge a new society, the Revolution implored its people to develop a *conciencia comunista* (communist consciousness), inculcated through voluntary labor, for example, the harvesting of sugar and coffee, and participation in neighborhood committees and newly created mass organizations such as the Federación de Mujeres Cubanas (Federation of Cuban Women; FMC) and the Federación Estudiantil Universitaria (Federation of University Students; FEU). The widely proclaimed mantra was that Cubans should put ego and themselves aside and, through activism and a revolutionary education, prioritize the creation of a more egalitarian society.[4]

From 1962 to 1965, a "Great Debate" took place in Cuba over the best road to socialism. Which economic model best suited the underdeveloped island's unique conditions? Should they follow the strategy prescribed by Marx and the Communist Party and beat a path to communism through the stages of capitalism and socialism? Or should they ignore the market and build a new utopian economy from scratch? At first, the model of a centralized economy advocated by Che Guevara won the day, promoting moral rather than monetary incentives. In reality, this economic plan soon proved an enormous mistake.

Mystery surrounds a visit to Cuba by Greene in 1961. In an extended interview, he said it came about due to the excellent U.S. ambassador that JFK sent to London, David Bruce. After receiving honorary membership of the American Academy of Arts and Letters in New York that year, Greene remarked to Ambassador Bruce at a lunch reception in London how contradictory it was that, despite the honor, he could still not obtain an ordinary visa for the United States. Within two weeks, he said, the U.S. embassy in London issued him an open visa, and he used it at once to visit Cuba after stopping in New York.[5] Evidence to support these claims includes a scheduled embassy lunch reception for Greene and other recipients of the honor on June 28, 1961. Greene's passport contains a non-immigrant visa issued by the American embassy in London on August 22, 1961, with an admission stamp in New York from the Immigration and Naturalization Service dated September 30, 1961.[6] Yet a trawl of his regular correspondence (e.g., with Catherine Walston) yields no mention of his visit to Cuba.

The timing of the impromptu visit raises suspicions. Is it possible he undertook the trip at the behest of SIS? Washington had broken diplomatic relations with the Castro government in January 1961. The Bay of Pigs fiasco followed in April 1961. The British embassy in Havana was providing good overviews of the situation in Cuba, all of them (minus any commercially sensitive content) shared with Washington.[7] But the Foreign Office had got it all wrong in late 1958 over the British arms sales to Batista. And according to what the CIA were telling Kennedy, a decisive section of the Cuban people were going to support the invasion force once it established a beachhead in Cuba, two assumptions that proved to be wishful thinking.

Did SIS therefore commission Greene to gather its own assessment of the situation in Cuba? Between 1960 and 1964, Maurice Oldfield was the main liaison between SIS and the CIA in the British embassy in Washington. Given the CIA-instigated debacle in April 1961, did he ask Greene to nose around in Cuba for him?[8] The author had the contacts in the island and the necessary cover: a left-leaning author of *Our Man in Havana* whose decisive intervention had interrupted British arms sales in late 1958. Were his "Lines on the Liberation of Cuba" in April 1961 a bid to reinforce his cover? The trip, assuming it happened, does appear a spur-of-the-moment decision.

✳

A veritable planeload of social and political scientists, cultural theorists, and economists—not to mention writers and journalists—descended on Cuba in the early 1960s to witness and analyze Castro's revolution in the Caribbean. Some were avowed Marxists, and others leftists of a different political stripe. Names included Lawrence Ferlinghetti, Waldo Frank, Allen Ginsberg, LeRoi Jones, Susan Sontag, and C. Wright Mills. All were intrigued to see the island's great experiment in tropical socialism. Greene's final three visits to Cuba were far more low-key than the tour of the island by French intellectuals Jean-Paul Sartre and Simone de Beauvoir in early 1960. They arrived during carnival season and toured the island with Fidel Castro, buzzing over the Zapata swamp with him in a helicopter. They met students, artists, writers, and port and agricultural workers. They had introductions to government ministers, including a midnight encounter with the head of the National Bank, Che Guevara. A black-and-white photograph shows Che—in beret, boots, and military fatigues—lighting his guest's cigar. Putting his thoughts into print, Sartre criticized colonialism and the U.S. role in Cuba's history, while supporting the 1959 Agrarian Reform Law and the Revolution generally. In his view, the Spanish had enslaved Cuba through sugar, and big U.S. business had perpetuated the island's monoculture dependency.[9] By the end of the 1960s, however, Sartre and de Beauvoir had grown disenchanted with Castro and the Cuban Revolution.

No longer in the mode of hedonistic holidaymaker, investigative novelist, or screenwriter, Greene traveled to Cuba in 1963 and 1966 as a newspaper correspondent to report on the evolution of the Revolution. He would make a final short visit in 1983, arriving as a political messenger, with Greene himself embodying "the message."

Thus far, his fictional portrayal of Cuba and Cubans in his novel and its film version had barely gone beyond the touristic experience. *Our Man in Havana* had actually perpetuated stereotypes of both the island and its people. These post-1959 visits enabled him to travel wider, delve deeper, and try to discern the true nature of the Revolution. Like others, he met important writers and artists in the country, and even its political leaders. However, his familiarity with the country under Batista meant he was in a better position to evaluate the island's transformation from capitalist excess to economic austerity in the years following the Revolution.

While he had evidently detested some aspects of the Batista dictatorship, supported by Washington, where did he stand on the 1959 Revolution and its leader Fidel Castro, soon an implacable enemy of the United States? Was his enemy's enemy his friend? To his frustration, it took years of waiting and missed opportunities before he finally met Fidel Castro. He twice saw him speak in public before then. Indeed, both occasions when he saw him speak, and his eventual face-to-face meetings with Fidel, were highlights of Greene's many experiences in the island.

THE "YEAR OF EDUCATION"

The Bay of Pigs fiasco was just one of several significant events in 1961. Castro deemed it the "Year of Education," and the ensuing Literacy Campaign was one of the Revolution's most enduring achievements. It mobilized 271,000 adolescent and adult students to every corner of the island to teach more than 700,000 illiterate Cubans to read and write. The campaign reduced the country's illiteracy rate from 23.6 percent to just 3.9 percent within twelve months. As well as the evident educational advance, the mass campaign radically changed social and political attitudes of instructors and the instructed alike, involving them all more fully in the revolutionary process. British ambassador Bill Marchant took a more cynical view, branding the campaign "a monster exercise in mass indoctrination."[10]

At the end of the year, Fidel Castro confirmed Washington's worst fears when he declared, "I am a Marxist-Leninist, and I shall always be one."[11] At pretty much the same time, President Kennedy authorized Operation Mongoose. Its chief of operations was General Richard Lansdale (incorrectly identified by some as a model for Greene's quiet American in Vietnam because he had served as the region's CIA counterinsurgency expert). Lansdale's CIA team designed the campaign of covert operations to sabotage the Cuban economy and unseat—or assassinate—Castro via proxies like the mafia and embittered Cuban exiles. It was vital to Washington to maintain "plausible deniability" of its hand in the operation at all times.[12]

Shifting political currents affected Cuba's cultural scene, with doctrinaire apparatchiks growing wary of the Revolution's new artistic and intellectual establishment. They viewed its leading figures as irredeemably bourgeois and susceptible to decadent Western values, and decided to rein them in. If intellectuals saw themselves as cultural arbiters at the vanguard of culture, radicals in the People's Socialist Party (PSP) and ICAIC wanted to use culture as a political weapon, to defeat imperialism, for example.[13] In this early period, *Lunes de Revolución* was a successful and well-received weekly cultural supplement (to the daily newspaper *Revolución*), edited by Guillermo Cabrera Infante[14] with Pablo Armando Fernández as assistant editor. When ICAIC banned the fifteen-minute black-and-white documentary *P.M. (Pasado Meridiano)* from exhibition, *Lunes* protested and organized a petition to defend the short film. Shot with a handheld camera, *P.M.* showed mostly black and mixed-race inhabitants of Havana's lower classes dancing and drinking to excess in down-at-the-heels bars in the disreputable dock area of the capital. Made by nineteen-year-old Orlando Jiménez Leal and twenty-eight-year-old Saba Cabrera Infante (Guillermo's younger brother), the authorities judged it an unflattering portrait of the city's underclass.[15]

Matters came to a head in 1961 in a series of meetings convened at the National Library in Havana, during which revolutionary leaders confronted Cuba's leading intellectuals and artists about the cultural direction of the Revolution. Fidel Castro attended the final encounter on June 30 and made a declaration later termed "Words to the Intellectuals." He uttered the oft-quoted formula, *"dentro de la Revolución todo; contra la Revolución, nada"* (within the Revolution everything; against it nothing), an apparent demarcation of the parameters of cultural expression in the new Cuba. Blaming a paper shortage, publication of *Lunes* soon ceased. The government established the National Union of Cuban Artists and Writers (UNEAC), a forum the Revolution's detractors viewed as a tool through which to exercise Soviet-style monopolistic control and censorship over cultural production.[16]

PICKPOCKETING AND RATIONING

A letter from Fleet Street in late 1962 led to Greene's next visit to Cuba the following year. According to *Sunday Telegraph* editor Donald McLachlan, the writer had once told him he would be interested in "a really difficult assignment." Now that it was possible to get into Cuba without a special visa, McLachlan asked if Greene would like to travel there on a writing assignment for his newspaper.[17] Greene was definitely interested in an all-expenses-paid trip to the island and replied, "You certainly put the most luscious temptation in my way. I've so far evaded prison and it would be interesting to see the inside of a Cuban one!"[18] While there was no mention of his previous visits to Cuba or his iconic 1958 novel, they were surely factors in the newspaper selecting him for the job. Furthermore, in various journalistic articles following 1950s trips to Indochina and Kenya, for example, he had more than proven himself an insightful newspaper correspondent.

First, Greene needed to pick travel dates, arrange routing (including visas), and agree on his fee and expenses, none of them straight-forward matters. In addition to his Cuban trip, Greene offered to travel on assignment to Haiti because the political situation under Papa Doc Duvalier's rule also appeared interesting. He could com-bine visits to both Caribbean countries and produce two articles for the *Sunday Telegraph*. Averse to traveling to Cuba via the United States, Mexico City and Prague were his two other options, although travel via Mexico necessitated a visa. As for expenses, Haiti would be cheaper with Cuba's currency pegged to the U.S. dollar, but he promised not to be "unduly expensive!"[19]

By May 1963, the Cuban government had extended an official invi-tation to Greene. This carried "advantages and disadvantages." His expenses would be lower and the government could hardly object to him traveling around the island if they had invited him. However, he feared they would want to show him "a great deal of dull things such as collective farms and new schools!" Still, he assured McLachlan he knew the island and the places he wanted to visit.[20] His literary agent Murray Pollinger negotiated with the *Sunday Telegraph* on his behalf and arranged the trip. Like some earlier visits, Greene's out-ward and return legs made for a circuitous itinerary: London > New York > Kingston > Mexico City > Havana > Mexico City > Kingston > Port-au-Prince > Santo Domingo > Kingston > London. Such a complicated routing, plus Cuba's political and economic isolation, all but guaranteed disruption to his journey.

✴

Greene lived between London, Paris, and Capri when he was not trav-eling in the early 1960s, a period when French companion Yvonne

Cloetta contextualized his personal life. He first met her in Africa following his Belgian Congo trip, shortly before his April 1959 visit to Cuba for on-location filming of *Our Man in Havana*. Like Catherine Walston before her, she was married. Her husband became aware of the relationship but was indifferent toward it, aided by the fact he worked abroad for much of the year. Yvonne Cloetta was unable to accompany Greene on his 1963 Caribbean trip, probably due to her two small children, but she was his principal correspondent during it. He did not travel there alone, however.

In his first letter from the Hotel Nacional, he informed Yvonne that both he and "Ted" were "completely sage . . . He is looking out of the window now—I think he likes Havana." Yet Greene left him in the hotel room to wander "old familiar streets alone." In the next letter, his traveling companion was still "sage & patient like his master."

"Ted" or "Teddy" was a teddy bear, an odd and perhaps perplexing sight for the large Jamaican immigration official who knocked at Greene's hotel room door in Kingston. Like his second visit to Havana in 1954, he had passed through Jamaican immigration control without surrendering his entry card.[21] Greene loved to challenge authority.

His teddy bear was not in the tradition of Aloysius, Lord Sebastian Flyte's teddy in Evelyn Waugh's *Brideshead Revisited*. Nor could there be any comparison to Sir John Betjeman's Archibald, the British poet's lifelong companion who inspired Flyte's stuffed friend. And neither was Greene's Ted a sign of homosexuality in the writer, as one biographer attests. Instead, Ted was a mere prop, a mascot received as a present earlier in the year from his close publishing friend A. S. Frere. Greene simply packed Ted and took him on his travels for harmless fun, a quirky surrogate for the mistress who could not accompany him to Cuba.[22]

✳

As with his first all-too-brief visit to the island, a stay in Mexico preceded Greene's eighth trip to Cuba. Yet he did not enjoy his first visit to the country since 1938. Part of the reason for this was a lengthy travel delay. He did at least fully indulge in the first-class BOAC flight service from London to New York. He imbibed everything offered to him: two whiskies in the departure lounge, "2 big dries" (i.e., dry martinis) before lunch on the plane, then red wine and brandy, another whisky, and another "dry" before dinner, plus more red wine and a second brandy. Such stiff drinks stood him in good stead for a rocky passage via Kingston and Mexico City to Havana. Following an earlier two-day delay in Jamaica, Cubana Airlines canceled his onward flight to Havana, marooning him in Mexico's capital city for five days.[23]

His second acquaintance with the country had an inauspicious start. Just after his midnight arrival under the bright lights of Mexico City's new airport, a dexterous pickpocket pilfered his U.S., British, and Jamaican cash, "about 100 dollars [$811] & 20 pounds [£398]." Luckily, his travelers' checks remained intact. Far from getting him down, however, the experience perversely lifted the difficult-to-bear melancholia he had suffered during his two-day delay in Jamaica. "I am grateful to the pickpocket who robbed me—he acted & I reacted," he wrote in his journal.[24] Such unexpected occurrences had the power to jolt the grateful writer out of despair.

He soon discovered that pressure from Washington made journeys for Cuba-bound and Cuban-origin passengers through Mexico "as uncomfortable as possible." Passengers' pictures were taken at the airport ("presumably for the FBI," according to Greene). After returning from Cuba, passengers only received transit visas for Mexico. Meanwhile, their luggage was subject to close inspection, with prohibited items confiscated. Greene's copy of Charles Dickens' *Pickwick Papers*, for example, received a lengthy examination.[25]

Mexico maintained an ambivalent relationship with Cuba, partly because the country's own relationship with the United States was ambivalent. While support for a socialist revolution shored up its own revolutionary legitimacy and internal leftist support, Mexico was keen to cooperate with Washington. Furthermore, its government was wary of Cubans using Mexico City as a bridge to export revolution to the rest of Latin America. Nevertheless, Mexican-Cuban relations were symbolically important in a period when other Latin American countries had severed their diplomatic relations with the island, although the Cuba-Mexico relationship was rather superficial. For example, to aid the U.S. intelligence effort, Mexican airport authorities compiled lists and photographs of every passenger traveling to and from Cuba and shared them with the CIA.[26] It is normal to receive an entry stamp when arriving in a country, but not for the stamp to state the country from where a passenger has arrived. A conspicuous Mexican stamp in Greene's passport proved his return from the blockaded communist island with three words: "LLEGO DE CUBA" (arrived from Cuba).[27]

Greene's delay in Mexico City reminded him of his three-day journey by mule in Chiapas in 1938, when a small plane failed to appear. On this occasion, he learned that Cubana Airlines' only two planes were fetching passengers from Prague. He became acquainted with his stranded fellow passengers, including senior Communist and Socialist Party figures from Uruguay and Argentina, respectively. His fruitless visit with them to the Cuban embassy in Mexico City, plus three unmanned typewriters at the Cubana Airlines airport counter, were a precursor to onerous bureaucracy in the island itself.

When he did land at Havana's airport after a five-day delay in Mexico, there was nobody from UNEAC to meet Greene, as arranged. And the prestigious Hotel Nacional, where he planned to stay for the first time, had no booking in his name. According to Jean-Paul Sartre, the noble six-story hotel was disdainful of towering incongruous neighbors like the Capri and Habana Hilton (now Habana Libre) hotels, which strained for a view of the sea. At least Greene found his room—a nice "Parisian retreat"—agreeable. Yet he was too exhausted to explore the city on his first evening, as was his usual custom. Instead, he suffered continual noise from loudspeakers in the street and room service without any beer.[28] Indeed, a main feature of this visit was the severe impact of the U.S. economic blockade and erratic local planning on the availability of consumer goods.

The year 1963 was relatively uneventful in Cuba following the two major Cold War events of the April 1961 Bay of Pigs invasion and the October 1962 Cuban Missile Crisis. Perhaps the most important occurrence in 1963 was Fidel Castro's lengthy trip to the Soviet Union between April 26 and May 4. Khrushchev used the opportunity to soothe Castro's hurt feelings after withdrawing nuclear missiles from the island without consulting him just months earlier. Cuba was now even more dependent on the Soviet bloc for its economic survival but was at pains not to show it. Upon his return, the Cuban leader declared that the island would again concentrate on sugar production. This followed poor results from efforts at industrialization and agricultural diversification away from the traditional sugar monoculture. Shortages of many consumer goods were becoming ever more conspicuous, and while there was talk of a U.S.-Cuban rapprochement, there was little sign of it happening. After a slight lull in anti-American rhetoric, Fidel Castro again launched several verbal salvos against the island's powerful northern neighbor during the year.

Cuba had changed considerably since Greene's April 1959 visit. His eventual published article in the *Sunday Telegraph* described the "poverty of consumer-goods" and the limited menu in his traditional haunt, the Floridita. He could consume a single beer, but only if he ate. He ordered bean soup, tinned langouste, and rice, plus coffee and beer, for an eye-watering $6.80 ($55). The fare and prices at the bar/restaurant in his 1963 and 1966 articles were a barometer to compare Batista's capitalist Cuba with Castro's communist Cuba.[29]

On another day, there was a line around the block for basketballs at one store and no limes at the Floridita, so daiquiris were off the menu. Greene noticed how a photograph of Fidel Castro and his rebel companions wading ashore had replaced the mirror that previously hung in the bar. He also recognized Floridita staff from before the revolution, a reassuring sign of continuity.[30] But for an establishment that prided itself as "la cuna del daiquiri" (the cradle of the daiquiri), the lack of one of the cocktail's key ingredients—a citrus fruit cultivated in Cuba—spoke volumes about economic management and shortages on the island. It was evidence of a worrying trend.

Greene detected a more pronounced reduction in glitzy and seedy establishments since his previous visit; Havana was no longer the "great open city for the bachelor on the loose." Victory at the Bay of Pigs and the definitive closure of the island's remaining gambling establishments in 1961 appeared to have finally extinguished the final flames of capitalist Cuba. But can we be sure that Greene was sincere about his "longer memories" of this "sad time"? Or was he nostalgic for happier memories of the brothel on the airport road, the now closed Blue Moon, and Superman's "nocturnal ritual" at the now moldering Shanghai Theater?[31]

He again satisfied his penchant for the unexpected and the famous when he encountered the "charming" Russian ambassador and Khrushchev's "extrovert & uninhibited" son-in-law Aleksei Adzhubei on an adjacent table at the Tropicana. He enjoyed their company. The establishment was much as in Batista's day, except for the poor drink offerings and an absence of gambling. Expensive-looking prostitutes still loitered on the drive outside, for "that was always the way" at the Tropicana. The girls could never solicit inside.[32] Again, Greene appeared keen to identify any relic of pre-1959 Cuba.

Overbearing Cuban bureaucracy was the largest burden Greene personally had to endure. After the difficulties flying into Cuba, he had to expend just as much—if not more—effort to leave. His first challenge was obtaining an exit permit from Cuban Immigration to get a reservation on a departing flight. He needed his passport to apply for the exit permit, but immigration officials had retained it upon his arrival at the airport. He went to retrieve his passport two days later, as they had instructed, only to find Cuban Immigration closed. He wasted another frustrating morning between the British embassy, Immigration, and the Mexican consulate, and seeking a passport photo. The next day, he scuttled two times between Cubana Airlines and a bank, perhaps to obtain a payment stamp for either Immigration or the airline, before returning to Cubana Airlines again. Despite meeting with airline officials three times, he would still have to present his documents the day before departure. In his *Sunday Telegraph* report, he wrote obliquely, "There must be times when the men from the mountains look back with nostalgia to the simple days of fighting before the days of forms." His diary's criticism was more direct, describing "[t]he real horror of bureaucracy" and the irony of an official dictum that "Bureau[cracy] is counter-revolutionary." His overriding private admonition was that "Kafka knew the future."[33]

Despite his continuing travel woes, Greene's first direct experience of Fidel Castro, a three-hour speech by the revolutionary leader in Havana's Revolution Square, was intoxicating. His first full day in Havana coincided with the tenth anniversary of the failed assault against Santiago's Moncada Barracks, and Castro's annual July 26 speech to commemorate it. This explained the presence of Latin American socialists and communists on his flight from Mexico. He witnessed a virtuoso performance in various acts in front of a "cheerful Bank Holiday crowd." Cubans came and went during the speech as in a "continuous movie," with "interludes of song, interludes of comedy, [and] interludes of farce."[34] They hissed at mentions of President Kennedy and made pig sounds about the Bay of Pigs defeat. A man beside Greene even dropped onto his haunches to mimic a pig. The consummate orator interacted with his audience. At times, the whole performance seemed more like a Mass than a political speech.[35] Castro appeared in touch with his crowd, spontaneous and interesting to all who listened, which included truckloads of small farmers who had come to Havana to debate changes to agricultural policy.[36]

On the other hand, Greene criticized the running of the economy on Marxist lines. Cubana Airlines was his most tangible example, doing "the smallest business of any air company with the greatest number of employees." An indication of poor agricultural planning was a poster whose slogan had transformed from "Eat what Cuba produces" to "Produce what Cuba eats." To emphasize his private thoughts, only at the end of the Revolution's first year had somebody realized that "in this fertile land" there were no seeds to sow.[37]

Indeed, in 1962—the year prior to Greene's visit—an accumulation of different factors had provoked an economic crisis in Cuba. These included nationalization of most land and all large businesses; vast expenditure on sweeping social reforms, the departure of many professionals, including managers and skilled workers; and general mismanagement of the Cuban economy. A double whammy of U.S. efforts to strangle the island economically added to these woes. The Economic Denial Program instigated in November 1960—termed a trade embargo by Washington and a blockade by Havana—ramped up Cuba's isolation incrementally. Full economic sanctions were in place by February 1963. In mid-1963, Washington invoked the Trading with the Enemy Act, freezing all Cuban assets in the United States and prohibiting all financial transactions with the island.[38]

Castro had promulgated a second Agrarian Reform Law in October 1962, but the island lacked the agricultural experts to manage the land already appropriated, let alone newly confiscated property. The British embassy's annual report for 1963 noted the lack of consumer goods, more severe rationing, and the lowest sugar harvest in eighteen years. It also reported a major reversal in economic policy. Cuba would slow—and later abandon—attempts to diversify agriculture and expand industry, and instead concentrate again on sugar as the main prop of its economy.[39]

Greene's musings indicate he blamed shortages of goods on both the economic blockade and flawed central planning. First, he noted there was more money than goods to spend it on. If beers or sodas reached a bar, a crowd soon gathered to consume them all. Rum sold at $15 ($122) a bottle and was so bad that the locals had nicknamed it rat poison. It was also now difficult to find a taxi in Old Havana. When Greene did locate one, it was broken down. The driver spent twenty minutes fashioning a washer from a sandal to get its engine running.[40]

Changes from within and without led to anomalies in the Cuban economy. Reduced production gravely affected consumer consumption. A larger population, despite the exodus of many Cubans, along with increases in employment and monetary income, meant there was more money in circulation and hence a rise in consumer demand, but the supply of consumer goods languished or declined. From 1962, this produced a mismatch between people's purchasing power and the availability of goods. Rather than allow market forces to determine price increases, or freeze prices and impose sales taxes, planners sought an egalitarian solution that would not harm lower-income families or benefit wealthy Cubans. They therefore chose to freeze prices on scarce goods but to ration them at the same time, while there were no qualms about increasing prices on unrationed luxury goods and services, such as meals in restaurants. This explains some of the exorbitant prices that Greene encountered. A negative effect of rationing in March 1962, meanwhile, was a burgeoning black market for consumer goods in high demand.[41]

Greene had met a traveling companion on his fourth full day: Polish-born and naturalized British artist Feliks Topolski. Together they visited a new Polynesian-style tourist resort three days later in the middle of crocodile-inhabited marshes at the end of a very dull road to the Bay of Pigs. It might be a big success if there were American tourists, but there were none in blockaded Cuba. Greene learned the holiday resort was "Fidel's idea." His diary notes suggest it was not a very good one (although he ignored the possibility that the resort was built for Cuban visitors).[42]

Meanwhile, he warmly praised developments in the arts, and made friends with several Cuban artists and writers during the visit. Abstractionism in art was on the rise and there were no Soviet-like pressures to conform. If such pressure did arise, Greene was given to understand that the minister of culture, Armando Hart, would ally himself to the artists, along with his wife, Haydée Santamaría. Both were acquaintances from Greene's 1957 visit to Santiago de Cuba.

Greene especially admired the different dream worlds of two cohabiting artists whose home he visited. Paintings by both René Portocarrero and Raúl Milián combined native Cuban and African influences. Fortunately, in his opinion, there was no danger here of socialist realism in art. Portocarrero took him to the now transformed country club, the haunt of millionaires in *Our Man in Havana*. Its buildings and golf course were now a sprawling art school with African, Italian, Cuban, and even Chinese influences.[43] Unlike other socialist countries, Cuban artists were free of ideological restraint and thus enjoyed greater creative freedom. There was more control from above in the field of literature, later highlighted in a controversial case surrounding the poet Heberto Padilla.

Greene acknowledged the huge and laudable effort to educate the population, both children and adults. All education was free. Domestic servants, each with a typewriter, attended school at the Hotel Nacional, as did thousands of agricultural laborers.[44] He was indeed witness to the construction of a new society. The level of participation and debate was astounding and led him to comment on the "touch of ancient Athens" in contemporary Havana. As opposed to the Agora of ancient Greece, however, the principal assembly point in Cuba appeared to be the capital's most luxurious hotel.[45]

When arranging his trip, Greene appeared to fear dull visits to new workplaces and schools. In reality, they were highlights of his 1963 and 1966 stays in Cuba. What he found revolting were the foreigners on the island. Initially, a British embassy second secretary carrying diplomatic bags on the Mexico City–Havana flight had proved a salvation by helping him avoid trouble, presumably at immigration. The payback for the second secretary's assistance was an invitation to a diplomatic party in Havana. Greene found himself talking to two foreign diplomats of "inexpressible ugliness," one with a swollen face and eyes. Separately, an ex-ambassador with "a hawk-like gaze" talked to him interminably about the English character. Meanwhile, a very serious Japanese man grilled a diplomatic counterpart about sugar statistics. Fortunately, Cuban author Virgilio Piñera[46] rescued Greene from further tedium. On another evening, in Topolski's company, he met a "hysterical" Danish journalist at the Riviera Hotel. Her presence induced him to forsake a restaurant dinner—albeit a poor one—for a sandwich back at the Hotel Nacional.[47]

Following their brief encounter outside Sloppy Joe's in April 1959, interior decoration at Hemingway's Finca Vigía home and his library left Greene unimpressed when he visited on August 4, 1963. In the intervening period, of course, the American man of letters had committed suicide, suffering the ill effects of depression, paranoid delusions, and electroconvulsive shock treatments. "How ignoble a library of books," Greene remarked to himself, although it is unclear if he was viewing the library as its owner had left it when he abandoned the island for the last time in 1960. Worse than his book collection were the "hideous heads & slain in H[emingway]'s house: the black bison coming from the bedroom wall: the cheetah spread-eagled like a bat head down."[48] The Englishman confessed his distaste for "such carnage" and the writer's "hairy-chest romanticism" in an interview six years later.[49] Still, he did harbor a grudging admiration for Hemingway's writing, admitting in the same decade that all writers of his generation owed him a debt, particularly with regard to dialogue.[50]

A DIFFERENT POLITICS

Greene's published 1963 article "Return to Cuba" pointed to a new tropical variant of Marxism, less dogmatic and philosophically and geographically distant from its nineteenth-century origins. He described how the Cuban Revolution was in intimate contact with its people. Furthermore, despite reports to the contrary from the United States, the Catholic Church appeared to be coexisting well with the state, or at least better than in Poland, a more "strictly Catholic" country. His article ended on an upbeat note, remarking that Cuba's was "a new voice in the Communist world."[51]

His article at best underplayed—if not fully ignored—the serious rupture between the Catholic Church and the Cuban state that had occurred in the first years of the Revolution. Surprisingly, the Catholic writer appeared largely dispassionate about religion in Cuba. This might have been due to its rather foreign and bourgeois character, the opposite of the poor, pious, and persecuted Catholics he had witnessed in Mexico in 1938. About two-thirds of priests practicing in Cuba at the point of Revolution had received their training in Franco's Spain. During the Revolution's early period, the church approved of humanitarian policies that benefitted the poor and opposed subsequent changes that impinged on the Church—for example, the nationalization of all education and the closure of religious colleges. However, it reserved its greatest fear for the atheistic communism emanating from Moscow.

Meanwhile, the Church's support for Christian ideals emanating from the United States alienated the Cuban government. But the final straw for the revolutionary authorities was the participation of three Spanish Falangist priests in the failed Bay of Pigs invasion. Only the Vatican's appointment of Cesare Zacchi as papal nuncio in Havana and his intelligent intervention from 1962 began to reverse a thus far disharmonious process. He recognized that the Church was behind the times in Cuba and developed a frank and cooperative relationship with Castro that included long games of chess and presents of cheese from Italy. Under Zacchi, a period of rapprochement developed between the Catholic Church and the Cuban state.[52]

For Greene, then, the Cuban Revolution's way of doing politics was direct and invigorating, a world away from the staid parliamentary party politics of Great Britain, dominated by old men in suits like Prime Minister Harold Macmillan. Dressed in olive-green military fatigues, the dynamic orator and revolutionary Fidel Castro oversaw Cuban politics. He enjoyed a direct connection with his people, explaining policy with vivid examples in various acts to a receptive crowd. The Revolution was not beyond reproach, due to economic mismanagement and Kafkaesque bureaucracy. Yet on balance, Greene supported the huge social experiment. The young revolutionaries—led by thirty-seven-year-old Castro—were making errors, he judged, but such was the ambitious and radical nature of the process. Representing the same British newspaper for his next visit in 1966, he would provide an update on the Revolution's progress—or perhaps its regression.

Greene filed his copy to the *Sunday Telegraph* on his return to Britain. Cuba's communist revolution and its bearded leader appeared at odds with the politics of an arch-Conservative newspaper. Probably for this reason, he included an accompanying note with his draft in which his own allegiance appeared clear: "I hope that you won't find my first article too politically repugnant. I suppose you can always put an editorial disclaimer of the views, but it's impossible if one has known Cuba aforetime to spend any length of time there today without feeling in favour of the Castro revolution."[53] The assignment earned him a first-class, all-expenses-paid trip to the Caribbean, and a healthy fee to boot.

✳

Greene planned a less comfortable but more provocative journey to Cuba in 1964. At the beginning of the year, the Cuban government had signed a deal with the Leyland Motor Company to purchase four hundred single-deck British buses, with an option for another thousand vehicles. The island was desperate to remedy a serious lack of urban transport caused by regular breakdowns of Eastern European buses and insufficient supplies of spare parts. Bus numbers halved between 1961 and 1963, leaving just eight hundred vehicles on Havana's roads. Cuba also suffered a serious lack of foreign exchange, despite Soviet economic assistance. For the bus deal to go ahead, the revolutionary government needed the British government to approve export credit backing in order to repay bus purchases over five years. Ahead of a finely balanced meeting at the top of the British government that approved the deal, the cabinet secretary advised the prime minister, "This is a clash between economic policy on the one hand and a particularly sensitive area of foreign policy on the other hand."[54] The deal would undoubtedly cause serious displeasure in Washington because Kennedy's government was trying to enlist Western support for a watertight trade blockade of the communist island. The Anglo-American disagreement over the bus exports to Castro's Cuba overlapped the final months of JFK's presidency, when the British government agreed to the deal, and the first months of Lyndon B. Johnson's presidency, when Havana announced the controversial $11 million ($88 million) deal.

Economic departments in the British government such as the Board of Trade were philosophically opposed to using an economic blockade for political purposes—that is, to topple Castro's government in Cuba. They were loath to deny Britain's balance of trade a healthy injection of dollars. Meanwhile, the Foreign Office needed U.S. support, particularly in the rapidly decolonizing Third World. British diplomats were keen to assuage Washington's wrath over Western trade with Cuba.

Newly installed President Lyndon Johnson saw red over the Leyland buses to Cuba deal. British foreign secretary Richard Austen
("Rab") Butler felt the full force of his anger when he visited Washington in late April 1964. The president argued that Britain should
prioritize its relationship with the United States over an export deal
with Soviet-backed Cuba. He produced a wad of dollar bills from his
pocket. If Britain was so desperate for money, the president raged, he
would pay the Leyland bill himself.[55] With the deal already agreed
and signed, it was too late. Johnson's impassioned plea only elicited
a phlegmatic and negative British response.

Leyland had trouble chartering a cargo boat willing to break the
U.S. trade blockade and ship the buses to Cuba, but eventually contracted East German shipping. A few weeks after Butler's visit to
Washington, Greene wrote to the Cuban ambassador in London to
sort out the finer details of a sea journey to accompany a consign-
ment of Leyland buses to Havana. He was "looking forward to the
journey immensely" and proposed that Cuban poet and cultural
attaché Pablo Armando Fernández accompany him on the voyage,
considering that Greene spoke little Spanish and no German. On
arrival, he would travel around the island with Fernández as "a visitor and not as a newspaper correspondent," and write at length
about Cuba on his return.[56] Unfortunately, his planned journey never
occurred. A clash between sailing dates and work on a play precluded it.[57]

If the Foreign Office knew about Greene's provocative plan, they
would surely have objected in the strongest terms. They were keen
to suppress all publicity about the bus exports. Greene liked to poke
a twig in the spokes of U.S. foreign policy. On this occasion, his own
government had poked a thick branch into Washington's policy of
economic isolation against communist Cuba.

The Cuban public welcomed with enthusiasm the arrival of new
buses that resolved a serious public transport shortage on the island.
In October 1964, however, an inbound Japanese vessel struck an

outbound East German boat on the River Thames, just minutes after setting sail with a cargo of forty-two Leyland buses destined for Cuba. The controversial nature of the Leyland deal and the timing of the incident gave rise to speculation about a CIA-backed sabotage operation.[58] With different scheduling, Greene and the Cuban poet might have found themselves on the East German freighter, beached and partially capsized in London's River Thames.

"SHADOW AND SUNLIGHT IN CUBA": FINALLY MEETING FIDEL

A confluence of Cold War events and political realignments ensured that Greene's lengthiest visit to Cuba in 1966 occurred at a contentious juncture of the Revolution. With Washington's encouragement, the island now stood in almost perfect hemispheric isolation. By 1964, every member country of the Organization of American States (OAS) minus Mexico had broken diplomatic relations with Havana. Three years after President Kennedy's assassination in Dallas in November 1963, there was little indication of a U.S.-Cuban rapprochement. In fact, the invasion of the Dominican Republic by forty-two thousand U.S. marines in 1965 exacerbated Cubans' siege mentality. In Southeast Asia, meanwhile, a mass deployment of U.S. troops was fully engaged in attempts to suppress communism in Vietnam. Greene's 1955 novel *The Quiet American* had of course prophesized U.S. involvement in the country.

Fidel Castro announced in 1965 that Che Guevara had left the country. The Argentine-born revolutionary visited Algeria and other African countries that year and supported a rebel movement in the Congo. Cuba continued to celebrate the heroic guerrilla Che, although it abandoned his more impractical and unsuccessful Marxist economic policies, for example, reducing the emphasis on moral over material incentives. In this regard, Cuba's revolutionary government cherry-picked what it viewed as the more progressive elements of Chinese and Soviet communism and abandoned strategies it now perceived as regressive. With increasing dependence on the Soviet Union, Castro renamed his ruling party the Partido Comunista Cubano (Communist Party of Cuba; PCC) in 1965. It promoted loyal members of the Ministry of the Interior and the armed forces to leading positions in its Central Committee.

With Soviet encouragement, Cuba had tried to cultivate better cultural and economic relations with Western countries other than the United States. The island had also ameliorated its continental isolation through links with the non-aligned movement, a concentration of mostly developing and/or Third World countries. In January 1966, Havana hosted the Tri-Continental Conference. Its aim was to coordinate subversion and guerrilla activity and thus foment a revolutionary process leading to the liberation of peoples in Africa, Asia, and Latin America. Under pressure to side with either Moscow or Beijing, Castro denounced the latter. Cuban-Chinese relations deteriorated, while Cuban-Soviet relations improved, although Castro showed more loyalty to the Third World than he did to allies in Moscow, from whom he was keen to maintain autonomy.

Shortages continued to drag down the Cuban economy. Availability of spare parts for industry worsened, and there were fewer consumer goods to buy. The loss of much of the island's middle (and thus technical) class continued to weigh heavily on the sugar industry as it struggled to increase production. In 1964, after the worst sugar harvest for two decades, the country produced an impressive six-million-ton harvest the following year. Unfortunately, a reduced world price for the commodity offset the achievement. This and other economic problems resulted in a severe lack of foreign exchange on the island. Nevertheless, the country continued to devote significant resources to health and education, including a renewed campaign to reduce illiteracy.

✳

The year 1966 also marked an important point in Greene's life: he abandoned his Mayfair flat in London, never to live in England again. He continued to maintain his properties in Capri and Paris but would now reside principally in Antibes on the French Côte d'Azur. He declared tax- and health-related reasons for his decision. In the case of the former, Greene would enjoy reduced tax liability in France, after discovering his British accountant had stolen most of his savings. In the case of the latter, a doctor advised him that the climate would help offset a recent bout of pneumonia and help prevent another one.

In addition to such comforts as the local Chez Felix restaurant for fine food and wine, he now lived close to Yvonne Cloetta. In time, she would come to spend many of her daytime hours with Greene, returning to her family nest every evening. The arrangement worked well because it avoided the domesticity to which his character was so ill suited. Unfortunately, a five-year-long feud from 1979 between Greene and the ex-husband of Yvonne's daughter Martine later soured his experience on the French Riviera. Greene accused him of receiving protection from the local mafia and corrupt local politicians.

Following his tumultuous affair with Catherine, and thanks to Yvonne's companionship, his depression became "much lighter" and his mania "less exaggerated" in the 1960s. His personal life was now less complicated, and Yvonne's regular presence helped him arrive "at a kind of plateau."[1] She was also a very different character from Catherine. This became evident to Greene after a pleasant dinner in Paris early in their relationship. He took her and another female friend to a brothel in the red-light district, but Yvonne reacted badly, and Greene never repeated the experiment.[2]

The death of a close friend and a leading literary light also affected Greene in 1966. His Catholic writing contemporary Evelyn Waugh died in April after celebrating Easter Sunday Mass. The Second Vatican Council's aggiornamento had recently abolished the traditional

Latin liturgy for a new vernacular version, greatly distressing Waugh. As a more conservative Catholic, he viewed the updated Mass as irredeemably prosaic. Thankfully, however, he did hear his very last Sunday Mass in Latin. Greene considered him the best writer of his generation and likened his passing to hearing "one's commanding officer was dead."[3]

✳

Greene's longest trip to Cuba came about when the *Weekend Telegraph* asked him to write "Back to Cuba" articles in the summer of 1966. They would pay his first-class airfare, out-of-pocket expenses, and a £400 (£7,100) fee for each published piece. The proposal received a favorable reception. Greene was "always interested" in Cuba and had contacts there. He advised them he could probably "make personal contact with Castro," an elusive ambition thus far. However, given his previous difficulties flying via Mexico he now preferred a routing via Prague or Madrid. Whereas Greene had decided the theme of his 1963 commission, this time the *Telegraph* specified interest in "the Cuban political situation and possibly an interview with Castro." The magazine's editor, John Anstey, offered to supply Greene with sufficient 35mm Ektachrome film to take photographs of his trip. This is odd, because no photographs appeared to accompany Greene's two published articles.[4]

His 1966 visit was of a completely different order from that of 1963. The bulk of the sixty-one-year-old English author's three-week visit consisted of an extensive road trip around the island. Two Cuban writers in their mid-thirties and a twenty-six-year-old photographer accompanied him, their large Packard chauffeured by Ángel, a French-speaking naturalized Cuban of Spanish origin. His traveling companions were the poet Pablo Armando Fernández and writer Lisandro Otero,[5] both former cultural attachés at the Cuban embassy in London and thus fluent English speakers. The photographer was Ernesto Fernández, who began his career at *Carteles* magazine and had shot iconic images during the Bay of Pigs invasion. While Greene was happy with this hospitality, he declined the offer of "a large house with a garden and swimming pool, three or four servants and a guard at the door."[6] He preferred to stay in a hotel, and he again chose the Hotel Nacional. He evidently liked the freedom this gave him. Ahead of the trip he informed Catherine Walston, "I think it will be a sadder Cuba than even three years ago, though perhaps a little more to eat!" He also hoped the British had "a nice ambassador in Havana!"[7]

"ON THE ROAD"

The three-week journey around the island between his arrival in Havana via Madrid on Iberian airlines on August 28 and departure on September 19, 1966, was his longest and most extensive. He traveled as far as the city of Guantánamo in the east, to the Isle of Pines off Cuba's southern coast, and many other points. He was in turns disappointed and pleasantly surprised by the quality of food and flabbergasted at its cost. Likewise, the poor organization of the journey frustrated him, and his opinions varied on accommodation in hotels, motels, and houses belonging to the Communist Party. Most frustrating of all were missed opportunities to meet Fidel Castro. At times, his experience resembled the "comedy of errors" that defined his visit to Santiago de Cuba in November 1957. Castro had either departed ahead of them or arrived after they left. To his growing frustration, it appeared as if Greene might never meet Comandante Fidel Castro.

Despite changes in Greene's personal circumstances, a propensity for irritability and hypercriticism was still evident. His complaints and praise at various points during the long road trip made him appear at times like a fastidious travel writer and food critic. The lack of coffee at breakfast in the Hotel Nacional was the first of several disappointing culinary experiences. A hotel lunch including a shrimp cocktail, a fried egg "with a few bits of ham & peas," and a beer came to a grand and extortionate total of $6.70 ($52). He tried to have lunch the next day with Haitian poet René Depestre at the Habana Libre Hotel, but there was no air-conditioning in its empty Polynesian restaurant. They ate instead at La Room, where shrimp and fruit cocktails, two rump steaks, and mixed ices came to "$22! [$171]" But a few days into his trip, at a Communist Party guesthouse outside Santa Clara, he bathed in its pool, drank "lots of rum," and "ate the best steak [he could] remember eating."[8]

At a hotel in Cienfuegos, he disparaged the "lukewarm water" in his room's "so-called" thermos flasks and a single bottom bed sheet that offered little protection from air-conditioning "as loud as a train." Yet he drank "beautiful coffee" at Otero's aunt's house in Morón, and they ate "the most excellent salty ham as an aperitif" at a nearby motel, followed by an "excellent dinner of local steaks." There was a carnival that evening in Holguín, "an ugly rich town," where they drank "bad rum" from "improvised mugs filled with ice." In Manzanillo's main café the next morning, there were only banana milkshakes, hot dogs "made with potatoes," and salami sausages. Later, at a guesthouse in the foothills of the Sierra Maestra, they again ate "excellent steaks."[9]

The all-encompassing figure of Fidel Castro bookended Greene's three-week stay. Greene had seen the revolutionary leader speak in Revolution Square in 1963, and Castro was at full voice again on the first full day of Greene's 1966 visit. For a second time, he found the leader's oratory skills and performance mesmerizing, despite Greene's only rudimentary comprehension of Spanish. The speech inside the Lázaro Peña Theater was part of the closing ceremony for the Revolution's third congress of the Central de Trabajadores de Cuba (CTC), equivalent to a Trades Union Congress. The detailed journal Greene kept describes the audience, including peasants in straw hats and uniformed female students from the School of Fertilizer.

Like in 1963, Greene again divided Castro's speech into phases or "acts" (so described in the first of his published *Telegraph* articles). He began the four and a half hours like a "headmaster," monotonous in the fashion of Dr. Fry or the Days of Lincoln and holding forth on the subject of "conscience." His hands remained on either side of the desk. A leftwards military turn presented his profile to television cameras.[10]

Then he transformed into an "enthusiast" and later a "clown." He used the six microphones "like metal flowers," leaning into them, at times purring, leering, smiling. He interacted with the audience through questions, and they called back answers. In the later stages, he used his arms constantly, acting and mimicking. He broached topics as diverse as the price of beer and French bulldozers, and then laid into Chilean President Eduardo Frei "with savage humor."[11]

The traveling party of five—Greene, Pablo Armando Fernández, Lisandro Otero, Ernesto Fernández, and their driver, Ángel—set out from Havana on Greene's sixth full day in Cuba. The Packard, due to depart at eight a.m., was not ready until midday. They traveled eastward from the capital along the north coast to Varadero but arrived too late to see Cubans departing the island for voluntary exile on two daily planes. The recent establishment of an air bridge between Varadero and Miami facilitated the emigration of 250,000 Cubans between 1966 and 1973. This relieved migratory pressure built up since the suspension of flights to the United States during the Cuban Missile Crisis. Our traveling correspondent noted provision of a free buffet but no ill feeling toward the Cubans leaving for exile. The group stayed at the resort's International Hotel and enjoyed the evening cabaret. After a boat trip the following morning, they visited the former Xanadu beachfront mansion of U.S. chemicals magnate Irénée du Pont, "ugly as only a millionaire's house can be." An eternal bibliophile, Greene perused its library with books by

Kipling and Twain, but detective and popular novels dominated.[12] Otero described their English guest as unmoved by the opulence on display.[13]

They drove on to Cienfuegos on the southern coast, where Greene had first traveled with Rocky in 1957, and he now met Tomás Gutiérrez Alea, the island's foremost film director. That evening they stayed at a motel in the hills above Trinidad, "beautifully built & atrociously managed." Greene's room had a fused bathroom light, no drinking water, and a frog dying noisily under the bed. This was only the beginning of a "surrealist night."[14]

A noise at two a.m. woke him. Outside were the shadows of two soldiers with tommy guns. The minister of education, José Llanusa, had been expecting the travel party in the Escambray Mountains and had sent a jeep to pick them up. He had organized a student performance for them. They made a forty-five-minute journey by jeep to Topes de Collantes, a large tuberculosis sanatorium built by Batista during his populist phase in 1937. Their jeep passed a cavalcade of three horsemen dressed in white in the dark and crushed yellow crabs under its tires. The minister was keen for their English guest to see Cuba's education policy in practice. Greene did indeed appreciate what he witnessed the next morning, after staying up for a talk until three thirty a.m.[15]

The former sanatorium was now a seminary for trainee primary schoolteachers, part of an ambitious Countryside Schools initiative. After a year of "severe training" in the Sierra Maestra, the students—70 percent of them female—spent two years in Topes de Collantes, followed by more training in Havana. Teacher training was combined with productive agricultural work, fully involving youth in the revolutionary experience. Here in the temperate mountains they were planting a million coffee plants by a river alongside local peasants. This was revolution in action, and it resonated with Greene. Here there was "none of the cynicism of Rumania," the eastern European communist Soviet satellite. His journal described "the sense of happiness that comes from full occupation, & sense of usefulness [. . .] In this place one felt that revolution had not tired." The head of workers' and peasants' education strummed a guitar and sang about the fight against illiteracy. Greene continued, "This is something incontestably right—they have no doubts, they experiment, they learn & alas they 'analyse.'"[16]

Along with his pre-revolutionary visits to the Shanghai Theater, this was among the highlights of all his trips to Cuba. Many thousands of miles away—literally and figuratively—from Berkhamsted School and decades after his own troubled school days on either side of the green baize door, Greene was witnessing revolution at its most utopian under a verdant canopy of trees. The experience led him to quote both Wordsworth and Hazlitt in his published article.[17]

Llanusa altered the group's plans, and they returned to the motel outside Trinidad to rebuke its manager, whom they held responsible for the previous evening's muddle. The minister told Greene a party militant had probably appointed the manager, but not because he was the best man for the job. Somebody would nevertheless hear the man's case and "analyze" the reasons for his failure. They subsequently bumped into the man responsible for the manager's appointment on the road. They drove away laughing after he confirmed the manager did indeed attain his job because of party affiliation.[18]

The five men were alone again the following day and for the fourth time drove along the road to Trinidad. The colonial town's cobbled streets were not kind to their Packard, and following a pizza lunch in neighboring Sancti Spíritus, it left its exhaust pipe at the side of the road. It belonged to another vehicle anyway. They were glad to leave Las Villas at last and cross a bridge into the flat cattle province of Camagüey and later the Isla de Turiguano, an artificial island reached by a causeway. Here Greene realized that due to poor planning and/or communication, the group had missed a rendezvous with Fidel Castro. He had stayed in the model revolutionary village the previous night, but due to the minister of education's intervention, the group arrived there twenty-four hours late. According to Greene, Pablo Fernández had promised to keep in touch with Castro's close confidante Carlos Franqui and his secretary Celia Sánchez. To his frustration, a phone call to Havana the next day confirmed that Castro was traveling with Armando Hart and Sánchez. Greene recorded in his diary, "I felt slightly sour at the mismanagement of the trip which made us a day late." The sense of improvisation was evident again when Otero had to run around the next evening to find rooms in a Communist Party house in Holguín. It was carnival in the city, which meant all hotel accommodations were full.[19]

Pablo was apparently in charge of arrangements and was Greene's main contact ahead of the trip, responsible for gaining him access to Castro. Greene surmised later in the journey that along with Ernesto the photographer, Otero had attached himself to the group, and a "complicated relationship" existed between the two Cuban writers. Pablo had earlier informed Greene about Lisandro's "failed marriage & his plunge into politics." Greene wrote about the fellow writer, "Lisandro writes for hours on end about his 'situation.' He said it helps to get it off his mind & one day perhaps the notes will be useful for a book."[20]

Speaking about the trip decades later, photographer Ernesto described Lisandro Otero as a difficult character, "very juvenile" and prone to arrogant outbursts. Pablo said he planned the group's itinerary with Celia Sánchez, with the intention that Castro would accompany them on part of the trip. Then Otero changed the itinerary in consultation with Minister Llanusa but only communicated this arrangement to the group late in the day. This caused the misunderstanding in Topes de Collantes and the post-midnight jeep ride. It also meant the group were now a day behind schedule, with Castro and his aides following the original itinerary. Ernesto says the men quarreled a few times during the trip, once in Greene's presence. Overall, however, the writer, although disappointed to have missed meeting Castro, appeared very enthused about the revolutionary process and the advances he saw on the island.[21]

Otero's autobiography *Llover sobre mojado* (*It Never Rains but It Pours*; 1999) relates how he and Greene conversed about their personal lives and melancholia during the trip. The Cuban writer was recovering from his broken marriage while the Englishman fretted about his son-in-law's poor management of the farm he had bought for his daughter and her husband in Canada. At one point, Otero had an epiphany about the perfect life he could lead on the Isla de Turiguano, but Greene disabused him of his false impression of idyllic lives in exile, using the examples of French painter Paul Gauguin and English author W. Somerset Maugham.[22]

The trip was not all strife and missed appointments. There were more than a few opportunities for boyish fun, despite the generational gap between the English author and his Cuban travel companions. After visiting Santiago de Cuba, they chatted in the car after drinks and "the young men discovered themselves a little more." According to Greene's diary, subjects of conversation included blue films "in the old days," the red-light Colón area of Havana, and promiscuity. The juvenile banter continued on the trip. Their sexagenarian English guest noted the favorite English swear words of his two principal traveling companions, both writers and former cultural attachés at the Cuban embassy in London.[23]

At the port of Manzanillo, close to the *Granma* landing spot in December 1956, Greene admired a new town for fishermen. Its little colored houses surrounded by trees and flowers were examples of Cuban-modern architecture, inspired by "the ephemeral butterfly fashion of the art schools." Five hundred families lived there, "rescued literally from the swamps." There were crowds of children and a "sense of gaiety & happiness." Greene judged, "Whoever is against the revolution it is not these." He romantically mused on the triumph against adversity of the guerrillas who had landed nearby to overthrow Batista ten years earlier.[24] It is more than evident that Greene valued the revolution's utopian dreams and early social achievements.

Tracks made impassable by rain and mud even for four-wheel trucks prevented Greene's traveling party from reaching Minas de Frío, high in the Sierra Maestra hills. This was a key teacher training installation in the Revolution's ambitious education program, where fifteen- and sixteen-year-old students spent their first grueling year under austere conditions before graduating—if passing the year—to Topes de Collantes for a further two years training in their chosen specialization. A final fourth year of practical teaching took place near Havana. The only access to Minas de Frío was a four- to five-mile journey on foot, a hike the children had to complete on arrival. Nevertheless, Greene could cite the ambitious plans for seven educational villages in the area, with schools to educate a target of twenty thousand students with five thousand instructors. Colorful architectural design inspired by the landscape would blend installations into the surrounding hills and trees. Greene appeared to share the plan's idealism and practical benefits for education.[25]

They then arrived at Santiago de Cuba, the cradle of rebellion that Greene had last visited in the midst of the anti-Batista insurrection in November 1957. The group stayed outside the city at the recently opened Motel de Versailles with "beautiful rooms, excellent food." They visited the Morro Castle, where Santiago's bay opens onto the Caribbean, and a Russian plant for the prefabrication of flats. There were plans for a new housing complex for seven hundred families, with rents set at one-fiftieth of income. Greene wondered if this and Castro's recently declared plan to abolish all rents in 1970 were "wild dreams" and if the government could pay for them out of sugar, tobacco, and coffee. Seven blocks already stood completed in a tasteful variety of colors, after Castro had "rightly" overruled technicians' plans to paint them all white.[26]

The group received a military welcome at their next stop in the city of Guantánamo. A jeep carried them to the Cuban observation post overlooking the U.S. naval base in Guantánamo Bay. It would appear that Greene had almost free rein to reconnoiter the parts other foreigners could not reach. The 116-square-kilometer facility under perpetual lease was a legacy of an article in the 1901 Platt Amendment that two years later ceded to the United States the right to build "coaling and naval stations" on Cuban soil. Greene spotted three U.S. warships in the harbor. His hosts informed him that seven U.S. tanks had approached the border that morning and that a Cuban platoon was stationed six hundred meters from the American side behind a deep earth wall. Tellingly, Greene wanted to visit the nearest border point, where only yards separated Cuban from U.S. guards, but his hosts preferred to avoid such provocation. Photographs by Ernesto Fernández show Greene alongside military personnel, inspecting defense positions and their outlook, with binoculars and a Rolleiflex camera to hand. The visit to this strategically important military zone raises suspicions he was gathering intelligence for SIS. If these photographs do prove his involvement in "enhanced tourism"—i.e., informal espionage—it is doubtful the evidence proved very useful to either SIS or their intelligence partners in the United States. Both the Cubans and the Americans had their adversaries' sides of the fence well surveyed. Following his visit to the observation post, Greene made toasts to the Cuban and Vietnamese armies at battalion headquarters: a provocative act, with the U.S. intervention in Southeast Asia in full flow.[27]

The next day they drove up to Gran Piedra in the hills between Guantánamo and Santiago de Cuba and visited the museum home of former French coffee planters, escapees from Haiti's late eighteenth-century revolution. Despite slippery tracks, their skidding vehicles, and vertiginous drops, Greene was completely indifferent to risk and death, according to Otero. In the style of his 1938 trip to Mexico, they proceeded by mule from where the road ended. The road trip section of Greene's trip was over, and they flew back to Havana that afternoon.[28]

Back in the capital, he took photos near the Hotel Nacional in Vedado. He perused the scant offering of pavement booksellers with "strays from the past" such as the *Hilton Bedside Book*, the *Blue-jackets Annual* from 1946, and strip cartoons of Russian cosmonaut Yuri Gagarin. He met with Haydée Santamaría for the first time since seeing her in the safe house in Santiago in November 1957. She told him of the "need to restrain Fidel from plunging in," in reference to some of Castro's boyishly overambitious but impractical dreams for the Revolution. She had "tremendous enthusiasm for everything," despite the trauma of witnessing drowned women and children after Hurricane Flora had ravaged central and eastern Cuba in October 1963.[29] The island's worst natural disaster provoked widespread loss of life and damage, destroying crops and aggravating economic difficulties.

Following two nights in Havana, Raúl Castro lent Greene and his companions a military plane to fly to the Isle of Pines. Against Greene's will, they visited the "grim black circular old blocks" of the Modelo Prison, where the Castro brothers had been incarcerated for twenty-one months (August 1953–May 1955) after their failed attack on the Moncada Barracks in July 1953. The English visitor noted that war criminals currently imprisoned there, some with maximum thirty-year sentences, received up to two visits a month. But many refused rehabilitation in the hope that a further U.S. military invasion would succeed and free them from prison.

A plan to travel around the island's keys led to more frustration after a four a.m. start. Despite having to abandon the plan due to rain and rough waters, they were all "exhilarated . . . by the uselessness & absurdity of the trip" that had made them spend a total of five hours in a jeep only "to get wet and tossed about for 40 minutes" at sea.[30]

Back in Havana again, Greene spent the last few days of his visit in the company of many of the Revolution's most important political and cultural figures. He also took advantage of the opportunity to stroll the streets of Old Havana again. He visited the Museum of Art and the Museum of the Revolution, housed in the old Presidential

Palace. He met artist René Portocarrero, Carlos Franqui, and author Alejo Carpentier, at a big party at Pablo's house. Still in Pablo's company, he spent the following morning out with Portocarrero and Raúl Milián, two homosexual artists whose twenty-six-year-long partnership was stronger than ever. They gave him several paintings and drawings as gifts. Milián's was a personal present from Castro. The Pen Club held a cocktail party for Greene at the luxury house with a porter where the Cuban government had expected him to stay. Greene spent the evening at the Tropicana, its "fantastic luxury of bad taste . . . made possible to endure only by the beauty of some of the mulatta women."[31] It was as close as he would come to reliving his pre-revolutionary jaunts in the vicious city under Batista's rule.

His final full day on September 18 was frantic and action-packed, but ultimately satisfying. After interviews for radio stations in Haiti and Havana, he met young anthropologist Miguel Barnet.[32] Time was running out for him to meet Castro and fulfil his commitment to the *Telegraph*, but the revolutionary leader was in contact with Celia Sánchez, and it appeared Greene would finally realize his ambition.

After lunch he viewed Tomás Gutiérrez Alea's "excellent" *Death of a Bureaucrat* (1966), a high-spirited black-and-white satire that ridiculed overbearing pen and paper pushers in Cuba in slapstick fashion. During a tropical downpour that turned Havana's streets into rivers, Greene was "proudly passed by the Leyland buses," the same vehicles he had planned to accompany on a cargo boat from London to Cuba.[33] He evidently admired the fact that his country had driven a fleet of buses through the U.S. economic blockade of the communist island.

Before his departure for the Isle of Pines, new British ambassador to Cuba Dick Slater had met Greene for drinks and gave him two bottles of whisky. Now he received him for dinner at the ambassadorial residence in Vedado. Another dinner guest at the residence on this final evening was the Vatican's representative in Havana, Monsignor Cesare Zacchi. Greene heard the religious position was worse than it had been in 1963. The three men's dinner conversation turned to the Military Units to Aid Production (UMAP) forced labor camps. He learned that in addition to the "vicious [presumably prostitutes] & homosexual," there were three priests currently in the camps. However, a recent speech by Castro suggested possible abolishment of the camps. They were an exercise, Greene annotated, a form of military service not involving the privileged classes.[34]

Finally, after missed opportunities spanning nine years, Carlos Franqui arrived to whisk Greene to a guarded house outside Havana and a meeting with Castro. It was already eleven p.m. Minister of Education José Llanusa was in attendance, as well as Dr. René Vallejo as interpreter, described by Greene as "the angel." As Greene told an interviewer sixteen years later, "He translated so quickly and rapidly, that one had no sense of there being a break in the conversation."[35] Vallejo was Castro's personal physician and aide de camp. He had served with the Third U.S. Army in Germany after the Second World War and abandoned a successful medical practice in Manzanillo to join the rebels in the Sierra Maestra, where he rose to the rank of *comandante* (major).[36]

According to Greene, unlike a typical politician, Castro showed a private side in public and a public side in private. He spoke first without interruptions for about forty-five minutes on the subject of the countryside and agriculture. They then tackled Catholicism and communism. Castro praised the nuncio. Greene lauded *Death of a Bureaucrat* "via humor versus cynicism," therein criticizing revolutionary Cuba's rampant bureaucracy, of which he had been a victim in 1963. Vallejo shared the praise, and Castro simply acknowledged it. On the subject of cinema, he offered Greene "all facilities free of charge" to shoot a film version of his new novel *The Comedians* (1966) in Cuba. The offer came too late for the Haiti-based story, with agreement already in place to shoot the film in Dahomey, Africa. Castro's generous offer demonstrated there were no hard feelings about the troubled filming of *Our Man in Havana* seven years earlier.

Before departing at two a.m., after three hours of conversation, Greene's bearded host gifted the writer a Portocarrero painting inscribed on its frame by the revolutionary leader. The work of art would hang behind his writing desk at his Antibes flat for the remainder of his days in the South of France.[37] It is no exaggeration to say that the long-anticipated meeting had gone extremely well, with genuine affection displayed on both sides.

Pablo Fernández and Carlos Franqui accompanied Greene to the airport early the next morning. Nuncio Zacchi and film director Alea also came to bid him farewell. First and tourist class were packed. Greene noticed how a young bourgeois couple, abandoning the island for exile, did not "give a last look at their country." While the bourgeois might support a revolution with cash, he judged, they do not stay behind in discomfort to influence and fight it when it changes course. Greene completed his notes on the late-night meeting with Castro during his plane journey home.[38]

CUBA IN "SHADOW AND SUNLIGHT"

Greene wrote to Catherine Walston about his meeting with Fidel Castro, "we got on very very well. I liked him a lot & was very impressed. I was fetched away by a messenger from a private dinner with the British Ambassador who was quite jealous as he hasn't spoken more than two words to Castro yet."[39]

Dick Slater had only commenced his ambassadorial posting in Havana three months earlier, in June 1966, and did not have to be jealous of Greene for long. He bumped into Castro on a beach the very day after the writer's meeting with him. According to Slater:

[H]e waxed eloquent in Graham Greene's praise. Of course it must be gratifying to him that an eminent author from the capitalist world—and a Roman Catholic to boot—should take

this benevolent interest in the Cuban revolution, but Graham
Greene evidently struck a personal chord.

The ambassador was accurate when he predicted that Greene's
Weekend Telegraph articles would contain "sympathetic but not
wholly uncritical" judgments on the revolution. Slater's guess that
Greene might return for the Party Congress in 1967 was wrong, but
through no fault of his own. The first Party Congress did not actually
take place until 1975.[40]

Greene's 1966 visit produced two articles for the *Weekend Telegraph* magazine in successive weeks: "Fidel: An Impression" (later
published in his *Collected Essays* as "The Marxist Heretic"[41]) on
December 2 and "Shadow and Sunlight in Cuba" on December 9.
As Slater had predicted, this second article contained generally positive impressions of the Revolution tempered by some negative observations. The first, largely laudatory piece concentrated by definition
on the personage of Fidel Castro. It starts with commentary on his
elusiveness akin to the Scarlet Pimpernel, mainly due to security
considerations. The roving revolutionary refused ties to an office.
Instead he wandered purposefully around the countryside, "discovering his own country for the first time," an island that was no
longer Havana-centric. Castro's character was not suited to Soviet
discipline. He was a young and energetic revolutionary given to
impulse, experiment, and utopian dreams. In Greene's eyes, he was
"a Chestertonian man," traveling around his own island like a for-
eigner. His speeches were "nearer to Cobbett than Churchill" and in
the author's opinion, "greater for that." Indeed, they were "full of
information, down to earth, filled with detail."[42]

The alliterative bracketing of Fidel Castro with William Cobbett
and G. K. Chesterton (but not Churchill) deserves analysis. Whimsical English writer G. K. Chesterton (1874–1936) loved argument
and was convinced that the best possible adventure involved redis-
covering the familiar. As with Castro, his adherents—at least in

Chesterton's earlier life—never knew what he was going to say next, a quality that also differentiated the Cuban leader from British politicians. Political writer and farmer William Cobbett (1763–1835), meanwhile, always maintained a strong sense of national identity. He was often critical of the United States, a country where he had resided, and championed the English countryside and agricultural workers throughout his life.

It would appear Greene had found a kindred spirit with regard to his unorthodox interpretation of communism. Castro construed the doctrine as he saw fit, adapting it to local circumstances. He was "an empirical Marxist, who plays Communism by ear and not by book." Of course, despite Cuba's economic dependence on Russia, Castro was no faithful lapdog of the Soviet Union. This was especially the case after the Cuban Missile Crisis, when Khrushchev informed Kennedy but not Castro about the withdrawal of Soviet nuclear missiles from Cuba. In subsequent visits to Moscow, its leaders advised Castro to reduce his country's dependence on them, giving him freer rein to chart Cuba's political course. Noting Russia's drift toward "a managerial revolution" and state capitalism and China toward "some fantastic variant" of its own, Cuba—in Greene's opinion—"may well become the real testing ground of Communism." Repeating what he had written in his 1963 article, he identified the island's "Athenian" quality, small enough for its people to be "consulted, informed, confided in: they can see their leaders day by day in the streets of their towns and villages."[43] Mass participation and assembly—for example, in Havana's Revolution Square, where Greene saw Castro speak in 1963—were indeed important and continuing features of the Cuban Revolution.

Greene was fascinated about possible cooperation between Communism and Catholicism. (His witnessing of Liberation Theology in action in Central America in the following decade would satisfy this curiosity). He correctly noted that Catholicism in Cuba was the religion "of the bourgeoisie." The more popular religion among peasants in the island, just as in Haiti, was a syncretism of Afro-Christian beliefs. According to Greene's vision, the church's enemies in Cuba were Cardinal Francis Spellman and Bishop Fulton J. Sheen (also cited in his 1963 article), "those doughty champions of cold war and counter-revolution."[44] He evidently felt disdain for these Catholic cold warriors, fellow travelers of the Catholic senator Joe McCarthy.

Greene's largely positive first article ended on a more ambivalent note. He recognized how a "sympathetic visitor" like himself lived "in the bright sunlight of the revolution." Cubans who had chosen exile, meanwhile, "must have seen the shadows, some of them imaginary, some of them real enough."[45]

His second article, "Shadow and Sunlight in Cuba," picked up where his first article had left off. It was a more thorough analysis of the Cuban Revolution itself, its priorities, achievements, and mistakes. It started with a particular obsession of Greene's: the price of food in the Floridita restaurant. Suffice to say, prices had risen extraordinarily since the days of Batista. And for the majority of Cubans who could not afford to eat at the restaurant, severe rationing was a daily reality, given the U.S. blockade and the recent devastation of Hurricane Flora. Among these ordinary Cubans was Rocky, his long-trusted taxi driver of pre-revolutionary days. After his vehicle fell apart in 1962, Rocky had joined the army for three years and was now training to be an accountant. Along with his passenger of old, he criticized "odd eating habits" for some Cubans' problems. They generally shunned fish and eggs, and even fruit and vegetables rotted away in markets due to lack of interest. Although Rocky was ostensibly worse off, with a wife unable to work due to two small children, Greene reported him "not against the revolution" and with "new social freedom."[46]

The economy had improved because of the wise decision to abandon the "bad error" of industrialization. Greene noted a particular improvement in the countryside, where peasants now owned and cultivated their own land. The neglect of Havana was an "official policy," and its tall hotels stood as "bourgeois tombs." Greene, however, was dismissive of Cubans' tendency to "grumble," particularly the "real poor" with disposable income for the first time but little to spend it on. He also appeared to disparage those black Cubans who yearned for exile in the United States but who ignored daily local press photographs of blacks beaten up by white policemen.[47] This was of course the era of Dr. Martin Luther King Jr. and civil rights protests in the United States.

On a positive note, the "war against illiteracy" was "a genuine crusade with a heroic quality of its own." Along with defense and agriculture, education was now the most important ministry in Cuba, and its new head, José Llanusa, was proving as energetic as Castro as he toured the island. Greene described what he had seen in the Escambray and Sierra Maestra mountains. During his 1957 stay, they were the refuge of two rival guerrilla bands fighting Batista's forces, but they were now the site of a battle for education.[48] This definitely constituted one of the "sunshine" elements of his article. Meanwhile, the "dark shadow" of his 1966 trip and article was the Military Units to Aid Production (UMAP) camps, "worse than blockade or rationing or hit-and-run raids," and with a name that sounded like "something from science fiction."[49]

The flawed UMAP initiative was an attempt to resolve a number of different social, economic, and even military challenges concurrently. The issue caused enduring damage to the Revolution, particularly its image abroad, repeatedly used by embittered Cuban exiles and others to condemn the Revolution and its leader Fidel Castro. Socially, UMAP was a strand of obligatory military service (SMO) for Cuban males, with the first UMAP call-up in November 1965 and the second in June 1966, shortly before Greene's visit. The third planned call-up never occurred, and the last camp closed in June 1968. During the two years and seven months of their existence, twenty-five thousand people passed through the seventy UMAP camps in the central eastern province of Camagüey.[50] The initiative particularly targeted individuals deemed social deviants and therefore unsuitable for standard military service. These included religious zealots and homosexuals, as well as other groups viewed as living on the margins of society such as hippies and layabouts. Of the religious groups, Jehovah's Witnesses were a particular target, alongside Protestants like Seventh-day Adventists and evangelical pastors, due to their links with counterrevolutionary groups in the United States. Catholics constituted only a very small minority among the religious internees.[51]

A three-year stint of compulsory service under military discipline wherein these marginalized individuals would undertake collective agricultural work was supposed to reeducate them though inculcation of revolutionary values, facilitating their later reintegration into Cuba's new revolutionary society. Its instigators considered hard physical work in the countryside a moral virtue. In fact, there was already a tradition in revolutionary Cuba of sending university students to the countryside, for example, to participate in coffee harvests. The UMAP policy also formed part of a general initiative to prioritize the countryside over urban centers and exalt virtuous *campesinos* (peasants) and their work ethic.[52]

A twin objective of the policy was to fill a labor shortage in the countryside and contribute to economic production. Under a sugar trade agreement with Moscow in 1964, Cuba needed to export 24 million tons of sugar to the Soviet Union between 1965 and 1970. But structural changes to the Cuban economy and internal migration from countryside to urban centers had created this severe labor shortage, just as the country's leaders decided to concentrate again on the island's traditional agricultural strength, the planting and harvesting of sugarcane and other crops. Sugar industry workers had always faced seasonal unemployment and low wages, but newly created posts in the military, state security, the police, mass state organizations, and the state's burgeoning bureaucracy drew

Cubans to towns and cities. To combat the shortage of workers in the countryside, the revolutionary state had long mobilized its citizens to fill some of this gap thorough voluntary work. A problem with voluntary work, however, was that it had proved woefully inefficient and had not raised agricultural production to desired levels.[53]

Certain camps or platoons within camps were designated for homosexual internees, adding to their stigmatization and harsh treatment by certain guards. Indeed, many questioned the evident homophobia of a policy that identified homosexuals as requiring incarceration and reeducation in the first place. It is tempting to conclude the experiment of forced labor and reeducation for homosexuals sprang from the same moralizing minds responsible for the Revolution's early puritanism, including the Bureau of Public Order's attempts to censor filming of *Our Man in Havana*, though views differ as to how such a wrongheaded policy came about. Among Cubans, Guillermo Cabrera Infante suggested the Revolution's early moralism stemmed from a Cuban variant of exaggerated Latin machismo. Carlos Franqui described "Operation P" in 1961, when police undertook mass street arrests of those suspected as pederasts, prostitutes, or pimps. Forced to wear uniforms with a huge P across their backs, they were then subject to questioning at a Spanish colonial fort-cum-prison. Among those arrested was the homosexual writer Virgilio Piñera, later released after the protests of influential friends. Franqui placed particular blame for this earlier phase of homosexual persecution on "power-mad *machistas*."[54]

One foreign commentator identified in 1960s Cuba "a combination of a heterosexual masculinist tradition, on one hand, and a socialist morality that identified certain forms of sexual behavior with bourgeois decadence and a lack of productivity."[55] When asked about homosexuals by U.S. journalist and photographer Lee Lockwood in an extended series of interviews in 1965, Fidel Castro told him nothing prevented a homosexual from "professing revolutionary ideology." Yet he also affirmed:

> [W]e would never come to believe that a homosexual could embody the conditions and requirements of conduct that would enable us to consider him a true Revolutionary, a true Communist militant. A deviation of that nature clashes with the concept we have of what a militant Communist must be.

Viewing some homosexuality as pathological, Castro judged his country should inculcate its young people with the spirit "of discipline, of struggle, of work."[56] Such antiquated views need to be set against the legal position of homosexuals in Greene's home country. Only in 1967 did the Sexual Offences Act for the first time decriminalize sexual relations between men over twenty-one years old in England and Wales. Men in the armed forces and merchant navy were exempt from the Act.

Greene's description and analysis of the UMAP camps in his second *Weekend Telegraph* article are certainly a denunciation. He quoted the four-and-a-half-hour speech he had witnessed on August 29 when Castro employed the term *campo de concentración* (concentration camp) in what many hoped was as an allusion to the UMAP camps. The policy in Greene's estimation was more serious than a tactical mistake like the attempt at industrialization. The camps constituted a moral mistake that "compromises the revolution." By implication, if the revolution was prepared to devour its own citizens, it could soon devour itself. Nevertheless, he was optimistic the government would reverse the serious policy error, which indeed it did two years later.[57]

The UMAP camps and the incarceration of marginalized individuals therefore led Greene to his strongest published criticism of the Revolution. Otero recalls that early in their road trip around the island, their English guest broached the subject over a bottle of whisky at a Cienfuegos hotel, asking if foreign reports of repression of homosexuals in Cuba were true. His Cuban host told him the country's intellectuals were certainly opposed to a policy incompatible with revolutionary ethics. They signed documents opposing the senseless harassment and pressured those in positions of political power.[58] The Cuban Union of Writers and Artists (UNEAC), of which Otero and Fernández were leading members, was very active in this regard.[59] Also influencing Greene's decision to put pen to paper about the camps was the fact that several of his best friends in Cuba's cultural sphere during his 1963 and 1966 trips were well-known homosexuals, including writer Virgilio Piñera and the cohabiting artists René Portocarrero and Raúl Milián. Greene's denunciation of the UMAP camps demonstrated personal loyalty to them and gratitude for their generous hospitality.

His article contributed to foreign pressure on the Cuban government to reverse the mistaken policy. The government recognized their error and phased out the camps in 1968. Ultimately, the attempt to resolve a number of different domestic difficulties through the UMAP policy proved a disaster. A policy conceived as a win-win—to bring marginalized Cubans into the revolutionary process and improve agricultural production—seriously tarnished the Revolution's image abroad.

One commentator is correct in her analysis that the 1966 "Shadow and Sunlight" article was a "more sombre" and "less effusive" overview of the revolution. Greene had been "almost ecstatic" about the Revolution in 1963, but by 1966 he complained about its "authoritarianism."[60] The earlier article alludes to bureaucracy and economic shortcomings, while the second denounces abuses of human rights. In the balance of his judgments on Batista's Cuba and Castro's Cuba, there was no doubt he preferred the latter—although he did lament the demise of the Shanghai Theater and other "vicious" pleasures. When the wife of former ambassador Stanley Fordham wrote to him a few months after publication of his 1966 articles, Greene replied unequivocally: "I must say I remain firmly a pro-Fidelist after what I saw of the Batista regime and what I have found wandering round Cuba recently."[61]

To Catherine Walston, whom he now saw only rarely, he was even more effusive. On his return to France, he described his "four hours sleep a night & hours & hours of motoring," and overall a "wildly energetic and fatiguing time." As well as the military plane lent by Raúl Castro, he listed all the paintings received as presents from Cuban artists. With Fidel, meanwhile, whom he "liked enormously," he had talked for three hours on his final evening. It was all "[r]eal red carpet treatment."[62]

✳

Ironically, Catherine's husband soon outdid the former rival for his wife's affections when he met Fidel Castro on his first-ever visit to Cuba. A life peer since 1961, Harry Walston was Foreign Office parliamentary undersecretary of state from 1964 to 1967. The lord from the Labour Party had discussed the possibility of a visit to Cuba with Dick Slater before the new ambassador took up his post in Havana in 1966. Senior British diplomats had reservations, and the Foreign Office sought and received approval from the U.S. State Department for what would be the first NATO-country ministerial visit since the Revolution. It received approval on the understanding that Walston would tackle Castro on that year's Tri-Continental Conference and efforts to export his revolution to other parts of the Third World. Ambassador Slater extended the invitation, and Lord Walston made "a 'private' visit" to Cuba from December 18 to 22, 1966.[63]

Castro and Walston hit it off due to a mutual interest in agriculture. The Labour peer was a recognized authority on the subject, owning a two-thousand-acre Cambridgeshire farm and an estate in the West Indies. In fact, he had even authored a 108-page book titled *Agriculture under Communism*.[64] According to Slater, the revolutionary leader regarded himself as an expert on pretty well everything, but "his real love" was agriculture. Walston and Castro were a match made in a furrowed Caribbean field. As with Greene's visit, the superb interpretation skills of Castro's charming personal physician and confidant Major René Vallejo smoothed their warm dialogue. Outdoing by some margin Greene's mere three late-night hours with the revolutionary leader, Lord Walston enjoyed an impressive twenty-five hours in his company. They visited farms and agricultural experimental stations together in the provinces of Havana and Pinar del Río.

Yet only at the midpoint of the trip did Castro learn that Walston owned and farmed an estate on the Caribbean island of St. Lucia. This gratifying information ignited talk of a possible exchange of seeds, cuttings, and even respective technical experts. A proud Castro took Walston on a tour of a Cavendish banana planation, where closely planted trees were producing impressive yields owing to a special fertilization formula. His British guest then trumped the boastful revolutionary leader with news about a recent experiment at his St. Lucia estate that had yielded even better results. Castro was "rather jealous," according to Slater's account, and asked Walston if he could send a female banana expert to St. Lucia to see the new method in action.[65]

Following the visit, Lord Walston sent Castro a Fortnum & Mason fruitcake along with a copy of his book. To colleagues in the Foreign Office, he remarked on Castro's vitality, energy, and leadership powers. He judged that "both fear and hatred of the United States" dominated his thinking. Like Greene, the Cuban leader's security arrangements fascinated him, including a car "bristling with automatic weapons."[66]

Unfortunately, Foreign Office unease prevented a Cuba/St. Lucia exchange of agricultural experts on banana and tobacco growing and compromised a follow-up visit by Walston. He was no longer a minister by 1968. His former department fretted about both

Washington's reaction and the sensitivity of rival Caribbean agricultural producers in receipt of generous U.S. aid. In any event, the
St. Lucia government denied visas for Castro's agricultural experts
to visit their island. The decision turned Walston red. With his own
high-level contacts in St. Lucia, he informed the British foreign secretary in April 1968 that he was "under no illusions" as to who had
forced the decision. Accompanied by his wife, he did visit Cuba from
February 23 to March 1, 1968, but in Slater's words, "Castro kept us
dangling and then dropped us flat on our faces." The keen if amateur
agriculturist in olive-green military fatigues evidently felt snubbed by
the denial of visas for his banana experts and never surfaced to greet
the Walstons in Cuba.[67] Catherine therefore never met Fidel Castro,
a decade after accompanying Greene to licentious Havana in late
1954 and 1956.

12

FROM HAVANA WITH LOVE

In January 1979, Greene received a surprise postcard from Havana. A former SIS colleague and professed friend had breached the Iron Curtain to holiday in one of the few countries open to him. Its message simply read, "New Year Greetings from Your Fan in Havana. Muchos Daiquiris en la Floridita! KP"[1] Greene guessed correctly that his admirer was British traitor and defector Kim Philby, writing from Hemingway's haunt of double-frozens. In further correspondence, the first-time visitor lauded Cuba's "general ebullience," but grumbled about "infernal ice-chips [that] interfered with serious drinking." Despite escaping a harsh Moscow winter for the tropics, temperature and humidity fluctuations still played "merry Hell with [his] bronx."[2] Such gripes would have elicited little sympathy from other former SIS colleagues. Indeed, most were probably heartened to know that for the rest of the year, the traitor was doubly frozen out in Moscow—pining for the latest *Times* crossword and English cricket, and drinking himself to an early grave.

Philby's betrayal of confidential information to the Russians had condemned numerous British-trained agents to death. For example, Rodney Dennys, SIS head of station in Istanbul (and Elisabeth Greene's husband) and his colleagues could not understand why every one of the hundreds of agents they meticulously trained found themselves arrested as soon as they landed in Albania. More than three hundred agents were killed, and many more sent to labor camps.[3]

Greene and his former Section V boss maintained a regular if infrequent correspondence following the traitor's defection from Beirut to Moscow in 1963. The writer even visited Philby in the Soviet Union three times in 1986 and 1987 to chat about old times over drinks. For many, his support for Kim Philby was hard to swallow. Worse still, he wrote an introduction to Philby's autobiography *My Silent War* (1968). Greene appeared to sympathize with the traitor's dilemma through the rhetorical question, "who among us has not committed treason to something or someone more important than a country?"[4]

Their friendship was not all it appeared, however. Head of SIS Maurice Oldfield hoped that Philby, fed up with life in Moscow, might defect a second time, back to his native England. This would provide a moral defeat for the KGB, and a late but hollow propaganda victory for SIS. Oldfield, often the "F.O. man" that Greene met before and after his SIS-financed missions abroad, used the writer as a go-between with the traitor in Moscow. As part of this work, Greene passed all his correspondence with Philby to Oldfield via his brother-in-law Rodney Dennys.[5]

After release of *The Third Man*, there was speculation that Kim Philby and Graham Greene had inspired the character and name of the duplicitous Harry Lime. Four years after Foreign Office diplomats Burgess and Maclean defected to Moscow in 1951, Prime Minister Harold Macmillan had to deny speculation in the House of Commons that Philby had tipped off the British traitors and was "the so-called 'third man.'"[6]

In a late scene in the film adaptation of *Our Man in Havana*, Wormold borrows a pistol belonging to semiconscious Captain Segura and abandons their drunken game of checkers. He phones Carter to invite him around the "hot spots" of nocturnal Havana. (Carter, of course, was the name of one of Greene's bullies at Berkhamsted

School.) The two men end up at "a house" (a brothel), where Wormold draws Segura's pistol, points it at Carter, and shoots:

> CARTER: You're ma-making a mistake. I'm not important. I was
>   under orders, like you. My pipe! You broke my pipe!
> WORMOLD: Beginner's luck.
> CARTER: I'm not even armed. Wormold, we're just private
>   soldiers, you and I.[7]

This scene contains clues hidden in plain sight to implicate Carter as Philby, the notorious worm at the heart of British intelligence. As well as his deadly combination of overt charm and hidden treachery, other Philby hallmarks were a debilitating stammer and a pipe. Indeed, Greene's introduction to his ex-colleague's autobiography described Philby's propensity to interject "a halting stammered witticism" into conversation. When Philby was working as a correspondent for *The Times* in France at the beginning of the Second World War, his expenses claim for a lost Dunhill pipe and a camel-hair overcoat became a Fleet Street legend.[8]

The storylines of both *The Third Man* and *Our Man in Havana* conclude in similar fashion, with Lime and Carter at the sharp end of a pistol. Carter ends his days backed against a brothel entrance door, its round glass apertures resembling the eyes of a night owl. Rather than enter the gates of sin, Carter has presumably gone to hell. What is the viewer supposed to see and read into Carter's death scene? Could it be that Carter is Philby, an agent working for the other side? Given that *Our Man in Havana*—both the novel and film—were written and produced between 1957 and 1959, was their author confirming Philby as the "third man," years before his actual defection to Moscow in 1963? This would provide further evidence that sympathy expressed in his glowing introduction to Philby's autobiography in 1968 was insincere, and likewise, his meetings with the intelligence traitor in Moscow in the late 1980s were not all they seemed.

In a preceding scene in *Our Man in Havana*, a mysterious enemy targets Wormold at the European Traders' Association annual lunch. As Carter conspires to poison him, Wormold rises to speak:

> "We hear a lot nowadays about the cold war. But any trader will tell you that the war between two manufacturers can be quite a hot war. [He spills his drink] Sorry. Uh—take Phastkleaners and Nu-cleaners for instance . . . there's no fundamental difference between the two machines any more than there is between two human beings. There'd be very little competition and certainly no war, if it wasn't for the ambitions of a few men. I don't suppose that Mr. Carter even knows the name of the man who sent him here to put an end to Phastkleaners for the good of Nu-cleaners." [9]

During his speech, Wormold intentionally knocks his whisky to the floor, already primed with poison by the stammering Carter. A dachshund at his feet laps up the spilt spirit, whimpers, and promptly dies.

The pivotal Traders' Lunch is a metaphor for global East versus West rivalry. Carter's rival vacuum cleaner company, named Nu-cleaners, even evokes the specter of Cold War nuclear confrontation. On the one hand, we learn that rival private soldiers Wormold and Carter take their orders from nameless men. On the other, we conclude that while the possibilities for satire in a fantasy Cold War story are endless, real espionage is a serious and sometimes mortal business. In this fictional instance, the victims of faceless rivalry are an enemy agent endeavoring to poison a rival agent, and an innocent dog. Philby's real victims were far more numerous.

CHAMPIONING UNDERDOGS

Greene held a long fascination with Panama. During his schooldays at Berkhamsted, he had first learned about Francis Drake's exploits at Nombre de Dios bay on its Caribbean coast. The Elizabethan privateer's plunder of spices and treasure from Spanish ships and ports in the Americas made him a romantic figure for British schoolchildren. For the Spanish crown, meanwhile, Drake was an enduring bête noire. Once he had traveled there, Panama became for Greene a "bizarre and beautiful little country, split in two by the Canal and the American Zone."[10] Indeed, the isthmian republic's history and geography, straddling the continents of South and North America, epitomized Latin America's fractious relationship with the United States.

Greene accepted a mysterious invitation and visited Panama for the first time in 1976. Yet he was reluctant to leave Yvonne and his Paris flat when he came to embark on the long journey to Central America (Paris > Amsterdam > Zurich > Madrid > Caracas > Curaçao > Panama City). Initially, at least, the seventy-one-year-old author feared he "had lost for ever the excitement of a long plane journey to an unknown place." A complimentary whisky in the Van Gogh room at Amsterdam's Schiphol Airport helped awaken the feeling. Two Bols gins—"one young, one old"—in first class on the connecting Amsterdam-Zurich KLM flight also allowed "the old sense of adventure" to return. He had booked with the Dutch airline in remembrance of his post-midnight departure from Rancho Boyeros Airport at the end of his accidental two-day visit to "vicious" Havana in September 1954.[11]

Akin to his four consecutive winter journeys to Indochina in the early 1950s, Greene would fly across the Atlantic to the Central American republic like a migratory bird. He visited four times between 1976 and 1980 and once again in 1983. General Omar Torrijos had ruled Panama since coming to power through a military coup in 1968 and received Greene as his personal guest. They spent many days traveling the country and, the general in his hammock, hours conversing about its fractious relationship with the United States. Both men had schoolmaster fathers in common. Greene enjoyed the general's company and appreciated his sense of humor, his humility, and his courage. He also hit it off with the general's charismatic personal advisor, the former university professor of Marxist philosophy José "Chuchu" Martínez.

During these years, Torrijos was involved in drawn-out negotiations with the United States over the transference of Panama Canal Zone control to his country. Greene's many experiences in Latin America reached their climax in 1977 when he received an official invitation to join the Panamanian delegation at the signing of the Canal Treaty in Washington. In a highly symbolic moment for inter-American relations, the U.S. government was about to agree to relinquish eventual control over the canal and transfer authority to a Latin American country. It appeared as if Greene had lived all his life for this climactic moment of exquisite awkwardness and Latin pride. Torrijos arranged a temporary Panamanian diplomatic passport for Greene. Thus, for a few days at least, he was a proud citizen of the small republic. Moreover, he was traveling on a Latin American passport to the political heart of a country that had deported him from its territorial possession Puerto Rico two decades earlier.

Gabriel García Márquez, the Colombian author of *One Hundred Years of Solitude* and a mutual friend of Torrijos, was a fellow honorary guest. A former Communist Party member in Colombia, he had been barred earlier in his life from the United States. Greene and García Márquez sniggered like mischievous schoolboys at their predicament: two left-leaning novelists mingling with Washington's establishment of Anglo-Saxon politicians and policymakers as they clinked glasses with a veritable rogues' gallery of Latin American despots. Among the invitees at the treaty signing event was Argentine dictator Jorge Videla, whose right-wing junta had already rounded up, tortured, and disappeared—in the verb's transitive sense—many thousands of Argentinians suspected of left-wing activism in a period labeled the Dirty War. Augusto Pinochet of Chile was another foreboding military presence. At one point, somebody attempted to introduce Greene to a minister in Alfredo Stroessner's government. The minister recalled a visit by the author to Paraguay and his support for Castro's Cuba. He therefore aborted a handshake, leaving the Englishman's hand to dangle in the air, a rebuke that instilled pride in Greene.[12]

The rise of Liberation Theology—a melding of Marxist theory and Christian theology—in 1970s Latin America fascinated Greene. It highlighted the socioeconomic structures that led to inequality and proposed a theology of salvation to liberate the poor from injustice through their active participation in political and civil affairs. Like politics, he considered that religion had the potential to force real change in the continent. The concept that the Catholic Church could reinterpret its role and lead the struggle for economic and social justice for the poor made perfect sense to him. It was a philosophy he considered both enlightened and practical, combining his political and Christian instincts. In Central America, he would witness liberation theology in action.

In the 1980s, Greene and García Márquez involved themselves in peace negotiations in the region, then a locus of Cold War confrontation. Left-wing guerrillas in El Salvador and Nicaragua had overthrown long-standing right-wing dictatorial regimes, but with exaggerated fears about Communist subversion in the hemisphere, President Ronald Reagan provided their opponents with substantial military aid, some of it illegally. Long and bloody insurgency wars ensued. Pronouncements by Pope John Paul II that criticized the involvement of the church in political struggles appalled Greene. He suspected Poland's Cold War experiences had colored the Polish pope's opinions, as the Soviet Union had tried to introduce a national Catholic Church in his country. In Nicaragua, on the other hand, priests had participated in its civil war of liberation.[13]

Torrijos died in a plane crash in Panama in 1982, just as Greene was packing his bags for another visit to the country. The following year, he traveled to Central America once again to assist in a delicate peace process in the region. As part of these negotiations and in advance of a key election in Panama, Greene traveled to Cuba for the final time in 1983 as an unofficial envoy of the Central American peace process. Like his first 1954 visit, he spent only one night in Havana, nostalgic for the Old Havana he had discovered three decades earlier. To his evident disappointment, however, his hosts housed him in an unfamiliar area. Hence his annotation to himself, "no chance of seeing the Havana of my memories." A "more matured" Otero was one of the old acquaintances to greet him at the airport. Also present in Havana was Gabriel García Márquez, recipient of the Nobel Prize for Literature the previous year, as well as Armando Hart, now minister of culture, whose hair had turned white.[14] Greene had a keen eye for such detail.

Castro appeared late in the evening following a dinner with the Spanish ambassador. The Cuban leader struck him as "much more *détends*" (relaxed/carefree). This time the topic of conversation ranged from contemporary politics to Russian roulette. In an article for Spanish newspaper *El País*, García Márquez said Greene and Castro were "a little intimidated" on meeting each other. To break the ice after a discussion of the forthcoming elections in Panama, García Márquez broached the topic of Russian roulette. Greene had played it so many times that Fidel found it hard to believe he was still alive.[15] Such manly risk evidently aroused the interest of a revolutionary leader who had spent more than two years surrounded by arms in the Sierra Maestra hills and was a target for CIA assassination attempts and numerous plots thereafter.

Probably on the recommendation of García Márquez, the Cuban leader had read about one-third of Greene's new novel *Monsignor Quixote* (1982), inspired by several wine-fueled summer trips around Spain with a Galician priest in a chauffeured car. He questioned Greene about his knowledge of Spanish wines and his regimen: he did not exercise and ate and drank whatever he liked. Castro was also interested in the author's long-running feud with Yvonne Cloetta's ex-son-in-law and Greene's allegations against the local mafia and politicians in Nice. Castro made him a generous offer: "If you have to leave France come & live here." In his diary, Greene remarked that Fidel was "very friendly" and displayed a "feeling of affection" for him.[16]

Following years of frustrations, therefore, Greene had managed to meet Castro on his final two visits to Cuba. He was worth the wait. The pair got on well, understood each other—albeit through a translator—and shared a sharp political intuition. Castro evidently admired Greene's courage and peculiarity, while Castro's charisma and energy charmed the writer. Castro had readily understood Greene's declaration when greeting him with "I am not a messenger. I am the message"—i.e., his journey from Central America came with the blessing of political leaders in Panama and Nicaragua and indicated their continued support for the ideas of Torrijos. Like their 1966 encounter, they said goodbye in the early hours of the morning, and Castro instructed Greene, "Tell them that I have received the message."[17] It was the last time they saw each other.

WHERE DID GREENE STAND?

It is obvious Greene both enjoyed and disliked Cuba before and after the Revolution, but for very different reasons. On the one hand, he had indulged in—and later felt nostalgic for—some of Cuba's vicious capitalist trappings under Batista, but he abhorred its cruel repression and accommodation with the United States. Meanwhile, he admired Castro's Cuba for its communist heresy and impressive social and cultural achievements, yet he was uncomfortable with its puritanism. He found its bureaucracy crushing, and short-lived Stalinist policies such as the UMAP camps appalled him.

Greene wrote an unused opening to his second 1966 article that neatly sums up his nostalgia for pre-revolutionary Cuba:

> What centuries of change seem to have passed since I came to Havana, having been arrested & deported from Puerto Rico by the American authorities on my way from Haiti to England, & was momentarily mistaken by one of Batista's police for a German called Kreuger—wanted for I never learned what: the Havana of Superman performing nightly to American tourists: the Shanghai Theater: the Mambo Club: roulette tables in all the best hotels . . .[18]

In addition to American tourists, the truth was that Greene had also enjoyed Superman's performances at the Shanghai. It is also notable that he misremembered (and misspelled) the German name Kreuger instead of Strippling from his unplanned visit in 1954. Kruger was the Conradian passenger who spilled out his life story and philosophy to Greene on a return transatlantic voyage from Mexico to Europe in 1938, when their German liner called at Havana en route. The similarly named corrupt financier Krogh was a character in his 1935 novel *England Made Me*, based on the real Swedish "Match King" millionaire and swindler Ivar Kreuger (1880–1932).[19]

When Evelyn Waugh's son Auberon quizzed Greene in 1968 about the many thousands of political prisoners in Cuba, he retorted that its "forced labour camps" for layabouts, homosexuals, and Catholic priests worried him more. Greene underlined the fact that Cubans could "paint or write what they please." (Events in coming years would disprove this assertion with regard to writers.) His overriding admiration for Cuba was its "element of Utopianism."[20]

Greene openly criticized Batista but was more circumspect in criticizing Castro. In an interview over several days in 1981, he said he had felt "very close to the Fidelistas' struggle" at the time of the Revolution. But he also admitted he was "very much of two minds" about Castro, declaring, "I admire his courage and his efficiency, but I question his authoritarianism."[21]

Just weeks before Greene's final visit to Havana at the beginning of 1983, a provocative article by London-domiciled Cuban exile Guillermo Cabrera Infante in the *London Review of Books* led to a fractious literary chain reaction. The lengthy piece was more a denunciation of Castro and his foreign hagiographers than it was a review of a new anthology of poems by Cuban exile Heberto Padilla. After the aforementioned shuttering of the *Lunes de Revolución* in 1961, its co-editor Cabrera Infante had served as cultural attaché in Brussels from 1962, before returning to Cuba for his mother's funeral three years later. He then resigned his diplomatic post in 1966 to go into permanent exile, firstly in Barcelona and later in London, where he lived for the rest of his life, authoring such books as *Tres Tristes Tigres* (*Three Sad Tigers*) (1967) and *La Habana para un Infante Difunto* (*Infante's Inferno*) (1979). The poet Padilla had courted serious controversy in 1968 when he wrote a positive review of Cabrera Infante's *Tres Tristes Tigres*, because the exiled author was already an enemy of the Revolution. At the same time, he criticized a prize-winning novel by Lisandro Otero, Greene's traveling partner in 1966, and then a vice minister in the National Council of Culture.

Further official criticism of Padilla in the following years led to his house arrest and an enforced public confession in which he criticized his own and others' counterrevolutionary behavior. Alleged counterrevolutionaries included his own wife! These events made the poet an international cause célèbre and led to the so-called Padilla Affair in 1971. Hitherto supportive foreign intellectuals broke with the Cuban Revolution at this point. Renowned philosophers and literary figures such as Jean-Paul Sartre, Simone de Beauvoir, Susan Sontag, and Peruvian novelist Mario Vargas Llosa addressed a letter of protest to Castro condemning Stalin-like repression of intellectual freedoms in the island.

Employing his customary convoluted wordplay, Cabrera Infante's extended 1983 article denounced the "tyrant" Fidel Castro and supported the now exiled poet Heberto Padilla. He also laid into Castro's foreign supporters, including Greene, whose 1966 article he labeled "a paean to Castro," summarizing it as "Graham Greene chasing after Fidel Castro all over Cuba." His overriding criticism was that "Greene chose to be inimical to Batista and amicable with Castro." Unfortunately, he committed serious factual mistakes that undermined the case he was trying to make. Apparently, he had arranged "Greene's final meeting with Castro in Cathedral Square" in 1959 and ironed out "censorship problems" with his film. There was truth in the second assertion but not in the first. It was one of several wild claims.[22]

The first published response in the *London Review of Books* came from a black Cuban poet, living in voluntary exile in London. He lambasted a "deliriously self-indulgent/lyrical" article by "a much embittered and out-of-touch man." He accused Cabrera Infante of hailing from Cuba's pre-revolutionary bourgeois cultural elite, resistant to change and blind to the Revolution's cultural achievements.[23]

Greene normally stayed above such noise. He had certainly not involved himself in the controversial Padilla Affair and did not break with the Revolution in the manner of other early supporters. Yet this time the author made a succinct response to Cabrera Infante:

> When one attacks one should get one's facts correct. This Mr. Cabrera has failed to do. I last visited Cuba in 1966 (the only time I encountered Castro) and I met Torrijos for the first time in 1976. I never visited Castro on my way to Panama.[24]

Cabrera Infante's excuse for confusing Carol Reed and Alec Guinness with Greene at Cathedral Square in May 1959 was that "all Englishmen looked alike." He again criticized Greene's "admiration for a cruel and ruthless tyrant." On firmer factual ground, he cited those "shot by firing-squad" at the beginning of the Revolution, as well as its "rampant, blind and total" censorship. Yet he weakened his case once again when he accused Greene of overlooking Cuba's large labor camps for homosexuals as he crisscrossed the island in 1966.[25] It appeared he had only read Greene's first *Telegraph* article that year. UMAP was writ large in the second.

A week after his 1983 meeting with Castro and Greene in Havana, Gabriel García Márquez's Spanish newspaper article also wrongly described a first meeting between the Englishman and Castro in 1959, although in other respects, his version closely resembled Greene's. However, García Márquez's article was more than Cabrera Infante could bear, and the Cuban named for his literary Latin American cousin a long list of compatriot writers living in enforced exile from the island.[26]

It is true that Greene viewed left-wing authoritarian regimes in a much rosier light than their right-wing counterparts. British essayist Christopher Hitchens had an interest in both Greene and in Cuba. He worked as a voluntary *brigadista* on the island in 1968 during his undergraduate studies at Balliol College, Oxford, where Greene had also studied. In fact, Hitchens wrote a new introduction to a Penguin Classics edition of *Our Man in Havana* in 2007. In this and published articles, he struggled to find any consistency in Greene's political posturing, either about Castro and Cuba, or about left-wing regimes elsewhere. He judged Greene conservative, at odds with authority, a dissident Catholic, and reactionary. According to the self-declared polemicist, Greene's most fervent loyalty was to betrayal, and his most eternal attachment to the underdog. In Hitchens's final analysis, while "frenziedly inconsistent . . . on everything else, Greene was unwaveringly hostile to the United States." The most shining example of this was his portrayal of naïve U.S. foreign policy in Vietnam in *The Quiet American*.[27]

Yet there is little anti-Americanism to discern in *Our Man in Havana*. This is odd, considering pervasive economic and cultural

U.S. influence in Cuba prior to the Revolution, and indeed the ubiquitous presence of North Americans when Greene first discovered
Havana as a location and then researched and wrote his story there.
North American characters make only fleeting appearances in his
novel: Mr. Humpelnicker, Harry Morgan, Thomas Earl Parkman Jr.,
and his father, Vincent C. Parkman.

Even Greene's three articles and his personal notes from his time
in post-revolutionary Cuba make little reference to the United States
or foreign policy toward the island. Important exceptions are his
post–Bay of Pigs verse, and criticism of U.S. Catholic Church tirades
against Cuba. Following his Vietnamese novel's characterization of
U.S. policy through quiet American Alden Pyle, and the ensuing criticism for his anti-Americanism stance, it appears Greene studiously
avoided U.S. characters and influences in his Cuban novel.

Where did Greene stand, therefore, on Cuba and the Castro-led
Revolution? He declared himself a friend of Castro and appeared
desperate to meet him, both before and after the Revolution. He
finally satisfied his ambition, twice over. Demonstrating solidarity
with the rebel movement, he interceded to block British arms sales
to Batista shortly before the triumph of the Revolution. He planned
to break the Washington-imposed trade blockade by accompanying
Leyland buses to Cuba in 1964. On the other hand, he denounced
the UMAP camps in print in 1966. Yet one could view this action
as an effort by Greene to help his homosexual Cuban friends and
correct Castro's serious policy mistake. Meanwhile, it is possible
that Greene carried out intelligence-gathering work for SIS in Cuba,
hardly supportive of the Revolution. Although in the light of the
British arms to Batista policy mistake and the Bay of Pigs debacle,
one could be very charitable and view any intelligence as helping
his government gain an informed picture of the island. It is also evident that Greene was very mercenary when it came to foreign travel.
From youth through to old age, he preferred others to finance his
expensive trips to a multitude of destinations.

More generally, trying to identify a consistent thread in Greene's political expression is a fool's errand. In letters to newspaper editors and in interviews until the end of his life in 1991, he was apt to make provocative, contradictory, and diversionary statements. The maverick Catholic pronounced on every subject imaginable. Topics ranged from the 1959 Street Offences Act (and the freedom of prostitutes to solicit clients on London's streets), to his declared preference to live in the USSR rather than the United States, to the British Army's "deep interrogation" of Irish Republican Army prisoners during the Troubles in Northern Ireland.[28] One could conclude it was all a willful attempt to create a smokescreen around his political persona, and distract from his intelligence gathering activities.

CONCLUSION

13

CONCLUSION

Greene's story has an afterlife, as well as a few imitators. These go beyond the frequent "our man"/"our woman" monikers employed by news organizations and diplomatic corps in eternal homage to Greene's title.

For example, John le Carré recognized his debt to Greene in his 1996 novel *The Tailor of Panama*. He conceded that after reading *Our Man in Havana*, "the notion of an intelligence fabricator" never left his head.[1] Cuban "dirty realist" Pedro Juan Gutiérrez reimagined a foreign author's presence in pre-revolutionary Havana in *Our GG in Havana* (2004). The jacket copy to his short novel describe "GG—who may or may not be Graham Greene—arrives in Havana in 1955 in search of a good time." Many of the main protagonist's experiences in the city closely mimic Greene's in Batista's day.

In the world of cinema, Richard Lester's *Cuba* (1979) and Sydney Pollack's *Havana* (1990) share themes with *Our Man in Havana* (both novel and film), as well as Greene's experiences in Cuba.[2] The two films portray capitalist avarice, dictatorial brutality, and rebel heroism in the lead up to the Cuban Revolution, with love affairs that reach consummation in tandem with sociopolitical events. Revolution triumphs on New Year's Eve and pent-up passions spill over like champagne in wild and vengeful scenes of liberation. Storylines of pursuit and conquest of local women by foreign men end when the British and American lead male characters abandon the island, leaving their Cuban love interests to an uncertain future under a new regime.

In Lester's *Cuba*, British military officer and counter-insurgency specialist Major Robert Dapes (played by Sean Connery), with experience in Kenya and Malaya, savors a drink on the rocks as he flies into Havana on a Cubana de Aviación twin-prop airliner. General Bello of Batista's army has hired Dapes to help defeat Castro's rebels. A Cuban army captain and a British embassy official await Dapes at the Havana airport, where the diplomat informs Dapes that the British government is content to support Batista by "flogging him clapped-out old tanks and Leyland buses," summoning up Greene's involvement and near involvement, respectively, with these two British exports to pre- and post-revolutionary Cuba. But he warns the major he is a potential embarrassment to the embassy and should keep a low profile. Paying increasingly less heed to the official, Dapes spots old flame Alexandra Pulido departing the terminal building in a large convertible.

With most Cubans fully on the rebels' side, Dapes realizes the insurrection is beyond the point of no return. Nevertheless, he pursues Alex, and they finally evoke old times when they make love in his hotel. The major travels into the interior with the army and meets a Cuban army officer who collects dead rebels' severed ears for trophies, not unlike Captain Segura and his cigarette case covered in human skin. Dapes begins to despise Batista's amoral rule and switches sides to aid the rebels.

In Pollack's movie *Havana*, Jack Weil (played by Robert Redford) tells us "anything is possible" in the city, just as Greene had in 1958. He sails into the troubled island paradise by ferry to seek out "high-rollers" and play one last big poker game. Through the beautiful Bobby and her husband, Arturo Durand, he learns about Cuba's incipient revolution.[3] Mimicking Captain Segura in Greene's story, Arturo tells Jack there are two classes of people in Batista's Cuba: "the torturable and the non-torturable." Police thugs arrest the Durand couple, and it appears Arturo dies at their hands. During a card game, Jack pays off a corrupt official to seek Bobby's release.

The big poker game is set up, but Bobby's fate distracts Jack. He travels to the heart of conflict in the island's interior, meets up with the now-released Bobby, and they make love in Jack's apartment. He organizes a boat to carry them away from the violence, but then her partner Arturo turns up alive. As revolution erupts with mobs wrecking Havana's casinos and parking meters, Jack accepts his fate and leaves the island alone. The final scene jumps to 1963, with Jack contemplating a sunset in Key West, his departure point for Havana five years earlier. Alas, the ferry no longer sails to communist Cuba.

In common with other foreign productions set in Cuba since *Our Man in Havana*, neither Lester's nor Pollack's films were filmed there. Due to various restrictions, including those of the U.S. government, Pollack shot his movie in Santo Domingo in the Dominican Republic, just like Coppola's Havana scenes in *The Godfather, Part II*. Lester chose Andalusia in southern Spain for his film, using some of the locations scouted by Carol Reed and Graham Greene in late 1958. With similar baroque architecture, Cadiz, Jerez de la Frontera, and Seville stood in for Havana. For the same reason, Cadiz masqueraded as Havana for scenes in the 2002 James Bond film *Die Another Day*, starring Pierce Brosnan and Halle Berry.

Another cinematic trend set by *Our Man in Havana* is rooftop swimming pools. To the soundtrack of a strumming mandolin, Captain Segura inspects a raven-haired female swimming languid backstroke in the opening pool scene of Reed's film. Havana's stunning skyline provides the backdrop. Different commentators have misidentified this high-rise swimming pool, one saying it is the Hotel Capri, while another bizarrely locates the pool at both the Capri and the Habana Hilton.[4] In fact, the irregular, heptagon-shaped pool at the Habana Hilton (now Habana Libre) is at mezzanine level (a glazed terracotta mural by René Portocarrero decorates its interior bar). A topographical analysis of the scene's adjacent buildings and streets identifies it as the roof terrace of the Someillán residential building, opened just two years earlier in 1957 at the intersection of O & 17th Streets in Vedado.

Richard Lester's *Cuba* has ground-level hotel and private swimming pool scenes near its beginning and end. But perhaps the most impressive example of an ivory tower rooftop pool scene begins two minutes into the 1964 film *Soy Cuba* (*I Am Cuba*), shot by Soviet director Mikhail Kalatozov at the Hotel Capri. The noisy pool party is one of several extended sequences in this cinematic critique of pre-revolutionary decadence, foreign imperialism, and inequality on the island. Martin Scorsese and Francis Ford Coppola rescued the black-and-white Soviet-Cuban jewel from obscurity in the 1990s and reissued it. Pool scenes in both Lester's *Cuba* and Kalatozov's *Soy Cuba* highlight the social gulf between the affluent/corrupt and the poor/disadvantaged in Cuba.

As for protagonists in the Reed/Greene film, chameleon-like actor Alec Guinness transformed from poacher—agent Wormold—to gamekeeper, as molehunter George Smiley in the 1979 TV adaptation of John le Carré's Cold War thriller *Tinker, Tailor, Soldier, Spy*. Unlike his performance under Carol Reed's direction exactly twenty years earlier, his assured rendition of bespectacled Smiley attracted wide critical acclaim. To inform his portrayal of a high-ranking SIS spook, he had lunched with Maurice Oldfield alongside John le Carré before filming.[5]

Tragically, U.S. comedian Ernie Kovacs died three years after playing Captain Segura when his Chevrolet Corvair careered into a telephone pole on a wet road. He was trying to light a cigar while driving, following a Beverly Hills party at Hollywood director Billy Wilder's home.[6]

In deciding where in the world to visit and where to set his stories, common features inspired the pleasure-seeking Greene. During his 1963 visit to Cuba, he described to Yvonne Cloetta how he twinned Havana with Brighton in his mind. Both had produced novels—*Our*

Man in Havana and *Brighton Rock*—and offered "the sea, a sense of fun & the unexpected."[7] Their unique cocktail of charms appealed and led him to set stories of intrigue and human failing in both. In their different ways, they afforded convalescence to the writer, of a physical nature in Brighton and a psychological nature in Havana. Both locales also cured his writer's block. After a few aborted attempts, Greene made a definitive start to *Our Man in Havana* in the city's Hotel Sevilla-Biltmore in November 1957. He then wrote and finessed the screenplay for *Our Man in Havana* with Carol Reed in Brighton's Metropole Hotel in late 1958.

The thriller *Brighton Rock* starts with "the holiday crowd" streaming off trains and down the hill from the station to the sea-front beach and promenade. The English south-coast resort's straight promenade has its airy Havana equivalent in the sweeping Malecón. Meanwhile, the "cheerful Bank Holiday crowd" in Havana thronged its Revolution Square for political assembly and a speech by Fidel Castro when Greene visited in 1963.[8]

※

As well as the Cuban Missile Crisis, Greene's Cuban story has another important real-world sequel. After the major terrorist attacks against the United States on September 11, 2001, a political process began that led to the Iraq War two years later. Washington and London alleged that Iraqi dictator Saddam Hussein posed an imminent military threat to the West due to possession of chemical and biological weapons—i.e., weapons of mass destruction (WMDs). But their assessment relied on intelligence supplied by sources later revealed as fabricators. In one instance, Iraqi asylum seeker Rafid Ahmed Alwan al-Janabi—codenamed Curveball—told Western intelligence services the Iraqi dictatorship possessed mobile production facilities for biological agents. Embarrassingly, U.S. secretary of state Colin Powell made a presentation to the UN Security Council shortly before the

invasion of Iraq that included rough color sketches of supposed biological trucks, all drawn by Curveball. Yet it became evident to the
CIA when they finally gained direct access to the agent in March
2004 that his information was unreliable and his reporting a fabri-
cation.[9]

British prime minister Gordon Brown ordered a public inquiry
into his country's involvement in the Iraq War. After many delays, the
2016 Chilcot Inquiry report revealed that SIS had used intelligence
on Saddam Hussein's chemical weapons from another "sub-source"
in June 2003. This subsource denied having supplied the information and SIS concluded he was "a fabricator who had lied from the
outset." His description of chemical agents stored in "spherical glass
containers" appeared to mimic scenes from the 1996 film *The Rock*.
It is evident that SIS had fretted about the damage his false reports
would cause to the intelligence community, particularly his much
publicized but later discredited claim that deployment of chemical
weapons against the West could happen within forty-five minutes, a
falsehood that Prime Minister Tony Blair repeated to Parliament in
September 2002. A dossier published the day after—with a signed
foreword by Blair—repeated the claim. A second dossier published
in February 2003, later labeled the "dodgy dossier," added to people's skepticism, especially after the discovery it contained material
plagiarized from a PhD thesis.[10]

Of course, the ends justified the means for American and British
political leaders who sought a casus belli. They welcomed intelligence
that told them what they needed to hear and suited their agenda
to invade Iraq and topple Saddam Hussein. A poisonous climate of
infighting within the U.S. intelligence community also worked against
clear-headed analysis.[11] Inside the British government, meanwhile,
the relationship between SIS and Defence Intelligence staff was dys-
functional. In normal circumstances, interdepartmental cooperation
and intelligence sharing would have led to second opinions and less
subjective analysis before reaching politicians at the decision-making

stage. However, during the heightened atmosphere leading up to the war, senior intelligence chiefs enjoyed unusually direct access to ministers. Others inside the intelligence system did not have sufficient opportunity to pull the information apart.[12]

In several aspects, therefore, the WMD debacle mimicked Greene's fictional tale about an amateur spy who supplies false intelligence to gullible superiors in London, based on an Atomic Pile vacuum cleaner.[13] This proves that Greene's tale about "concrete platforms and unidentifiable pieces of giant machinery" augured more than just the Cuban Missile Crisis.

Indeed, there is a curious circularity to Greene's experiences in Cuba and his Cuban story. The author properly discovered the island after his deportation from Puerto Rico, due to his former membership of the Communist Party. Havana's capitalist excess enthralled the author and persuaded him to resurrect a spy story and relocate it in the vicious Caribbean city. A revolution then triumphed to send the right-wing U.S.-backed dictator into permanent exile. The Castro-led Revolution soon turned socialist and then communist with Soviet support. The British military hardware exports that Greene had protested against in late 1958 fell into new ownership and helped sink a CIA-backed invasion in the water at the Bay of Pigs in 1961. The United States did not regain control over Cuba. A year and a half later, Wormold's invention of "big military installations under construction" in the mountains of eastern Cuba turned disconcertingly real. The island became the locus of a potentially white-hot Cold War conflagration between Washington and Moscow in the Cuban Missile Crisis. It is likely that the author of the spy fiction satire himself then spied on the communist island for SIS during post–Cuban Revolution visits to the island in the 1960s.

Our Man in Havana satirized bungling British officialdom and decision making. This reflected the preceding Suez Crisis, soon paralleled the British arms to Batista controversy, and resonated again more than four decades later in the buildup to the Iraq War. Of course, Greene worked for different government departments during the Second World War and saw how large bureaucracies reached decisions. He worked for SIS in Africa and in London, witnessing how those in the head office often viewed intelligence from the field in a different light. These experiences aided his accurate portrayal of British intelligence and officialdom. Aspects of *Our Man in Havana* are therefore realistic and prophetic.

When the BBC invited Ian Fleming to review the Greene/Reed film, he chose instead to discuss the wider business of intelligence. He argued that any fictional work about the espionage world had to choose between the incredible or the farcical, and his preference was for the former. He judged that Graham Greene preferred the latter "more truthful" and "modern" approach. His literary contemporary had taken "the splendid myth of centuries and kick[ed] it hilariously downstairs." In fact, Fleming felt the dissembling Wormold was "almost too close to those who served in wartime intelligence to be funny." Evidence presented here demonstrates how aspects of fictional James Wormold and his fabricated intelligence approximate reality, unlike James Bond, the aspirational but implausible shaken-not-stirred figure of Ian Fleming's imagination.[14]

While it is tempting to overplay Greene's clairvoyance, it is clear that various small prophecies in his story—along with the H-bomb-sized prophecy linking vacuum cleaner designs to the Cuban Missile Crisis—amalgamate into a resonant whole of eerie Cold War atmospherics. *Our Man in Havana* mirrors the paranoia of the period and expresses a universal truth about mistakes committed by decision makers when irrationality dominates their thinking. It was paranoia about communism, after all, that resulted in rigid U.S. Immigration rules about former members of the Communist Party. Strict adherence to these rules is what led immigration officials to deport Graham Greene from San Juan in the first place. Yet had this not happened, he would never have written *Our Man in Havana*.

ACKNOWLEDGMENTS

Most of Graham Greene's archives are located an ocean away from his and my home country, making research an expensive undertaking. Without the generous British Studies Fellowship awarded by the Harry Ransom Center at the University of Texas at Austin, I would not have embarked on this fascinating journey in the first place. The Harry Ransom Center's rich collection of Greene archives, its knowledgeable and efficient staff, and the camaraderie of other fellows, provided the perfect research environment in which to commence my detective work.

I mined further rich veins of Greene material during two trips to Washington, DC and Boston, in the pleasant surroundings of the Booth Family Center for Special Collections (Georgetown University Library), and the John J. Burns Library (Boston College). Lisette Motano at Georgetown deserves a special mention. Natalie Baur at the Cuban Heritage Collection (University of Miami) kindly copied key press articles for me that were unobtainable in Cuba itself.

For permission to quote from archives and writing under copyright, I am grateful to the above institutions plus the President and Fellows of Trinity College, and the Bodleian Library, Oxford (The Sutro Papers), to the Graham Greene Estate, the Alec Guinness Estate, the Noël Coward Estate, the Selwyn Lloyd Estate, and the Ernest Hemingway Foundation and Society.

Several Cubans went the extra mile to help me. Estela Rivas at the Hotel Nacional provided invaluable leads when I began knocking on doors in Cuba. These included the late Nydia Sarabia, who was generous with her time on three occasions in Havana. Ernesto Fernández Nogueras, Pablo Armando Fernández, and Natalia Bolívar, also welcomed me into their homes to reminisce about their time alongside Greene. Also in Havana, I am grateful to

Pablo Estrada Rodríguez for ad hoc taxi services, to Maximiliano Trujillo Lemes (Universidad de La Habana) for his advice, and Rogelio Letusé La O for his legwork.

Former newspaper correspondents and Greene acquaintances Bernard Diederich and the late Jay Mallin Sr. answered my email enquiries patiently. Jonathan Wise at the Graham Greene Birthplace Trust generously provided me with copies of the 1963 Greene diary in Havana I had missed at Texas. Also at the Trust, Mike Hill was a constant source of encouragement, and his expertise on Greene enabled me to correct several mistakes in my draft manuscript. Likewise, Yan Christensen answered questions big and small, or put me in touch with those that could. Richard Greene (no relation) has been generously collaborative with his research findings. My uncle Richard Joscelyne read a whole draft of my manuscript and made valuable observations and suggestions. My good friend and ex-colleague James Clifford Kent (Royal Holloway) also gave me expert feedback on my manuscript.

I am indebted to Jens Hentschke (Newcastle University) and Tony Kapcia (University of Nottingham) for their expert guidance during my earlier postgraduate studies. Bernard McGuirk and Mark Millington encouraged my Greene research when it commenced at Nottingham. Colleagues in the Modern Languages Department at the University of Chester have also been supportive.

Michele Rubin at Cornerstones helped me finesse my draft submission package. Kevin O'Connor of the O'Connor Literary Agency in New York has been a model agent, offering insightful feedback on my manuscript. I am very grateful to the excellent team at Pegasus Books in New York, particularly my wise and proficient editor Katie McGuire.

I thank David Freire García of Vigo for his continuing loyalty. I likewise thank my family for their support. In my spiritual Cuban home of Oriente in the east of the island, I am grateful to my own band of rebels: Misclaidy Fernández Lescay, Idalmis Garbey Tallart, Dania López Angulo, and Elianis González Nolasco.

I should not ignore Graham Greene himself, a complex and peripatetic Englishman who left an abundant wealth of written archival material for researchers like me to fathom/puzzle over.

Tollemache Terrace, Chester, UK

ENDNOTES

CHAPTER 1

1 2nd draft of "The Pleasure of Being Deported," 20 Dec. 1973, Graham Greene Collection, Box 26, Folder 4, Harry Ransom Center, The University of Texas at Austin; Graham Greene, *Ways of Escape* (London: Bodley Head, 1980), p. 211.

2 Greene, *Ways of Escape*, p. 240.

3 *Our Man in Havana*. Directed by Carol Reed (screenplay by Graham Greene). Kingsmead Productions: Columbia Pictures, 1959; Our Man in Havana film script (Shepperton Studios, ca. 1960), British Library shelfmark Cup.410.c.68.

4 Norman Sherry, *The Life of Graham Greene: Volume Two, 1939–1955* (London: Jonathan Cape, 1994), p. 109; Michael Shelden, *Graham Greene: The Man Within* (London: Minerva, 1995), pp. 361–62. Brian Wormald later become a Catholic like Greene and Walston.

5 "Addendum from Miss Reid to Mr Greene's letter of 3rd January 1972 . . . ," Box 74, Folder 33, Graham Greene papers, MS.1995.003, John J. Burns Library, Boston College.

6 In Ian Fleming's *Casino Royale* (London: Penguin, 2004 [1953], p. 45), James Bond requests a dry martini with three measures of Gordon's gin, one of vodka, and half a measure of Kina Lillet, shaken very well until ice-cold, and served with a large thin slice of lemon peel. So a dry martini without Martini vermouth, Kina Lillet being a different brand of aromatized wine.

7 Dedication by Grechko, "7.9.85," in *Our Man in Havana* (Harmondsworth: Penguin 1962), p. 6, PR6013.R44 O8 1962, Greene's Library, John J. Burns Library, Boston College.

8 Greene, *Our Man in Havana* (London: Penguin, 2007 [1958]), p. 5.

9 Greene, *Our Man in Havana*, p. 7.

10 Greene, *Our Man in Havana*, p. 58.

11 Greene, *Our Man in Havana*, pp. 95, 74.

12 Greene, *Our Man in Havana*, p. 204.

13 *The Times Literary Supplement*, 10 Oct. 1958, p. 573.

CHAPTER 2

1 Marie-Françoise Allain, *The Other Man: Conversations with Graham Greene* (London: Bodley Head 1983), p. 25; "Double Agent: A Conversation with Graham Greene," written, narrated, and produced by Alan Cooke, Thames Television, 30 Dec. 1975, video at British Film Institute, Stephen St. London W1.

2 Graham Greene, *A Sort of Life* (London: Vintage, 2002 [1971]), p. 60.

3 Greene, *Our Man in Havana*, p. 159.

4 Greene, *A Sort of Life*, p. 41.

5   Greene Panama Diary, 7 Sept. [1977], Graham Greene Papers, Box 1, Folder 11, Booth Family Center for Special Collections, Georgetown University Library, Washington, D.C.

6   Greene, *A Sort of Life*, pp. 86–91.

7   Greene, *A Sort of Life*, pp. 75–76.

8   Greene, *A Sort of Life*, p. 76; "The Graham Greene Trilogy: Part I, England Made Me," directed by Donald Sturrock, BBC TV Arena, 1993.

9   Christopher Burstall, "A Writer at Work," BBC Radio 4, broadcast 14 Aug. 1969, P475W BD 1, British Library Sound Archive.

10   "The Waugh Trilogy: Part I, Bright Young Things," narrated and written by Nicholas Shakespeare, BBC2 TV, 1987.

11   Sherry, *Life of Graham Greene: Volume Two*, p. 134.

12   Sherry, *Life of Graham Greene: Volume Two*, pp. 150–53.

13   In an ironic and tragic reversal of fate, a German shell killed Lieutenant Reginald St. George Lake (1887–1916) outside his battalion headquarters on the penultimate afternoon of the Battle of the Somme—a 141-day battle of attrition and futility on the Western Front in which the British army advanced less than seven miles and failed to achieve its prime objective of breaking the German defensive line. Oxfordshire & Buckinghamshire Light Infantry's 1/4th Battalion War Diary or Intelligence Summary, Martinpuich (Pas-de-Calais, France), Nov 17 (1916), The National Archives of the UK [henceforward: TNA] WO95/2764/1.

14   Graham Greene, "The Revolver in the Corner Cupboard," in *The Lost Childhood, and Other Essays* (London: Penguin, 1962 [1951]), pp. 201–06; "Nigel Lewis interview with Graham Greene, Part I, Antibes, 17–18 April 1982," C829/6, British Library Sound Archive.

15   Greene, *A Sort of Life*, p. 94.

16   Burstall, "A Writer at Work."

17   Greene, *A Sort of Life*, pp. 97–98; Graham Greene, *Journey without Maps* (London: Vintage, 2006 [1936]), p. 24,

18   Sherry, *Life of Graham Greene: Volume Two*, pp. 179–82.

19   Greene, *Ways of Escape*, pp. 70–71; Ian Thomson, "Our Man in Tallinn: Graham Greene's Chance Encounter with a Model Spy," in *Articles of Faith: The Collected Tablet Journalism of Graham Greene* (Oxford: Signal Books, 2006), pp. 165–79; Deborah McDonald and Jeremy Dronfield, *A Very Dangerous Woman: The Lives, Loves and Lies of Russia's Most Seductive Spy* (Richmond: Oneworld, 2015), pp. 317–20.

20   Greene, *Ways of Escape*, pp. 70–71; Thomson, "Our Man in Tallinn," pp. 165–79.

21   David ParkInson (ed.), *Mornings in the Dark: The Graham Greene Film Reader* (Manchester: Carcanet, 1993), p. 234, 449–52. His review in *Night and Day* was dated 28 Oct. 1937; Graham Greene (Clapham Common, London) to Hugh [Greene], 16 Jan. 1938, in Richard Greene (ed.), *Graham Greene: A Life in Letters* (London: Little Brown, 2007), p. 87.

22   Graham Greene, *The Lawless Roads* (London: Penguin, 2006 [1939]), p. 134

23   Greene, *The Lawless Roads*, pp. 109, 118–20, 123–24.

24   Graham Greene, *Getting to Know the General: The Story of an Involvement* (London: Vintage, 2005 [1984]), p. 23.

25   Greene, *The Lawless Roads*, pp. 168, 211–14.

26   Greene, *The Lawless Roads*, pp. 113, 207.

27   Hugh Thomas, *Cuba: Or the Pursuit of Freedom* (London: Eyre & Spottiswoode, 1971), p. 12.

28   "A Mexican Diary," f54 "May 3 [1938]," The Catherine Walston/Graham Greene
     Papers, Box 51, Folder 7, Booth Family Center for Special Collections, Georgetown
     University Library, Washington, D.C.
29   Greene, *The Lawless Roads*, pp. 215–17.
30   Greene, *The Lawless Roads*, pp. 215–17.
31   Greene, *The Lawless Roads*, pp. 180, 201.
32   Judith Adamson, *Graham Greene: The Dangerous Edge: Where Art and Politics
     Meet* (Macmillan: London, 1990), p. 47.
33   "Mexico City" journal, 21 July [1963], Graham Greene Papers, Box 20, Folder 5,
     Harry Ransom Center, The University of Texas at Austin.

CHAPTER 3

1   "The Defenders," f3, Graham Greene Collection, Box 20, Folder 4, Harry Ransom
     Center, The University of Texas at Austin.
2   Lara Feigel, *The Love-charm of Bombs: Restless Lives in the Second World War*
     (London: Bloomsbury Publishing, 2013), pp. 18, 90–91.
3   Malcolm Muggeridge, *Chronicles of Wasted Time: Part 2, The Infernal Grove*
     (London: Fontana, 1975), pp. 78–79, 104.
4   "Paul Vaughan speaks to Graham Greene for Kaleidoscope," n.d., NP6249W TR 1,
     British Library Sound Archive.
5   "Graham Greene in conversation with Ronald Harwood," BBC Radio 4, 12 March
     1975, P1097, British Library Sound Archive; Feigel, *The Love charm of Bombs*, p. 87.
6   Shelden, *The Man Within*, pp. 87–88.
7   Jeremy Lewis, *Shades of Greene: One Generation of an English Family* (London:
     Vintage, 2011), pp. 8–9.
8   Sherry, *Life of Graham Greene: Volume Two*, pp. 496–500.
9   Japanese Naval Attaché (London) to Director of Naval Intelligence (Tokio), No. 2,
     29 Jan. 1934; Japanese Naval Attaché (London) to Director of Naval Intelligence
     (Tokio), No. 7, 16 Feb. 1934, TNA KV 2/636.
10   n.d., TNA KV 2/634 f13A.
11   Minute Sheet, Minute No. 9 by HW, 10 March 1934, TNA KV 2/636.
12   "re: William Herbert GREENE," 15 Aug. 1934, TNA KV 2/634 f25A.
13   "Arthur" [Captain Oka] to [Herbert] Greene (Plumpton, Lewes), 10 Dec. 1934, TNA
     KV 2/634 f62A.
14   Lewis, *Shades of Greene*, pp. 174–80.
15   Herbert Greene, *Secret Agent in Spain* (London: Robert Hale, 1938). For an excellent
     summary of the book, see Michael G. Brennan, *Graham Greene: Political Writer*
     (New York: Palgrave Macmillan, 2016), pp. 47–48.
16   "'I was in the pay of Japan': A Secret Agent Tells His Story to *The Daily Worker*,"
     Daily Worker, 22 Dec. 1937, p. 1.
17   Graham Greene (Clapham Common, London) to Hugh [Greene], 16 Jan. 1938, in
     Richard Greene (ed.), *Graham Greene: A Life in Letters*, p. 87.
18   Memorandum by Roland C. Allen "Interview with Mr. Greene," n.d., TNA KV 2/635 f109A.
19   Letter from Pte. Greene (Huyton Camp, Nr. Liverpool) [no addressee], 9 July 1940,
     TNA KV 2/635 f169A; Letter to Lt. Commander J. F. Anderson, RSNI, War Office,
     26 March 1946, TNA KV 2/635 f227.
20   Minute Sheet [no folio number], minute by F. V. A. Laing, 29 Nov. 1942, TNA KV
     2/635; Police Constable Percy Chapman (East Sussex Constabulary) to The Supt. of
     Police, Lewes, 4 Sept. 1942, TNA KV 2/635 f195A.

21 Memorandum by Courtenay Young, 24 Apr. 1943, f227; Letter to Lt. Commander
    J. F. Anderson, RSNI, War Office, 26 March 1946, TNA KV 2/635 f216A.
22 Graham Greene, *England Made Me* (London: William Heinemann, 1935).
23 Julian Maclaren-Ross, *Memoirs of the Forties* (London: Alan Ross, 1965), p. 16.
24 Julian Maclaren-Ross, *Of Love and Hunger* (London: Penguin, 2002 [1947]), pp. 6–7.
25 *The Spy's Bedside Book. An Anthology edited by Graham Greene and Hugh Greene*
    (London: Rupert Hart-Davis, 1957), p. 31.
26 Herbert Greene, *Secret Agent in Spain*, p. 18.
27 The slightly longer actual front-page report from the *Mid-Sussex Times* (11 Jan.
    1938) also states he was the author of the soon-to-be published *Secret Agent in Spain*,
    that he was found "on the hill near the Plough Inn" and was "making satisfactory
    progress" in hospital.
28 Christopher Hawtree, "Elisabeth Dennys obituary," *Guardian*, 10 Feb. 1999; "The
    Defenders," f5, Graham Greene Collection, Box 20, Folder 4, Harry Ransom Center,
    The University of Texas at Austin.
29 Kim Philby, *My Silent War* (St. Albans: Panther, 1969 [1968]), p. 47.
30 Muggeridge, *Infernal Grove*, p. 124.
31 Allain, *The Other Man*, p. 67.
32 Keith Jeffery, *MI6: The History of the Secret Intelligence Service, 1909–1949*
    (London: Bloomsbury, 2010), pp. 479–80.
33 Greene to Betjeman, 18 Oct. [1941], in Richard Greene (ed.), *A Life in Letters*, pp. 109–10.
34 Sherry, *Life of Graham Greene: Volume Two*, pp. 103–09; Graham Greene, "The
    Soupsweet Land," in *Collected Essays* (London: Bodley Head, 1969), pp. 455–63
    (455–57).
35 Sherry, *Life of Graham Greene: Volume Two*, pp. 150–51; Draft Introduction to
    Our Man in Havana, 1963, Graham Greene Papers, Box 25 Folder 4, Harry Ransom
    Center, The University of Texas at Austin; Greene, "The Soupsweet Land," pp. 458–59.
36 Greene (Freetown, Sierra Leone) to Raymond [Greene], 23 July [1942], in Richard
    Greene (ed.), *A Life in Letters*, pp. 117–18; Graham Greene (Freetown, Sierra
    Leone) to Hugh [Greene], 1 Aug. [1942], in Richard Greene (ed.), *A Life in Letters*,
    p. 119.
37 Greene to Raymond Greene, 4 Jan. [1943], in Richard Greene (ed.), *A Life in Letters*,
    p. 123.
38 "Nigel Lewis interview with Graham Greene, Part II, Antibes, 17–18 April 1982,"
    C829/7, British Library Sound Archive; Greene, "The Soupsweet Land," p. 459.
39 Graham Greene, *In Search of a Character: Two African Journals* (New York: Viking
    Press: 1962), In "II, Convoy to West Africa," p. 91 (footnote 1), Greene tells us that
    Denyse Clairouin died a year later in a German concentration camp after her arrest as
    a British agent.
40 Sherry, *Life of Graham Greene: Volume Two*, pp. 119–20; Greene to Sherry, 27
    Feb. 1991, in Richard Greene (ed.), *A Life in Letters*, pp. 420–22; Greene, "The
    Soupsweet Land," p. 460.
41 Nigel Clive, "Philby, Harold Adrian Russell [Kim] (1912–1988)," rev. Oxford
    Dictionary of National Biography, Oxford University Press, 2004, http://www
    .oxforddnb.com/view/article/40699, accessed 6 Aug 2013.
42 Philby, *My Silent War*, p. 47.
43 Greene to Norman Sherry, 20 March 1991, in Richard Greene (ed.), *A Life in Letters*,
    pp. 422–23.

44   Robert Cecil, "Five of Six at War: Section V of MI6," *Intelligence and National Security* 9, no. 2 (Apr. 1994), pp. 345–53.

45   Nigel West and Oleg Tsarev, *The Crown Jewels: The British Secrets at the Heart of the KGB Archives* (London: HarperCollins, 1998), p. 313.

46   West and Tsarev, *The Crown Jewels*, pp. 219, 312–13.

47   Sherry, *Life of Graham Greene: Volume Two*, p. 171; Anthony Cave Brown, *The Secret Servant: The Life of Sir Stewart Menzies: Churchill's Spymaster* (London: Michael Joseph, 1988), pp. 225–28.

48   "Security in Room 51" by Graham Greene, Graham Greene Papers, Box 30 Folder 1, Harry Ransom Center, The University of Texas at Austin.

49   Greene, *Ways of Escape*, pp. 238–39.

50   F. H. Hinsley and C. A. G. Simkins, *British Intelligence in the Second World War: Vol. 4, Security and Counter-Intelligence* (London: HMSO, 1990), pp. 199–200; Ben Macintyre, *Double Cross: The True Story of the D-Day Spies*, pp. 184–85, 314; Tomás Harris, "Summary of the Garbo Case 1941–1945" in *Garbo: The Spy Who Saved D-Day* (Kew: National Archives, 2004), p. 73.

51   Michael Howard, *British Intelligence in the Second World War: Vol. 5, Strategic Deception* (London: HMSO, 1990), pp. 18–19; Macintyre, *Double Cross*, pp. 21–24; "Appendix II: List of Reference Books on which Bovril based his Lisbon traffic," C. B. Mills to Major F. Foley, 5 May 1942, TNA KV 2/4190 f35A.

52   Howard, *British Intelligence in the Second World War: Vol. 5*, p. 19; Macintyre, *Double Cross*, pp. 77–78; Mark Seaman, "Introduction" in *Garbo: The Spy Who Saved D-Day* (Kew: National Archives, 2004), p. 17; J. C. Masterman, "Twenty Committee," 29 May 1942, TNA KV 2/4191 f89A.

53   "A Summary of the Garbo Case from 1.8.42–28.2.43," Bishop to Hart, 15 March 1943, TNA KV 2/4197 f569; Howard, *British Intelligence in the Second World War: Vol. 5*, pp. 231–33; Macintyre, *Double Cross*, pp. 79, 114, 186, 257; Tomás Harris, "Summary of the Garbo Case 1941–1945," p. 70.

54   Macintyre, *Double Cross*, pp. 116, 315–17; Juan Pujol García and Nigel West, *Operation Garbo: The Personal Story of the Most Successful Spy of World War II* (London: Biteback, 2011), pp. 167–69.

55   Greene, *A Sort of Life*, p. 30.

56   22/23 June, 2/3 July 1944, "During the Second Siege of London," Graham Greene Collection, Box 20 Folder 4, Harry Ransom Center, The University of Texas at Austin.

57   Pujol García and West, *Operation Garbo*, pp. 176–80.

58   Macintyre, *Double Cross*, pp. 174, 343–44. At the denouement of *Our Man in Havana*, MI6 award Wormold an OBE. For more detail on Garbo, see https://www.mi5.gov.uk/agent-garbo.

59   Len Scott, "Human Intelligence," in Rob Dover, Michael Goodman, and Claudia Hillebrand (eds), *Routledge Companion to Intelligence Studies* (Abingdon: Routledge, 2014), pp. 96–104.

CHAPTER 4

1   George Orwell, "You and the Atomic Bomb," *Tribune*, 19 Oct. 1945.

2   Greene, *Our Man in Havana*, p. 6.

3   Philby, *My Silent War*, p. 92.

4   Philby, *My Silent War*, pp. 93–99.

5   "Kim Philby: by Graham Greene," in Philby, *My Silent War*, p. 9.

6   Allain, *The Other Man*, p. 91.
7   Philby, *My Silent War*, p. 13.
8   Greene, *Ways of Escape*, pp. 238–39.
9   Graham Greene, *Nobody to Blame*, pp. 18–22 [included in Graham Greene, *The Tenth Man* (London: Bodley Head, 1985)].
10   Greene, *Nobody to Blame*, pp. 26–30.
11   Greene, *Nobody to Blame*, pp. 28–30.
12   Greene, *Nobody to Blame*, pp. 30–32.
13   Graham Greene, *The Third Man and Other Stories* (London: Collectors Library, 2011 [1950]), p. 19.
14   Shelden, *The Man Within*, pp. 317–21.
15   "The Third Man Music" by Rob White, www.screenonline.org.uk/film/id/591639/index.html; Quentin Falk, *Travels in Greeneland: The Complete Guide to the Cinema of Graham Greene* (London: Reynolds & Hearn, 2000), pp. 67–68.
16   Sherry, *Life of Graham Greene: Volume Two*, pp. 243–49; Greene, *Ways of Escape*, p. 125.
17   Greene, *Ways of Escape*, p. 122.
18   *The Third Man*. Directed by Carol Reed (screenplay by Graham Greene). London Film Productions, 1949.
19   Philip French, "The Third Man Review—A Near-Perfect Work," *Guardian*, 2 Aug. 2015, www.theguardian.com/film/2015/aug/02/the-third-man-review-philip-french.
20   William Cash, *The Third Woman: The Secret Passion that Inspired* The End of the Affair (London: Little, Brown, 2000), pp. 3–14.
21   Evelyn Waugh to Nancy Mitford, 4 Oct. 1948, p. 283; Evelyn Waugh to Ann Fleming, [7 Apr.] 1953, p. 397; Ann Fleming (Dover) to Evelyn Waugh, Good Friday [3 Apr. 1953], p. 126; Mark Amory (ed.), *The Letters of Ann Fleming* (London: Collins, 1985).
22   Email Caroline Bourget to Yan Christensen, 31 May 2018.
23   Cash, *The Third Woman*, p. 21.
24   Editorial note about Graham Greene's relationship with Catherine Walston in Richard Greene (ed.), *A Life in Letters*, pp. 137–38.
25   Sherry, *Life of Graham Greene: Volume Two*, p. 282.
26   Oliver Walston, "The End of the Affair," *The Spectator*, 30 July 1994, p. 15.
27   Greene, *Ways of Escape*, p. 139.
28   Greene (London WC2) to Vivien Greene, 3 June 1948, in Richard Greene (ed.), *A Life in Letters*, p. 159.
29   Undated notes by Gillian Sutro, Papers of Gillian and John Sutro, MS. Eng. c.7234 f35, Department of Special Collections, Bodleian Library, University of Oxford.
30   Rough notes by Gillian Sutro after telephone conversation with Yvonne Cloetta at 9 p.m. on 14 June 1990, MS. Eng. c.7231 f197, Undated notes by Gillian Sutro, Papers of Gillian and John Sutro, MS. Eng. c.7234 f171, Department of Special Collections, Bodleian Library, University of Oxford.
31   A London to New York return fare in 1950 with BOAC was $630 ($6,600 today) in peak season and $466 ($4,900 today) off-peak, when all transatlantic flights were still in a one-class configuration. Charles Woodley, *Golden Age: Commercial Aviation in Britain 1945–1965* (Shrewsbury: Airlife, 1992), p. 43.
32   Undated notes by Gillian Sutro, Papers of Gillian and John Sutro, MS. Eng. c.7263 f192, Department of Special Collections, Bodleian Library, University of Oxford.
33   Shelden, *The Man Within*, pp. 29–32.
34   Frederick Forsyth, *The Outsider: My Life in Intrigue* (London: Transworld, 2015), pp. 226–27.
35   Forsyth, *The Outsider*, p. 335.

36   Graham Greene (C.6 Albany) to Catherine Walston (Newton Hall), Friday
     [postmarked 13 Sept. 1957], The Catherine Walston/Graham Greene Papers, Box 24,
     Folder 13; Graham Greene (Paris) to Lady Walston (Newton Hall), 16 Nov. [1962],
     The Catherine Walston/Graham Greene Papers, Box 34, Folder 14: Booth Family
     Center for Special Collections, Georgetown University Library, Washington, D.C.;
     Shelden, *The Man Within*, pp. 393–94, 424.
37   Yvonne Cloetta, *In Search of a Beginning: My Life with Graham Greene* (London:
     Bloomsbury, 2005), p. 144.
38   Greene, *Ways of Escape*, pp. 147–52.
39   Greene, *Ways of Escape*, pp. 154–62.
40   "Nigel Lewis interview with Graham Greene, Part V, Antibes, 17–18 April 1982,"
     C829/10, British Library Sound Archive.
41   Greene, *Ways of Escape*, pp. 165–6; Burstall, "A Writer at Work."
42   France created the territory of Indochina in 1887 out of its four colonies: Cochin
     China, Annam, Tonkin (all now part of Vietnam), and Cambodia. Laos was added
     in 1893. In the 1954 Geneva Accord the Communists agreed to recognize Laos and
     Cambodia as independent countries and withdraw their forces from both.
43   Greene, *Ways of Escape*, pp. 163–64; Edward W. Said, *Culture and Imperialism*
     (London: Chatto and Windus, 1993), pp. 7–8.
44   Brian Diemert, "The Anti-American: Graham Greene and the Cold War in the
     1950s," in Andrew Hammond (ed.), *Cold War Literature: Writing the Global
     Conflict* (London: Routledge, 2006), pp. 212–25 (p. 220).
45   Greene, *Ways of Escape*, pp. 163–64, 170.
46   Sherry, *Life of Graham Greene: Volume Two*, pp. 463–64.
47   Greene, *Ways of Escape*, pp. 188–91.
48   Verne W. Newton, *The Cambridge Spies: The Untold Story of Maclean, Philby, and
     Burgess in America* (Lanham, MD: Madison Books, 1991), p. 81.
49   Newton, *The Cambridge Spies*, p. 149.
50   Christopher Andrew, *The Defence of the Realm: The Authorized History of MI5*
     (London: Penguin, 2012), pp. 423–24.
51   Greene, *Our Man in Havana*, p. 153.
52   Allain, *The Other Man*, p. 93.
53   Albert Fried (ed.), *McCarthyism: The Great American Red Scare: A Documentary
     History* (New York; Oxford: Oxford University Press, 1997), pp. 85–87.
54   Greene to Mary [Pritchett], 12 Sept. 1952, in Richard Greene (ed.), *A Life in Letters*,
     p. 198.
55   BBC2 TV Newsnight, "Is James Bond's Britishness Part of His Attraction?," 31
     May 2012, www.bbc.co.uk/news/av/entertainment-arts-18281667/is-james-bond-s-
     britishness-part-of-his-attraction.
56   "Eden 'Was on Purple Hearts during Suez Crisis,'" *Independent* (UK), Nov. 2006,
     www.independent.co.uk/news/uk/politics/eden-was-on-purple-hearts-during-suez-
     crisis-6230247.html.
57   Brian Diemert, "The Anti-American: Graham Greene and the Cold War in the 1950s,"
     in Andrew Hammond (ed.), *Cold War Literature: Writing the Global Conflict* (London:
     Routledge, 2006), pp. 212–25 (p. 221); Greene, *Our Man in Havana*, pp. 193–94.

CHAPTER 5

1   Rosalie Schwartz, *Pleasure Island: Tourism and Temptation in Cuba* (Lincoln:
     University of Nebraska Press, 1997), pp. 113–14, 138–39, 182–83.

2   Somerville-Smith, "Cuba: Leyland buses" [memorandum], 8 Feb. 1951, TNA
     FO371/90793 AK1372/4.
3   Holman to Eden, No. 36, 1 Apr. 1954, TNA FO371/108991 AK1016/1.
4   Betty Holman, *Memoirs of a Diplomat's Wife* (York: Wilton 65, 1998), pp. 142–45.
5   Louis A. Pérez Jr., *Cuba: Between Reform and Revolution* (New York: Oxford
     University Press, 2015), pp. 236–37.
6   Helen Lawrenson, "The Sexiest City in the World," *Esquire*, 1 Feb. 1955; Eve
     Arnold, *Eve Arnold: In Retrospect* (London: Sinclair-Stevenson, 1996), pp. 34–38.
7   Ulises Carbó, "Desfile," *Prensa Libre*, 29 Nov. 1955, p. 7.
8   Jon Erickson, "Havana, Police Wink at Vice, and Legalized Gambling Helps to
     Support the Government," *Chicago Tribune Magazine*, 25 Sept. 1955, pp. 34–35.
9   "La Habana, Ciudad Abierta al Vicio y al Juego," *Diario Nacional*, 4 Oct. 1955.
10   Greene (El Rancho Hotel, Pétionville, Port-au-Prince, Haiti) to Catherine Walston,
     23 Aug. 1954, The Catherine Walston/Graham Greene Papers, Box 18 Folders 3,
     4, 7, Booth Family Center for Special Collections, Georgetown University Library,
     Washington, D.C.
11   Greene (El Rancho Hotel, Pétionville, Port-au-Prince, Haiti) to Catherine Walston,
     n.d. [ca23 Aug. 1954], The Catherine Walston/Graham Greene Papers, Box 18
     Folder 7, Booth Family Center for Special Collections, Georgetown University
     Library, Washington, D.C.; Journal—Haiti and Havana, 21 Aug.–3 Sept. 1954,
     Graham Greene Papers, Box 1, Folder 5, Booth Family Center for Special Collections,
     Georgetown University Library, Washington, D.C.
12   Ibid.
13   "Adultery Can Lead to Sainthood," 29 Oct. 1951, *Time* magazine interview.
14   Greene, *Ways of Escape*, pp. 210–11; Shelden, *The Man Within*, pp. 395–96
     (including extracts from *New Statesman*, 22 Nov. 1952, and *New Republic*, 22 Nov.
     1952); Norman Sherry, *The Life of Graham Greene: Volume Three, 1955–1991*
     (Jonathan Cape: London, 2004), p. 14.
15   Greene (El Rancho Hotel) to Catherine Walston, 30 Aug. 1954, The Catherine
     Walston/Graham Greene Papers, Box 18, Folder 5, Booth Family Center for Special
     Collections, Georgetown University Library, Washington, D.C.
16   Greene, *Ways of Escape*, pp. 210–13; Edward Scott, "U.S. Shows Red Light for
     Greene," *Havana Post*, 2 Sept. 1954, p. 4. Greene was twenty years old, not nineteen,
     when he joined the Communist Party in January 1925.
17   Shelden, *The Man Within*, pp. 395–97; Greene to Natasha and Peter [Brook] (244
     East 49th Street, NY), 6 Sept. 1954, Box 12, Folder 70, Graham Greene papers,
     MS.1995.003, John J. Burns Library, Boston College; Journal—Haiti and Havana,
     30 Aug. 1954, Graham Greene Papers, Box 12, Folder 5, Booth Family Center for
     Special Collections, Georgetown University Library, Washington, D.C.
18   Greene, *Ways of Escape*, pp. 211–14. An FBI Radiogram from San Juan on 31 Aug.
     1954 details these events (see final page): http://investigatingtheterror.com/documents/
     files/greene%201.pdf.
19   Greene, *Ways of Escape*, pp. 211–14; Bernard Diederich, *Seeds of Fiction: Graham
     Greene's Adventures in Haiti and Central America, 1954–1983* (London: Peter
     Owen, 2012), p. 88; Bernard Diederich, email to author, 10 May 2013; 2nd draft of
     "The Pleasure of Being Deported," 20 Dec. 1973, Graham Greene Collection, Box
     26 Folder 4, Harry Ransom Center, The University of Texas at Austin. While Greene
     stated in his autobiography that the flight's final destination was Miami, *The Official*

Airline Guide 10, no. 11 (Aug. 1954) makes it clear that the routing for this Delta flight was San Juan > Ciudad Trujillo > Port-au-Prince > Havana > New Orleans. Greene's recollection of exactly what happened in Haiti changed three decades later. See "Freedom of Information," *Spectator*, 7 Apr. 1984, in Graham Greene, *Reflections* (London, 1991), pp. 303–05. He wrote that he "refused to leave the plane when it reached Haiti and flew on free of charge to Havana."

20   Greene, *Ways of Escape*, pp. 215–16.

21   "Novelist Sent Back by U.S.: Puerto Rico Bans Graham Greene," 1 Sept. 1954, *Daily Telegraph*, p. 1.

22   Greene, *Ways of Escape*, pp. 215–16.

23   Greene, *Our Man in Havana*, p. 53.

24   *Our Man in Havana* film script (Shepperton Studios, ca. 1960), British Library shelfmark Cup.410.c.68.

25   Lars Schoultz, *That Infernal Little Cuban Republic: The United States and the Cuban Revolution* (Chapel Hill: University of North Carolina Press, 2009), pp. 16–18.

26   Luis Martínez-Fernández, *Revolutionary Cuba: A History* (Gainesville: University Press of Florida, 2014), pp. 24–25.

27   Greene, *Ways of Escape*, p. 240.

28   Oliver to Lloyd, No. 64, "Political Situation in Cuba," 29 May 1956, TNA FO533/10 AK1015/21; "Former Cuban Officer Esteban Ventura Novo Dies," *Miami Herald*, 23 May 2001.

29   *Havana Post*, 1 Sept. 1954, p. 1.

30   Fulgencio Batista, *The Growth and Decline of the Cuban Republic* (New York: Devin Adair, 1964), p. 194.

31   Claudia Lightfoot, *Havana: A Literary and Cultural Companion* (Oxford: Signal, 2002), p. 125.

32   "Havana Journal," 8 Nov. 1957, Graham Greene Papers, Box 1, Folder 8, Booth Family Center for Special Collections, Georgetown University Library, Washington, D.C.

33   John Dorschner and Roberto Fabricio, *The Winds of December* (London: Macmillan, 1980), p. 15.

34   Ted Scott obituary by Don Grady, *Evening Post* (New York), 2 Nov. 1989, p. 7; "Deported Editor Calls Panama President U.S. Foe," Feb. 5, 1941, *New York World-Telegram & Sun Collection*, Library of Congress Prints & Photographs Division, Washington, DC.

35   Ted Scott obituary by Don Grady, *Evening Post* (New York), 2 Nov. 1989, p. 7; Bill Macdonald, *The True Intrepid: Sir William Stephenson and the Unknown Agents* (Vancouver: Raincoast, 2001), p. 201; Matthew Parker, *Goldeneye: Where Bond Was Born: Ian Fleming's Jamaica* (London: Windmill, 2014), p. 22.

36   Lewis's biographer tells us his subject claimed to have seen Greene in the Sevilla-Biltmore's ground-floor bar in December 1957, yet his fellow writer had departed the island on November 21. *The Sunday Times* published two articles by Lewis in April 1959 about the early months of Castro's Revolution, yet the same biography doubts he even traveled to Cuba that year, instead basing them on what he had seen in 1957. Julian Evans, *Semi-Invisible Man: The Life of Norman Lewis* (London: Jonathan Cape, 2008), p. 441, 448.

37   "A Mission to Havana," in Norman Lewis, *A View of the World: Selected Journalism* (London: Eland, 1986), pp. 247–58.

38   "Interesting *if* True: A Lion There Was" by Edward Scott, *Havana Post*, 24 July

1954, p. 4; Ernest Hemingway (Finca Vigia, San Francisco de Paula, La Habana) to Ed [Scott], 24 July 1954, Box OC10 Ernest Hemingway Collection: Personal Papers, John F. Kennedy Presidential Library, Boston, MA.

39   "Interesting *if* True: Frailty, They Name Ain't . . ." by Edward Scott, *Havana Post*, 20 Aug. 1954, p. 4; Ernest Hemingway (Finca Vigia, San Francisco de Paula, La Habana) to Mr [Edward] Scott, 20 Aug. 1954, Box OC10 Ernest Hemingway Collection: Personal Papers, John F. Kennedy Presidential Library, Boston, MA.

40   "U.S. Shows Red Light for Greene," *Havana Post*, 2 Sept. 1954, p. 4. Greene actually joined the Communist Party in January 1925.

41   Journal—Haiti and Havana, 31 Aug. 1954, Graham Greene Papers, Box 1, Folder 5, Booth Family Center for Special Collections, Georgetown University Library, Washington, D.C.

42   Greene (Colour postcard with glitter of "HAVANA: MARTI OR PRADO PROMENADE THE SEVILLA BILTMORE—HAVANA, CUBA) to Catherine Walston (n.d.), The Catherine Walston/Graham Greene Papers, Box 18, Folder 27, Booth Family Center for Special Collections, Georgetown University Library, Washington, D.C.

43   Greene, *The Lawless Roads*, p. 61.

44   Greene to Natasha and Peter [Brook] (244 East 49th Street, NY), 6 Sept. 1954, Box 12, Folder 70, Graham Greene papers, MS.1995.003, John J. Burns Library, Boston College.

45   Journal—Haiti and Havana, 1 Sept. 1954, Graham Greene Papers, Box 1, Folder 5, Booth Family Center for Special Collections, Georgetown University Library, Washington, D.C.; "British Author Reserves Passage on KLM for London," *Havana Post*, 2 Sept. 1954, p. 1; Greene, *A Sort of Life*, p. 57.

46   Rosa Lowinger and Ofelia Fox, *Tropicana Nights: The Life and Times of the Legendary Cuban Nightclub* (Los Angeles: In Situ, 2016), p. 387.

47   *Our Man in Havana* composite holograph and typescript draft with author revisions, Graham Greene Collection, Box 25, Folder 6. Harry Ransom Center, The University of Texas at Austin.

48   BBC website, Witness: "Sixties Soho's Dancing Nudes," 15 Nov. 2017. www.bbc .co.uk/news/av/magazine-41987825/sixties-soho-s-dancing-nudes.

49   Muggeridge, *The Infernal Grove*, p. 109.

50   "Double Agent: A Conversation with Graham Greene," written, narrated, and produced by Alan Cooke, Thames Television, 30 Dec. 1975, video at British Film Institute, Stephen St, London W1.

51   Dick Cluster and Rafael Hernández, *The History of Havana* (Basingstoke: Palgrave Macmillan, 2006), 8, 195.

52   *Our Man in Havana* screenplay Tms/mimeo, f78, Graham Greene Collection, Box 26, Folder 3, Harry Ransom Center, The University of Texas at Austin. The reference to non-Cuban blacks is probably to British West Indians living/working in the island.

53   Greene to Natasha and Peter [Brook] (244 East 49th Street, NY), 6 Sept. 1954, Box 12, Folder 70, Graham Greene papers, MS.1995.003, John J. Burns Library, Boston College.

54   Carlos Franqui, *Family Portrait with Fidel* (London: Cape, 1983), p. 139.

55   Journal—Haiti and Havana, 2 Sept. 1954, Graham Greene Papers, Box 1, Folder 5, Booth Family Center for Special Collections, Georgetown University Library, Washington, D.C.

56   Journal—Haiti and Havana, 2 Sept. 1954, Graham Greene Papers, Box 1, Folder

5, Booth Family Center for Special Collections, Georgetown University Library, Washington, D.C.

57   "Thank You, America for Throwing Me Out Says Graham Greene," *Daily Express*, 4 Sept. 1954, p. 2.

58   "Irked U.K. Author Here on Unscheduled Visit," *Montreal Star*, 3 Sept. 1954, p. 1.

59   "Greene 'Thanks' U.S.," *New York Times*, 4 Sept. 1954, p. 2.

60   Journal—Haiti and Havana, 3 Sept. 1954, Graham Greene Papers, Box 1, Folder 5, Booth Family Center for Special Collections, Georgetown University Library, Washington, D.C.; "GREENE op Schiphol na Amerikaans anontuur," *de Volkskrant*, 4 Sept. 1954, p. 3; "Thank You, America for Throwing Me Out Says Graham Greene," *Daily Express*, 4 Sept. 1954, p. 2.

61   Greene (C.6 Albany) to Natasha and Peter [Brook], 27 Sept. 1954, Box 12, Folder 70, Graham Greene papers, MS.1995.003, John J. Burns Library, Boston College.

62   Greene to Catherine Walston (Newton, Cambridge), 19 Sept. 1954, The Catherine Walston/Graham Greene Papers, Box 18, Folder 10, Booth Family Center for Special Collections, Georgetown University Library, Washington, D.C.

63   Graham Greene Passports 1951–77, Box 81, Graham Greene papers, MS.1995.003, John J. Burns Library, Boston College. The stiff passport also contains a three-month visa for Haiti from the country's London embassy on 22 October. His entry stamp for Jamaica is dated 30 Oct. 1954, and his Haiti stamp is dated 20 Nov. 1954, indicating a three-week stay in Jamaica followed by three nights in Haiti.

64   Greene, *Ways of Escape*, pp. 241–42.

65   Greene (C.6 Albany) to Natasha [Brook], 2 Dec. 1954, Graham Greene Papers, Box 12, Folder 70, Graham Greene papers, MS.1995.003, John J. Burns Library, Boston College.

66   For an in-depth study of Superman in Havana, see http://roadsandkingdoms .com/2015/superman-of-havana.

67   *The Godfather, Part II*. Directed by Francis Ford Coppola. Paramount Pictures Corp: The Coppola Company, 1974.

68   Greene mentioned "her" in reference to the friend who accompanied him to Havana, inhaling what they thought was cocaine in their hotel room. See Allain, *The Other Man*, p. 59.

69   The establishment had originally opened as "La Piña de Plata" (The Silver Pineapple) in 1817. Lightfoot, *Havana: A Literary and Cultural Companion*, p. 97.

70   John Pearson, *The Life of Ian Fleming, Creator of James Bond* (London: Cape, 1966), p. 395.

71   Diary entry, 25 Nov. 1956, in Graham Payn and Sheridan Morley (eds.), *The Noël Coward Diaries* (London: Macmillan, 1982), pp. 337–38.

CHAPTER 6

1   Graham Greene (The Royal Albion, Brighton) to Catherine Walston (Newton Hall, Cambridge), 31 August 1956, The Catherine Walston/Graham Greene Papers, Box 22, Folder 4, Booth Family Center for Special Collections, Georgetown University Library, Washington, D.C.

2   Only a month before definitively beginning the novel in Havana, he dined with Michael Anderson, director of *The Dam Busters* (1955), *1984* (1956), and *Around the World in 80 Days* (1956), and stated to Catherine, "Name of film 'Our Man in Havana.'" Greene (C.6 Albany) to Catherine Walston (Newton, Cambridge), Sunday

[6 Oct. 1957], The Catherine Walston/Graham Greene Papers, Box 24, Folder 17, Booth Family Center for Special Collections, Georgetown University Library, Washington, D.C.

3   Greene (C.6. Albany) to René de Berval, 8 Oct. 1956, Box 11, Folder 82; Graham Greene passport (issued 10 Sept. 1954), p. 10, Box 81: Graham Greene papers, MS.1995.003, John J. Burns Library, Boston College; email from Oliver Walston (son) to author, 16 Oct. 2014.

4   Greene, *In Search of a Character: Two African Journals*, p. 19.

5   Graham Greene (Calgary, Alberta, Canada) to Catherine Walston (Newton Hall, Cambridge), 27 Dec. 1956, Box 22, Folder 15; Graham Greene (Hotel Algonquin, New York) to Catherine Walston (Newton Hall), 11 Jan. 1957, Box 23, Folder 4; Graham Greene (C.6 Albany, London) to Catherine Walston (Glitter Bay, St. James, Barbados), 1 Feb. (1957), Box 23, Folder 8: The Catherine Walston/Graham Greene Papers, Booth Family Center for Special Collections, Georgetown University Library, Washington, D.C.

6   Graham Greene (C.6 Albany, London) to Catherine Walston (Newton Hall, Cambridge), n.d. (postmarked 19 June 1957), Box 23, Folder 31: The Catherine Walston/Graham Greene Papers, Booth Family Center for Special Collections, Georgetown University Library, Washington, D.C.

7   Graham Greene (C.6 Albany) to Catherine Walston (St. Anne's Bay, Jamaica), n.d. (postmarked 27 Feb. 1957), The Catherine Walston/Graham Greene Papers, Box 23, Folder 11, Booth Family Center for Special Collections, Georgetown University Library, Washington, D.C.

8   Graham Greene (Martinique) to Catherine Walston (Marquis Estate, St Lucia), 18 July 1957, Box 24, Folder 5; Graham Greene (Hôtel du Vieux Moulin, Martinique) to Catherine Walston (Newton Hall, Cambridge), 27 July 1957, Box 24, Folder 6: The Catherine Walston/Graham Greene Papers, Booth Family Center for Special Collections, Georgetown University Library, Washington, D.C. What made Greene feel worse was that Catherine was present in the Caribbean, and even in Martinique for a few days at the same time.

9   Greene was a frequent visitor to the ancient house Stonor Park in the Chiltern Hills. Following the Reformation, the Stonors had been one of the great British Catholic families. See Cash, *The Third Woman*, pp. 313–14.

10   "Introducing the Hostess," 27 May 1953, *Daily Express*, p. 3; Greene to Dr. Mendoza (Cuban Embassy, London W2), 21 Oct. 1957, Box 28, Folder 15, Graham Greene papers, MS.1995.003, John J. Burns Library, Boston College.

11   Roberto de Mendoza (Cuban Embassy, London W2) to Greene, 22 Oct. 1957, Box 28, Folder 15, Graham Greene papers, MS.1995.003, John J. Burns Library, Boston College.

12   Greene (Greene-Park Ranch, Cochrane, Alberta) to Mrs John Sutro (London SW1), 4 Dec. 1957, Papers of Gillian and John Sutro, MS. Eng. C. 7227 f43, Department of Special Collections, Bodleian Library, University of Oxford.

13   "Havana Journal," 7 Nov. 1957, Graham Greene Papers, Box 1, Folder 8, Booth Family Center for Special Collections, Georgetown University Library, Washington, D.C.

14   "Havana Journal," 7 Nov. 1957, Graham Greene Papers, Box 1, Folder 8, Booth Family Center for Special Collections, Georgetown University Library, Washington, D.C.

15   Greene, *Our Man in Havana*, p. 12.

16   "Havana Journal," 8 Nov. 1957, Graham Greene Papers, Box 1, Folder 8, Booth

Family Center for Special Collections, Georgetown University Library, Washington, D.C.

17 Greene (Hotel Sevilla-Biltmore, Havana) to Catherine Walston (Newton, Cambridge), Nov. 8 [1957], The Catherine Walston/Graham Greene Papers, Box 24, Folder 22, Booth Family Center for Special Collections, Georgetown University Library, Washington, D.C.
    Due to a misreading of this letter, biographer Norman Sherry (*The Life of Graham Greene: Volume Three*, pp. 93–94) asserts incorrectly that Anita Björk accompanied Greene to Havana.

18 Greene (Hotel Sevilla-Biltmore, Havana) to Catherine Walston (Newton, Cambridge), Nov. 8 [1957], The Catherine Walston/Graham Greene Papers, Box 24, Folder 22, Booth Family Center for Special Collections, Georgetown University Library, Washington, D.C.

19 "Havana Journal," 8 Nov. 1957, Graham Greene Papers, Box 1, Folder 8, Booth Family Center for Special Collections, Georgetown University Library, Washington, D.C.

20 The refurbished and expanded Grand Packard Hotel reopened on the Paseo del Prado in 2018, standing shoulder to shoulder with the narrower Edificio Bolívar on a neighbouring street.

21 Fordham to Selwyn Lloyd (Foreign Secretary, London), No. 28, 20 March 1957, TNA FO533/11 AK1015/13; Ramón L. Bonachea and Marta San Martín, *The Cuban Insurrection, 1952–1959* (New Brunswick, NJ: Transaction, 1974), p. 114, 119–20; R. Hart Phillips, *Cuba: Island of Paradox* (New York: McDowell Obolensky, n.d.), p. 306.

22 Greene, *Our Man in Havana*, p. 21.

23 "Mr. Graham Greene Honor Guest at British Embassy Luncheon," *Havana Post*, 15 Nov. 1957, p. 3.

24 "Havana Journal," 8 Nov. 1957, Graham Greene Papers, Box 1, Folder 8, Booth Family Center for Special Collections, Georgetown University Library, Washington, D.C.

25 Fordham to Selwyn Lloyd (Foreign Secretary, London), No. 28, 20 March 1957, TNA FO533/11 AK1015/13.

26 "Havana Journal," 8 Nov. 1957, Graham Greene Papers, Box 1, Folder 8, Booth Family Center for Special Collections, Georgetown University Library, Washington, D.C.

27 "Havana Journal," 8 Nov. 1957, Graham Greene Papers, Box 1, Folder 8, Booth Family Center for Special Collections, Georgetown University Library, Washington, D.C.

28 Greene annotations (n.d.) in Stendhal, *On Love* (Garden City, NY: Doubleday, 1957), HQ21.B6 1957, Greene's Library, John J. Burns Library, Boston College.

29 Graham Greene, *Our Man in Havana*, p. 113.

30 "Havana Journal," 8 Nov. 1957, Graham Greene Papers, Box 1, Folder 8, Booth Family Center for Special Collections, Georgetown University Library, Washington, D.C.

31 "Havana Journal," 8 Nov. 1957, Graham Greene Papers, Box 1, Folder 8, Booth Family Center for Special Collections, Georgetown University Library, Washington, D.C.

32 Allain, *The Other Man*, p. 59.

33 Greene, *Ways of Escape*, p. 242.

34 "Havana Journal," 8 Nov. 1957, Graham Greene Papers, Box 1, Folder 8, Booth Family Center for Special Collections, Georgetown University Library, Washington, D.C.

35 "Havana Journal," 10 [*sic*: 9] Nov. 1957, Graham Greene Papers, Box 1, Folder 8, Booth Family Center for Special Collections, Georgetown University Library, Washington, D.C.

36 Ibid.

37 Greene, *Our Man in Havana*, p. 36.

38 *Our Man in Havana* film script (Shepperton Studios, ca. 1960), British Library shelfmark Cup.410.c.68.

39 "Havana Journal," 10 [*sic*: 9] Nov. 1957, Graham Greene Papers, Box 1, Folder 8, Booth Family Center for Special Collections, Georgetown University Library, Washington, D.C.

40 "Havana Journal," 10 [*sic*: 9] Nov. 1957, Graham Greene Papers, Box 1, Folder 8, Booth Family Center for Special Collections, Georgetown University Library, Washington, D.C.

41 "Havana Journal," 10 Nov. 1957, Graham Greene Papers, Box 1, Folder 8, Booth Family Center for Special Collections, Georgetown University Library, Washington, D.C.; Greene, *Our Man in Havana*, p. 12.

42 It was a significant coincidence if Greene saw Mass at the Santo Angel Convent, because this was a key location in Cuba's classic nineteenth-century novel *Cecilia Valdés or El Angel Hill*. Set in 1830s Havana, main character Cecilia Valdés is a beautiful fair-skinned *mulata* pursued by the son of a slave owner. Yet both Cecilia and her suitor are unaware they share the same father. Unwittingly, therefore, the main female character of Greene's novel has a plausible literary connection with Cuba's most renowned literary female character and novel. Cirilo Villaverde, *Cecilia Valdés or El Angel Hill* (Oxford: Oxford University Press, 2005) (translated from the Spanish by Helen Lane).

43 "Havana Journal," 10 Nov. 1957, Graham Greene Papers, Box 1, Folder 8, Booth Family Center for Special Collections, Georgetown University Library, Washington, D.C.; Greene, *Our Man in Havana*, p. 21.

44 "Havana Journal," 10 Nov. 1957, Graham Greene Papers, Box 1, Folder 8, Booth Family Center for Special Collections, Georgetown University Library, Washington, D.C.

45 Peter C. Whybrow, *A Mood Apart: Depression, Mania, and Other Afflictions of the Self* (New York: Basic Books, 1997), pp. 106–07.

46 "Havana Journal," 11 Nov. 1957, Graham Greene Papers, Box 1, Folder 8, Booth Family Center for Special Collections, Georgetown University Library, Washington, D.C.; Greene, *Our Man in Havana*, p. 112; Greene (Hotel Sevilla-Biltmore, Havana) to Catherine Walston (Newton, Cambridge), Nov. 8 [1957], The Catherine Walston/ Graham Greene Papers, Box 24, Folder 22, Booth Family Center for Special Collections, Georgetown University Library, Washington, D.C. Greene annotations (n.d.) in Stendhal, *On Love* (Garden City, NY: Doubleday, 1957), HQ21.B6 1957, Greene's Library, John J. Burns Library, Boston College.

47 "Havana Journal," 11 Nov. 1957, Graham Greene Papers, Box 1, Folder 8, Booth Family Center for Special Collections, Georgetown University Library, Washington, D.C.; Greene annotations (n.d.) in Stendhal, *On Love* (Garden City, NY: Doubleday, 1957), HQ21.B6 1957, Greene's Library, John J. Burns Library, Boston College.

48 Author interview with Natalia Bolívar and Nydia Sarabia, Playa, Havana, 9 January 2012. For more detail see Mark Gollom, "Natalia Bolivar, 82, Unsentimental about Role in Cuban Revolution," CBC News, 4 Dec. 2016, www.cbc.ca/news/world/natalia-bolivar-cuban-revolution-women-1.3877753.

49 "Havana Journal," 11 Nov. 1957, Graham Greene Papers, Box 1, Folder 8, Booth Family Center for Special Collections, Georgetown University Library, Washington, D.C.

50 Hermes Mallea, *Great Houses of Havana: A Century of Cuban Style* (New York: Monacelli Press, 2011), p. 85.

51 "Havana Journal," 11 Nov. 1957, Graham Greene Papers, Box 1, Folder 8, Booth Family Center for Special Collections, Georgetown University Library, Washington, D.C.

52 Greene (Trinidad, Cuba) to s.n, 12 Nov. [1957], Papers of Gillian and John Sutro, MS. Eng. C. 7227 f67, Department of Special Collections, Bodleian Library, University of Oxford.

53 "Havana Journal," 12 Nov. 1957, Graham Greene Papers, Box 1, Folder 8, Booth Family Center for Special Collections, Georgetown University Library, Washington, D.C.; Jay Mallin Sr. e-mail to author, 22 May 2013.

54 Anthony DePalma, *The Man Who Invented Fidel: Cuba, Castro, and Herbert L. Matthews* of The New York Times (New York: Public Affairs, 2006), pp. 36–37.

55 Greene, *Ways of Escape*, p. 241.

56 Samuel Farber, "Cuba before the Revolution," 9 June 2015, www.jacobinmag .com/2015/09/cuban-revolution-fidel-castro-casinos-batista; Luis Salas, *Social Control and Deviance in Cuba* (New York: Praeger, 1979), p. 64.

57 Typescript version of Introduction (to *Our Man in Havana*) with holograph author revisions, 1963, Graham Greene Collection, Box 25 Folder 4, Harry Ransom Center, The University of Texas at Austin.

58 Interview with Natalia Bolívar, Playa, Havana, 9 January 2012; Bonachea and San Martín, *The Cuban Insurrection, 1952–1959*, p. 175.

59 Author interview with Nydia Sarabia (Vedado, La Habana), 7 Jan. 2012; Nydia Sarabia, "El Equivocado Graham Greene," *Revolución* (La Habana), 6 Mar. 1959, p. 2.

60 Sarabia, "El Equivocado Graham Greene"; Greene, *Ways of Escape*, p. 244.

61 Greene, *Ways of Escape*, pp. 243–44.

62 Thomas G. Paterson, *Contesting Castro: The United States and the Triumph of the Cuban Revolution* (New York: Oxford University Press, 1994), pp. 88–92.

63 The younger brother of Frank País—another urban guerrilla in the same movement—had been killed by Batista's forces a month earlier.

64 Paterson, *Contesting Castro*, pp. 94–96.

65 Greene, *Ways of Escape*, p. 244.

66 Gallienne (British Embassy, Havana) to H. Macmillan (Foreign Secretary, London), No. 76, "Cuba: Heads of Foreign Missions," 3 June 1955, TNA FO533/9 AK1902/1.

67 "Del Caso Lojendio al por qué No Te Callas: Precedentes de Crisis Diplomáticas," 26 Jan. 2018, *El País* (Madrid, Spain). https://elpais.com/politica/2018/01/26/actualidad/1516993219_211689.html

68 American Consulate (Santiago de Cuba) confidential despatch No. 26 to Department of State, November 25, 1957, NARA RG59 1956–1959 Central Decimal File, Box 3077, 737.00/12-457; Vilma Espín, quoted in Lois M. Smith and Alfred Padula, *Sex and Revolution: Women in Socialist Cuba* (New York: Oxford University Press, 1996), p. 27.

69 Sarabia, "El Equivocado Graham Greene."

70 Greene, *Ways of Escape*, pp. 244–45.

71 Sarabia, "El Equivocado Graham Greene."

72 Greene, *Ways of Escape*, p. 245.

73 Greene, *Our Man in Havana*, p. 63.

74 Greene, *Ways of Escape*, p. 244.

75 Sarabia, "El Equivocado Graham Greene."

76 Greene, *Ways of Escape*, pp. 245–46.

77   Jay Mallin Sr. email to author, 12 June 2013.
78   Greene, *Ways of Escape*, p. 246.
79   Author interview with Nydia Sarabia (Vedado, La Habana), 7 Jan. 2012.
80   Julia E. Sweig, *Inside the Cuban Revolution: Fidel Castro and the Urban Underground* (Cambridge, MA: Harvard University Press, 2002), p. 54.
81   Author interview with Sarabia, 7 Jan. 2012.
82   Sarabia, "El Equivocado Graham Greene."
83   Greene, *Ways of Escape*, p. 247.
84   Patricia Calvo González, "La Sierra Maestra en las Rotativas. El Papel de la Dimensión Pública en la Etapa Insurreccional Cubana (1953–1958)" (PhD thesis, Universidade de Santiago de Compostela, Spain, 2014), 218, 327.
85   Sweig, *Inside the Cuban Revolution*, pp. 14, 78; Author interview with Sarabia, 7 Jan. 2012.
86   Mallin email to author, 14 June 2013; Sarabia, "El Equivocado Graham Greene."
87   William Shakespeare, *The Comedy of Errors* (1594), Act 3, Scene 2.
88   Author interview with Sarabia, Vedado, Havana, 7 Jan. 2012; Author interview with Natalia Bolívar and Nydia Sarabia (Playa, La Habana), 9 Jan. 2012.

CHAPTER 7

1   Greene (Greene-Park Ranch, Cochrane, Alberta) to Catherine Walston (Newton, Cambridge), 7 Dec. 1957, The Catherine Walston/Graham Greene Papers, Box 24, Folder 23, Booth Family Center for Special Collections, Georgetown University Library, Washington, D.C.; Graham Greene (Greene-Park Ranch, Cochrane, Alberta) to Mrs. John Sutro (London SW1), 4 Dec. 1957, Papers of Gillian and John Sutro, MS. Eng. C. 7227 f43, Department of Special Collections, Bodleian Library, University of Oxford; Greene (Greene-Park Ranch, Cochrane, Alberta) to Catherine Walston (Newton, Cambridge), 23 Dec. 1957, The Catherine Walston/Graham Greene Papers, Box 24, Folder 24, Booth Family Center for Special Collections, Georgetown University Library, Washington, D.C.
2   Greene (C.6 Albany) to Catherine (Newton, Cambridge), n.d. [postmarked London W1, 15 Jan. 1958], Georgetown, Box 25, Folder 4; Greene (C.6 Albany) to Catherine Walston (St. Lucia, BWI), 4 Feb. 1958, Box 25, Folder 5: The Catherine Walston/Graham Greene Papers, Booth Family Center for Special Collections, Georgetown University Library, Washington, D.C.
3   Norman Sherry, *The Life of Graham Greene: Volume Three*, pp. 97, 101, 105.
4   Greene (C.6 Albany) to Catherine Walston (Newton, Cambridge), 25 Feb. 1958, The Catherine Walston/Graham Greene Papers, Box 25, Folder 10, Booth Family Center for Special Collections, Georgetown University Library, Washington, D.C.
5   Francis Greene (C.6 Albany) to Graham Greene, 24 Nov. 1957; Graham Greene to Francis Greene, 22 May 1958: Box 8, Folder 3, Graham Greene papers, MS.1995.003, John J. Burns Library, Boston College.
6   Greene, *Our Man in Havana*, p. 102.
7   *Our Man in Havana* holograph draft with author revisions and inserts; and composite holograph and typescript draft with author revisions, Graham Greene Collection, Box 25, Folders 5 and 6, Harry Ransom Center, The University of Texas at Austin; Cuba Clippings include *Paris Match*, 6 March 1958, with report of the Cifuentes crash in the 1958 Habana Gran Prix, Box 73, Folder 13, Graham Greene papers, MS.1995.003, John J. Burns Library, Boston College.

8   *Our Man in Havana* holograph draft with author revisions and inserts; and composite holograph and typescript draft with author revisions, Graham Greene Collection, Box 25, Folders 5 and 6, Harry Ransom Center, The University of Texas at Austin.

9   Graham Greene, *Our Man in Havana* (London: William Heinemann, 1958), 31, 44. In the simultaneously published U.S. Viking Press first edition (New York, 1958) the room number was 510 both times (30, 42).

10 Colonel Felix Cowgill (Austria) to Greene, 22 June 1959, Box 58, Folder 11, Graham Greene papers, MS.1995.003, John J. Burns Library, Boston College.

11 One of Hemingway's many biographers informs us that while the author was living at the Ambos Mundos Hotel in 1939, he found more peace to start writing *For Whom the Bell Tolls* by registering concurrently at the Sevilla-Biltmore Hotel. See Michael Reynolds, *Hemingway: The 1930s* (New York: W. W. Norton, 1997), pp. 299, 352n39.

12 *Our Man in Havana* 1st draft handwritten manuscript with revisions, Graham Greene Collection, Box 25 Folder 5, Harry Ransom Center. The published sentence (Greene, *Our Man in Havana*, p. 21) became, "the President's régime was creaking dangerously towards its end."

13 Gillian Sutro comment (n.d.) on Graham Greene letter of 3 Nov. 1957, Papers of Gillian and John Sutro, MS. Eng. C. 7320, Department of Special Collections, Bodleian Library, University of Oxford; Quentin Falk, *Travels in Greeneland*, pp. 96–97.

14 Carol Reed telegram to Greene (Sweden), 25 July 1958; Greene telegram to Pollinger, 29 July 1958: Box 58, Folder 16, Graham Greene papers, MS.1995.003, John J. Burns Library, Boston College.

15 Greene (Stockholm, Sweden) to Catherine (St. Lucia), 14 July 1958, Box 25, Folder 24; Greene (Hotel Eden au Lac, Zurich) to Catherine (Newton, Cambridge), 22 Aug. 1958, Box 25, Folder 25: The Catherine Walston/Graham Greene Papers, Booth Family Center for Special Collections, Georgetown University Library, Washington, D.C.

16 Agreement between the Holborn Literary Company Limited and Kingsmead Production Limited, 21 Oct. 1958, Graham Greene Collection Box 92, Folder 8, Harry Ransom Center, The University of Texas at Austin.

17 Greene (Algonquin Hotel, New York) to Catherine Walston (Newton, Cambridge), 12 Oct. 1958, The Catherine Walston/Graham Greene Papers, Box 26, Folder 10, Booth Family Center for Special Collections, Georgetown University Library, Washington, D.C.

18 Ibid.

19 Ibid.

20 "Actress's Baby in Death Drama," 8 Aug. 1962, *Daily Express*, p. 1; "Former Actress 'Was Suicidal,'" 11 Aug. 1962, *The Times*, p. 4; "Pat Marlowe Money Shock," 30 Oct. 1962, *Daily Mirror*, p. 24; "Max Bygraves and His Lovechildren," 26 July 2011, *Daily Express*.

21 Greene (Havana) to Catherine Walston (Newton, Cambridge), 16 Oct. 1958, The Catherine Walston/Graham Greene Papers, Box 26, Folder 11, Booth Family Center for Special Collections, Georgetown University Library, Washington, D.C.

22 "Extract from BBC Radio Programme in Which Film Director Sir Carol Reed Is Interviewed by Gordon Gow . . . about His Collaborations with Graham Greene among Other Subjects," 22 Dec. 1959, British Library, 1CDR0017547 BD2.

23   "Interesting *if* True: The Quiet Englishman" by Edward Scott, *Havana Post*, 17 October 1958, p. 4.

24   "El Hombre del Tercer Hombre," 2 Nov. 1958, "Las Entrevistas de Carteles," in Guillermo Cabrera Infante, *Obras Completas I. El Cronista de Cine: Escritos Cinematográficos I* (Barcelona: Galaxia Gutenberg, 2012), p. 1388.

25   "Quentin Falk Interview with Graham Greene, Antibes, May 1983," C1669, British Library Sound Archive; "Extract from BBC Radio Programme in Which Film Director Sir Carol Reed Is Interviewed by Gordon Gow . . . about His Collaborations with Graham Greene among Other Subjects," 22 Dec. 1959, British Library, 1CDR0017547 BD2.

26   Greene (London, W1) to Catherine (St. Lucia, BWI), 20 Nov. 1958, Box 26, Folder 13; Greene (London, W1) to Catherine (St. Lucia, BWI), 1 Dec. 1958, Box 26, Folder 15: The Catherine Walston/Graham Greene Papers, Booth Family Center for Special Collections, Georgetown University Library, Washington, D.C.

27   Greene, *Ways of Escape*, pp. 101–13.

28   "A Memory of Indo-China," *Listener*, 15 Sept. 1955 (*Reflections*, pp. 185–88).

29   On MAP and US attempts to pressure Batista, see Mark Phythian and Jonathan Jardine, "Hunters in the Backyard: The UK, the US and the Question of Arms Sales to Castro's Cuba, 1959," *Contemporary British History* 13, no. 1 (spring 1999): 32–61 (pp. 33–35).

30   Havana to FO, 24 July 1957, TNA FO371/126467 AK1015/31.

31   P.R. Oliver (Havana) to FO, 11 Oct. 1957, TNA FO371/126479 AK1192/1.

32   Wieland (Director of the Office of Middle American Affairs) to Roy Rubottom, 17 Jan. 1958, *FRUS: 1958–60*, p. 11.

33   For the background and outcome to U.S. internal debate on arms embargo, see Morley, *Imperial State and Revolution*, pp. 58–61; Paterson, *Contesting Castro*, pp. 130–38. For the reason for and effects of embargo, see the analysis by former U.S. diplomat to Havana Wayne S. Smith, *The Closest of Enemies: A Personal and Diplomatic Account of US/Cuban Relations since 1957* (New York: W. W. Norton, 1987), pp. 16–18.

34   Christian A. Herter to Embassy in Cuba, 14 March 1958, *Foreign Relations of the United States* [henceforward: FRUS], *1958–60: Volume VI Cuba* (Washington, DC, 1991), p. 60.

35   Greene to Delargy, 2 Apr. 1958, Box 16, Folder 36, Graham Greene papers, MS.1995.003, John J. Burns Library, Boston College.

36   Anthony Sampson, *The Arms Bazaar* (London: Hodder & Stoughton, 1977), pp. 107–08.

37   Viscount S. Hood (H.M. Minister, Washington) to Sir H. A. C. Rumbold (London), 14 Dec. 1957, TNA FO371 126479/AK1192/23. On Anglo-American discussions over arms sales to Batista, see Harold Bush-Howard, "Coming to Terms with Castro: Britain and the Cuban Revolution, 1958–1965" (PhD thesis, London School of Economics and Political Science, 1997), 49–52.

38   Fordham to Hankey, 19 Nov. 1957, FO371/126479 AK1192/8.

39   Robert Cecil, *A Divided Life: A Biography of Donald Maclean* (London: Bodley Head, 1988), p. 116.

40   Fordham to Hankey, 22 Feb. 1957, TNA FO371/126467 AK1015/8; "Cuban Rebel Is Visited in Hideout," *New York Times*, 24 Feb. 1957, p. 1; Minute by Pease, 12 July 1957, TNA FO371/126467 AK1015/28; Hone (Santiago de Cuba) to Fordham, 6 May 1958, TNA FO371/132164 AK1015/28.

41   Fordham to Hankey, 2 Apr. 1958, TNA FO371 132164/AK1015/20.

42   *The Times*, 5 Apr. 1958, p. 5.

43   Fordham to Lloyd, Havana, 15 Apr. 1958, TNA FO371 132164/AK1015/25.

44   Fordham to FO, Havana, 23 May 1958, TNA FO371 132174/AK1191/10.

45   Fordham to FO, Havana, 25 May 1958, TNA FO371 132174/AK1191/11.

46   *The Times*, 4 July 1958, p. 11. An article in *The Times* on 19 May (p. 8) highlighted
      the difficulties in reporting from Cuba. While reporting that "superficially, the scene
      in Havana looks normal enough," it also said it was "virtually impossible to know
      what is happening in Oriente and other disturbed centres."

47   Oliver to FO, Havana, 25 July 1958, TNA FO371 132175/AK1192/4.

48   FO memorandum by Hankey, London, 6 Aug. 1958, TNA FO 371 132175/
      AK1192/6.

49   FO memorandum (anonymous), 15 Jan. 1959, TNA FO371 139459/AK1192/25.
      This memo says the US report was dated 15 August 1958—before the sale of Sea
      Fury aircraft was concluded.

50   Royal Court telegram received at Buckingham Palace, 17 Oct. 1959, TNA FO371
      132179/AK1223/9.

51   FO371/132165 AK1015/47, enclosing "BBC Monitoring" transcriptions from Radio
      Rebelde broadcasts (19 and 20 October 1958).

52   TNA FO371/132176 AK1192/64, Benest (Washington) to Hildyard, enclosure "Coopera
      al Boycott Revolucionario: No Compres Productos Ingleses," 23 December 1958.

53   FO memorandum by Hankey, 23 Oct. 1958, TNA FO 371 132175/AK1192/28. A
      minute by Norman Brain (assistant undersecretary of state for foreign affairs) on 24
      Oct. agreed with the proposal and raised the likelihood of an imminent parliamentary
      question on the subject. A minute by Sir F. Hoyer-Miller on 24 Oct. expressed his
      unhappiness at this "surrendering to blackmail by the rebels and denying resistance to
      the legitimate force."

54   Greene to Delargy, 24 Oct. 1958, in Richard Greene (ed.), *A Life in Letters*, pp. 232–33.

55   Hankey, "Anglo-Cuban Relations" [memorandum], 4 Nov. 1958, TNA
      FO371/132168 AK1051/14.

56   See Oliver to Hankey, 24 Sept. 1958, TNA FO371/132168 AK1051/1. On the
      chances of Castro coming to power, the chargé d'affaires in Havana wrote, "in
      view of [his] declared opposition to U.S. economic and commercial interests in
      Cuba, Washington would probably go to very considerable lengths to prevent this
      happening."

57   Memorandum by Hankey, 11 Nov. 1958, TNA FO371/132175 AK1192/38; Sir John
      Taylor (Canning House) to Hankey, 17 Nov. 1958, TNA FO371/132175 AK1192/35.

58   *Hansard Vol. 595, Parliamentary Debates—House of Commons*, 19 Nov. 1958, pp.
      1133–34.

59   Greene to Mallin (sent via Monica McCall), 24 Nov. 1958, Box 27, Folder 13;
      Greene to Hugh Delargy, 24 Oct. 1958, Box 16, Folder 36: Graham Greene papers,
      MS.1995.003, John J. Burns Library, Boston College.

60   Hankey, "Arms for Cuba" [memorandum], 18 Nov. 1958, TNA FO371/132175
      AK1192/36; Fordham to Hankey, 2 Dec. 1958, TNA FO371/132165 AK1015/72.

61   R. Hart Phillips, *Cuba: Island of Paradox* (New York: McDowell Obolensky, n.d.), p.
      386.

62   *Hansard Vol. 597, Parliamentary Debates—House of Commons*, 15 Dec. 1958, pp.
      763–66, 770–75.

63 Oliver (Havana) to Watson (Ministry of Supply), 17 Nov. 1958; Oliver (Havana) to Barnes (Ministry of Supply), 18 Dec. 1958, FO371/132176 AK1192/45; Chancery (Havana) to American Dept, 20 Aug. 1958, FO371/132179 AK1223/6.

64 Paterson, *Contesting Castro*, pp. 206–11, 223–24.

65 FO memorandum by Hankey, 12 Dec. 1958, TNA FO371/132176 AK1192/57.

66 Brain to Hood, 22 Dec. 1958, TNA FO371/132176 AK1192/58.

67 Chris Hull, "Our Arms in Havana: British Military Sales to Batista and Castro, 1958–59," *Diplomacy and Statecraft*, 18/3 (2007), pp. 593–616 (601–02).

68 Greene to Hugh Delargy, 19 Dec. 1958, Graham Greene Papers, Box 16, Folder 36, Graham Greene papers, MS.1995.003, John J. Burns Library, Boston College.

69 Fordham to Hankey, 31 Dec. 1958, TNA FO371/139398 AK1015/14.

70 Dorschner and Fabricio, *The Winds of December*, pp. 385–86.

CHAPTER 8

1 Greene (C.6 Albany) to Catherine Walston (St. Lucia, BWI), 3 Jan. [1959], The Catherine Walston/Graham Greene Papers, Box 27, Folder 1, Booth Family Center for Special Collections, Georgetown University Library, Washington, D.C.

2 Greene to Sir William Haley, 2 Jan. 1959, Box 73, Folder 12, Graham Greene papers, MS.1995.003, John J. Burns Library, Boston College; "Cuba's Civil War: To the Editor," *The Times*, 3 January 1959, p. 7.

3 Greene to Sir William Haley, 5 Jan. 1959, Box 73, Folder 12, Graham Greene papers, MS.1995.003, John J. Burns Library, Boston College; "Were the British Government Misinformed? From Our Diplomatic Correspondent," *The Times*, 5 Jan. 1959, p. 8; "Cuba's Civil War: To the Editor," *The Times*, 6 January 1959, p. 9.

4 Greene to Phyllis Bewley (London, SW10), 12 Jan. 1959, Graham Greene Papers, Box 11, Folder 88, Graham Greene papers, MS.1995.003, John J. Burns Library, Boston College.

5 "Our Men in Havana," *Guardian*, 8 Jan. 1959, p. 8; *The Economist*, 10 Jan. 1959, p. 108.

6 "Foreign Office Defended: Critics on the Wrong Lines" by Richard Scott, 21 Jan. 1959, *Guardian*, p. 8.

7 Greene, Our Man in Havana, p. 60; "Our Men in Havana," *Guardian*, 8 Jan. 1959, p. 8. The *Economist* asserted ("Cuba: Hindsight Wisdom," 10 Jan. 1959, p. 108) that the affair "made Whitehall look pretty silly, and it will scarcely help to get Britain's relations with the victorious regime in Havana off to a good start."

8 FO memorandum by Hankey, 15 Jan. 1959, TNA FO371/139459 AK1192/25; Second Report from the Select Committee on Estimates, "Sale of Military Equipment Abroad," Session 1958–59, 11 March 1959 [published by HMSO, London, 5 August 1959].

9 Greene, *Our Man in Havana*, p. 214.

10 Oliver to Hildyard (FO, London), 27 Jan. 1959, TNA FO371/139400 AK1015/58; Fordham to Lloyd, 3 July 1959, TNA FO371/138897 AK10113/3.

11 Greene (Paris, France) to Lady Fordham (Royston, Herts.), 11 Jan. 1967, Box 19 Folder 15, Graham Greene papers, MS.1995.003, John J. Burns Library, Boston College.

12 "'Complete Surprise' to Ambassador," 2 Jan 1959, *The Times*, p. 8; Memorandum by Brain, 8 Jan. 1959, TNA FO371/139519 AK1903/3; "Cuban Embassy Surprise: Ambassador's Services Terminated," *The Times*, 17 Jan. 1959, p. 4.

13 Fordham to Foreign Office, telegram no. 16, 6 Jan. 1959, TNA FO371/139429

AK1051/7; Edwin Tetlow, "'Straight Questions' by Cuba to Britain," *Daily Telegraph*, 7 Jan. 1959, pp. 1, 15. Another source affirms that the planes did see action in the last great battle of the insurrection at Santa Clara in late December. See Dorschner and Fabricio, *Winds of December*, pp. 347, 358.

14 Fordham to FO, T. No. 31, 13 Jan. 1959, TNA FO371/139430 AK1051/16.

15 Havana Chancery to American Dept. (FO), 11 Feb. 1959, enclosure "Extracts from Dr. Fidel Castro's speech at the Shell refinery on Friday, February 6, 1959," TNA FO371/139431 AK1051/37.

16 "On-Again Off-Again Casinos Are on Again," *Times of Havana*, 17 Jan. 1959, p. 1.

17 "Editorial Note," *FRUS 1958–60: Volume VI Cuba*, p. 476.

18 "Gala Ceremony Due to Open Plush Hotel Capri, Casino," *The Times of Havana*, 21 Nov. 1957, p. 8; "Our Man in Havana: Guinness Was Logical Choice," *Aberdeen Express*, 2 May 1960.

19 "Riviera Hotel Opening to Attract Celebrities," *The Times of Havana*, 25 Nov. 1957, p. 3.

20 "Our Man in Havana: Guinness Was Logical Choice," *Aberdeen Express*, 2 May 1960.

21 "Our Man in Havana: Guinness Was Logical Choice," *Aberdeen Express*, 2 May 1960.

22 "Shooting 'Our Man in Havana' on the Spot," 26 Apr. 1959, *New York Times*, p. X7.

23 "The Face You Don't Know in This Pack of Talent," *Daily Express*, 22 Apr. 1959, p. 6; Nicholas Wapshott, *The Man Between: A Biography of Carol Reed* (London: Chatto & Windus, 1990), pp. 297–98.

24 Greene (Monlogo River, Belgium Congo) to Gillian [Sutro], 24 Feb. 1959, Papers of Gillian and John Sutro, MS. Eng. c.7320 f63, Department of Special Collections, Bodleian Library, University of Oxford.

25 "Graham Greene interviewed by David Lodge," n.d., 1CD0197190, British Library Sound Archive.

26 Date Book *2nd trimester 1959*, Graham Greene Papers, Box 39, Harry Ransom Center, The University of Texas at Austin; Oswald Morris, *Huston, We Have a Problem: A Kaleidoscope of Filmmaking Memories* (Lanham, MD: Scarecrow, 2006), pp. 135–6.

27 Cited in Quentin Falk, *Travels in Greeneland*, p. 107.

28 Date Book *2nd trimester 1959*, Graham Greene Papers, Box 39, Harry Ransom Center, The University of Texas at Austin

29 "Graham Greene en La Habana," 24 May 1959, "Las Entrevistas de Carteles," in Guillermo Cabrera Infante, *Obras Completas I. El cronista de Cine: Escritos Cinematográficos I* (Barcelona: Galaxia Gutenberg, 2012), p. 1409.

30 Noël Coward diary entry, 16 Apr. 1960, in Payn and Morley (eds.), *The Noël Coward Diaries*, p. 406; Alec Guinness (Hotel Capri, Havana) to Merula Guinness, Wednesday [date incomplete], British Library Western Manuscripts, Alec Guinness Archive, Add MS 89015/2/1/13.

31 Alec Guinness (Hotel Capri, Havana) to Merula Guinness, Wednesday [date incomplete]; Alec Guinness to Merula Guinness, Sunday 26 Apr. [1959], British Library Western Manuscripts, Alec Guinness Archive, Add MS 89015/2/1/13.

32 "The Name Dropper," *The Times of Havana*, 7 May 1959, p. 6.

33 Guinness, *Blessings in Disguise*, pp. 204–05.

34 Alec Guinness to Merula Guinness, Sunday 26 Apr. [1959]; Alec Guinness (Hotel

Capri, Havana) to Merula Guinness, 29 Apr. [1959], British Library Western Manuscripts, Alec Guinness Archive, Add MS 89015/2/1/13.

35 "Extract from BBC Radio Programme in Which Film Director Sir Carol Reed Is Interviewed by Gordon Gow . . . about his collaborations with Graham Greene among Other Subjects," 22 Dec. 1959, 1CDR0017547 BD2, British Library Sound Archive.

36 Alec Guinness to Merula Guinness, Sunday 26 Apr. [1959], British Library Western Manuscripts, Alec Guinness Archive, Add MS 89015/2/1/13.

37 Halsley Raines, "Shooting 'Our Man in Havana' on the Spot," 26 Apr. 1959, *New York Times*, p. X7.

38 Noël Coward diary entry, 16 Apr. 1960, in Graham Payn and Sheridan Morley (eds.), *The Noël Coward Diaries* (London: Macmillan, 1982), p. 406.

39 Jay Mallin Sr., *Covering Castro: Rise and Decline of Cuba's Communist Dictator* (New Brunswick, NJ: Transaction, 1994), p. xi.

40 Edward Scott, "Interesting *if* True: Our Man Has Stormy Passage in Havana," *Havana Post*, 17 Apr. 1959, p. 4.

41 Noël Coward diary entry, 16 Apr. 1959, in Payn and Morley (eds.), *The Noël Coward Diaries*, pp. 406–07; Nicholas Wapshott, *The Man Between: A Biography of Carol Reed* (London: Chatto & Windus, 1990), p. 300.

42 Kenneth Lynn, *Hemingway* (New York: Simon & Schuster, 1987), pp. 502–04; Paul Hendrickson, *Hemingway's Boat: Everything He Loved in Life, and Lost, 1934–1961* (London: Vintage, 2013), pp. 323–24.

43 Norman Sherry, *The Life of Graham Greene: Volume One, 1904–1939* (London: Jonathan Cape, 1989), pp. 614–15.

44 George Plimpton (ed.), *Writers at Work: The Paris Review Interviews. Second Series* (New York: Penguin, 1977), pp. 238–39.

45 Elaine Dundy, "Our Men in Havana," *Guardian*, 9 June 2001, www.theguardian.com/world/2001/jun/09/cuba.humanities.

46 Dundy, "Our Men in Havana."

47 "Havana" journal, 26 July [1963], Graham Greene Papers, Box 20, Folder 5, Harry Ransom Center, The University of Texas at Austin.

48 Greene, *Our Man in Havana*, p. 170.

49 Fordham (Havana) to Selwyn Lloyd (FO, London), 28 Oct. 1959, TNA FO371/139503 AK1635/1.

50 "Their Men Watch Our Men in Havana," *Daily Express*, 16 Apr. 1958, p. 8.

51 "Será Supervisado el Rodaje de Nuestro Hombre en La Habana," *Diario de la Marina*, 16 Apr. 1959, p. B1; "Ventura's Shadow Haunts Film: Our Man in Ciudad Trujillo Never Like This, Say Cubans," 16 Apr. 1959, *The Times of Havana*, p. 3.

52 Edward Scott, "Interesting *if* True: Our Man Has Stormy Passage in Havana," *Havana Post*, 17 Apr. 1959, p. 4.

53 An Old Habanero, "Saturday's Sofrito," *The Times of Havana*, 18 Apr. 1959, p. 9.

54 "Round the Dives with Graham Greene," *Daily Express*, 20 Apr. 1959, p. 8.

55 Kenneth Tynan, "A Visit to Havana," *Holiday* 27 (Feb. 1960): 50–58; Stanley Price, "Cuban Heel," *Oldie*, no. 175 (Oct. 2003): 20–21. Tynan had a personal predilection for flagellation. His wife, Elaine Dundy, tried but failed in the practice. Their marriage later ended in divorce. See www.telegraph.co.uk/news/obituaries/1933071/Elaine-Dundy.html.

56 Halsley Raines, "Shooting 'Our Man in Havana' on the Spot," *New York Times*, 26 Apr. 1959, p. X7.

57 "Their Men Watch Our Men in Havana," *Daily Express*, 16 Apr. 1958, p. 8.

58 Edward Scott, "Interesting *if* True: Our Man Has Stormy Passage in Havana," *Havana Post*, 17 Apr. 1959, p. 4; "Ventura's Shadow Haunts Film: Our Man in Ciudad Trujillo Never Like This, Say Cubans," 16 Apr. 1959, *The Times of Havana*, p. 3.

59 "Shooting 'Our Man in Havana' on the Spot," 26 Apr. 1959, *New York Times*, p. X7.

60 Gonzalo de Quesada y Miranda, "Cuban Sidelights," *Havana Post*, 24 Apr. 1959, p. 4; Edward Scott, "Interesting *if* True: Our Man Has Stormy Passage in Havana," *Havana Post*, 17 Apr. 1959, p. 4.

61 Guinness, *Blessings in Disguise*, p. 203.

62 Tynan, "A Visit to Havana," p. 56; Kenneth Tynan, *Tynan Right and Left: Plays, Films, People, Places, and Events* (London: Longman, 1967), pp. 332–34. For a very different version of the episode, describing Tynan flying into a rage when American captain Herman Marks (the actual executioner) invited them, see George Plimpton, *Shadow Box* (London: Deutsch, 1978), pp. 140–49.

63 G. Cain [Guillermo Cabrera Infante], "Los Avatares de un Director y una Película," *Carteles* (La Habana), no. 23, 7 Jun. 1959, pp. 42–44.

64 G. Cain [Guillermo Cabrera Infante], "Los Avatares de un Director y una Película."

65 "'Our Man in Havana' Runs into Trouble: Demand for Script," *Daily Telegraph*, 26 Apr. 1959, p. 11.

66 G. Cain [Guillermo Cabrera Infante], "Los Avatares de un Director y una Película."

67 "Actors Upstaged by Fidel Castro," *Times of Havana*, 14 May 1959, p. 3.

68 Date Book *2nd trimester 1959*, Box 39, Greene Collection, Harry Ransom Center.

69 Greene to Nick Mendoza, 13 May 1959, Box 28, Folder 14, Graham Greene papers, MS.1995.003, John J. Burns Library, Boston College.

70 "The Hemisphere: His Men in Havana," *Time*, 27 Apr. 1959; Halsley Raines, "Shooting 'Our Man in Havana' on the Spot," *New York Times*, 26 Apr. 1959, p. X7.

71 Alec Guinness speaking on his return to England from Cuba, May 1959, www.youtube.com/watch?v=_pM1cxbaZC8.

72 "No Trouble in Cuba for Carol Reed," *Kinematograph Weekly*, 14 May 1959.

73 Alec Guinness (Hotel Capri, Havana) to Merula Guinness, Tuesday 5 May [1959], British Library Western Manuscripts, Alec Guinness Archive, Add MS 89015/2/1/13.

74 Robert Emmett Ginna, "Our Man in Havana," *Horizon II* (Nov. 1959), pp. 27–31, 122–26.

75 Graham Greene to Francis Greene, 24 Apr. 1959, Box 8, Folder 4, Graham Greene papers, MS.1995.003, John J. Burns Library, Boston College.

76 William N. Graf (London W1) to Greene, 25 May 1959, Box 70, Folder 37, Graham Greene papers, MS.1995.003, John J. Burns Library, Boston College.

77 "Nuevos Prostíbulos Fueron Clausurados," *Revolución*, 24 Apr. 1959, p. 7.

78 E. J. Hobsbawm, *Revolutionaries: Contemporary Essays* (London: Weidenfeld & Nicolson, 1973), p. 218.

79 Greene's review of "*Deuxième Bureau*" (directed by Pierre Billon, 1935) in the *Spectator*, 17 January 1936, cited in David Parkinson, *Mornings*, pp. 64–66.

80 "All talent and no technique," *Guardian*, 2 Jan. 1960, p. 3.

81 Ibid.

82 Kenneth Von Gunden, *Alec Guinness: The Films* (Jefferson, NC: McFarland, 2002), pp. 125–26.

83   Guinness to Coward, 5 Jan. 1960, in Barry Day (ed.), *The Letters of Noël Coward* (London: Methuen, 2007), pp. 658–59.

84   Guinness quoted in Quentin Falk, *Travels in Greeneland*, p. 107.

85   Wapshott, *A Biography of Carol Reed*, p. 297.

86   Falk, *Travels in Greeneland*, p. 107; "Quentin Falk interview with Graham Greene, Antibes, May 1983," C1669, British Library Sound Archive.

87   Greene quoted in Barry Day (ed.), *The Letters of Noël Coward*, p. 657.

88   "Nigel Lewis interview with Graham Greene, Part V, Antibes, 17–18 April 1982," C829/10, British Library Sound Archive.

89   "Picture Stealer!," *Daily Mirror*, 7 Jan. 1960, p. 15.

90   Coward to Greene, Aug. 1959: Barry Day (ed.), *The Letters of Noël Coward*, pp. 659–60.

91   Diary entry 1 Jan. 1960 in Payn and Morley (eds.), *The Noël Coward Diaries*, p. 427.

92   "The Face You Don't Know in This Pack of Talent," *Daily Express*, 22 Apr. 1959, p. 6.

CHAPTER 9

1   Greene, *Our Man in Havana*, p. 132.

2   "Fidel Castro As I Knew Him" by Sergio Rojas Santamaria, *Daily Telegraph*, 27 Oct. 1960.

3   Fordham to FO, 24 Feb. 1959, TNA FO371/139400 AK1015/68.

4   Fordham to Lloyd, 21 Aug. 1959, TNA FO371/139402 AK1015/139. James Bond novelist Ian Fleming (1908–64) needs little introduction. Writer Eric Ambler (1909–98) earned renown for maturing the spy thriller genre in the 1930s through his employment of realism. Politically inclined to the left, he later received acclaim as "the father of the modern spy novel." Michael Barber, "Ambler, Eric Clifford (1909–98)," *Oxford Dictionary of National Biography* (Oxford University Press, Sept. 2004).

5   There had been speculation in the British press in early 1959 that Fordham would be replaced. See memorandum by Campbell, 12 Jan. 1959, TNA FO371/139517 AK1891/1.

6   FO to Havana, London, 26 March 1959, TNA FO371/139470 AK1223/4.

7   Hull, "Our Arms in Havana," p. 603.

8   Phythian and Jardine, "Hunters in the Backyard?," p. 41.

9   Brain to Hood (Washington), 20 Aug. 1959, TNA FO371/139472 AK1223/37.

10   This assertion is repeated in several documents, including FO memorandum "The Cuban Request for Hunters" by Hildyard, 22 Oct. 1959, TNA FO371/139473/AK1223/76.

11   Minute by Hildyard, 2 Apr. 1959, TNA FO371/139400 AK1015/77.

12   Draft memorandum by Hildyard, "The Cuban Case," n.d. [ca. 27–29 Oct. 1959], TNA FO371/139473 AK1223/75.

13   Christian A. Herter to Embassy in the United Kingdom, 14 Oct. 1959, *FRUS 1958–60: Volume VI Cuba*, p. 624.

14   "U.S. Objecting to British Arms Sales to Cuba," *The Times*, 17 Oct. 1959, p. 6.

15   Minute by Hildyard, London, 19 Oct. 1959, TNA FO371/139473 AK1223/73. Permanent undersecretary Derick Hoyer Millar commented (19 Oct.) that the US handling of the issue had been "lamentable" but thought the embargo should continue for the present.

16   *The Times*, 19 Oct. 1959, p. 11.

17   Christian A. Herter to Foreign Secretary Selwyn Lloyd, 17 Nov. 1959, *FRUS 1958–60: Volume VI Cuba*, pp. 670–71; Personal "confidential" diary entry for 23 Nov. 1959, The Papers of Selwyn Lloyd, 4/33, Churchill Archives Centre, Cambridge University.

18   Cabinet Secretary's Notebooks, 26 Nov. 1959, TNA CAB195/18 C.C.60 (59).
      The 1959 upturn in British exports to Cuba was short-lived, halving in 1960 and
      declining further in 1961.

19   Selwyn Lloyd "confidential" diary entry for 26 Nov. 1959, The Papers of Selwyn
      Lloyd, 4/33, Churchill Archives Centre, Cambridge University.

20   Fordham to Hankey, 11 Dec. 1959, enclosing "Extract from 'Revolución' dated
      December 3, 1959," "England against Cuban interests," "Extract from 'Revolución'
      dated December 4, 1959," and "Perfidious Albion and the Jet Planes" by Jacobino,
      TNA FO371/139475 AK1223/131.

21   The term la perfide Albion is attributed to the Marquis de Ximenès (1726–1817).
      J. A. Simpson and E. S. C. Weiner (eds.), The Oxford English Dictionary: Volume I,
      A–Bazouki (Oxford: Clarendon Press, 1989), p. 297.

22   "New Zealander Held in Havana," The Times, 4 June 1960, p. 4; "Cuban Expulsion
      of Journalist," The Times, 6 June 1960, p. 6. On the same day that Scott was held the
      authorities deported a Daily Express journalist from Havana only a day after his arrival.

23   Greene (C.6 Albany) to Nick Mendoza, 7 July 1960, Box 28, Folder 14, Graham
      Greene papers, MS.1995.003, John J. Burns Library, Boston College.

24   Nick Mendoza (St. Louis, MO) to Graham Greene, 3 Apr. 1961; Graham Greene
      to Nick Mendoza, 22 Apr. 1961: Box 28, Folder 14, Graham Greene papers,
      MS.1995.003, John J. Burns Library, Boston College.

25   Nick Mendoza (Blytheville, Arkansas) to Greene, 29 May 1961, Box 28, Folder 14,
      Graham Greene papers, MS.1995.003, John J. Burns Library, Boston College.

26   Jay Mallin, Fortress Cuba: Russia's American Base (Chicago, IL: H. Regnery Co., 1965).
      A later book by Mallin was Covering Castro: Rise and Decline of Cuba's Communist
      Dictator (New Brunswick, NJ: Transaction Publishers, 1994). In Feb. 1961, Mallin
      wrote to tell Greene he had thought it prudent to send his wife and son into exile in
      Miami months before. Jay [Mallin] (Vedado, Havana) to Greene, 20 Feb. 1961, Box 27,
      Folder 13, Graham Greene papers, MS.1995.003, John J. Burns Library, Boston College.

27   William Millward, "Life in and out of Hut 3," in F. H. Hinsley and Alan Stripp (eds.)
      Codebreakers: The Inside Story of Bletchley Park (Oxford: Oxford University Press,
      1994), pp. 17–29 (p. 26).

28   "Obituary: Sir Herbert Marchant," Independent, 15 Aug. 1990.

29   Guardian, 23 Jan. 1961, p. 9; Sutherland to FO, 19 Jan. 1961, TNA FO371/156138
      AK1015/6.

30   Marchant to FO, 6 Apr. 1961, TNA FO371/156140 AK1015/41.

31   Luis Báez, Secretos de Generales, mentioned at www.granma.cu/cuba/2014-03-20/
      el-peso-que-llevo-sobre-mis-hombros-es-el-mismo-peso-que-llevan-todos-los-
      revolucionarios.

32   For a detailed account of Sea Fury engagements, see Howard Jones, The Bay of Pigs
      (Oxford: Oxford University Press, 2010), pp. 106–07; Peter Wyden, Bay of Pigs: The
      Untold Story (London: Cape, 1979), pp. 250–55; Hugh Thomas, Pursuit of Freedom,
      pp. 1358–59.

33   Marchant to Home, "Annual Review for Cuba 1961," 11 Jan. 1962, TNA
      FO371/162308 AK9843/5.

34   Marchant to Home, 10 May 1961, TNA FO371/156147 AK1015/184.

35   Marchant to Brain, 24 May 1961, TNA FO371/156149 AK1015/207.

36   Greene, Our Man in Havana, 74, 81.

37   Rediscovered and first published posthumously in Parkinson (ed.), Mornings in the
      Dark (1993).

38 Peter Hennessy, *Having It So Good: Britain in the Fifties* (London: Allen Lane, 2006), p. 581.
39 Francis Greene (C.6 Albany, London) to Graham Greene, 24 Nov. 1957; Graham Greene to Francis Greene, 22 May 1958: Box 8, Folder 3, Graham Greene papers, MS.1995.003, John J. Burns Library, Boston College.
40 Cedric Watts, "Greene, Dunne, Dreams and Precognition," pp. 187–208, in William Thomas Hill (ed.), *Lonely without God: Graham Greene's Quixotic Journeys of Faith* (Bethesda, MD: Academica Press, 2008).
41 Burstall, "A writer at work"; Greene expressed his dislike of New York in "Nigel Lewis interview with Graham Greene, Part II, Antibes, 17–18 April 1982," C829/7, British Library Sound Archive.
42 Cedric Watts, "Greene, Dunne, Dreams and Precognition," p. 196.
43 *Our Man in Havana* screenplay composite holograph and proof sheets with author revisions, f72b, Graham Greene Collection, Box 26 Folder 2, Harry Ransom Center.
44 Raul Dominguez becomes Montez in the film version, a play on the Spanish word *montes,* meaning mountains. He flies over the "snow-covered mountains of Cuba" in an attempt to obtain photographic evidence of "concrete platforms and unidentifiable pieces of giant machinery." *Our Man in Havana* film script (Shepperton Studios, ca1960), British Library shelfmark Cup.410.c.68.
45 TNA FO371/168135 AK1011/1, Marchant to Home, "Annual Review for 1962," No. 3, 23 Jan. 1963.
46 Marchant to FO, 18 Jan. 1961, TNA FO371/156218 AK1192/8/G.
47 Sutherland to Edmonds, 6 July 1961, TNA FO371/156219 AK1195/5/G.
48 Minute by Hankey, 17 July 1961, TNA FO371/156219 AK1195/5/G.
49 The embassy occupied the Edificio Bolívar on Calle Capdevila, only moving to the diplomatic quarter in the residential suburb of Miramar in the mid-1990s.
50 Scott, p. 28; TNA 371/156177 AK103145/46, Sutherland (Havana) to Hankey, 2 Feb. 1961.
51 TNA FO371/162374 AK1201/2, Havana Chancery to American Dept. (FO), 4 Jan. 1962; G. G. Brown (Washington) to Sutherland (Havana), 17 Jan. 1962.
52 TNA FO371/162374 AK1201/15, G. R. Way (JIB) to Head of Chancery (Havana), 7 May 1962.
53 Interview with Michael Brown in Leicester (UK), 9 Sept. 2010.
54 TNA FO371/162374 AK1201/11, J. M. Brown (Havana) to Miss G. G. Brown (Washington), 19 Apr. 1962.
55 Domingo Amuchastegui, "Cuban Intelligence and the October Crisis," in James G. Blight and David A. Welch (eds.), *Intelligence and the Cuban Missile Crisis* (London: Frank Cass, 1998), pp. 101, 116n41.
56 Philip M. Williams, *Hugh Gaitskell: A Political Biography* (London: Cape, 1979), pp. 693–94. Gaitskell reportedly received much anti-American correspondence. Healey initially doubted that Washington had much evidence of missiles.
57 Greene, *Our Man in Havana*, 61, 63.
58 Byatt (Havana) to Parsons, 10 Nov. 1962, enclosing minute and drawings by Capie (26 Oct. 1962), TNA FO371/162374 AK1201/26.
59 Sutherland (Washington) to Scott (Havana), 27 Dec. 1962, TNA FO371/162435 AK1962/20(E).
60 Sutherland (Washington) to Slater, 5 Nov. 1962, enclosing "Intelligence Reports from Her Majesty's Embassy, Havana" for 2–8 Nov. 1962, sent to G. Summ (Office

of Caribbean Affairs, State Department, Washington, DC), TNA FO371/162399 AK1261/497.

61   Marchant to FO, 14 Dec. 1962; Greenhill (Washington Embassy) to FO, 19 Dec. 1962: TNA FO371/162373 AK1193/33(A)&(B).

62   D. R. Thorpe, *Alec Douglas-Home* (London: Sinclair-Stevenson, 1997), pp. 236–37; Thorpe says the foreign secretary regarded Marchant "as one of the unsung heroes of the Cuban crisis." See p. 517n7. Marchant to Home, 24 Oct. 1962, TNA FO371/162377.

63   Marchant to Home, 10 Nov. 1962, TNA FO371/162408 AK1261/667.

64   Greene, *Our Man in Havana*, p. 146.

CHAPTER 10

1   *New Statesman*, 28 Apr. 1961, p. 671.

2   His U.S. agent wrote to him about an unpublished short story: "When JFK was nominated, you did a little beauty called THE PRINCE OF LAS VEGAS . . ." Mary Pritchett (Deep River, CT) to Greene, 3 July 1962, Box 31, Folder 52, Graham Greene papers, MS.1995.003, John J. Burns Library, Boston College.

3   Speech by Fidel Castro in Havana's Revolution Square, 28 Sept. 1961, www.cuba.cu/gobierno/discursos/1961/esp/f280961e.html.

4   Geraldine Lievesley, *The Cuban Revolution: Past, Present, and Future Perspectives* (Basingstoke: Palgrave Macmillan, 2004), p. 94.

5   Allain, *The Other Man*, p. 93.

6   Memberships and honors: American Academy of Arts and Letters, 1961–1970, Box 67, Folder 1, Graham Greene papers, MS.1995.003, John J. Burns Library, Boston College; Passport (issued Apr. 21, 1960), Box 81, Graham Greene papers, MS.1995.003, John J. Burns Library, Boston College. The final two pages of the FBI file on Greene demonstrate how the agency continued to keep tabs on the writer's movements through the United States: www.spyculture.com/graham-greenes-fbi-file/.

7   Sutherland (Havana) to Hankey (FO), 2 Feb. 1961, TNA FO371/156177 AK103145/46.

8   Richard Deacon, *"C": A Biography of Sir Maurice Oldfield* (London: Macdonald, 1985), pp. 117–18.

9   William Rowlandson, *Sartre in Cuba—Cuba in Sartre* (n.p.: Palgrave Macmillan, 2017).

10   Marchant to Home, 31 July 1961, TNA FO371/156151 AK1015/252.

11   Marchant to Home, No. 63.S, 7 Dec. 1961, TNA FO371/156153 AK1015/282.

12   Lars Schoultz, *That Infernal Little Cuban Republic: The United States and the Cuban Revolution* (Chapel Hill, NC: University of North Carolina Press, 2009), pp. 175–83. Both Shelden (*The Man Within*, pp. 399–400) and Sherry (*Vol. II*, pp. 416–17) affirm that Colonel Lansdale came to Vietnam well after Greene had finished the first draft of *The Quiet American*.

13   Antoni Kapcia, *Cuba in Revolution: A History since the Fifties* (London: Reaktion, 2008), pp. 58–59.

14   Guillermo Cabrera Infante (1929–2005): famed for his "extensive wordplay and the pun," major themes in his writing are "betrayal, machismo, the cinema, nostalgia for the Havana of his youth, and the creativity of language." Julio A. Martínez (ed.), *Dictionary of Twentieth-Century Cuban Literature* (New York: Greenwood, 1990), pp. 361–70.

15   Michael Chanan, *Cuban Cinema* (Minneapolis: University of Minnesota Press, 2004), pp. 133–35.

16 Kapcia, *Cuba in Revolution*, p. 59.

17 Donald McLachlan (*The Sunday Telegraph*, London EC4) to Greene (C.6 Albany), 29 Dec. 1962, Box 28, Folder 6, Graham Greene papers, MS.1995.003, John J. Burns Library, Boston College.

18 Greene to Donald McLachlan, 4 Jan. 1963, Box 28, Folder 6, Graham Greene papers, MS.1995.003, John J. Burns Library, Boston College.

19 Greene to Donald McLachlan, 4 Apr. 1963, Box 28, Folder 6, Graham Greene papers, MS.1995.003, John J. Burns Library, Boston College.

20 Greene to Donald McLachlan, 10 May 1963, Box 28, Folder 6, Graham Greene papers, MS.1995.003, John J. Burns Library, Boston College.

21 Greene (Kingston) to Yvonne Cloetta, 19 July 1963, Box 1, Folder 2; Greene (Hotel Nacional, Havana) to Yvonne Cloetta, 27 July 1963, Box 1, Folder 4; Graham Greene (Hotel Nacional, Havana) to Yvonne Cloetta, 6 August 1963, Box 1, Folder 5: Yvonne Cloetta/Graham Greene Papers, Booth Family Center for Special Collections, Georgetown University Library, Washington, D.C.

22 Cloetta, *In Search of a Beginning*, pp. 50–51; Shelden, *The Man Within*, pp. 68–70.

23 Greene (Kingston) to Yvonne Cloetta, 19 July 1963, Box 1, Folder 2; Graham Greene (Kingston) to Yvonne Cloetta, 20 July 1963, Box 1, Folder 3; Graham Greene (Mexico City) to Yvonne Cloetta, 22 July 1963, Box 1, Folder 3: Yvonne Cloetta/Graham Greene Papers, Booth Family Center for Special Collections, Georgetown University Library, Washington, D.C.

24 "Mexico City" journal, 21 July [1963], Graham Greene Papers, Box 20, Folder 5, Harry Ransom Center, The University of Texas at Austin; Graham Greene (Hotel Luma, Mexico City) to Josephine Reid, 22 July [1963], Graham Greene-Josephine Reid Papers, GGJR/10, Balliol College Archives, University of Oxford.

25 "Return to Cuba" by Graham Greene, *Sunday Telegraph*, 22 Sept. 1963.

26 Renata Keller, *Mexico's Cold War: Cuba, the United States, and the Legacy of the Mexican Revolution* (New York: Cambridge University Press, 2015), pp. 85–86, 164–65.

27 Graham Greene passport (issued 21 April 1960) p. 26, Box 81, Graham Greene papers, MS.1995.003, John J. Burns Library, Boston College.

28 "Mexico City" journal, 22 July [1963]; Jean-Paul Sartre, *Sartre on Cuba* (Westport, CT: Greenwood Press, 1961), p. 8; "Havana" journal, 25 July [1963].

29 Greene, "Return to Cuba."

30 "Havana" journal, 27 and 31 July [1963], Graham Greene Papers, Box 20, Folder 5, Harry Ransom Center, The University of Texas at Austin.

31 Greene, "Return to Cuba."

32 "Havana" journal, 26 July [1963], Graham Greene Papers, Box 20, Folder 5, Harry Ransom Center, The University of Texas at Austin.

33 "Havana" journal, 29, 30, and 31 July [1963], Graham Greene Papers, Box 20, Folder 5, Harry Ransom Center, The University of Texas at Austin; Graham Greene, "Return to Cuba."

34 Greene, "Return to Cuba"; Fidel Castro speech in Revolution Square, Havana, 26 July 1963. www.cuba.cu/gobierno/discursos/1963/esp/f260763e.html.

35 "Havana" journal, 26 July [1963], Graham Greene Papers, Box 20, Folder 5, Harry Ransom Center, The University of Texas at Austin.

36 Greene, "Return to Cuba."

37 "Havana" journal, 28 and 31 July, 4 Aug. [1963], Box 20, Folder 5, Harry Ransom Center, The University of Texas at Austin.

38 Martínez-Fernández, *Revolutionary Cuba*, p. 83; Schoultz, *That Infernal Little Cuban Republic*, pp. 205–07.

39 Watson to Butler, "Cuba: Annual Review for 1963," 7 Jan. 1964, TNA FO371/174002 AK1011/1.

40 "Havana" journal, 28 and 29 July [1963], Graham Greene Papers, Box 20, Folder 5, Harry Ransom Center, The University of Texas at Austin.

41 Carmelo Mesa-Lago, "Economic Policies and Growth," pp. 277–338 (p. 290); Carmelo Mesa-Lago and Luc Zephirin, "Central Planning," pp. 145–84 (p. 173) in Carmelo Mesa-Lago (ed.), *Revolutionary Change in Cuba* (Pittsburgh: University of Pittsburgh Press, 1971).

42 "Havana" journal, 1 Aug. [1963], Graham Greene Papers, Box 20 Folder 5, Harry Ransom Center, The University of Texas at Austin.

43 "Havana" journal, 28 and 31 July, 1 and 6 Aug. [1963], Graham Greene Papers, Box 20 Folder 5, Harry Ransom Center, The University of Texas at Austin.

44 "Havana" journal, 1 Aug. [1963], Graham Greene Papers, Box 20 Folder 5, Harry Ransom Center, The University of Texas at Austin.

45 Greene, "Return to Cuba."

46 Virgilio Piñera Llera (1912–79): lived in the early 1950s in Argentina. Famed for his skepticism, a major theme of his writing was that "life is a succession of terrible blows." Julio A. Martínez (ed.), *Dictionary of Twentieth-Century Cuban Literature* (New York: Greenwood, 1990), pp. 361–70.

47 "Havana" journal, 27 and 1 Aug. [1963], Graham Greene Papers, Box 20 Folder 5, Harry Ransom Center, The University of Texas at Austin.

48 "Havana" journal, 4 Aug. [1963], Graham Greene Papers, Box 20 Folder 5, Harry Ransom Center, The University of Texas at Austin.

49 Roy Perrot, "Graham Greene: A Brief Encounter," *Observer Review*, 16 Nov. 1969, p. 25.

50 Written annotation by Gillian Sutro re: conversation with Greene in early 1960s on Brighton seafront (n.d.), Papers of Gillian and John Sutro, MS. Eng. c.7234 f25, Department of Special Collections, Bodleian Library, University of Oxford.

51 Greene, "Return to Cuba."

52 John M. Kirk, *Between God and the Party: Religion and Politics in Revolutionary Cuba* (Tampa: University of South Florida Press, 1988), pp. 65–126.

53 Greene to Thackeray, n.d., Graham Greene Papers, Box 36, Folder 48, Graham Greene papers, MS.1995.003, John J. Burns Library, Boston College.

54 Trend to Macmillan, "Buses for Cuba," 24 Sept. 1963, TNA PREM11/4697.

55 R. A. Butler, *The Art of the Possible: The Memoirs of Lord Butler* (London: Hamilton, 1971), pp. 256–57; Christopher Hull, "'Going to War in Buses': The Anglo-American Clash over Leyland Sales to Cuba, 1963–64," *Diplomatic History* 34, no. 5 (Nov. 2010): 793–822.

56 Greene to Dr Ricardo Alonso, 25 May 1964, Box 73, Folder 12, Graham Greene papers, MS.1995.003, John J. Burns Library, Boston College.

57 "Places, ca1964," Graham Greene Collection, Box 26 Folder 4, Harry Ransom Center.

58 Morris H. Morley, *Imperial State and Revolution: The United States and Cuba, 1952–1986* (Cambridge: Cambridge University Press, 1987), p. 236; "CIA 'Waged Four-Year War against Cuba,'" *The Times* (UK), 18 July 1975, p. 5; "Was Magdeburg Sunk to Halt Buses for Cuba?," *Lloyd's List*, 2 June 2001, p. 6; "Leyland Buses, Cuba and the CIA," an episode in *Document*, BBC Radio 4, 30 March 2009;

E. John McGarry, *The Cuban Bus Crisis: Tales of CIA Sabotage* (self-published, 2011).

CHAPTER 11

1   "Graham Greene Takes the Orient Express" (interview with Christopher Burnstall, 1968), in Henry J. Donaghy (ed.) *Conversations with Graham Greene* (Jackson: University Press of Mississippi, 1992), p. 50. The writer's most acute period of manic depression during his affair with Catherine in the 1950s had predated the approval of lithium as a treatment for the affliction by two decades. It also predated a redefinition of the term to describe his illness. Manic depression became bipolar disorder in the 1970s. Kay Redfield Jamison, *An Unquiet Mind: A Memoir of Moods and Madness* (London: Picador, 1995), pp. 81, 181.
2   Cloetta, *In Search of a Beginning*, pp. 21–23.
3   "The Waugh Trilogy: Part III, An Englishman's Home," narrated and written by Nicholas Shakespeare, BBC2 TV, 1987.
4   Murray Pollinger (Laurence Pollinger Ltd., London W1) to Greene (Anacapri), 2 Aug. 1966; Greene (Anacapri) to Murray Pollinger, 4 Aug. 1966; Murray Pollinger (Laurence Pollinger Ltd., London W1) to Greene (Paris), 10 Aug. 1966; Murray Pollinger (Laurence Pollinger Ltd., London W1) to Greene (Antibes), 17 Aug. 1966: Box 73, Folder 12, Graham Greene papers, MS.1995.003, John J. Burns Library, Boston College.
5   Lisandro Otero González (1932–2008) studied journalism at the University of Havana, and philosophy and literature at Sorbonne University. He was active in Castro's underground movement before 1959. He was a controversial figure due to his ardent defense of the revolution, yet equal concern in his writing for individual freedom. Martínez (ed.), *Twentieth-Century Cuban Literature*, pp. 339–42.
6   Greene (Antibes) to Catherine (Newton, Cambridge), 28 Nov. 1966, The Catherine Walston/Graham Greene Papers, Box 40, Folder 28, Booth Family Center for Special Collections, Georgetown University Library, Washington, D.C.
7   Greene to Catherine (Newton, Cambridge), 16 Aug. [1966], The Catherine Walston/Graham Greene Papers, Box 40, Folder 23, Booth Family Center for Special Collections, Georgetown University Library, Washington, D.C.
8   Greene, 1/2 Sept. (1966) "Cuban Diary. [28] Aug.–[19] Sep. 1966," The Graham Greene Papers, Box 1, Folder 9, Booth Family Center for Special Collections, Georgetown University Library, Washington, D.C.
9   Greene, 4/5/6/8 Aug. "Cuban Diary. Aug.–Sep. 1966."
10 Greene, 29 Aug. "Cuban Diary. Aug.–Sep. 1966."
11 Greene, 29 Aug. "Cuban Diary Aug.–Sep. 1966."
12 Greene, 4 Sept. "Cuban Diary. Aug.–Sep. 1966."
13 Lisandro Otero, *Llover Sobre Mojado: Una Reflexión Personal de la Historia* (Madrid: Ediciones Libertarias, 1999), p. 237.
14 Greene, 4 Sept. "Cuban Diary. Aug.–Sep. 1966."
15 Greene, 4 Sept. "Cuban Diary. Aug.–Sep. 1966."
16 Greene, 4 Sept. "Cuban Diary. Aug.–Sep. 1966"; Rolland G. Paulston, "Education," in Carmelo Mesa-Lago (ed.), *Revolutionary Change in Cuba* (Pittsburgh: University of Pittsburgh Press, 1971), pp. 375–97 (p. 387).
17 Greene, "Shadow and Sunlight in Cuba."
18 Greene, 4 Sept. "Cuban Diary. Aug.–Sep. 1966."
19 Greene, 6 Sept. "Cuban Diary. Aug.–Sep. 1966."

20   Greene, 8/11 Sept. "Cuban Diary. Aug.–Sep. 1966."

21   Interview with Pablo Armando Fernández and Ernesto Fernández (Playa, La Habana), Apr. 2013.

22   Otero, *Llover Sobre Mojado*, pp. 238–40.

23   Greene, 8/12 Sept. "Cuban Diary. Aug.–Sep. 1966."

24   Greene, 8 Sept. "Cuban Diary. Aug.–Sep. 1966."

25   Greene, 8 Sept. "Cuban Diary. Aug.–Sep. 1966"; K. S. Karol, *Guerrillas in Power*, pp. 313–14.

26   Greene, 8/9 Sept. "Cuban Diary. Aug.–Sep. 1966."

27   Greene, 10 Sept. "Cuban Diary. Aug.–Sep. 1966."

28   Greene, 11 Sept. "Cuban Diary. Aug.–Sep. 1966"; Otero, *Llover Sobre Mojado*, pp. 241–43.

29   Greene, 13 Sept. "Cuban Diary. Aug.–Sep. 1966."

30   Greene, 14 Sept. "Cuban Diary. Aug.–Sep. 1966."

31   Greene, 16/17 Sept. "Cuban Diary. Aug.–Sep. 1966."

32   On Greene's recommendation, publishing house Bodley Head would two years later publish (in translation) Barnet's groundbreaking extended interview with an elderly ex-slave from nineteenth century Cuba: Miguel Barnet (ed.), *The Autobiography of a Runaway Slave, by Esteban Montejo [Biografía de un cimarrón]* (London: Bodley Head, 1968).

33   Greene, 18 Sept. "Cuban Diary. Aug.–Sep. 1966."

34   Slater to Edmonds, 22 Sept. 1966, TNA FO371/184888 AK1631/5; Greene, 18 Sept. "Cuban Diary. Aug.–Sep. 1966." Six years later in his diplomatic career, in 1972, the tyrannical Idi Amin expelled British high commissioner Richard Slater from Uganda, along with twenty thousand Asian Ugandans.

35   Greene, 18 Sept. "Cuban Diary. Aug.–Sep. 1966"; "Nigel Lewis interview with Graham Greene, Part II, Antibes, 17–18 April 1982," C829/7, British Library Sound Archive.

36   Lee Lockwood, *Castro's Cuba, Cuba's Fidel* (Boulder, CO: Westview Press, 1990), p. 74.

37   Greene, 18 Sept. "Cuban Diary. Aug.–Sep. 1966."

38   Greene, 19 Sept. "Cuban Diary. Aug.–Sep. 1966."

39   Greene (Antibes) to Catherine Walston, 3 Oct. 1966, in Richard Greene (ed.), *A Life in Letters*, pp. 285–86.

40   Slater to Edmonds, 22 Sept. 1966, TNA FO371/184888 AK1631/5.

41   Graham Greene, "The Marxist Heretic," *Collected Essays* (London: Penguin, 1981), pp. 303–10.

42   Graham Greene, "Fidel: An Impression," 2 Dec. 1966, *Weekend Telegraph Magazine*, pp. 9–10, 12.

43   Greene, "Fidel: An Impression."

44   Greene, "Fidel: An Impression."

45   Greene, "Fidel: An Impression."

46   Greene, "Shadow and Sunlight in Cuba."

47   Greene, "Shadow and Sunlight in Cuba."

48   Greene, "Shadow and Sunlight in Cuba."

49   Greene, "Shadow and Sunlight in Cuba."

50   Rafael Hernández, "La Hora de las UMAP: Notas Para un Tema de Investigación," *Temas*, 12 July 2015.

51   Joseph Tahbaz, "Demystifying las UMAP: The Politics of Sugar, Gender, and Religion

in 1960s Cuba," *Delaware Review of Latin American Studies* 14, no. 2 (31 Dec. 2013), www1.udel.edu/LAS/Vol14-2Tahbaz.html.

52 Rafael Hernández, "La Hora de las UMAP."

53 Joseph Tahbaz, "Demystifying las UMAP."

54 Guillermo Cabrera Infante, *Mapa Dibujado por un Espía* (Barcelona: Galaxia Gutenberg, 2013), pp. 86–87; Franqui, *Family Portrait with Fidel*, pp. 138–41.

55 Carrie Hamilton, *Sexual Revolutions in Cuba: Passion, Politics, and Memory* (Chapel Hill: University of North Carolina Press, 2012), p. 40.

56 Lee Lockwood, *Castro's Cuba, Cuba's Fidel: An American Journalist's Inside Look at Today's Cuba in Text and Picture* (New York, Vintage Books: 1969), p. 107.

57 Greene, "Shadow and Sunlight in Cuba."

58 Otero, *Llover Sobre Mojado*, pp. 237.

59 Marvin Leiner, *Sexual Politics in Cuba: Machismo, Homosexuality, and AIDS* (Boulder, CO: Westview, 1994), pp. 28–29.

60 Adamson, *Graham Greene: The Dangerous Edge*, pp. 146–47.

61 Greene (Paris) to Lady [Isabel] Fordham, 11 Jan. 1967, Box 19, Folder 15, Graham Greene papers, MS.1995.003, John J. Burns Library, Boston College.

62 Greene (Paris) to Catherine [Walston] (Newton, Cambridge), 10 Nov. 1966, Box 40, Folder 25; Greene (Antibes) to Catherine [Walston] (Newton, Cambridge), 28 Nov. 1966, Box 40, Folder 28: The Catherine Walston/Graham Greene Papers, Booth Family Center for Special Collections, Georgetown University Library, Washington, D.C.

63 Slater (Havana) to Robin Edmonds (FO), 21 Sept. 1966, TNA FO371/184889 AK1632/1; Edmonds (FO) to R. E. L. Johnstone (Washington), 16 Dec. 1966, TNA FO371/184889 AK1632/13.

64 Henry Walston, *Agriculture under Communism* (London: Bodley Head, 1962).

65 Slater (Havana) to Edmonds (FO), 21 Sept. 1966, TNA FO371/184889 AK1632/1; Slater (Havana) to G. Brown (FO), No. 2, 13 Jan. 1967, TNA FCO7/531 AK2/2; Slater (Havana) to Edmonds, 20 Feb. 1967, TNA FCO7/583.

66 Edmonds (FO) to R. Johnstone (Washington), 16 Dec. 1966, TNA FO371/184889 AK1632/13; Walston to Secretary of State (George Brown), 24 Dec. 1966, TNA FCO7/531; Edmonds (FO) to Slater (Havana), 15 Feb. 1967, TNA FCO7/531 f16.

67 Sir Paul Gore-Booth (FO) to Harry Walston (A14, Albany, Piccadilly), 8 Jan. 1968, TNA FCO7/531 f24; Michael Stewart (FO) to Lord Walston (A14 Albany), 20 March 1968, TNA FCO7/583 f65; Lord Walston (A14 Albany) to Michael [Stewart], 2 Apr. 1968, TNA FO7/583 f69.

CHAPTER 12

1 KP to Graham Greene, n.d. [London postmark 8 Jan. 1979], Box 71, Folder 24, Graham Greene papers, MS.1995.003, John J. Burns Library, Boston College.

2 Kim [Philby] (Moscow) to Graham [Greene], 2 Jan. [1979], Box 71, Folder 25, Graham Greene papers, MS.1995.003, John J. Burns Library, Boston College.

3 Martin Pearce, *Spymaster: The Life of Britain's Most Decorated Cold War Spy and Head of MI6, Sir Maurice Oldfield* (London: Transworld, 2016), pp. 120–21.

4 "Kim Philby: by Graham Greene," in Philby, *My Silent War*, p. 7.

5 Pearce, *Spymaster*, pp. 369–71; email Amanda Saunders (Rodney Dennys's daughter) to Richard Greene, 1 Apr. 2003.

6 Alistair Horne, *Macmillan, 1894–1956: Volume I of the Official Biography* (London: Macmillan 1988), pp. 365–66.

7   *Our Man in Havana* film script (Shepperton Studios, ca. 1960), British Library shelfmark Cup.410.c.68.
8   "Kim Philby: by Graham Greene," in Philby, *My Silent War*, p. 9; Ben Macintyre, *A Spy Among Friends: Kim Philby and the Great Betrayal* (London: Bloomsbury, 2014), p. 19.
9   *Our Man in Havana* film script (Shepperton Studios, ca. 1960), British Library shelfmark Cup.410.c.68.
10 Greene, *Getting to Know the General*, p. 9.
11 Greene Panama Diary, 3 Dec. 1976, Graham Greene Papers, Box 1, Folder 11, Booth Family Center for Special Collections, Georgetown University Library, Washington, D.C.
12 Greene, *Getting to Know the General*, p. 119.
13 Karel Kyncl, "Conversation with Graham Greene" in Henry J. Donaghy (ed.) *Conversations with Graham Greene* (London: University Press of Mississippi, 1992), pp. 169–70.
14 Greene "Panama etc." diary, 11–12 Jan. 1983, Graham Greene Papers, Box 1, Folder 14, Booth Family Center for Special Collections, Georgetown University Library, Washington, D.C.
15 Greene "Panama etc." diary, 11–12 Jan. 1983, Graham Greene Papers, Box 1, Folder 14, Booth Family Center for Special Collections, Georgetown University Library, Washington, D.C.; Gabriel García Márquez, "Las Veinte Horas de Graham Greene en La Habana," *El País*, 19 Jan. 1983. The odds are in fact longer than five to one because the weight of a bullet in one of the revolver's six chambers reduces the likelihood that it will spin into the uppermost firing position, although this bias can be eliminated if the weapon is pointed at the ground when spinning its chambers. Mechanism or ammunition malfunctions can also save a player's life.
16 Greene "Panama etc." diary, 11–12 Jan. 1983, Graham Greene Papers, Box 1, Folder 14, Booth Family Center for Special Collections, Georgetown University Library, Washington, D.C.
17 Greene, *Getting to Know the General*, pp. 213–15.
18 Greene, Sep. 2 [1966] "Cuban Diary. Aug.–Sep. 1966."
19 Sherry, *The Life of Graham Greene: Volume One*, pp. 484, 491.
20 "Profile by Auberon Waugh," 22 May 1968, *Daily Mirror*, p. 18.
21 Allain, *The Other Man*, pp. 60, 111.
22 Letter by G. Cabrera Infante (London SW7), 18 Nov. 1982, *London Review of Books* 4, no. 21. The whole article is also in G. Cabrera Infante, *Mea Cuba* (London: Faber & Faber, 1994), pp. 291–308.
23 Letter by Pedro Perez Sarduy (London N4), 30 Dec. 1982, *London Review of Books* 4, no. 24.
    One motive for Cabrera Infante's lifelong resentment against communism stemmed from the fact that his parents were among the founders of the Communist Party in Cuba. His father was also a journalist for Cuba's Communist newspaper *Hoy* in the 1940s. Martínez (ed.), *Twentieth-Century Cuban Literature*, p. 101.
24 Letter by Greene (Antibes), 10 Jan. 1983, *London Review of Books* 5, no. 1.
25 Letter by G. Cabrera Infante (London SW7), 3 Feb. 1983, *London Review of Books* 5, no. 2. Cabrera Infante also listed Noël Coward as somebody he introduced to Castro. Yet like Greene, he had also departed Havana weeks earlier. Carlos Franqui made a more measured contribution to the debate from exile in New York (21 Apr. 1983, vol. 5, no. 7).

26   García Márquez, "Las Veinte Horas de Graham Greene en La Habana"; Guillermo Cabrera Infante, "Nuestro Prohombre en La Habana," *El País*, 3 Feb. 1983.

27   Christopher Hitchens, "I'll Be Damned: Graham Greene's Most Fervent Loyalty Was to Betrayal," *The Atlantic*, March 2005.

28   See Graham Greene, *Yours etc.: Letters to the Press* (London: Reinhardt, 1989), pp. 90–91, 143, 154–56.

CONCLUSION

1   John le Carré, *The Tailor of Panama* (London: Hodder & Stoughton, 1996), p. 410.

2   *Cuba*. Directed by Richard Lester. United Artists Corporation, 1979; *Havana*. Directed by Sydney Pollack. Universal Pictures (an MCA Company), 1990.

3   The male/female Jack and Bobby pairing, of course, reminds us of the Kennedy brothers Jack and Bobby.

4   Peter Hulme, "Graham Greene and Cuba: Our Man in Havana?" *New West Indian Guide* 82, no. 3–4 (2008): 185–209 (see p. 193). http://repository.essex.ac.uk/1865/1/Grahan_Greene_Our_Man_in_Havana.pdf; Philip D. Beidler, *The Island Called Paradise: Cuba in History, Literature, and the Arts* (Tuscaloosa: University of Alabama Press, 2014), pp. 133, 138.

5   John le Carré, *The Pigeon Tunnel: Stories from My Life* (London: Viking, 2016), pp. 14–16.

6   David G. Walley, *Nothing in Moderation: A Biography of Ernie Kovacs* (New York: Drake Publishers, 1975), pp. 3–6.

7   Greene (Hotel Nacional, Havana) to Yvonne Cloetta, 27 July 1963, Yvonne Cloetta/Graham Greene Papers, Box 1 Folder 4, Georgetown University Library, Washington, D.C.

8   Graham Greene, *Brighton Rock* (London: Penguin, 1975 [1938]), p. 5; Greene, "Return to Cuba."

9   The Chilcot Inquiry (July 2016), Section 4.3 Iraq WMD Assessments, October 2002 to March 2003, p. 394.

10   The Chilcot Inquiry (July 2016), Section 4.3 Iraq WMD Assessments, October 2002 to March 2003, pp. 383–84, 500; Richard J. Aldrich, "Intelligence and Iraq: The UK's Four Enquiries," in Richard J. Aldrich, Christopher Andrew, and Wesley K. Wark (eds.), *Secret Intelligence: A Reader* (London: Routledge, 2009), pp. 229–44.

11   James Risen, *State of War: The Secret History of the CIA and the Bush Administration* (New York: Free Press, 2006), pp. 115–23.

12   Eddie Mair interviews and analysis with BBC diplomatic correspondent Mark Urban and Pauline Neville-Jones (former head of the defence and overseas, chairman of the Joint Intelligence Committee, minister of state for security and counterterrorism), "PM Programme," BBC Radio 4, 8 July 2016.

13   One might even identify clairvoyance in the fact that the first, middle, and final letters of Wormold's odd surname spell WMD.

14   Andrew Lycett, *Ian Fleming* (London: Weidenfeld & Nicolson, 1995), p. 362.

INDEX